# INQUIRIES
# into
# CHILD LANGUAGE

Diane Nelson Bryen
*Temple University*

Allyn and Bacon, Inc.
*Boston      London      Sydney      Toronto*

**Library of Congress Cataloging in Publication Data**

Bryen, Diane.
  Inquiries into child language.

  Bibliography: p.
  Includes index.
    1. Children—Language. 2. Language acquisition.
3. English language—Study and teaching (Elemen-
tary) I. Title.
LB1139.L3B76      155.4′13      81-14898
ISBN 0-205-07642-4          AACR2


Printed in the United States of America.

10  9  8  7  6  5  4  3  2  1    86  85  84  83  82

to my sons, Jonathan Zev and Benjamin Eli, who have been both a joy and a motivation to me in studying child language.

to my wonderful husband, Michael, who continually supported me and sacrificed many hours of time with me so that this book could be completed.

to students in my graduate classes, *Problems in Language Development,* at Temple University, who continually challenged me to approach the study of child language in a creative fashion.

# Contents

v

## APPENDIX
### Transcripts of Children's Language and Communication 367

# Preface

Just as the study of language has expanded from describing and analyzing the particular aspects of a language to including both the accompaniments and circumstances of language usage, the interested audience has also expanded. The study of child language was once considered to be the exclusive domain of linguists and psycholinguists. However, as the field of language expanded to include not just structural considerations (i.e., particular aspects), but functional considerations as well (i.e., accompaniments and circumstances), the interested audience began to include psychologists, sociolinguists, and educators. *Inquiries into Child Language* was written not only in recognition of the expanding conceptualization of language and language acquisition, but also in recognition of the new audience that has come to view language as a fundamental social, cognitive, and cultural phenomenon. This population includes educators of both normal and handicapped youngsters, psychologists, reading specialists, and language clinicians.

However, *Inquiries into Child Language* represents more than just an attempt to address new issues and new audiences. Beyond these purposes, its major significance lies in an attempt to approach learning about language from a slightly different perspective—perhaps best described as a Socratic one. At the end of each chapter are a series of inquiries that utilize, reinforce, and expand the substance of each chapter. The format of these mini-experiments allows the reader to go beyond the material presented in the text to begin to answer questions based upon language data from real language users. Therefore, the gap that sometimes opens up between theory and application never really evolves here.

*Inquiries into Child Language* is an introductory book about language, language development, language-related processes, and language problems and practices. Within this framework, the intention is to introduce the reader to expanding theories concerning the nature and development of communication, language, and speech (Chapters 1 through 6). This introduction includes both the *what* and *how* of language development. The remaining chapters (7 through 10) reflect the second major focus—that of identifying and understanding how language affects children's experiences as they enter and progress through school. Topically, the second section of the book introduces the reader to dialect variation (Chapter 7), language and reading (Chapter 8), the assessment of language (Chapter 9), and language problems and classroom practices (Chapter 10). Because language is an omnipresent human phenomenon, the reader should find both the contents and the approach of *Inquiries into Child Language* highly interesting and widely applicable.

### A Note about the Use of the Inquiries

The inquiries found at the end of each chapter are designed to actively engage the reader in studying about child language in a direct and forceful manner, that is, by studying language in use. Therefore, the reader is encouraged to actually observe, tape-record, and transcribe dyadic interactions as directed in each inquiry. The linguistic data obtained from these transcribed interactions can serve several functions in addition to those specified in the objectives section of each inquiry. However, having used these inquiries for several years, the author realizes that obtaining access to child-child and parent-child interactions is sometimes difficult. Consequently, transcripts of various interactions among children and between adults and children have been included in the appendix. These transcripts, while they are clearly a less powerful learning tool than progressing from observing and recording to transcribing, are useful as data for discussion and analysis. Finally, it should be mentioned that it is not necessary to follow the sequence of inquiries in the order given or the exact procedures specified within each inquiry. The intent of these inquiries is to provide a challenging, and *creative,* approach to the study of child language.

D.N.B.

# 1

# Introduction: Communication, Language, and Speech

In this chapter, the relationship among communication, language, and speech is delineated. The position taken and explored in the following pages is that communication is the broad, superordinate category through which language and speech derive their purpose. The position is also taken that the ability to communicate is not restricted to the use of language, but also includes the use of facial expressions, gestures, and actions. Similarly, language, as a conventional means for human communication, is not restricted to the verbal modality (i.e., speech). Language also includes manual signs and written symbols. Two transcribed interactions are presented in this chapter to illustrate the relationship among communication, language, and speech. At the end of the chapter are two inquiries that provide a format for further exploration.

Language is one of the most salient abilities of the human species, yet it is perhaps the least understood. What is language? When this question was asked of college students, it elicited a wide variety of responses reflecting commonly held conceptions about the complex nature of language. These varied responses can be grouped into the following three patterns.

### Pattern I

- Language is expression, *communication,* involvement in the culture of society. Language is the ability to meaningfully *communicate* one's thoughts to another.
- Language is a form of *communication*—whether spoken, written, or expressed by gestures. In order to *communicate,* we have to agree (socially and culturally) on a particular language (e.g., Spanish or English); otherwise each of us would be speaking only to be self-understood.
- Language is the *ability to express* one's thoughts and/or ideas, needs, and feelings. It must be understood by others.

- Language is any form of *communication* among people. It can be verbal, written, signing, or expressions. It is giving and receiving messages.

## Pattern II

- Language is the means, ability, or tool that we use to communicate *orally* with others.
- Language is *verbal* communication. It is the method—*spoken*—by which we make others aware of our feelings, wants, needs, etc., and the way in which we transmit information.
- Language is a means of communication, involving *sounds* produced by the vocal cords, lips, tongue, and teeth. The sounds of a language are common across a group of people. In other words, the sounds have a meaning that can be understood by the persons in the group.

## Pattern III

- Language is *a form of communication* from one person to another through the use of *symbols.*
- Language is *a means of communication* that uses either written or spoken *symbols* to convey meaning. Each language has a structure and an accepted arrangement of symbols to enhance the meaning of the communication.
- Language is *an avenue of communication* between two or more agents. It is not restricted to words or verbalizations, but includes any *symbol* to which shared meaning is attached. It usually has rules that govern it, even if not formally. Upon analysis, it can be broken down into basic, well-established components.
- Language is a *symbol system* that is capable of representing one's knowledge of the world.

Although, at first glance, each of the above groups of definitions of language appears to capture the essence of language, each pattern retains some ambiguity about the relationship between communication, language, and speech. Take, for example, Pattern I; there is a common element to these definitions, one that relates language exclusively to communication. In fact, language is viewed as being communication. In contrast, the definitions of language clustered in Pattern II reflect a different conception. Here, speech and communication define the nature of language, as in *Language is . . . ability to communicate orally. Language is verbal communication.* Finally, the definitions clustered in Pattern III come closer to a viable consensus on the nature of language. These definitions recognize that the relationship between language and communication can be put as "Language is an avenue of communication." However, in contrast to Patterns I and II, in Pattern III, language is defined as a *symbol system* that is (1) structured, (2) mutually agreed upon, (3) not restricted to speech, and (4) capable of representing one's knowledge of the world.

Clearly, the relationship among communication, language, and speech is not completely agreed upon by college students (or by linguists, psycholinguists, psychologists, speech and language clinicians, or teachers). However, there is a general body of information that enables us to understand how these three concepts interrelate.

## COMMUNICATION

Communication, simply, is that act of making one's thoughts, experiences, feelings, needs, and desires known to one or more other people (Stelle, 1978). In order for communication to occur, there must be at least two persons, a sender and a receiver. The sender can be a speaker, signer, or writer. Sending a message can also be accomplished via music, visual arts, pantomime, or actions. The receiver is the listener, the reader, the person being signed to, or the observer. Even when we make notes for ourselves, the "present me" (i.e., the sender) is writing to the "future me" (i.e., the receiver).

In the above definition of communication, the phrase *making one's thoughts . . . known* has an important implication. Communication, for both the sender and the receiver, is a cooperative and intentional process. "The sender must wish to share something with the receiver, and the receiver in turn must wish to be shared with" (Stelle, 1978, p. 1). A social interaction is thus intended, and if either the sender or the receiver chooses not to cooperate, communication will not take place.

It is as a result of the social nature of humans—their desire to interact and communicate—that language has evolved. In fact, language owes its raison d'être to the need to communicate, and language is only one vehicle for communication.

Traditionally, the study of communication has been restricted to the study of language, the underlying assumption being that communicative abilities are equivalent to linguistic competence. The cooperative or social aspect of communication was all but ignored. Similarly, the notion of intent received relatively little attention. The social and physical contexts of communication were viewed as being outside the parameters of linguistic study and were, therefore, relegated to a position of lesser importance. Until the early 1970s, language was studied as though it occurred in a social vacuum—detached from its communicative function. The realm of such study was restricted to only one aspect of the process of communication, that of the linguistic message itself.

As can be seen, in Figure 1.1 several critical elements of communication are not identified. First, the context of communication remains unspecified. Second, the relationship between the listener and the speaker is only superficially portrayed. Third, the message to be sent (**X**) is restricted exclusively to language and fails to take into account gestures and facial expressions, which act as supplements and extensions of language. This restricted model of communication also fails to take into account the notion of intent. The sender (**S**) does not simply code the message (**X**), but codes it with the intent of making it understood by the receiver (**R**).

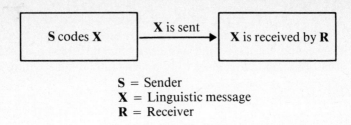

**S** = Sender
**X** = Linguistic message
**R** = Receiver

FIGURE 1.1    A Restricted Model of Communication

Similarly, the receiver **(R)** does not merely receive the message, but attempts to understand the intent of the speaker, which is just as important and may be more so than the exact message being sent. This intentionality is absent from Figure 1.1.

In contrast to this restricted model of communication, an expanded model of communication is graphically portrayed in Figure 1.2. Present in this model are both a social context **(SC)** and a physical context **(PC)** in which communication takes place. In coding (or recoding) the intended message **X**, the sender is not simply coding, but is coding the message *for* the receiver. In doing so, the sender takes into account both the current physical context and the social context (e.g., shared information and familiarity between **S** and **R**, perceived formality). It is the intentional quality of communication that motivates the sender to code the message not from a personal perspective but rather from the perspective of the receiver. Similarly, it is the intent to communicate that motivates the receiver also to take into account the physical and social contexts (frequently as important as the message **X**) in order to grasp the underlying intent. The cooperative and social nature of communication is further evidenced by the feedback from the receiver to the sender, which either confirms or disconfirms that the intended message has been understood or requests the sender to recode the message so that effective communication can take place. The vehicle for sending **X** is made up of more than language. Gestures that additionally specify intended referents, facial expressions, and eye contact are all utilized to ensure effective communication.

Therefore, the very nature of communication forces one to go beyond the study of language. Social and cognitive aspects of communication are equally significant. They will affect (albeit often tacitly) the basic decisions that one continually makes when engaged in the communication process.

To summarize thus far, communication is a social-interpersonal function that is not restricted to language or speech. In order for communication to take place, a minimum of three conditions must be fulfilled:

1. *why*—a reason for sending the message;
2. *what*—the content of the message; and
3. *how*—a way of sending the message.

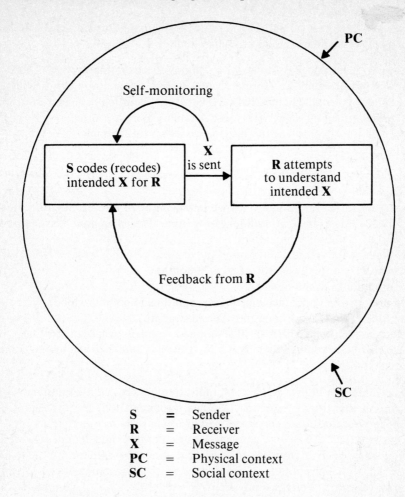

S = Sender
R = Receiver
X = Message
PC = Physical context
SC = Social context

FIGURE 1.2   An Expanded Model of Communication

As previously mentioned, the study of child language was traditionally restricted to the third condition, that is, the *how* of communication. Even this focus was further narrowed to the study of spoken language as the exclusive mechanism for transmitting a message. Although spoken language is a primary means of communication among competent, hearing adults, we must not so narrow our focus to include only spoken language. By doing so, we will not only have a restricted view of the communication process, but may also underestimate the influences of many critical variables that affect its development.

The following brief interaction between Teresa, who is seven months old, and her mother illustrates the three conditions given above as prerequisites for the communication process. This interaction was chosen because Teresa has not yet acquired language as a means of communication. In addition, the social-interpersonal aspects of communication are illustrated.

Setting: A middle-class home where the mother is in the process of feeding lunch to her daughter Teresa. Teresa is in a highchair, which is pulled up alongside the table in the kitchen. The mother is sitting in a chair in front of Teresa with food at her side on the table. There are three toys on the highchair tray in front of the baby—two small toy animals (a dog and a bear) and a rattle.

Teresa (banging the bear while having eye contact with her mother): "Ah–ah–ah." (rising pitch on the last ah).
(Mother smiles, looks at Teresa while putting food into her mouth.)
Teresa: "M–m–m ..." (while eating and then puts the bear in her mouth).
Mother: "Are you finished eating?" (eye contact with Teresa). "Don't eat the bear." (removes bear from Teresa's mouth).
(Teresa looks at the food.)
Mother (first, eye contact with Teresa, and then looks at the food): "Here's more food." (puts more food into Teresa's mouth).
Teresa: "Wh–wh." (high shrill sound and resumes banging the bear).
Mother: "Oh, you like that. You having a good time?" (while looking and smiling at Teresa).

There is little doubt that active communication between mother and baby took place during this brief interaction. Mother responded to Teresa's actions, eye contact, and vocalizations. Teresa derived meaning from her mother's communicative signals (i.e., smiles, eye contact, actions, context, and language). Mother and baby established an intimate, interactional atmosphere (the *why* of communication), wherein many different signals (the *how* of communication) served to make the thoughts, feelings, and needs of each (the *what* of communication) known to the other. It should be obvious from this interaction that communication is by no means restricted to the use of language. Eye contact, actions, smiles, and the physical context itself served the communicative functions of specifying *what* and indicating that both sender and receiver were ready to continue the cooperative act of communication.

Just as actions, eye contact, and gestures can serve as communicative signals, so too can language, in that it is one way in which an intended message can be transmitted and therefore shared by sender and receiver. However, as a result of the characteristics of a language system, the sender and receiver are freed to communicate about content that is not context-bound. In other words, the use of a language system enables both the sender and the receiver to communicate about objects and events that are distanced in time and space. The properties of language that make it context-free are described in the next section.

## LANGUAGE

Language is a rule-governed symbol system that is capable of representing one's understanding of the world. It is a shared social code and is generative. The primary, if not the exclusive, function of language is that of communication. Before becoming frustrated by this apparently elusive definition, let us examine each of the characteristics of language so that both its power and complexity begin to reveal themselves.

If someone were to write, sign, or say to you *Where is the ball?* in a context in which both the sender and you, as the receiver, knew the ball was generally found, an intended communication episode would begin to take place. Similarly, if the sender with a puzzled look and a shrug of the shoulders to underscore the puzzlement pointed to the same place, would not the potential for communication also exist? If so, what are the differences between the two communicative episodes? In the latter situation, signals that are socially agreed upon (i.e., pointing, raised eyebrows, shrug of the shoulders) are used to index a location and a state (puzzlement). Similarly, shared knowledge between sender and receiver (i.e., the recognition that something generally found there is presently absent) is called upon. However, the intended message (*Where is the ball? It is usually there. I want it.*) may not be adequately communicated; the nature of the pointing and shrugging signals (the *how* of communication) may not adequately represent the sender's intent. Language, if used to convey the same intended message, has the potential to convey that message more precisely due to its **symbolic nature.** As a symbol system—in fact, an arbitrary symbol system—language can represent (*re-present*) objects, events, relations, attributes, or actions that are either present or absent. Of course, this is true of other representations as well, such as photographs or line drawings. (See Figure 1.3 for various ways of indexing an object.) Unlike some other symbols, the symbols forming a language have no inherent relationship to the present, palpable world.

In addition to being a symbol system, any language is capable of representing one's understanding of the world. For example, even a child as young as two years old sees that all people are **agents** who act on **objects** (e.g., *Mommy pushes car*). Later, the child begins to understand that people can be not only agents of **actions** (e.g., *Mommy push*) but also **recipients** of actions (e.g., *Push Mommy*). Still later, the child understands that objects can be recipients of an action as well as being **instruments** that act upon other objects (e.g., *The knife cuts the bread*). As young children grow to more fully understand the physical and social world, their use of language reflects this growing understanding in that they use language that conveys relationships among agents, actions, objects, locations, instruments, and so on.

These symbols representing one's understanding of the world are not simply uttered in a random fashion, but rather are **rule-governed.** What does it mean when we say that all languages are rule-governed? Simply stated, it means that

To **point** as a signal requires the presence of the object or a representation of it.

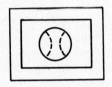

A **photograph** of ''ball,'' which has an inherent visual similarity to the referent (roundness, volume), is a nonarbitrary symbol.

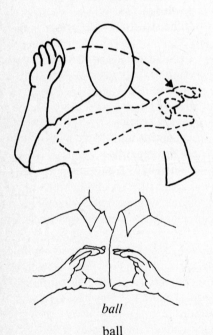

The **American-Indian Code** for ''ball'' (also for ''throw,'' ''game,'' ''play,'' and ''projectile'') is based on the concept of function (arbitrary?). (From Skelly, 1979.)

The **ASL sign** for ''ball'' is based on the shape of ball (arbitrary?). (From *An introduction to manual English,* 1972.)

*ball*     The **English spoken symbol** for ''ball'' is an arbitrary symbol.

ball     The **English written symbol** is an arbitrary symbol.

FIGURE 1.3   Ways of Signaling "Ball"

underlying all linguistic utterances are principles or organizing systems or tacit rules for combining the learned linguistic symbols. That is why the above-mentioned sender said or wrote *Where is the ball?* and not *The is ball where?* or *Where ball is the?* The rule-governed nature of language is not a fact of which any of us are consciously aware. In fact, most of us (including linguists) would find it to be a highly complex task to actually articulate and codify many of the rules underlying any language system. This is true even if we are highly competent in using that language.

The skeptical reader may find the following exercise to be revelatory of how English, as one language, is rule-governed. Fill in the missing blanks in the following:

1. The _____ twaggered down the tweb.
2. Where _____ the _____ clib?
3. Here is a nib. Here is another nib. Now there are two _____ .

Without going into detail about each of the above sentences, it is enough to say that you should have found it easy to complete them despite the fact that not all of the words presented are familiar. The ease with which you completed the sentences reflects your tacit or unconscious knowledge about how sentences are formed in English (i.e., its underlying rules). The structure (or rules) of English will be described in greater detail in Chapter 2.

Another characteristic of language is that it is a **generative system.** This means that the system possesses a finite set of linguistic rules that creates the potential for generating an infinite number of sentences. Let us return to the basic formulation of agent + action + object. Having learned this one linguistic rule, one is capable of generating an almost endless list of sentences. The only constraints are one's knowledge of the features of various words (e.g., agent must be animate) and the range of one's vocabulary. To fully understand the generative quality of this one linguistic relation, it is only necessary to make an exhaustive list of sentences representing this one relationship.

> *Boy push car.*
> *Dog push car.*
> *Boy hit car.*
> *Boy hit chair.*
>
> .
>
> .
>
> .

All languages must be generative, or else new ideas, relationships, or concepts have no way of being communicated via language.

The symbols that evolve to form any language system are **socially agreed upon.** This covers not only the vocabulary of a language, but also the rules for combining linguistic units and the melody of the language. The social nature of language accounts for the facts that infants of French-speaking parents grow up speaking French, that infants of deaf, signing parents grow up with sign language as one major language system, and so on. It also accounts for the existence of varieties of a particular language (i.e., dialects) within a larger language system. Languages and dialects, because they become the shared coin for communicative exchange, serve a particular sociocultural function. Members of a social or cultural group are identified with their linguistic community due to specific and shared language patterns. The sociocultural aspects of language will be explored further in Chapter 7.

To conclude this brief introduction to language, it is important to reiterate that language is not restricted to spoken language. If we agree with the above introductory remarks about language, we must also recognize that the language of manual signs employed by most deaf persons (i.e., American Sign Language or ASL) is also a formal language system. Linguists (e.g., Wilbur, 1976; Schlesinger & Namir, 1978) have consistently supported what deaf signers have long known; that is, that American Sign Language is a socially agreed upon, rule-governed symbol system that is generative in nature.

One of the major differences between a spoken language, such as English, and a manual language, such as ASL, is the modality through which it is serviced. This is not meant to deny or underestimate other differences, such as vocabulary or the rules governing the combination of linguistic units. Spoken English is serviced through speech, an organizational system that is auditory, vocal, and temporal in nature. In contrast, ASL is serviced through a system of manual signs that can be most easily described as visual and spatial in nature. So just as a person can communicate without language, a person can use a language without having speech.

## SPEECH

Just as language can be viewed as a symbol system in service of communication, speech can be viewed as one service system through which language is delivered. From the previous sections on language and communication, we know that communication and language are not restricted to spoken language or spoken communication. As previously stated, it cannot be convincingly argued that deaf persons have no language. All that can be argued is that most deaf people service their language system through a system of manual signs as opposed to a system of spoken symbols. Therefore, speech is only one system through which language can be serviced and transmitted between sender and receiver. In a literate society, a standard alphabet also serves as a delivery system for language.

What is speech? Speech, if viewed as a sound system in service of language, is the smallest significant unit of sound—significant, that is, from a linguistic perspective. This is in contrast to the wide variety of sounds that humans are capable of producing and hearing. **Speech-sounds,** or phonemes, are linguistically significant sounds because a change in one such sound can potentially affect the word itself. One example should suffice to illustrate what is here described as significant. Take the following English phonemes: /b/, /a/, /i/, /t/, and /h/. Three of these speech-sounds can be combined to produce the word *bat*. However, one phonemic change results in a change in the word (and the meaning it represents).

$$bat: /b/ \text{ changed to } /h/ \rightarrow hat$$
$$bat: /a/ \text{ changed to } /i/ \rightarrow bit$$

Of course, each speaker produces phonemes in a slightly idiosyncratic way. This idiolectic aspect of speech results in the recognizable uniqueness of an individual's speech. However, this variation in speech production is usually within the boundaries of a particular phoneme, so that the variation is *not* significant from a linguistic perspective.

As in language, these smallest significant units of sound making up speech are rule-governed in their combination, are generative, and are socially agreed upon. Speech, like language, has as its primary function that of communication. This is not to say that speech cannot exist without language or communication. The following brief interaction between Chris, who is twelve months old, and his mother illustrates how speech can exist without language and without intentional communication.

> (Chris carries a music box that is playing.)
> Mother: "Look at the picture." (points to the picture on the music box).
> Chris: "Ah–ah–ah." (while looking at the picture).
>
> .
>
> .
>
> .
>
> Mother (removes Chris's hand and points): "Look, look, Chris. Duck . . . quack, quack, quack."
> Chris: "Ah! Ah!" (grabs the box and walks away).
> Mother: "Okay."
> Chris: "Ga-ga." (continues walking away).

Both Chris and his mother use speech in this interaction; however, the variety, form, and function of their speech is qualitatively different. Mother's speech is linguistic in nature. That is, the speech-sounds the mother uses are servicing her language system. Spoken language is used by her for very specific and intentional communicative purposes, that is, persuading Chris to interact with Mother and the toy. Mother's speech is also quite varied in form. Many, many different phonemes are used. In contrast, Chris's speech is restricted in variety and form (i.e., *Ah-ah-ah, Ah! Ah!* and *Ga-ga*). It is unlikely that Chris's speech is linguistic. Speech-sounds have not yet begun to serve a symbolic function for him. In other words, the speech-sounds Chris uses do not yet reliably represent objects, events, or attributes of his environment. More likely, they are vocal reactions to Chris's internal states of excitement, displeasure, and so forth. It is unlikely that Chris's speech has the function of intentionally communicating his displeasure or excitement. (This does not mean that Chris's mother views his speech-sounds as meaningless or unintentional. In fact, mothers generally attribute meaning to their young children's early vocalizations.)

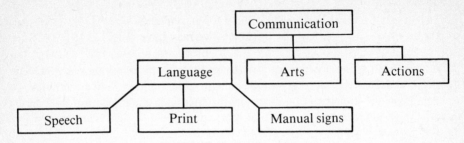

FIGURE 1.4   Relationship among Communication, Language, and Speech

## CONCLUDING REMARKS

The relationship among communication, language, and speech is a complex one that has been conceptually confused in the past and frequently continues to be confused in diagnosing and treating language-delayed or different youngsters. Without being either totally separate or identical systems, they do share many of the same features. They are all (1) rule-governed rather than random systems, (2) reflective of sociocultural conventions, and (3) generative in nature.

A useful way of viewing the relationship among communication, language, and speech is illustrated in Figure 1.4. Communication is viewed as the umbrella process or function and is motivated by the social and interpersonal nature of humans, as well as of other animals. We can communicate without using either language or speech. Because of the unique cognitive and social aspects of humans, a symbol system, language, has evolved. However, this linguistic system is derived from and in service of communication, and we would not have such a system without the motivating function of communication. Similarly, speech is but one vehicle for the delivery of language. American Sign Language and writing are other modalities for the delivery of language. Without language, speech has no raison d'être. Its usefulness is solely derived from its use as a linguistic instrument. Since each of the lower-level systems derives its meaning and function from the superordinate process, one can argue that speech is subordinate to language, which is in turn subordinate to communication. This relationship will be made more explicit throughout this book. However, the following inquiries will enable you to begin to explore these three concepts and to relate their definitions to their everyday use.

## INQUIRY 1.1

Each of us is an expert in the area of language. While this statement may seem at first to be rather bold, it is nonetheless true. Is it not true that each of us has the ability to process and understand that which is communicated to us? Furthermore, do we not communicate our needs, desires, points of view, and information to others with rather great facility? Whereas we may have only a tacit knowledge of our communication, language, and speech processes, as evidenced by the competency with which we use them, it is the purpose of this first inquiry to begin to develop our skills as observers of language and its use. These skills will enable us to begin a highly challenging *and* highly exciting study of children's communication, language, and speech.

**OBJECTIVES**   The objectives of this inquiry are to:

1. Begin to listen to and observe individuals in their use of speech and language.
2. Begin to develop skills in using transcripts as a means for systematically analyzing spontaneous language.
3. Explore the relationship among communication, language, and speech.
4. Explore the various roles of the speaker and the listener.

**PROCEDURES**   Tape-record and observe the spontaneous use of language by two persons (either two children or an adult and a child or two adults). The language interaction can be of short duration (five to ten minutes). Transcribe the tape using the following format:

1. Child (pointing to microphone): "Whusch your name?"
2. Mother (in a high-pitched voice): "My name is Missy Goldstein."
3. (Child giggles.)
4. Mother (voice at normal pitch): "Isn't that funny?"

(See Chapter 9, pages 253–265, for some useful conventions for obtaining and transcribing a spontaneous sample of language.)

**REPORT**   Include the following in your report:

1. Brief description of the participants.
2. Setting where interaction took place.
3. Actual transcript of tape. Do *not* edit it.

In addition, address yourself to the following questions:

1. How did the individuals communicate? Did they use spoken language, gestures, body language? Explain.
2. Were language and speech always successfully used for the purpose of communication? Explain.
3. Did the listener seem to understand the speaker? Explain.
4. Did the speaker seem to code the message for the listener? Explain.
5. Summarize the language episode.

**EVALUATION**   Did this inquiry develop the specific objectives? If so, how? If not, why? How could the effectiveness of this inquiry be increased?

## INQUIRY 1.2

Some psychologists and psycholinguists have argued that communication occurs prior to the onset of language and speech (e.g., Bates, Camaioni, & Volterra 1975). If this is so, then we have further evidence for the notion that language and speech derive their meaning from or grow out of the need to communicate.

**OBJECTIVES**   The objectives of this inquiry are to:

1. Begin to observe how a person without a language system communicates.
2. Begin to develop skills in using analyses of interaction as a means for systematically analyzing communication.
3. Explore the relationship among communication, language, and speech.

**PROCEDURES**   Tape-record and carefully observe communication occurring between a parent and a very young child (less than sixteen months). This communication should represent a time of high interaction, but may be of short duration (five to ten minutes). Transcribe the tape and integrate your observations using the following format:

1. Child (points down away from the chair): "Nunun uhnuh."
2. Mother: "You wanta get down? Huh?"

**REPORT**   Include the following in your report:

1. The participants' ages.
2. The context in which the interaction took place.
3. An actual account of the interaction. Include all uses of speech and language, as well as of other forms of communication.

Address yourself to the following questions when analyzing the communicative episode:

1. What was the role of speech in the communicative episode?
2. What was the role of language in the communicative episode?
3. What other factors contributed to the process of communication (e.g., context, pointing, etc.)?
4. How did communication, language, and speech interact in this episode?

**EVALUATION**   Did this inquiry develop the specific objectives? If so, how? If not, why? How could the effectiveness of this inquiry be increased?

# 2

# The Structure of Communication, Language, and Speech

If there were no structure underlying communication, language, and speech, we would still be learning the potentially infinite features and the combinations thereof that comprise our complex communication system. However, our communication system does have structure, and this chapter presents an analysis of the structures underlying communication, language, and speech. Without at least a basic understanding of these underlying structures, it is unlikely that one can truly comprehend the nature and the significance of the developmental process described in Chapters 3 through 5.

## THE STRUCTURE OF COMMUNICATION

Traditionally, investigators have studied communication from the perspective that language has the function of performing a universal set of communicative functions. Communication was studied in persons who had some mastery of language and speech systems. More recently, however, the study of communication has been extended to cover the periods prior to the onset of speech and language—the **perlocutionary phase**, which is characterized by unintentional use of signals (Austin, 1962), and the **illocutionary phase**, in which the child intentionally uses nonverbal signals to convey meaning (Bates, Camaioni, & Volterra, 1975).

In order to discover the roots of communication that is linguistic in nature, one must first explore the structure of prelinguistic communication. Let us begin by analyzing the following accounts of two adult-child interactions. The first interaction is between Serena, whose age is four months and twenty-nine days, and an adult observer (Bates, Camaioni, & Volterra, 1975, p. 213).

15

The adult observer moves close in front of Serena, who touches his face and grasps his hair. The adult pulls back. Serena agitates her arms vigorously. The sequence is repeated several times in succession. Throughout, Serena continues to smile and vocalize. . . .

The adult in this episode responds as if Serena were intentionally signaling *more play*. However, there is no evidence that Serena is aware of the signal value of her arm movement; consequently, the movement of her arms is unintentional. If, however, Serena had first looked towards the adult and then initiated arm-swinging, one would have a stronger case to consider her signaling behavior as intentional.

Snow (1977*a*) provides other examples of "conversation" between mothers and young babies. For example, the following interaction occurred between a mother and Ann, her three-month-old baby (Snow, 1977*a*, p. 12):

> (Ann smiles.)
> Mother: "Oh, what a nice little smile! Yes, isn't that nice? There. There's a nice little smile."
> (Ann burps.)
> Mother: "What a nice wind as well! Yes, that's better, isn't it? Yes. Yes."
> (Ann vocalizes.)
> Mother: "Yes! There's a nice noise."

This sequence demonstrates that certain classes of unintentional communicative infant behaviors, such as smiles, burps, yawns, and gazing at an object, are responded to by the mother as if they were intended to communicate something specific (Snow, 1977*a*).

The two interactions demonstrate one structure of early communication **(CS)**, which can be portrayed as follows:

**CS 1**                    Signal (U,P)   $\rightleftharpoons$   Signal (I)

This signifies that the child unintentionally (U) and prelinguistically (P) behaves in such a manner so as to be interpreted by the adult as behaving both intentionally (I) and meaningfully. Behaviors like crying, smiling, swinging of arms, and so forth, are initially reactions to internal physiological states, rather than actions emerging from an awareness that such behaviors have the value or effect of signaling these states. However, the adult attributes intentionality to these behaviors and responds to them as though they were in fact intentional and meaningful. This earliest structure of communication is referred to as the **perlocutionary structure.**

However, as we know from the introductory comments on communication presented in Chapter 1, communication has the quality of intentionality. That is, basic to the process of communication is an awareness that the action will affect the responses of the other person. The following scene between a mother (M) and her child, Carlotta (C), who is one year old, illustrates this basic quality (Bates, Camaioni, & Volterra, 1975, p. 217):

C is seated in a corridor in front of the kitchen door. She looks toward her mother and calls with an acute sound "ha." M comes over to her, and C looks toward the kitchen, twisting her body and upper shoulders to do so. M carries her into the kitchen, and C points toward the sink. M gives her a glass of water, and C drinks it eagerly.

Note that Carlotta used several behaviors to communicate with her mother. These behavioral schemes usually involve eye contact followed by either vocalization or some gesture, such as pointing. In the above episode, Carlotta looks toward her mother and then vocalizes *ha*. Later, she looks toward the kitchen and finally points toward the sink. It is the initial eye contact or looking that permits the reasonable inference of intentionality. The entire communicative episode had one apparent function for Carlotta—that of demanding *I want water and you mommy* (agent) *get* (action) *it* (object) *for me*. This interaction is representative of another structure of early communication, which can be characterized as follows:

(function)

**CS 2a**         Signal (I,P) ——————▶ Agent to obtain
                                                         desired objects or actions

Communicative structure 2a portrays an intentional (I) prelinguistic (P) signal serving the purpose of making another person act as an agent to obtain an object or continue an action. Bates, Camaioni, and Volterra (1975) refer to this structure as a **proto-imperative,** whereby the child's intentional behavior signals such requests as *Get the ball* or *Want water*. However, intentional prelinguistic communicative signals are not restricted to the proto-imperative structure. This can be seen in the following example of Carlotta's behavior as she interacts with an already obtained object (Bates, Camaioni, & Volterra, 1975, p. 217):

She would first orient toward the interesting object or event, extending her arm and forefinger in the characteristic pointing gesture while uttering a breathy sound "ha." Then she would swing around, point at the adult with the same gesture, and return to look at the object and point at adult, point at object. . . .

Here we see a characteristic pattern of behavioral schemes that permits us to infer that Carlotta's communication is indeed intentional. First, Carlotta uses eye contact to signal to the adult that her attention is requested. Only then does the child point or vocalize indexing the object or event. As stated before, it is this prior eye contact that allows us to reasonably infer that the subsequent communicative signal (i.e., pointing) is an intentional one. However, the signal, in this case, does not have the function of demanding that was evidenced by the proto-imperative structure. Instead, the apparent intent of Carlotta's communication is to use the object as a means of acquiring the adult's attention. Carlotta already has obtained the desired object. Therefore, she does not need to solicit adult help in obtaining or operating the object. Instead, the child shows or gives the object to the person for no other apparent reason than to solicit the person's attention, as if to say *Look at the object* or *Here (see) the object.* This is illustrated in the foregoing episode where Carlotta points at the object, points at the adult, and returns to look and point again at the object. One other interpretation is that the child is seeking adult affirmation of her concepts. (*The object is an entity. Look at it and acknowledge its existence as such.*)

This pattern is characteristic of what Bates et al. (1975) call the **proto-declarative,** as if the child is saying *Mommy, see the ball.* The structure of the proto-declarative is quite similar to that of the proto-imperative (CS 2a).

|            |                                   | (function) |                                                              |
| ---------- | --------------------------------- | ---------- | ------------------------------------------------------------ |
| **CS 2b**  | Signal (I,P)  $\longrightarrow$   |            | Object as means for obtaining adult attention or confirmation |

However, the underlying function differs. Because of the similarity of structure in CS 2a and CS 2b, that is, the signals are both intentional (I) and prelinguistic (P), both the proto-imperative and the proto-declarative are subsumed under the larger category of the illocutionary phase.

The final major communicative structures to be discussed in this section appear to have the same functions as those of the illocutionary phase, those of using persons as agents in obtaining desired objects (proto-imperative) and of using objects in obtaining adult attention and affirmation (proto-declarative). However, as can be seen from CS 3a and CS 3b, the signal is no longer nonverbal in nature but is now linguistic (L), or symbolic.

| **CS 3a** | Signal (I,L)  $\longrightarrow$ | Agent on object/events |
| --------- | ------------------------------- | ---------------------- |
| **CS 3b** | Signal (I,L)  $\longrightarrow$ | Objects/events on agent |

This change in structure marks the entrance into what has been called the **locutionary phase** of communication, in which linguistic symbols emerge as important communicative vehicles.

To summarize up to this point, the structure and function of communication has its origins in the prelinguistic period of development. The importance of this prelinguistic period will become increasingly obvious when we discuss language acquisition in Chapter 4. Inquiries 2.1 and 2.2 at the end of this chapter are designed to facilitate the analysis and further exploration of this early communicative functioning.

## THE STRUCTURE OF LANGUAGE

In this section, an introduction to the structure of language is presented. This includes the semantic component of language, which deals primarily with meaning. Included in the discussion of semantics are descriptions of (1) the most basic unit of meaning, the morpheme, (2) categories of meaning underlying words, and (3) the meaningful relationships among words. The structure of language, which governs the arrangement of words into sentences, is described in the section entitled "The Syntactic Structure." This section provides an overview of some rules of English structure that are quite complex in nature. Yet it is the syntactic structure of a language that permits the language user to convey his intended meaning to another member of his linguistic community. Although these two components—semantics and syntax—are inseparable in actual language usage, for ease of comprehension they are presented separately here. Similarly, although semantics and syntax are not naturally isolated from their communicative contexts (both physical and social), for ease of presentation they have been somewhat artificially treated here as distinct, separable components of communication.

**THE SEMANTIC STRUCTURE**   Semantics is the aspect of language dealing with meaning and how it is communicated through the use of language. Semantics is concerned with the meaning of words, the meaningful relations among words, sentences, and other linguistic entities such as intonation. Meaningful distinctions made at the linguistic level reflect cognitive distinctions that emerge in the prelinguistic period (Schlesinger, 1974).

The way we group objects, events, and states into categories and subsequently symbolize them through language is not always apparent or completely predictable. For example, on the basis of appearance alone, why do we categorize St. Bernards, Chihuahuas, Irish wolfhounds, and French poodles as dogs, excluding other animals, such as cows or horses? Certainly the large, loud-sounding, long-haired St. Bernard does not physically resemble the tiny, short-haired, high-pitched Chihuahua. In fact, the St. Bernard more closely resembles the cow in size and shape, than it does many other members of the category *dog*. Individuals must learn to utilize other cognitive distinctions in addition to perceptual attributes, such as size and shape, if their cognitive as well as semantic distinctions are to eventually correspond with those of the society of which they are members.

The semantic structure, at even the one-word level, is probably the least understood aspect of language, even though our knowledge base does not suffer from a dearth of facts about the dictionary meaning of isolated words. We can provide a definition of the word *dog* or the word *break,* but what structures or features permit us to know and use the term *dog* only when referring to certain animate, nonhuman, four-legged animals in contrast to other animate, nonhuman, four-legged animals? Similarly, what semantic features direct us to use the word *break* when describing an action upon an object as opposed to using the word *tear* when describing an action upon a different object? For example, of the following objects, which ones would you break and which ones would you tear?

| | |
|---|---|
| bread | leaf |
| cup | paper |
| ribbon | glass |
| pencil | door |
| dress | feather |

Our unconscious or tacit knowledge of the physical world and our language system produces immediately the following semantic categories:

| break | tear |
|-------|------|
| cup | dress |
| pencil | paper |
| glass | ribbon |
| door | |

Other distinctions are less clear. Does one break or tear bread, a leaf, or a feather?

The dictionary definition of tear is "to pull apart or separate by pulling." In contrast, the definition of break is "to separate into pieces or make a fracture in; divide into fragments." One must have some prior knowledge about the composition of physical objects to know whether an object is breakable or tearable, and these features are not always easily identifiable. This difficulty exists despite the two definitions provided above. If one *pulls* at a limb of a tree and therefore the limb becomes *separated* from the tree, according to the above definitions, does one tear the limb or does one break the limb?

The preceding example should demonstrate how complex the structure of semantics is even at the one-word level. Several theories have attempted to explicate a theory of semantics (see Chapter 6; Fillmore, 1968; Chafe, 1970). The **semantic feature theory** (Katz & Fodor, 1963), for example, provides us with a reasonable model with which to begin to understand the structure of semantics. The semantic feature model states that words and, for that matter, cognitive distinctions are a result of our understanding that actions, objects, states, events, and so forth, are differentiated on the basis of physical *or* social features occurring in the environment. Certain objects are included in one category and excluded from others on the basis of a "bundle" of core features shared by some and not shared by others, as illustrated in Figure 2.1.

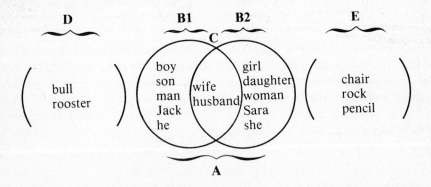

FIGURE 2.1   Sets of Words Illustrating the Semantic Feature Model

If we examine the sets of words shown in Figure 2.1, we see that a certain shared set of semantic features permits us to reasonably refer to all elements in Set A as [+human]. Each element of the Set A is [+human, +animate, +two-legged]. Sex, age, or the marital status of each are not core semantic features. However, for *boy, son, man, Jack,* and *he* to comprise a category, Set B1, separate from Set B2 (*girl, daughter,* etc.), the semantic feature [+human] is not sufficient. The feature [+human] is too global; the concept of a male would be overextended. Given this overextension, the word *boy* might well be used to refer to *man* and *Jack,* as well as *girl* and *daughter,* but not to *chair* [−human] or rooster [−human]. Therefore, a second semantic feature of [±female] has to be added to [+human] to differentiate the members of Set B2 from Sets B1, D, and E. What additional semantic features have to be added to differentiate Set C from the other sets? In addition to [+human], the features [+adult, +married] would be necessary.

Semantic features at the word level also influence how we judge the meaningfulness of a sentence. Although we will return to the topic of semantics at the multi-word level in a later section, a few examples will suffice here:

**(1)**     *The chair drank some water.*

**(2)**     *The dog thought about his bone.*

**(3)**     *My son was angry at herself.*

**(4)**     *Her husband is a bachelor.*

Each of these sentences is anomalous because in each one words that contain incompatible semantic features are used in conjunction with one another. These combinations violate what are called selection restrictions, which are semantic constraints governing word combinations. In simpler terms, the sentences simply do not conform to our notions of reality. For example, in sentence **(1)** *chair* [−animate] does not correspond with *drank* [+animate]. Similarly, *dog* [+animate, −human] and *thought* [+human] in sentence **(2)** do not correspond at the semantic features level because once again their juxtaposition contradicts our understanding of our world.

A complete set of semantic features has yet to be identified by linguists studying this aspect of semantics. Also, we do not fully understand how children learn which specific features are critical to the comprehension and production of language. We will consider this latter issue in Chapter 6.

**BASIC SEMANTIC RELATIONS.** Semantics depends on more than the individual meanings of isolated words. Consider this sentence used by Brown (1973*a*, p. 7): *Mr. Smith cut the rope with a knife.* Structurally there are four phrases: (1) *Mr. Smith,* (2) *cut,* (3) *the rope,* and (4) *with a knife.* Each phrase has a distinct semantic role in the sentence and a distinct semantic relation with other phrases in the sentence, as illustrated below:[1]

| Semantic relation | Description | Example |
|---|---|---|
| Agent | One who causes or performs an action | *Mr. Smith* |
| Action | The action taken | *cut* |
| Object | The recipient of an action | *the rope* |
| Instrument | Object used to play a part in action | *the knife* |

It is insufficient to analyze the above sentence from a syntactic perspective alone, even though three of the phrases are noun phrases (*Mr. Smith, the rope,* and *a knife*). The role that each noun phrase plays in a particular sentence is not identified using a strict syntactic approach. The same noun phrase may play quite a different semantic role depending on the particular sentence. As Brown (1973a) illustrates, the noun phrase *Mr. Smith* could also take the semantic role of experiencer (*Mr. Smith wanted a drink*) or the role of object (*They drowned Mr. Smith*) or beneficiary (*Mr. Smith owns a Rolls-Royce*).

It is also insufficient to analyze a sentence solely on the basis of syntactic structures such as its subject, verb, or object, for these categories are too abstract. For example, *Mr. Smith* is the subject of the following sentences:

**(5)**                              *Mr. Smith hit the ball.*

**(6)**                              *Mr. Smith wanted a raise.*

**(7)**                              *Mr. Smith has two homes.*

In each sentence above *Mr. Smith* plays a different semantic role: in **(5)** that of agent, in **(6)** experiencer, and in **(7)** beneficiary. Table 2.1 illustrates the basic semantic relations that characterize the semantic system of English.

MODULATION OF MEANING. In addition to basic semantic relations, there are meaningful linguistic elements that serve to modulate meaning. Examine the following clusters of meaningful elements.

| Cluster I | Cluster II | Cluster III |
|---|---|---|
| *boy* (agent) | *in, on* | *-ed* |
| *run* (action) | *and* | *-s* |
| *dirty* (attribute) | *is* | *re-* |
| *chair* (location) | *a, the* | *-ing* |

The words in Cluster I all represent basic semantic roles (i.e., agent, attribute, action, and location). These words are often referred to as **content words**. Although the morphemes in Clusters II and III also carry meaning, these meanings are less obvious or essential (i.e., are subordinate to the basic semantic roles identified in Cluster I).

TABLE 2.1   Basic Semantic Categories

| Category | Definition | Example* |
|---|---|---|
| 1. Agent | One who causes or performs an action | *Jon* pushes the truck. |
| 2. Action | Action taken | Jon *pushes* the truck. |
| 3. Object | Someone or something suffering a change of state or receiving an action | Jon pushes the *truck*. He hit the *girl*. |
| 4. Locative | Place or locus of an action or entity | The truck rolled under the *chair*. |
| 5. Entity | A person or thing having a distinct existence | *Mommy* is home. Here's a *dog*. |
| 6. Possession | Alienable or unalienable relationship between an object and a possessor | That's *mommy's sack*. See the *doggie's tail?* |
| 7. Attribution | Some characteristic of an entity, object, agent, or action that could not be known from its class characteristics alone | It's a *little dog*. The *yellow block* fell. |
| 8. State | A state of being | He *wants* more food. |
| 9. Experiencer | An animate object experiencing a temporary or durative state | *He* feels hungry. *Mr. Smith* wanted a raise. |
| 10. Beneficiary | One who is the beneficiary of a relationship | *Mr. Smith* has two homes. *I* have the cookie. |
| 11. Dative | The animate being affected by the state or action | He gave the book to *Ben*. |
| 12. Instrument | The inanimate force or object causally involved in the state or action | The *knife* cut the meat. |

Adapted from Brown (1973*a*), Fillmore (1968), and Chafe (1970).
* Italicized words represent the designated category.

Brown (1973*a*) argues that the grammatical morphemes (Clusters II and III) serve to modulate the meanings of the basic semantic terms in the following ways. First, certain grammatical morphemes (e.g., progressive *-ing,* past tense marker *-ed,* plural inflection *-s,* and articles *a* and *the*) modulate, or further specify, the references made by nouns and verbs (Brown, 1973*a*). In fact, these grammatical morphemes are so dependent on the words that they modulate that it is inconceivable for them to be used alone. These morphemes (Cluster III) are frequently referred to as **bound morphemes,** as they must occur joined to other morphemes (content words). Second, grammatical morphemes such as the locative prepositions *in, on,* and *under* modulate meaning in that they specify more precisely the relation of place. Third, grammatical morphemes such as the present tense copulas *is, are,* and *am* and the possessive marker *-s* add redundant information to relations already expressed by combining the basic semantic categories (e.g., *John'(s) shoe* or *The ball (is) big*). Fourth, auxiliary verbs such as *be* and *have* modulate the meanings of verbs (e.g., *run → is running, has run*) by further specifying tense, progression of action, and so on.

Morphemes such as those in Cluster II are frequently referred to as **structural words,** because they reliably signal the function of the syntactic structures in which they occur. (*A* and *the* mark a structure as a noun phrase; *is* marks a structure as a verb phrase; *in* and *on* mark structures as prepositional phrases; etc.)

To summarize thus far, semantics, whether at the single-word or sentential level, involves the ways in which we linguistically communicate subtle differences of meaning. Certain semantic categories have superordinate communication value (e.g., those words in Cluster I). Others, such as the grammatical morphemes in Clusters II and III, are less critical for communicating basic meanings. It should be noted, however, that extralinguistic features such as gestures, shared knowledge, and the physical and social contexts are all intricately tied into meaningful communication.

**SEMANTICS RECONSIDERED**   In contrast to previously conceived notions about semantics, the study of semantics is not the study of words used to simply name things. Semantic competence requires or is reflective of one's knowledge of the physical, linguistic, and social world. Bartel (1975) illustrates how this knowledge determines or disambiguates the meaning of a word by using the example *fair*. In isolation, the word *fair* does not have one specific meaning. Given different linguistic, social, or physical contexts, *fair* can denote a carnivallike event, a description of the weather of a particular day, one's hair coloring or skin pigmentation, or even-handed behavior. Similarly, how one refers to the object 10¢ is dependent on the particular context. While the object remains the same, given a particular set of alternatives, it can be referred to as (1) *a dime,* (2) *a coin,* (3) *money,* (4) *an artifact,* (5) *that thing,* (6) *it,* or (7) *a 1952 dime that is quite dull and has most of its lettering worn down* (Brown, 1958).

Therefore, semantic competence requires not only the knowledge of a particular intended object or event, but also knowledge of the alternatives from which it must be differentiated. This point is illustrated when one considers the following simple paradigm proposed by Olson (1970, p. 264):

A gold star is placed under a small, wooden block. A speaker who saw this act is then asked to tell a listener, who did not see the act, where the gold star is. In every case, the star is placed under the *same* block, a small white, . . . one. However, in the first case there is one alternative block present, a small, round, *black* one. In the second case there is a different alternative block present, a small, *square* white, . . . one. In a third case there are three alternative blocks present, a round black one, a square black one, and a square white one. These three cases are shown in the figure.

| | Event | Alternative | Utterance |
|---|---|---|---|
| Case 1 | ○ | ● | ...the white one |
| Case 2 | ○ | ☐ | ...the round one |
| Case 3 | ○ | ☐●■ | ...the round, white one |
| Case 4 | ○ | | (Look under) the round, white, wooden block that is about one inch across... |

In these situations, the speaker would say the following for Case 1: "It's under the *white* one"; for Case 2: "It's under the *round* one"; for Case 3: "It's under the *round, white* one." [From D. Olson, Language and thought: Aspects of a cognitive theory of semantics. *Psychological Review,* 1970, *77,* p. 264. Used with permission of the author. Figure copyright 1970 by the American Psychological Association. Reprinted by permission.]

Olson summarizes his conclusions as follows:

1. Words are not simple names for things. If this were the case, each sender would utilize the same word(s) in referring to the same thing. This clearly was not the case in the above situation.
2. Words do not name intended referents. In the example cited, the gold star is under the same block, which remains the intended referent. Yet in each case the utterances differ. "Words designate, signal, or specify an intended referent relative to the set of contextual alternatives from which it must be differentiated" (Olson, 1970, p. 264). It is as if the sender self-questions in this instance "What alternatives could confuse or distract the receiver; what do I need to mention so that this does not occur?" It is this

combined knowledge, as well as the factors described earlier, that makes the nature and structure of semantics so complex.

The area of semantics is pursued further in Inquiries 2.3 through 2.5 presented at the end of this chapter. Inquiry 2.3 is designed to investigate further the basic semantic relations used by a child in an informal conversation. Inquiry 2.4 looks once again at the semantic features theory, and Inquiry 2.5 investigates "what a thing is called."

## THE SYNTACTIC STRUCTURE

Linguistic knowledge is not restricted to the meaning, or semantic component, of language. It also includes those rules which permit the coding of intended meaning in acceptable sequences or constructions (i.e., syntactic structures). Syntax is that branch of language that deals with the arrangement of semantic elements into acceptable sequences. Syntactic sequences are not merely strings of words that define or comprise a sentence. As stated in Chapter 1, sentences are rule-governed structures. Without necessarily being able to state these syntactic rules, each of us acts as though we explicitly know them when we comprehend and produce acceptable sentences, as well as when we judge the acceptability of sentences. Take, for example, the following sequences of morphemes:

(8)                              *To John walked school*

(9)                              *Sake for ness good*

(10)                             *John is very well.*

It is easy not only to identify the one acceptable sequence from the above three, but also to order each sequence on the basis of how closely it follows the syntactic rules of English. Sequence **(10)** is considered an acceptable construction because it represents a rule-governed sentence. Although both sequences **(8)** and **(9)** are clearly not acceptable sentences, there is still a hierarchy of rule-governedness. In sequence **(8)**, there are violations of the rules governing word order. In sequence **(9)**, however, not only are there violations of the rules governing word order, but there are also violations concerning the sequencing of the morphemes. For example, *-ness* is a grammatical morpheme that cannot function independently of a more basic semantic element, such as the attribute *good*. To make sense, some grammatical morphemes such as *-ness* must be suffixed to particular words (e.g., *good*). The syntactic rules that govern our language system are described in the following sections.

**PHRASE STRUCTURES AND WORD ORDER**    The syntactic structure of sentences can be described by a finite set of rules that permit the generation of a potentially infinite number of sentences. Chomsky (1965) claims that one's abilities to identify grammatical versus ungrammatical sentences, to generate numerous sentences given just one syntactic rule, and to create and to understand sentences never spoken or heard before are due to the fact that one has internalized rules of sentence construction. In other words, speakers and listeners have a tacit or unconscious knowledge of grammatical rules. **Phrase structure rules** (PS rules) attempt to organize this tacit knowledge. A PS rule system is one way of relating as well as identifying basic elements or constituents of a sentence.

There are several levels of PS rules. Sentence **(13)** allows for the analysis of these levels.

**(13)**  *The woman drove to the store.*

At one level we can view sentence **(13)** as being composed of a *subject* and a *predicate.* Therefore, a sentence (S) can be represented as follows:

$$S \longrightarrow \text{Subject } (\textit{The woman}) + \text{Predicate } (\textit{drove to the store})$$

Because the subject of a sentence is comprised of at least a noun or a pronoun, many linguists refer to this constituent as a noun phrase (NP). Similarly, because the predicate of a sentence is comprised of a verb as its basic element, it is usually referred to as the verb phrase (VP). As a result, linguists suggest that the following is one of the most basic rules of grammar:

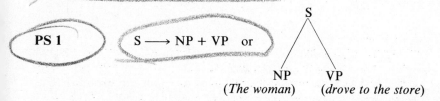

**PS 1**  $S \longrightarrow NP + VP$  or

S
/ \
NP       VP
(*The woman*)   (*drove to the store*)

The order of appearance in the actual sentence—or the relationship between these two constituents NP and VP    is implied in the left to right sequencing. This one PS rule, however, does not identify or delimit either the elements that may be constituted within the NP or the order for sequencing these elements. Therefore, the NP must be further specified. The NP of sentence **(13)** contains a determiner *the* (Det) plus a noun *woman* (N) in this order and is symbolized as follows:

$NP_1$
/ \
Det       N
(*the*)   (*woman*)

**PS 2**  $NP_1 \longrightarrow Det + N$  or

Similarly, the VP must be further specified to account for the actual elements of the phrase. The VP of sentence **(13)**, contains a verb *drove* (V) and a locative phrase *to the store* (Loc) and is symbolized as follows:

**PS 3**           VP $\longrightarrow$ V + Loc   or

$$
\begin{array}{c}
\text{VP} \\
\diagup\diagdown \\
\text{(tense)} \\
\text{V} \qquad \text{Loc} \\
(\textit{drove}) \quad (\textit{to the store})
\end{array}
$$

However, the locative phrase requires further analysis for it contains a preposition *to* (Prep) and another NP (*the store*). The PS rule representing this constituent is the following:

**PS 4**           Loc $\longrightarrow$ Prep + $NP_2$   or

$$
\begin{array}{c}
\text{Loc} \\
\diagup\diagdown \\
\text{prep} \qquad NP_2 \\
(\textit{to}) \qquad (\textit{the store})
\end{array}
$$

All that remains at a structural level is the specification of the NP (*the store*) in the locative phrase. The following PS rule describes this $NP_2$:

**PS 5**           $NP_2 \longrightarrow$ Det + N   or

$$
\begin{array}{c}
NP_2 \\
\diagup\diagdown \\
\text{Det} \qquad \text{N} \\
(\textit{the}) \qquad (\textit{store})
\end{array}
$$

At a final level of analysis, the actual lexical items or words are included. The following specifies some possible nouns that could appear in a NP:[3]

$$
\text{N} \longrightarrow \left\{ \begin{array}{l} \textit{woman} \\ \textit{man} \\ \textit{father} \\ \textit{store} \\ \textit{chair} \\ \textit{house} \end{array} \right\}
$$

The natural interaction between syntax and semantics should already be noted. In sentence **(13)**, $NP_1$ (*The woman*) is actually the agent of the sentence. Therefore, lexical items occuring in $NP_1$ must have the semantic feature [+animate] Similarly, because of the nature of the action (*drove the car*), entries into this NP must be not only [+animate] but also [+human]. Therefore, the [−animate, −human] nouns *store, chair,* and *house* would be anomalous if they appeared in $NP_1$. In contrast, $NP_2$ in the locative phrase may contain [−animate] nouns because of its semantic relationship in the sentence.

Some possible determiners are those shown in the following:

$$\text{Det} \longrightarrow \begin{Bmatrix} the \\ a \\ that \\ this \end{Bmatrix}$$

Some possible verbs are as shown.

$$\text{V} \longrightarrow \begin{Bmatrix} drove \\ rode \\ . \\ . \\ . \end{Bmatrix}$$

Some possible prepositions are as shown.

$$\text{Prep} \longrightarrow \begin{Bmatrix} to \\ at \\ . \\ . \\ . \end{Bmatrix}$$

The preceding PS rules were used to illustrate the syntactic structure of sentence **(13)**. However, linguists do provide more general rules, as can be seen below:

**PS 6** $\qquad$ $\text{NP} \longrightarrow \begin{Bmatrix} \text{Pronoun} \\ [\text{Det}] + \text{N} \\ [\text{Det}] + [\text{Adj}] + \text{N} \\ . \\ . \\ . \end{Bmatrix}$

**PS 7** $\qquad$ $\text{VP} \longrightarrow \begin{Bmatrix} \text{V} + [\text{NP}] \\ [\text{Aux}] + \text{V} \\ . \\ . \\ . \end{Bmatrix}$

These more general rules permit the generation of numerous phrases and sentences. To illustrate, generate as many noun phrases as possible given the NP rule outlined above. The following are just a few of the possible noun phrases:

| Agent [+animate] | Object [± animate] |
|---|---|
| He | him |
| She | them |
| They | the boy |
| The fat one | the truck |
| Many | Mark |
| My friend | it |
| The boy | that one |
| . | the store |
| . | the broken chair |
| . | . |
|  | . |
|  | . |

Phrase structure rules can be used to produce a tremendous number of sentences. This generative quality is further increased by the embedding of one sentence within another using the following PS rule:

**PS 8**                    $NP \longrightarrow \left\{ \begin{array}{c} \text{Pronoun} \\ \text{[Det] + N} \end{array} \right\} + [S]$

This yields such NPs as follow:

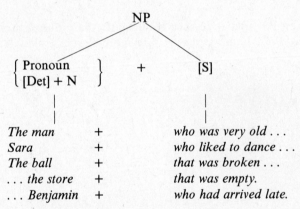

$$NP$$

$$\left\{ \begin{array}{c} \text{Pronoun} \\ \text{[Det] + N} \end{array} \right\} \quad + \quad [S]$$

| | | |
|---|---|---|
| *The man* | + | *who was very old . . .* |
| *Sara* | + | *who liked to dance . . .* |
| *The ball* | + | *that was broken . . .* |
| *. . . the store* | + | *that was empty.* |
| *. . . Benjamin* | + | *who had arrived late.* |

It is the recursive nature of a grammar that reflects the notion that language puts no arbitrary restrictions on sentence length.

**TRANSFORMATIONAL RULES**   Despite the capacity of phrase structure rules to codify much of one's knowledge about one's native language, according to linguists such as Chomsky, a phrase structure grammar could account neither for the infinite number of sentences of a natural language, nor for (1) internal grammatical relations, (2) relationships among sentences, and (3) ambiguous sentences. For example, PS rules cannot account for the fact that sentences **(14)** and **(15)** convey the same basic meaning or proposition **(deep structure)** even though the **surface structures** are quite different.[4]

**(14)**              *The girl hits the ball.*

**(15)**              *The ball is hit by the girl.*

This can be seen from the following tree diagrams of PS rules:

**Sentence (14)**

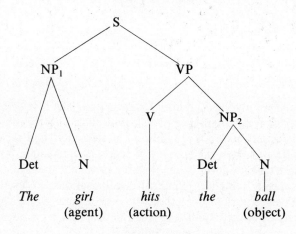

**Sentence (15)**

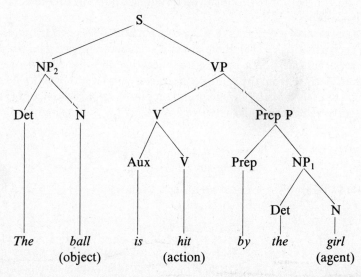

Although the PS rules for the above two sentences yield two different surface structures, how do we explain the fact that sentences **(14)** and **(15)** mean essentially the same (i.e., are derived from the same deep structure)? **Transformational rules** (T rules) specify how one deep structure of a sentence is related to various surface structures and how various sentences are related to each other. For example, sentence **(14)** is a simple **active sentence** that can be related to the **passive sentence (15)** through a series of transformational operations—adding elements, deleting some elements, rearranging elements, or substituting elements. The following passive transformation (T passive) shows how sentences **(14)** and **(15)** are related.

T passive:

| Sentence (14) | Sentence (15) |
|---|---|

$$NP_1 + V + \text{-}s + NP_2 \;\Rightarrow\; NP_2 + is + V + by + NP_1$$

*The girl hits the ball.*     *The ball is hit by the girl.*

Several operations are involved in this transformation. The first and second noun phrases are inverted (rearranging elements). *Is* is placed before the verb and the preposition *by* is added before $NP_1$ (addition of elements), and the grammatical morpheme *-s* is deleted from the verb *hit* (deletion of elements).

The foregoing transformation is one possible passive transformation for relating active and passive sentences. Similar transformations are used for relating both active and passive sentences to the same deep structure of a sentence. What is important here, however, is not a detailed description of various transformational rules, but rather a basic understanding that a PS grammar may not adequately show the way in which various sentences are related. Before leaving this section on transformational grammar, we should consider the relationship among other sentence types.

In addition to active declarative sentences such as sentence **(14)** and passive sentences such as sentence **(15)**, there are also sentences that negate a proposition and sentences that question a proposition. Negative and interrogative sentences are, however, derived from the same deep structure and are related to declarative sentences by various transformational rules. Let us return to sentence **(14)** and see how a negative sentence and an interrogative sentence are derived from the declarative.

**(16)**                      *The girl does not hit the ball.*
**(17)**                      *Does the girl hit the ball?*

Sentence **(14)**, using PS rules, is symbolized as follows:

$$NP_1 + V + \text{-}s + NP_2$$
*The girl hits the ball.*

To negate the proposition, the following transformational operations must be carried out: add the auxiliary *do* between $NP_1$ and V if an auxiliary verb is not already present in the declarative. The auxiliary verb (Aux) marks tense instead of being marked by the main verb (V). Add the negative morpheme *not* after the auxiliary verb. Finally, an optional transformation permits the contraction of *not* and the auxiliary. Symbolically, the transformational operations (T neg) to the negative sentence are as follows.

Declarative:

$$NP_1 + V + \text{-}s + NP_2$$
*The girl hits the ball.*

T neg 1 [Add Aux *do* if Aux not present]:

$$NP_1 + Aux + V + NP_2$$
*The girl does hit the ball.*

T neg 2 [Add negative morpheme *not* after Aux.]:

$$NP_1 + Aux + Neg + V + NP_2$$
*The girl does not hit the ball.*

T neg 3 [Contract Aux and *not* (optional)]:

*The girl doesn't hit the ball.*

Therefore, the following negative transformation relates sentences **(14)** and **(16)**.
T neg:

| Sentence **(14)** | | Sentence **(16)** |
|---|---|---|
| $NP_1 + V + \text{-}s + NP_2$ | $\Rightarrow$ | $NP_1 + Aux + Neg + V + NP_2$ |
| *The girl hits the ball.* | | *The girl does not hit the ball.* |

Similarly, to transform the declarative sentence **(14)** into its related question form **(17)**, the following transformational operations are applicable. First, the auxiliary verb *do* is added before the main verb if an auxiliary is not already present in the declarative sentence. Once again, the auxiliary verb marks the tense. Then, the auxiliary verb and the first noun phrase are inverted. These transformational operations (T quest) are symbolically represented below.

Declarative:

$$NP_1 + V + \text{-}s + NP_2$$
*The girl hits the ball.*

T quest 1 [Add Aux *do* if Aux is not present]:

$$NP_1 + Aux + V + NP_2$$
*The girl does hit the ball.*

T quest 2 [Invert Aux with $NP_1$]:

$$Aux + NP_1 + V + NP_2$$
*Does the girl hit the ball?*

Therefore, the following interrogative transformation relates sentences **(14)** and **(17)**.

T quest:

|        **Sentence (14)**        |        **Sentence (17)**        |
| :---: | :---: |

$$NP_1 + V + \text{-}s + NP_2 \Rightarrow Aux + NP_1 + V + NP_2$$

*The girl hits the ball.*      *Does the girl hit the ball?*

The purpose of the preceding discussion has not been to present a detailed description of all of the various PS rules and T rules. Rather the purpose has been to describe some of the underlying principles that permit one (1) to understand and produce novel sentences, (2) to relate various sentences to the same basic proposition, and (3) to relate variations of a sentence to each other. It is this set of underlying rules and operations that a child must and usually does learn, rather than a finite set of specific strings of words. In fact, many linguists argue that all speakers of a native language operate as if they know these underlying rules. It is this phenomenon of tacit knowledge that makes the study of language so exciting and so complex.

Inquiries 2.6 through 2.10, presented at the end of the chapter, are designed to provide a further exploration of the syntactic component of language and its interaction with the semantic component. Each inquiry addresses a different aspect of a speaker's knowledge of the language, so that the structure of language may be more comprehensible.

## SPEECH: THE PHONOLOGICAL STRUCTURES

The reason that humans are capable of producing such a wide variety of sounds is due to the physiological structure of their respiratory system. As can be seen in Figure 2.2, the structure of this system permits us to resonate our breath stream in either our nasal cavity or our oral cavity. The tautness or laxness of our vocal cords permits us to produce a variety of sounds. Changing the shape of our vocal cavity (mouth) permits further versatility in sound production. Various placements of the tongue in relationship to the teeth and palate further contribute to our ability to produce varied sounds.

Given the wide range of sound production, only a relatively small subset of these sounds fall within the parameters of speech, or what is called by many the phonological system of a particular language. Furthermore, the particular subset of sounds considered to be speech varies from language to language and, to a lesser extent, from dialect to dialect. As was mentioned in Chapter 1, the spoken language is made up of phonemes, which have been traditionally considered to be the smallest significant unit of sound in a word or phrase. By itself, each phoneme is meaningless and must be combined into words or with words to be meaningful.

There are approximately forty-four speech-sounds or phonemes in the English language. To a very limited degree, these phonemes may be represented in writing

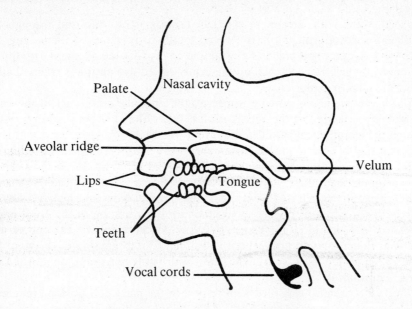

FIGURE 2.2   The Vocal Structure

by the letters of the English alphabet. Thus, in the spoken word *bat,* there are three phonemes: the sound /b/, the sound /a/, and the sound /t/.[5] In this example, the sounds of the spoken word are each represented in the written form of the word by a corresponding letter, that is, *b-a-t.* However, as will become clear in Chapter 8, this is not always the case.

There are two major classes of phonemes, **segmental features** and **suprasegmental features.** The segmental features apply to those phonemes that have traditionally been referred to as vowels, consonants, or semivowels. For each of the following words, we can actually analyze the segmental phonemes.

*pan* ⟶ /p/  /a/  /n/   (three segmental phonemes)

*belt* ⟶ /b/  /e/  /l/  /t/   (four segmental phonemes)

*lends* ⟶ /l/  /e/  /n/  /d/  /z/   (five segmental phonemes)[6]

*walnut* ⟶ /w/  /a/  /l/  /n/  /u/  /t/   (six segmental phonemes)

When **vowels** are produced, the air from the lungs passes through the vocal cords, causing them to vibrate, and then flows freely into the oral cavity. Changes in vowel sounds occur primarily as a result of changes in the shape of the mouth as air flows unobstructed through it. Vowels are represented by the alphabetical letters *a, e, i, o,* and *u.* However, varying vowel sounds are associated with each of these letters, making alphabetic representation of vowel sounds very difficult.

Another group of segmental phonemes is consonants. When **consonants** are produced, the breath stream, rather than flowing freely into and through the mouth as in vowel production, is blocked totally or partially by the tongue, the teeth, the lips, or the soft palate. For example, to produce the phoneme /p/, the air is temporarily held in check behind the firmly closed lips until it is released all at once with a sharp explosion.

Consonants are classified with respect to the presence or absence of the voice during the production of the speech-sound. When the air from the lungs passes through the closed vocal bands in the throat (see Figure 2.2), the vocal bands vibrate, causing a voiced sound. When the vocal bands are open, no vibration occurs when the air passes; hence the voiced sound is not produced. This can be easily demonstrated. Place your fingers on your throat where you can feel a slight swelling (sometimes referred to as the adam's apple). Now say the word *bat.* As you say this word, your fingers should pick up the vibration of the vocal bands associated with the initial phoneme /b/. Now say the word *pat.* In contrast, this time your fingers should not feel the vibration at the beginning of the word because /p/ is an unvoiced consonant (the vocal bands remaining open when the sound is produced).

Consonants are also classified with respect to the particular position they hold within a word. In the word *sing,* /s/ is in the **initial position;** in *lesson,* /s/ is in the **medial position;** and in the word *bus,* /s/ is in the **final position.** Vowels and semivowels can also hold a specific position in a word, however, all phonemes do not hold every position. For example, whereas /ŋ/ may be found in the medial or the final position of a word or syllable, such as in *singer* or *sing,* it does not occur in the initial position of English words.

Another feature of consonants is their nasal or oral character. Although most sounds of the English language are produced in the oral cavity, three consonants are considered to be nasal sounds. These are /n/, /m/, and /ŋ/. These nasal sounds are produced by forcing the air to escape through the nose rather than the mouth. If you place your hand lightly on your nose, you will be able to actually feel the air vibrating in your nose as you say the words *no, many,* and *thing.*

Different consonant sounds are produced depending on the place of the articulators—the teeth, tongue, and lips. Various combinations of the articulators, such as lips together (/p/, /b/, and /m/), teeth on lips (/f/ and /v/), tongue up against the teeth (/th/ and /n/), tongue up against the alveolar ridge (/t/, /d/, /s/, /z/, /ch/, and /j/), and so on, account for the various consonantal sounds.

Finally, consonants are also characterized by the manner in which the breath stream is obstructed as it flows through the mouth. If the flow of air is totally blocked (e.g., /t/, /g/, and /b/), the consonant is called a **stop.** If the flow is only partially blocked, the consonant is called a **fricative** (e.g., /f/, /th/, and /s/).

Each consonant, and each vowel for that matter, is comprised of a set of those features described above. Jakobson (1941) has argued that it is this bundle of **binary distinctive features** (i.e., voicing, place of articulation, etc.) that makes one segmental phoneme distinct from another. Let us examine several phonemes to understand the notion of binary distinctive features. The phoneme /d/ can be characterized by the presence or absence, that is, the binary quality, of certain features. The /d/ phoneme is consonantal not vowellike in nature [+consonantal]. It is voiced not unvoiced [+voiced] and oral not nasal [+oral]. It is produced using the articulators tongue and alveolar ridge [+tongue, +alveolar], and the breath stream is totally stopped as it passes through the mouth [+stop]. In contrast, the features comprising the phoneme /m/ are as follows:

[+consonantal]
[+voiced]
[−oral], that is, [+nasal]
[+bilabial]

If we compare the bundles of binary features of the /d/ and /m/ sounds, we can see that they are distinctive on the basis of three features—nasality, place of articulation, and the manner in which the breath stream is diverted. If we were to analyze each of the segmental phonemes of the English language, we would see that each phoneme represents a different and unique set of binary features.

Semivowels are segmental phonemes that fall between vowels and consonants and have some of the characteristics of both. In this book, the following sounds are considered to be semivowels: /w/, /y/, and /r/. Although /r/ has not been classified as a semivowel by some linguists (Schane, 1973; Chomsky & Halle, 1968), Fasold (1972) has argued that /r/ acts like a semivowel and can be grouped with /w/ and /y/. Since these phonemes fall between vowels and consonants, they are sometimes considered to be consonantal (consonantlike) and at other times vocalic (vowellike). These semivowels are generally consonantal when they precede vowels within a syllable (e.g., *quick* is pronounced *qwik; million* is pronounced *milyon*) and vocalic when they follow vowels (e.g., *car, cow,* and *joy*).

In addition to the segmental phonemes, there are also aspects of speech called **suprasegmental phonemes**. These suprasegmental phonemes are more commonly referred to as phonemes of pitch, intonation, juncture, and stress and constitute the "melody" of a language. **Pitch** is the relative height of tone with which an utterance is spoken. There are four pitches in English, ranging from low to high. In English, rather than having an effect on the literal meaning of a word or sentence, pitch signals affective states. For example, when one is nervous or excited, the pitch of one's utterances is usually higher than when one is calm and at ease. Brown (1977) suggests that a higher pitch is also used when speaking to a very young child, to plants, to pets, or when in a very intimate interaction. The reasons for this heightened pitch are still somewhat unknown, although Brown (1977) and Snow (1977b) suggest that it may, among other functions, serve to signal intimacy.

The use of pitch in some languages does affect meaning. For example, in Chinese the word *ch'i*, depending on the pitch used when pronouncing it, can mean "seven," "period of time," "use," or "breath."

**Intonation**, that is, the rise and fall of the voice, is a very important feature of English (or of any language, for that matter). Lieberman (1967) has argued that the intonational contour of a language serves to segment the continuous flow of speech into sentences or phrases. Our knowledge of these ups and downs of spoken English enables us to know when a declarative sentence ends (with a final fall in intonation) or when a question is asked (with a final rise in intonation).

In addition to segmenting the continuous flow of speech into sentences and phases, intonation adds to the literal meaning of an utterance. Lindfors (1980, p. 121) provides an example of this.

> Various intonation patterns differentiate between at least the "Oh" of sudden surprise, the "Oh" of challenge ( . . . ya' wanna bet?), the "Oh" of uncertainty ( . . . well . . . I don't know really), the "Oh" that means "How beautiful," the "Oh" of understanding ( . . . so *that's* what it means), the "Oh" of disappointment, the "Oh" of knowing a sly secret.

Juncture and stress are the final suprasegmental features we will consider here. Juncture and stress play an important role in English. Consider the following words: *desért, désert; presént, présent; convért, cónvert*. These verbs and nouns are not distinguished by their segmental phonemes, but in terms of the placement of the main stress, that is, which vowel is produced with the most articulatory force (Falk, 1973), and by where a pause or juncture occurs. Juncture and stress, in combination with specific intonational contours, frequently aid us in clarifying potentially ambiguous sentences. Take for example the following sentences:

**(18)**                          *Visiting relatives can be a nuisance.*
**(19)**                          *They are eating apples.*

Each of these sentences, as they appear out of a specific context and in writing, is ambiguous. Sentence **(18)** can mean either of the following:

**(18a)**                    *They are eating apples.*

                          (juncture) (stress)

**(18b)**                    *They are eating apples.*

                          (juncture)        (stress)

Similarly, sentence **(19)** can mean either of the following:

**(19a)**                    *Visiting relatives can be a nuisance.*

                          (juncture)        (stress)

**(19b)**                    *Visiting relatives can be a nuisance.*

                          (stress)              (juncture)

The differences in meaning between **(18a)** and **(18b)** and between **(19a)** and **(19b)** are cued by the differential placement of juncture and stress.

It is one's knowledge of the suprasegmental features of a language that makes that language sound familiar no matter what other native speaker is speaking it and no matter how unfamiliar the content of what is being said. What sounds to us when we hear an unknown foreign language like noise or gibberish is not just due to our unfamiliarity with the words and syntactic structures of that langauge. It is our unfamiliarity with the tune or rhythm of that language, that is, our lack of knowledge of its suprasegmental features.

**PHONOLOGICAL RULES**    As was mentioned in Chapter 1, each language community shares a common set of linguistic rules that are reflected at the semantic, syntactic, and phonological levels. Speech-sounds or phonemes similarly are rule-governed. In all languages there are tacitly agreed upon rules covering what and how phonemic features can be combined. For example, in English there is an upper limit to how many and which consonant sounds can be combined in a particular position of a spoken word. English speech permits an upper limit of three consonants clustering together in either the initial or final position of a spoken word, as can be seen in the following examples:

| Initial position | Final position |
|---|---|
| *stroke* (three) | *sinks* (three) |
| *bleak* (two) | *bump* (two) |
| *crane* (two) | *rest* (two) |

Not only do phonological rules specify *how many* phonemes can be combined in a particular position of a word, but they also indicate *which* phonemes comprise a particular speech system and which phonemes can be combined with others. Certain speech sounds may be combined, while other combinations are ungrammatical. Take for example the following phonemes: /b/, /l/, /r/, /s/, and /t/. Each of these phonemes can be combined with the others; however, only certain combinations are considered to be grammatical in English. This is illustrated in Table 2.2.

In addition to being rule-governed, our speech or phonological system is generative. Given that English has approximately forty-four phonemes, its generative quality results in an astoundingly large set of words made up from the various phonemic combinations. To comprehend the generative nature of our phonemic system, try to make an exhaustive list of all the words that can be formed by any combination of the following phonemes: /b/, /l/, /r/, /s/, /t/, /o/, and /e/.

The relationship between the phonological rules and the actual pronunciation (i.e., the phonetic representations) of words requires a brief explanation. Some grammatical morphemes, such as the past tense marker and the plural marker, can be easily added to familiar words as well as to nonsense words such as *trom* $\longrightarrow$ *tromd* and *nad* $\longrightarrow$ *nadz*. This quality is not simply the result of our

TABLE 2.2   Rules Governing the Combinations of
/b/, /l/, /r/, /s/, and /t/ Consonants

| Initial position in word | Final position in word |
|---|---|
| /b/ + /l/ (as in *black*) | /b/ + /l/ [*] |
| /b/ + /r/ (as in *break*) | /b/ + /r/ [*] |
| /b/ + /s/ [*] | /b/ + /s/ [a] |
| /b/ + /t/ [*] | /b/ + /t/ [*] |
| /l/ + /b/ [*] | /l/ + /b/ (as in *bulb*) |
| /l/ + /r/ [*] | /l/ + /r/ [*] |
| /l/ + /s/ [*] | /l/ + /s/ (as in *pulse*)[b] |
| /l/ + /t/ [*] | /l/ + /t/ (as in *wilt*) |
| /r/ + /b/ [*] | /r/ + /b/ [c] |
| /r/ + /l/ [*] | /r/ + /l/ [*] |
| /r/ + /s/ [*] | /r/ + /s/ [a, c] |
| /r/ + /t/ [*] | /r/ + /t/ [c] |
| /s/ + /b/ [*] | /s/ + /b/ [*] |
| /s/ + /l/ (as in *slide*) | /s/ + /l/ [*] |
| /s/ + /r/ [*] | /s/ + /r/ [*] |
| /s/ + /t/ (as in *stew*) | /s/ + /t/ (as in *list*) |
| /t/ + /b/ [*] | /t/ + /b/ [*] |
| /t/ + /l/ [*] | /t/ + /l/ [*] |
| /t/ + /r/ (as in *try*) | /t/ + /r/ [*] |
| /t/ + /s/ [*] | /t/ + /s/ (as in *hats*) |

* Denotes an ungrammatical combination.
[a] These combinations, although permissible in writing (e.g., ru*bs*, sta*rs*) are not permissible in spoken language. The written forms *rubs* and *stars* are pronounced as *rubz* and *starz*. Think pronunciation not spelling.
[b] In the written word *pulse*, the letter *e* is in the final position of the word. However, in its spoken form *puls*, the phoneme /s/ is in the final position. Think pronunciation *not* spelling.
[c] The letter *r* in the final position or cluster of a word such as *stir, girl,* or *herb* is pronounced as a semivowel rather than a consonant.

semantic and syntactic knowledge. If that were the case, the following formations would all be acceptable:

$$\text{plural of } nad \longrightarrow nadz$$
$$nads$$
$$nadiz$$

$$\text{past tense of } trom \longrightarrow tromd$$
$$tromt$$
$$tromid$$

How then can we explain the fact that only the first responses (*nadz* and *tromd*) are acceptable? The basis for this knowledge is portrayed in the following paradigm:

| Underlying representations | Phonological rules $\longrightarrow$ | Phonetic representations |
|---|---|---|

The underlying representational level provides general markers for both past tense /-d/ and plurality /-z/. It is, however, the phonological rules that account for the variations in the actual pronunciation (i.e., the *phonetic representations*). Without these phonological rules, all nouns would be pluralized using the /-z/ marker as in *nadz, hotchz,* and *lutz,* and all verbs would be marked for past tense using the underlying representation /-d/, as in *tromd, glopd,* and *flestd.* Two phonological rules spell out the relationship between the underlying representations of past tense and plural marking and their phonetic variations. The first phonological rule states that if more than one consonant are clustered together, there is a tendency for both consonants to be either voiced or voiceless (Dale, 1976). The following demonstrates how this rule is operationalized when pluralizing a word:

| Voiced | Unvoiced |
|---|---|
| cab + /z/ | cap + /s/ |
| bug + /z/ | duck + /s/ |
| bed + /z/ | bet + /s/ |
| hem + /z/ | |

However, this phonological rule does not account for plural words such as *glasses* (pronounced *glasiz*) or *churches, judges,* and *mazes* (pronounced *churchiz, jujiz,* and *maziz,* respectively). An additional phonological rule is needed.

The second phonological rule states that it is necessary to insert an /i/ before the plural /-z/ marker whenever the final consonant of the root word is a stop or fricative that is articulated at the same place in the mouth as the ending being added. The phonemes /s/, /z/, /sh/, /zh/, /ch/, and /j/ are all produced at approximately the same place as the /-z/ plural marker (Dale, 1976). Therefore, this rule yields the following:

$$church + /iz/$$
$$judge \ (juj) + /iz/$$
$$loss \ (los) + /iz/$$
$$wish + /iz/$$

Underlying representations and phonological rules also account for the phonetic variations between root words and their derivations, such as *sign* $\longrightarrow$ *signature, critic* $\longrightarrow$ *critical* and *criticize, medical* $\longrightarrow$ *medicine,* and so on. Although it is beyond the scope of this book to explicate the many relationships between underlying representations and phonetic representations, it is important to note that the two phonological levels do exist and that various phonological rules are applied to explicate specified phonological contexts or environments.

**PHONOLOGICAL ENVIRONMENT**   The actual pronunciation of a word depends, to a large extent, on the specific sounds that precede and follow a phoneme either within a word or between words, even though the underlying representation of the phoneme is the same. (This factor was mentioned in the discussion on plural and past-tense marking.) Different phonetic realizations of a phoneme are the result of the preceding and following phonological environments. This can be better understood by reading the following words:

> *let*
> *let go*
> *let alone*

If read naturally, the final phoneme /t/ in the word *let* has different phonetic realizations depending on its phonological environment. In the first instance, the phoneme /t/ is preceded by a vowel and followed by a pause and is most likely to be unaspirated (the breath stream is stopped, rather than first stopping and then bursting out). In *let go, the phoneme* /t/ is probably not realized (pronounced) because of the influence of the following consonantal phoneme /g/ in *go*. In contrast, in the phrase *let alone,* the /t/ is both aspirated and realized because the sound immediately following it (the /a/ in *alone*) is a vowel sound.

One last example should suffice to show how the influence of the environment surrounding a phoneme actually influences its pronunciation. Read the following sentences:

**(20)**                         *He walked to the store.*

**(21)**                         *He walked so fast.*

**(22)**                         *He walked all alone.*

In sentence **(20),** the past tense marker /t/ in *walked* (pronounced *wakt*) was not pronounced because it was merged with the following phoneme /t/ in *to*. In sentence **(21),** the past tense marker /t/ is only barely realized because the influence of the following consonantal sound ( /s/ in *so*) results in the unaspiration of the final /t/ in *walked*. In contrast, the /t/ in *walked* is both realized and aspirated in sentence **(22)** because the following sound is a vowel ( /a/ in *all*).

In summary, this section on phonology presents the structure of the phonological system as described by many linguists. It is our knowledge of this system that enables us (1) to recognize the familiarity of English in contrast to Chinese or Hebrew, (2) to generate acceptable phonemic combinations, and (3) to be aware that various phonetic representations are derived from the same underlying phonemic representations. We act as though we know the rules of the phonological system, even though the actual explication of these rules is a rather complex undertaking. Inquiries 2.11 through 2.13 provide a better understanding of the phonological system. Each inquiry focuses on a different aspect of phonology.

## CONCLUDING REMARKS

The primary focus of this chapter has been one of developing a basic understanding of the structure underlying our speech and language systems. The intent has not been one of teaching the specific rules of either semantics, syntax, or phonology. To assume that such was possible would be naïve and misleading. First, a complete and agreed upon statement of these underlying rules does not yet exist. Second, it takes years of study to fully understand the body of knowledge that does exist. Third, it is unlikely that educators need a complete and detailed understanding of all of the linguistic rules to adequately approach the linguistic needs of students. What *is* needed is the recognition that all languages and dialects are rule-governed systems, not simply accumulations of isolated sounds, words, and sentences. In order to be a competent language user, one must learn both these underlying rules and their applications for communication purposes. Recognition of the existence of and a basic understanding of the structures of communication, language, and speech enable educators to understand more fully (1) the nature and complexities underlying the developmental processes, (2) the importance of viewing communication as a necessary component in all classroom decisions, and (3) the problems encountered by language-handicapped youngsters. Readers who wish to study more intensively the structures of the spoken language system should consult the following sources: Brown (1973a), Chafe (1970), Chomsky (1957, 1965, 1972), Fillmore (1968), Nelson (1973), Schane (1973), and Schlesinger (1974).

## INQUIRY 2.1

It has been argued (e.g., Bates, Camaioni, & Volterra, 1975) that language has its roots in the structure and function of prelinguistic communication. This argument is further supported by Slobin's (1973) contention that new forms grow out of old functions.

**OBJECTIVES**   The objectives of this inquiry are to:

1. Learn to analyze the nonverbal, prelinguistic behavior of developing infants.
2. Analyze the nature of intentional versus unintentional communicative signals.
3. Speculate about the relationship between prelinguistic communicative structure and function and their linguistic counterparts.

**PROCEDURES**   Select an infant between the ages of nine and fourteen months who is still not "talking" (this determination can be made by the infant's mother or caretaker). Observe the mother or caretaker interacting with the infant. While observing, write down a detailed account of your observations including the following:

1. The context of the interaction (i.e., where the interaction took place).
2. Any infant-initiated signals (e.g., looking at caretaker, object, or location; pointing; pulling; vocalizations; etc.).
3. What the caretaker does in reaction to the infant's signals (e.g., picking up the infant, bringing an object to the infant, talking to the infant, etc.).
4. What the infant does in reaction to the caretaker's response(s) or lack of response(s).

**REPORT**   In addition to the detailed account of your observations, address yourself to the following questions:

1. Were the infant's communicative signals intentional or unintentional? Explain.
2. What function did these communicative signals serve (e.g., declare, demand, etc.)?
3. What do you believe to be the relationship between prelinguistic communication and later linguistic communication?

**EVALUATION**   Did this inquiry develop the specific objectives? If so, how? If not, why? How could the effectiveness of this inquiry be increased?

_____                    **INQUIRY 2.2**                    _____

Bates, Camaioni, and Volterra (1975) and Snow (1977*a*) suggest that mothers attribute much more to their infants' signals than is intended by the infants. Snow further argues that this phenomenon helps to establish the basis for later evolving linguistic and communicative structures.

**OBJECTIVES**   The objectives of this inquiry are to:

1. Observe the "conversation" between caretaker and infant.
2. Observe and analyze the effects that the unintentional, behavioral signals of infants have on familiar adults, especially the mother.
3. Explore the "intent" that the caretaker attributes to these signals.

**PROCEDURES**   Select an infant from five to nine months old and observe as the caretaker and infant are interacting. While observing the caretaker and infant interacting, tape-record any "conversation" taking place and write down a detailed account of your observations, including the following:

1. The context(s) in which the interaction(s) take place.
2. Any infant-initiated behaviors (e.g., burps, smiles, vocalizations, eye contact with mother or looking at an object, gestures, etc.).

3. What the caretaker does or says in reaction to the infant-initiated behaviors.

Following any infant-initiated interaction, ask the caretaker what the infant's behavior means and on what this interpretation is based. For example, if the infant coos while looking at an object, watch to see what the caretaker's response is. After the caretaker responds in some fashion, ask for an explanation of what the baby's coo meant. Repeat this procedure until you have collected three or four interactional episodes.

**REPORT**   In addition to the detailed account of your observations, address yourself to the following questions:

1. To what kinds of infant-initiated behaviors did the caretaker respond? Describe and explain.
2. How did the caretaker respond to infant-initiated behaviors? Did he or she talk to the infant, hold the infant?
3. Would you consider these interactions to be communicative? If so, why? If not, why not?
4. Describe and analyze the communicative intent that the caretaker attributed to the infant's behaviors.

**EVALUATION**   Did this inquiry develop the specific objectives? If so, how? If not, why? How could the effectiveness of this inquiry be increased?

—————          **INQUIRY 2.3**          —————

One way of analyzing the language of children is to investigate the kinds of objects, events, relationships, and so forth, that they talk about among themselves. In so doing, one useful way of analyzing and understanding the linguistic data is to employ the basic semantic relations model as described by Brown (1973a).

**OBJECTIVES**   The objectives of this inquiry are to:

1. Observe and analyze what children talk about when they are engaged in informal conversation.
2. Utilize Brown's (1973a) semantic categorical system to analyze a corpus of language.
3. Evaluate the adequacy of Brown's semantic categorical system in accounting for what children talk about.

2 children

**PROCEDURES**   Tape-record and observe an informal spontaneous conversation between two children. Transcribe the tape using the format described in Inquiry 1.1. Now, using the basic semantic categories provided in Table 2.1, analyze the kinds of things that the children talk about. The following format may be useful for presenting your data:

| Semantic relation | Frequency | Examples |
|---|---|---|
| 1. Entity | 5 | *That's the block.* |
| | | *It's a coin.* |
| 2. Action/Object | 8 | *Put the block . . .* |
| 3. Action-object-dative | 1 | *Hand me the coin.* |

**REPORT**   In addition to the transcript of your tape and an analysis of the basic semantic relations used, address yourself to the following questions:

1. What kinds of semantic categories were most frequently used in the children's conversations? In other words, what do the children you observed talk about? Use your data to support your discussion.
2. What kinds of semantic categories were least frequently used in the children's conversation? Again, use your data to support your discussion.
3. How adequately do Brown's semantic categories account for the things children talk about? Use examples to support your view.

**EVALUATION**   Did this inquiry develop the specific objectives? If so, how? If not, why? How could the effectiveness of this inquiry be increased?

_____                       **INQUIRY 2.4**                       _____

One way of understanding semantic competence at a one-word level is through the use of the semantic features paradigm (see pages 20–21). The use of this paradigm permits one to explore what semantic features are the most essential in defining the meaning of a word (e.g., [±function], [±animate], [±human], attributes such as shape, color, and size, [±numerality], etc.).

**OBJECTIVES**   The objectives of this inquiry are to:

1. Analyze the various semantic features used by a child who is shown a specific object and asked to talk about it.
2. Analyze the various semantic features used by a child who is given a word that has no specific referent and asked to tell you about it.
3. Analyze the value of the semantic features theory in accounting for the meanings that children attribute to objects and words.

**PROCEDURES**[7]   Select two children (preferably between the ages of six and nine). Present each child separately with the following series of objects and words (the use of additional objects and words is optional), and ask each child to tell you about each object or word. For example, show the child a nail and say "Tell me about this." After the child has said some things about the nail, probe further by saying, "Tell me more." or "What else can you tell me about this?" Record all responses.

After you have completed the exercise with the objects, proceed to the words, which have no specific referent. Present each word to the child by saying "Tell me about _____." Probe further to obtain additional responses from the child. Record all responses.

| Objects (referents) | Words without specific referents |
|---|---|
| 1. Nail | 1. Animal |
| 2. Ball | 2. Toy |
| 3. Block | 3. Happy |
| 4. Envelope | 4. Hungry |
| 5. Pencil | 5. Numbers |
| 6. Button | 6. Knowledge |

**REPORT**   Include the following in your report:

1. The ages of the children involved.
2. A transcript of the children's responses.

In addition, address yourself to the following questions:

1. How did each of the children describe the objects that were presented to them? In other words, what semantic features did the children invoke when describing the objects?
2. How did each of the children describe the words presented without specific referents? What semantic features did the children invoke when talking about these words?
3. Were there any major differences between the way the children talked about the objects and the way they discussed the words without specific referents? Explain.
4. How adequately does the semantic feature theory account for the meanings that the children attributed to the objects and words?

**EVALUATION**   Did this inquiry develop the specific objectives? If so, how? If not, why? How could the effectiveness of this inquiry be increased?

---

## INQUIRY 2.5

Olson (1970, p. 264) has convincingly argued that words are not simply names for things, but rather "words designate, signal, or specify an intended referent relative to the set of alternatives from which it must be differentiated." If this is the case, then not only must one have a knowledge of the intended referent and how it may be referred to, but also one must have a knowledge of the alternatives from which the intended object must be differentiated.

**OBJECTIVES**   The objectives of this inquiry are to:

1. Observe just how words function with respect to specifying present objects.
2. Analyze what knowlege the speaker must possess to effectively designate or specify an intended referent relative to the alternatives from which it must be differentiated.

**PROCEDURES**[8]   Select two children (one to be the listener and one to be the speaker). The object of the task is for the speaker to tell the listener where the gold star is in three different contexts, as follows (Olson, 1970, p. 264):

> A gold star is placed under a small, wooden block. The speaker who saw this act is then asked to tell the listener, who did not see the act, where the gold star is. In every case, the star is placed under the *same* block, a small, round, white . . . one. However, in the first case there is one alternative block present, a small, round *black* one. In the second case there is a different alternative block present, a small *square* white . . . one. In the third case there are three alternative blocks present, a round black one, a square black one and a square white one.

(See the figure on page 25 for the three cases.) Record the speaker's directions for each of the three contexts.

**REPORT**   Include the following in your report:

1. A transcript of the child's directions for each of the three contexts.
2. The ages of the children involved.

In addition, address yourself to the following questions:

1. How did the alternatives affect the way in which the intended referent was described?
2. What knowledge must the speaker possess to effectively designate or specify an intended referent relative to a set of alternatives from which it must be differentiated?

**EVALUATION**   Did this inquiry develop the specific objectives? If so, how? If not, why? How could the effectiveness of this inquiry be increased?

----------                                     **INQUIRY 2.6**                                     ----------

One's tacit knowledge of the underlying rules of a language not only enables one to produce and comprehend sentences never heard or uttered before, but also accounts for our ability to judge the grammaticalness of various sentences, even though we are unable to consciously identify these underlying rules.

**OBJECTIVES**  The objectives of this inquiry are to:

1. Analyze the responses of older children and adults to sets of grammatical and ungrammatical sentences.
2. Speculate as to which linguistic structures, either semantic or syntactic, influence our judgments concerning grammaticalness.

**PROCEDURES**  In this inquiry, you will be asking two older children and an adult to respond to various sets of sentences. You will present six series of three sentences that vary in their degree of grammaticalness first to a child between the ages of eight and ten, next to a child between the ages of eleven and fourteen, and finally to an adult.

Read each set of three sentences to the first youngster and ask him or her which sentence sounds best and which sentence sounds worst. Probe to find out how the child arrived at the decision. Continue through all sets of sentences, using the same procedure. Tape-record all responses for later transcription and analysis. Repeat the series with the second youngster and with the adult.

The following four sets of sentences should be used with each person.[9] Develop fifth and sixth sets such that they too contain three sentences varying in degree of grammaticalness.

### Set 1

**(1)**    *Gadgets simplify work around the house.*

**(2)**    *On trains hive elephants the simplify.*

**(3)**    *Accidents carry honey between the house.*

### Set 2

**(1)**    *Across bears eyes work the kill.*

**(2)**    *Gadgets kill passengers from the eyes.*

**(3)**    *Accidents kill motorists on the highways.*

### Set 3

**(1)**    *Around accidents country honey the shoot.*

**(2)**    *Bears steal honey from the hive.*

**(3)**    *Bears shoot work on the country.*

### Set 4

**(1)**    *Trains steal elephants around the highways.*

**(2)**    *Between gadgets highways passengers the steal.*

**(3)**    *Trains carry passengers across country.*

**REPORT**   Include the following in your report:

1. The ages of the persons involved.
2. A transcript of the individuals' responses.

In addition, address yourself to the following questions:

1. Describe each person's responses to the degree of grammaticalness of each of the sets of three sentences.
2. Analyze each person's set of explanations of how they judged each of these sets of sentences.
3. What linguistic knowledge, either syntactic or semantic, influenced their judgments concerning grammaticalness?

**EVALUATION**   Did this inquiry develop the specified objectives? If so how? If not, why? How could the effectiveness of this inquiry be increased?

_____                    **INQUIRY 2.7**                    _____

Katz and Fodor (1963) have formulated a theory of meaning that is unique because it takes into account two aspects of semantics—semantic features and selection restrictions. The first aspect of semantics, semantic features, relates to the features of meaning of a particular word. For example, *father* has, among other semantic features, the set [+ human, + male, + parent]. In addition, there are semantic restrictions defining the possible combinations of words used to form a meaningful sentence. For example, the sentence *She is my father* is anomalous because it violates these semantic restrictions. That is, the semantic features of *she* [+human, +female] do not match the semantic features of *father* [+human, +male, +parent]. Semantic competency, therefore, must include both a tacit knowledge of semantic features and a knowledge of selection restrictions.

**OBJECTIVES**   The objectives of this inquiry are to:

1. Examine how semantic features and selection restrictions affect the grammaticalness of sentences.
2. Investigate how children use their semantic and syntactic competency when analyzing various sentences.

**PROCEDURES**   Select two children (between the ages of six and ten) and present the following stimulus sentences to each child individually. Have each child determine whether each sentence is a "good sentence" or a "bad sentence." After the child has made a judgment about each sentence, ask the child "Why is it a good sentence (or a bad sentence)?" For those sentences which the child has judged to be "bad," ask the child to "correct it" or "make it better." Record and transcribe all responses.

**Stimulus sentences**

| | |
|---|---|
| **(1)** | *She is my father.* |
| **(2)** | *My mother has no children.* |
| **(3)** | *The pony rides the girl.* |
| **(4)** | *His sister has no brother.* |
| **(5)** | *The candy eats Carol.* |
| **(6)** | *My brother's name is John.* |
| **(7)** | *My father is a bachelor.* |
| **(8)** | *My dog writes nice stories.* |
| **(9)** | *The academic liquid became an odorless audience.* |
| **(10)** | *The sun danced lightly through the clouds.* |

**REPORT**   Include the following in your report:

1. The ages of the two children to whom you presented the task.
2. A transcript of the children's judgments, justifications, and corrections for each of the ten sentences.

In addition, address yourself to the following questions:

1. What are the various roles played by semantic features and selection restrictions in affecting the grammaticalness of a sentence? Be specific.
2. What strategies did the children use to make judgments about each sentence? Explain the basis for their judgments and the strategies they used to correct anomalous sentences. Be specific and use examples.

**EVALUATION**   Did this inquiry develop the specified objectives? If so, how? If not, why? How could the effectiveness of this inquiry be increased?

---

## INQUIRY 2.8

By the age of four or five most children have mastered the rules governing the use of grammatical morphemes. These rules vary among dialects and languages. However, at a remarkably young age, most speakers of a particular language have not only discovered these rules but also can use them to generate novel utterances. The purpose of this inquiry is to analyze how children utilize morphological rules when they are presented with both novel and familiar words.

**OBJECTIVES**   The objectives of this inquiry are to:

1. Analyze children's production of grammatical morphemes from unfamiliar words.
2. Analyze children's production of grammatical morphemes from familiar words.

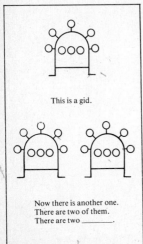

This is a gid.

Now there is another one.
There are two of them.
There are two _____.

**FIGURE 2.3** *Gid*
(Plural /*z*/ Marker)

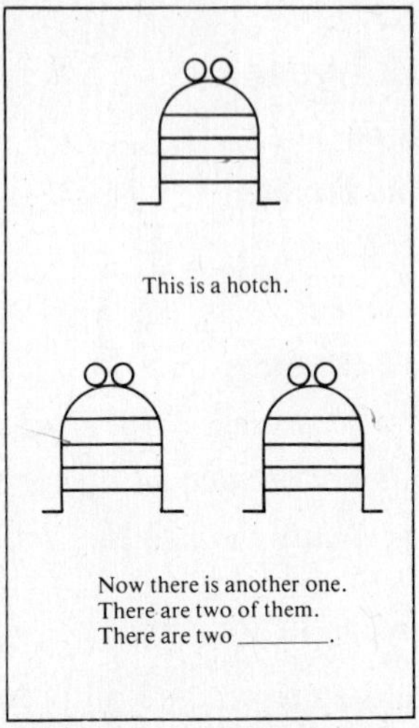

This is a hotch.

Now there is another one.
There are two of them.
There are two _____.

**FIGURE 2.4** *Hotch*
(Plural /*iz*/ Marker)

This is a hotch who knows
   how to lop.
He is lopping.
He did the same thing yesterday.
What did he do yesterday?
   Yesterday, he _____.

**FIGURE 2.5** *Lop*
(Past Tense /*t*/ Marker)

This is a gid who knows how to grom.
She is gromming.
She did the same thing yesterday.
What did she do yesterday?
Yesterday, she _____.

**FIGURE 2.6** *Grom*
(Past Tense /*d*/ Marker)

This is a gid who knows how to tine.
What is she doing?
She is _____.
What would you call a gid whose
   job it is to tine?
She is a _____.

**FIGURE 2.7** *Tine*
(Progressive /-*iŋ*/ and
Agentive /-*er*/ Markers)

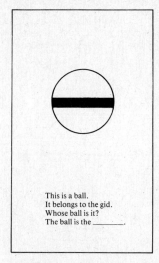

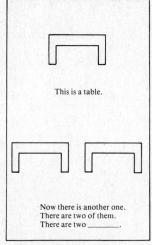

FIGURE 2.8   *Gid*
(Possessive /z/ Marker)

FIGURE 2.9   *Table*
(Plural /z/ Marker)

FIGURE 2.10   *Walk*
(Past Tense /t/ Marker)

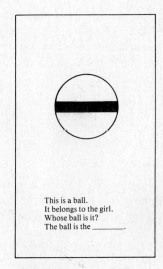

FIGURE 2.11   *Swim*
(Progressive /-iŋ/ and
Agentive /er/ Markers)

FIGURE 2.12   *Girl*
(Possessive /z/ Marker)

3. Compare the performances of children on both the novel and familiar words.

**PROCEDURES**[10]   Figures 2.3 through 2.12 are a series of pictures with accompanying stories. The first six figures represent unfamiliar or novel situations, whereas the last four figures should be quite familiar to the children. Presenting the novel pictures first, say to the first child:

"I'm going to tell you a story about some pictures. I'm going to leave out a word, so listen carefully. Your job is to fill in the missing word."

Read the stories that accompany the pictures and record precisely the responses that the child gives. For example, if the child answers *gidziz* for the blank in Figure 2.3, record *gidziz*, not *gidz* or *gidses*.

Repeat the entire process with another child in order to compare the responses of two children.

**REPORT**   Include the following in your report:

1. The ages of the two children.
2. The exact responses that each child made to each of the picture-stories.

In addition, address yourself to the following questions:

1. Were the children able to generate the appropriate grammatical morphemes? Explain. For example, in the picture-story about more than one *gid,* did the child generate the plural morpheme, and, if so, was the appropriate phoneme used? Illustrated below is the morphemic-phonemic relationship.

| Morpheme | Phonological realization |
|---|---|
| cat | /s/ |
| bed $\rightarrow$ plural morpheme $\leftarrow$ | /z/ |
| house | (yes/no) | /iz/ |

2. How did the children's performance on the novel words compare with their performance on the familiar words?
3. What knowledge must a child have in order to generate the appropriate grammatical morpheme?
4. What are the implications of each of the testing situations, that is, novel versus familiar, for evaluating children's understanding and use of grammatical morphemes? What information does this procedure elicit? What information about children's knowledge of grammatical morphemes is not tapped by this procedure?

**EVALUATION**   Did this inquiry develop the specified objectives? If so, how? If not, why? How could the effectiveness of this inquiry be increased?

## INQUIRY 2.9

We have already discussed how active sentences can be transformed into passive sentences without changing the basic meaning.

**(1)**                          *The boy chased the girl.*

**(2)**                          *The girl was chased by the boy.*

Although the surface structure of sentence **(1)**, which is symbolized as follows:

$$S \longrightarrow Det + N + V + \textit{-ed} + Det + N$$

is different from the surface structure of sentence **(2)**, which is symbolized as follows:

$$T \longrightarrow Det + N + Aux + V + \textit{-ed} + by + Det + N$$

the deep structure of both sentences is essentially the same. Transforming an active sentence to a passive one or vice versa is only one type of transformation.

**OBJECTIVES**   The objectives of this inquiry are to:

1. Study the difference between surface structure and deep structure when the surface structure is transformed from the active to the passive voice and vice versa.
2. Determine the relative difficulty of two different surface structures when the deep structure remains essentially the same.

**PROCEDURES**   Select two children, preferably between the ages of four and seven. Using the stimulus sentences below in conjunction with Figures 2.13 through 2.16, ask each child first to repeat the sentence after you and then to point to the picture that goes with the sentence. For each sentence, say to the child:

"I'm going to say a sentence and when I'm finished you repeat exactly what I said. If I say, 'The cat is big,' you say 'The cat is big.' After you repeat the sentence, choose the picture that goes with the sentence."

### Stimulus sentences

**(1)**          *The car is bumped by the bike.* (Figure 2.13)

**(2)**          *The boy is pushed by the girl.* (Figure 2.14)

**(3)**          *The turtle is carried by the girl.* (Figure 2.15)

**(4)**          *The bike bumps into the car.* (Figure 2.13)

**(5)**          *The boy pushes the girl.* (Figure 2.14)

**(6)**          *The boy is chased by the dog.* (Figure 2.16)

**(7)**          *The dog is chased by the boy.* (Figure 2.16)

**(8)**          *The girl pushes the boy.* (Figure 2.14)

FIGURE 2.13

FIGURE 2.14

FIGURE 2.15

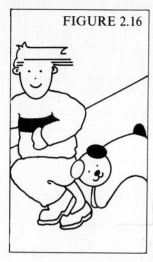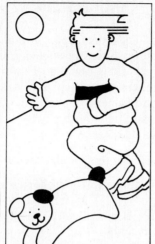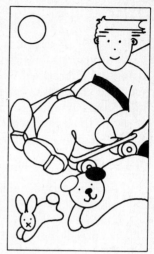

FIGURE 2.16

**(9)**          *The dog chases the boy.* (Figure 2.16)
**(10)**          *The girl is carried by the turtle.* (Figure 2.15)

Tape-record and transcribe *exactly* how the children imitated each sentence, and note whether each child was able to identify the correct picture representing the stimulus sentence.

**REPORT**   Include the following in your report:

1. The ages of the children to whom you presented the task.
2. The transcripts of the children's exact repetitions of the stimulus sentences, and your notations as to whether their picture selections were correct or incorrect.

In addition, address yourself to the following questions:

1. What was the relationship between the children's accuracy in repeating the stimulus sentences and their accuracy in selecting the correct picture? Explain. Did the relationship between their repetition and comprehension vary as the surface structure varied from active to passive?
2. What is the function of word order in the conveying of meaning? As a syntactic strategy, is it sufficient to account for sentence comprehension?
3. Which appeared to be the more difficult surface structure to process—active or passive voice? Speculate as to the reasons for this.
4. What do you consider to be the difference between surface structure and deep structure?

**EVALUATION**   Did this inquiry develop the specified objectives? If so, how? If not, why? How could the effectiveness of this inquiry be increased?

## INQUIRY 2.10

The meaning of sentences is dependent upon several linguistic structures (e.g., phrase structure rules, transformational rules, and grammatical morphemes). In Inquiries 2.6 through 2.9 the various functions of word order, transformational rules, and grammatical morphemes were explored. An additional linguistic function of some grammatical morphemes is that of providing important information indicating the logical or temporal relationship between words (*He runs and plays*) and phrases (*He ran fast then fell down*).

**OBJECTIVES**   The objectives of this inquiry are to:

1. Analyze how certain grammatical morphemes affect the meaning of a sentence.
2. Explore the relative levels of difficulty of different grammatical morphemes as they affect meaning.
3. Explicate the underlying meaning of specific grammatical morphemes.

**PROCEDURES**   Select two children, preferably between the ages of four and seven. Show the first child a book and a pencil and say:

"Here is a pencil and a book. I'm going to say something about the book and pencil and you repeat exactly what I say. Then you do exactly what the sentence says. So listen carefully. You say and do exactly what I say."

Say each stimulus sentence to the child and observe and record what the child says and does in response. Take note of whether or not the child performs the task correctly, and also analyze the types of errors the child makes (e.g., temporal errors). After the child completes each sentence, place the book and the pencil back on the table and present the next stimulus sentence. Tape-record and transcribe the child's repetitions of each sentence. Repeat the entire procedure with the second child.

### Stimulus sentences

| | |
|---|---|
| **(1)** | *Give me the book and the pencil.* |
| **(2)** | *Pick up and wave the book.* |
| **(3)** | *Put the book under the table, or hand me the pencil.* |
| **(4)** | *Pick up the book or the pencil.* |
| **(5)** | *Stand up, then pick up the pencil.* |
| **(6)** | *Put the book under the table, and hand me the pencil.* |
| **(7)** | *Show me the pencil but not the book.* |
| **(8)** | *Stand up, or wave the book.* |
| **(9)** | *Give me the book, then put the pencil under the table.* |
| **(10)** | *Hand me the pencil then the book.* |
| **(11)** | *Put the book but not the pencil under the table.* |

**REPORT**   Include the following in your report:

1. The ages of the children who participated in the task.
2. A transcript of each child's repetitions of the stimulus sentences, along with your evaluation of the child's success in performing the indicated action. Use the following format:

| **Repetition of sentence** | **Correct performance** |
|---|---|
| 1. Give me the pencil and book. | Yes |
| . | |
| . | |
| . | |
| 11. Put the book *and* the pencil under the table. | No |

In addition, address yourself to the following questions:

1. What is the relationship between the repetitions of the stimulus sentences and performances of the actions for each child? Analyze any errors made by each of the two children and any discrepancies between their repetitions of the sentences and their performances of the actions indicated.
2. What syntactical structures affected the children's success in their performances of the actions—sentence length, type of grammatical morpheme used, placement of the grammatical morpheme between two NPs, verbs, phrases, and so forth?
3. How do each of these morphemes affect the meaning of a sentence?

**EVALUATION**   Did this inquiry develop the specified objectives? If so, how? If not, why? How could the effectiveness of this inquiry be increased?

---

## INQUIRY 2.11

Native speakers' tacit knowledge of their speech system includes their ability to recognize acceptable and unacceptable phonemic combinations. Phonemic combinations permissible in one language may be quite unacceptable in another. This knowledge of the phonological system goes beyond one's knowledge of the meaning of particular words.

**OBJECTIVES**   The objectives of this inquiry are to:

1. Analyze the possible phonemic combinations acceptable in English.
2. Explore the tacit underlying phonological rules that characterize the English phonemic system.

**PROCEDURES**   There are two tasks involved in this inquiry.

*Task 1:* First, given a series of phonemes, generate as many acceptable English words as possible. The phonemes for this first task are as follows: /ŋ/, /a/, /b/, /i/, /s/, /p/, and /e/. To generate your list of acceptable words, use any combina-

tion of these seven phonemes. For the purpose of this inquiry, the /a/ will be pronounced as in *at,* the /i/ will be pronounced as in *hip,* and the /e/ will be pronounced as in *bet.* Remember in generating these words, think about
pronunciation *not* spelling. Also, you should concentrate on generating acceptable
phonemic combinations, not necessarily known or presently used English words.

*Task 2:* A series of unfamiliar words is provided below. Some represent acceptable phonemic combinations in English; others do not. Indicate which words are
not acceptable in English and explain what phonological rule they violate, including both specific phonemic combinations and word position. Remember,
think about pronunciation *not* spelling.

| | | |
|---|---|---|
| *blenk* | *klantz* | *ngat* |
| *brilk* | *prag* | *flung* |
| *tsin* | *ptit* | *srunk* |
| *stant* | *wilb* | *fromt* |
| *blibz* | *lbuet* | *rsat* |
| *strible* | *trount* | *burbs* |

**REPORT**   Include the following in your report:

1. The list of words generated for Task 1.
2. The list of words in Task 2, indicating which words represent acceptable
   phonemic combinations in English and which do not.

In addition, address yourself to the following questions:

1. What phonological rules did you unconsciously use when generating acceptable English words in Task 1? Give specific examples, including specific phonemic combinations, voicing, position in a word, and so on.
2. For those unfamiliar words found to be unacceptable in Task 2, specify
   which phonological rules these phonemic combinations violate.

**EVALUATION**   Did this inquiry develop the specified objectives? If so, how? If
not, why? How could the effectiveness of this inquiry be increased?

---

### INQUIRY 2.12

When two words differ in just one phoneme, such as *tuck* and *tug,* and also differ
in meaning, we can conclude that the two varying sounds (/k/ and /g/) differ significantly. Word pairs that differ in only one phoneme are called **minimal pairs.**
Native speakers' knowledge of the phonological system enables them to recognize
word pairs that differ in only one significant sound and those that are essentially
the same.

**OBJECTIVES**   The objectives of this inquiry are to:

1. Analyze the discrimination (reception) of phonemes in children's language.

2. Analyze the articulation (production) of phonemes in children's language.
3. Analyze the relationship between the reception and production of phonemes in the English language.
4. Evaluate the use of minimal pairs and the same/different paradigm as a methodology for assessing one's knowledge of phonology.

**PROCEDURES** Generate a list of minimal word pairs, so that their voicing, word position, place of articulation, and so forth, can be contrasted. For example, if we want to contrast the voicing component of a set of phonemes, we could use any one of the following minimal pairs:

> *ten* and *den* (/t/ is unvoiced; /d/ is voiced)
> *bag* and *back* (/g/ is voiced; /k/ is unvoiced)
> *vat* and *fat* (/v/ is voiced; /f/ is unvoiced)

If we want to analyze place of articulation, we could use any of the following minimal pairs:

> *think* and *fink* ( /th/ is articulated with tongue and teeth; /f/ is articulated with teeth and lips)
> *best* and *zest* ( /b/ is articulated with the lips; /z/ is articulated with the tongue and alveolar ridge)

Develop a list of approximately twenty minimal pairs to be used in the following tasks. Insert randomly throughout your list, five word pairs that are exactly the same (e.g., *bat* and *bat*). These will act as distracters.

Select a child between the ages of six and nine. Using your list of word pairs, present each pair to the child and ask the child to make a judgment concerning whether the words in the pair sound exactly the same or different. For example, say to the child:

"I'm going to say two words and when I'm done, you say *same* if the two words sound exactly the same. Say *different* if the two words do not sound the same. Let's try a few for practice. Listen . . . *dog-cat.* Do they sound the same or different? . . . *Say-day.* Do they sound the same or different?"

Once the child has responded to all word pairs, go back to the beginning of your list and ask the child to repeat each pair after you. For example, say to the child:

"I'm going to say two words and when I'm done, you say the words just the way I did. Wait until I say both words before you say them. Let's try a few for practice. Listen . . . *day-say.* Now you say them, just the way I did."

Tape-record all of the child's responses.

**REPORT** Include the following in your report:

1. The child's age.
2. The word pair lists developed, including the phonological feature that each word pair contrasts.

3. An exact transcript of both the articulation task and the same/different judgments on the discrimination task.

In addition, address yourself to the following questions:

1. What were the types of errors, if any, that the child made on the discrimination task? For example, were they errors involved in voicing (e.g., *tuck/tug*)? Errors in discriminating sounds occurring in the final, medial, or initial position of words? Errors involving place of articulation (e.g., *meat/neat*)? Describe.
2. What were the types of articulation errors, if any, that the child made on the articulation task? Use the same criteria used in the discrimination task to analyze these errors.
3. Describe the relationship between the child's performance on the receptive task and on the productive task. Were the errors similar in both the receptive and productive tasks?
4. Evaluate this procedure as a paradigm for assessing children's reception and production of phonemes. For example, what additional knowledge does this presuppose of the child? How does a minimal-pair paradigm compare to natural or connected speech? What kinds of information does this procedure yield that would enable a teacher or clinician to plan an intervention program?

**EVALUATION**   Did this inquiry develop the specified objectives? If so, how? If not, why? How could the effectiveness of this inquiry be increased?

_____                  **INQUIRY 2.13**

The linguistic environment of any phoneme influences the way in which that phoneme will be realized in pronunciation. This is especially true of the environment following a particular phoneme, which might be a pause, consonant, or vowel. Different following environments can result in a particular consonant being unaspirated, merged with the following consonant, or completely unrealized. The purpose of this inquiry is to study the influence of the following linguistic environment on the realization of consonants.

**OBJECTIVES**   The objectives of this inquiry are to:

1. Analyze the influence of following pauses, consonants, and vowels on the realization of the word-final consonants /t/ and /d/.
2. Examine the effects of using either a sentence-repetition paradigm or a spontaneous sample of speech in studying the influence of the following linguistic environment on the word-final consonants /t/ and /d/.

**PROCEDURES**   Select two children and ask each child to repeat exactly each of the following series of sentences.

**Series I:** /t/

*I bet!* (prepausal)

*I bet you, you can't.* (preconsonantal)

*I bet that you can.* (preconsonantal)

*I'll bet all of my money.* (prevocalic)

**Series II:** /d/

*Let's bed down.* (preconsonantal)

*My bed is old.* (prevocalic)

*Time for bed.* (prepausal)

*We have no bed bugs.* (preconsonantal)

Also obtain an informal spontaneous sample of speech from each child. Tape-record all responses.

When listening to the taped responses, analyze the children's imitations of the eight sentences. Pay special attention to word-final /t/ and /d/. Try to analyze how /t/ and /d/ were realized (pronounced) in each of the various linguistic environments. (Note that tape recordings sometimes distort the sounds of speech, so while engaging in the activity, you might also want to take some notes.) Also analyze the spontaneous samples of speech, noting all instances of word-final /t/ and /d/ along with the linguistic environments that followed.

**REPORT**    Include the following in your report:

1. The ages of the children who participated.
2. Transcripts of both the children's repetitions of the sentences presented in Series I and II and the spontaneous samples of speech.

In addition, address yourself to the following questions:

1. What was the influence of the linguistic environment that followed word-final /t/ and /d/ on the realization of these two phonemes?
2. Were there any differences in the realizations of /t/ and /d/ in the various linguistic environments? Explain.
3. Were there any differences in the realizations of /t/ and /d/ in the sentence repetition task and in the spontaneous samples of speech? Explain.

**EVALUATION**    Did this inquiry develop the specific objectives? If so, how? If not, why? How could the effectiveness of this inquiry be increased?

### NOTES

1. The terms are based on Roger Brown's *A first language: the early stages* (Cambridge, Mass.: Harvard University Press, 1973).

2. Square brackets [ ] indicate that the enclosed constituent is optional in this particular syntactic rule.

3. $\left\{ \quad \right\}$  Braces indicate that any one member of this set of lexical items can occur in the sentence.

4. There is some substantial argument against Chomsky's position that sentences **(14)** and **(15)** derive from the same deep structure. For example, Gruber (1967) makes the distinction between the *topic* and the *comment* in a sentence. The *topic* of the sentence usually appears in the subject NP, regardless of whether the subject NP is the agent (*The girl*) or the object (*ball*) of the action, and is the focus of the sentence. The *comment* of the sentence usually occurs in the VP, or predicate, and tells something about the *topic* of interest. Thus, in sentence **(14)**, what is of primary interest—the topic of the sentence—is *the girl* (agent). In contrast, the focus of sentence **(15)** is not *the girl* (agent) but *the ball* (object).

5. / / indicates the spoken sounds (phonemes) as opposed to the graphic symbols (graphemes).

6. Think pronunciation *not* spelling!

7. The procedures for this inquiry are adapted from the Verbal Expression Subtest of the *Illinois Test of Psycholinguistic Abilities* (Urbana, Ill.: University of Illinois Press, 1968).

8. The procedures for this inquiry are taken from Olson (1970, p. 264).

9. These sentences come from Miller and Isard (1963).

10. The format of this inquiry is based on Berko (1958).

# 3

# The Development of Communication

The beginning of communication takes place months prior to the onset of language and speech, and communication continues to develop throughout childhood into adulthood. Developmental variation in communication is not restricted to what the child proposes, but also includes how the child makes certain propositions and to whom. In addition, the precision and flexibility of children's communication increases as their linguistic, cognitive, and social abilities develop. The why of communication also expands, enabling growing children to more effectively influence their widening social world. The following communication vignettes globally illustrate some developmental changes in communication that occur as a child emerges as a socially, linguistically, and cognitively competent person.

### Vignette I

(Child looks at and reaches for a squeak toy.)

Adult: "Ya gonna squeak it?"

(Child tries to squeak the toy, then looks at adult.)

Adult (reaches and squeaks the toy): "Uh, there it goes." (looks at child).

(Child watches adult's actions.)

Adult: "Squeak, squeak." (while squeaking the toy).

(Child after watching adult's actions, leans over and squeaks the toy.)

Adult: "Oh! You made it squeak."

### Vignette II

"Dat." (points to a stuffed dog in a truck).

"Dat." (points to pick-up sticks; reaches for the sticks and all but two fall on the floor).

"Allgone." (looks at mother).

"Tick." (looks at mother and then at the sticks on the floor).

65

## Vignette III

"Where my ice cream is?"
"I want dat samich."
"It good."
"Mommy, want some?"
"It good ice cream."

## Vignette IV

Child 1:   "Le's make sumin else. Le's make da airplane."
Child 2:   "I know, le's make da jet. Le's make da jet."
Child 1 (pointing to the cover of the lego box): "Wanna make dis" (points) "an dis" (points) "and dat?" (points).
Child 2:   "Yeah, le's make dis." (pointing to one of the demonstration pictures on the lid of the box).
Child 3:   "Yeah, an le's make dose." (pointing to lid).
Child 1:   "Okay, le's go. Come on get ta work."

## Vignette V

Child 1:   "I watch Marine Boy; I watch Star Track."
Child 2 (smiling and moving hands in acknowledgement): "That's great!"
Child 1:   "My cousin, that's his favorite guy, and I can even do this." (makes a peace sign with two fingers). "It's some kind of peace sign for Vikings. You know Spock, that guy who's a Viking?"
Child 2:   "Do you like Spock? I do. Except that Spock is not a Viking."
Child 1:   "Yes he is! He's half Viking and half human."

These vignettes should make apparent the changes that occur as a child develops into a competent communicator. In fact, your intuitions about the communicative capabilities of each of these young persons would most likely result in modifications of your style of communication if you were to interact with any of them (see Chapter 6 for an analysis of modifications in adult linguistic input to children). Beyond intuitive insights, we can begin to explicate some of the factors differentiating the developmentally young communicator (Vignette I) from the more competent communicator (Vignette V). Before doing so, it is equally important to highlight some similarities among these communicators.

In all five vignettes, communication occurs in a physical and social context. This context includes senders and receivers who apparently have as a goal the desire to interact with each other (i.e., the why of communication). Even when the sender dominates the conversational episode (as in Vignettes II and III), the goal of influencing the social or physical environment is present. Similarly, in all five vignettes communicative signals are used as a means (i.e., the how of communication) for sending messages. These signals include eye contact, vocalization, pointing, facial expression, and spoken language. Finally, even though the nature of the communicative message or content (i.e., the what of communication) varies, both unintentional and intentional messages are continually being sent.

In what explicit ways then do differences in communication exist? Developmental differences in communication reflect the following factors:

1. Nature and variety of the signals used.
2. Content of the message.
3. Spatial and temporal orientation of the message.
4. Presuppositional quality of the message.
5. Precision and elaborateness of the linguistic message.
6. Stylistic variation.
7. Use of conversational postulates.

Although not all of the factors listed above are represented in the previous vignettes, the first five are.

One of the most obvious differences among Vignettes I through V is in the nature and variety of the communicative signals used. In Vignette I, looking, body posture, and actions are the only signals used for the purposes of communication. Although these signals continue to be used in subsequent vignettes, others emerge (e.g., smiling, pointing, vocalizations, and spoken language). In Vignette V, spoken language is the primary vehicle for communication, although smiling, gestures, and eye contact accompany the interaction. Not evident in any of the vignettes is a whole array of nonverbal communicative signals that have a compelling effect on communication. These include facial expression and visual interaction (Eibl-Eibesfeldt, 1972; Cook, 1977), body movements and gestures (Birdwhistell, 1970; Kendon, 1970; Condon & Sander, 1974; Knapp, 1978), paralinguistic features of tone and pitch (Davitz, 1969; Ostwald, 1973), and proximity (Hall, 1968; Montagu, 1977; Stern, 1977). Therefore, as children develop, so does their ability to produce and interpret a wider variety of verbal and nonverbal communicative signals.

Along with expanding the types of signals, one witnesses an expansion of the content of the communicative message. Interest in objects, states, and actions (as evidenced in Vignettes I through IV) expands to include events, attitudes, and attributes (Vignette V). The content of the message changes as a preoccupation with communicating about (and understanding) the present, palpable physical environment evolves to discussing (and trying to understand) the somewhat subjective and partially hypothetical physical and social world.

In Vignettes I through IV, communication is oriented to the ongoing temporal and spatial context. There is little distancing between *I* and *it* or *you*. Objects and people that are present are indexed by either eye contact, gestures, or pointing. Even when the child begins to develop a linguistic symbol system (Vignettes II through IV), its primary function is one of communicating about the here-and-now world of objects, people, actions, and events. This phenomenon of present-orientation is a major characteristic of communication occurring during the preschool years. It only gradually gives way to communication that concerns that which is distanced in both time and space. This gradual decentration of *I* and *it* is evidenced in Vignette V. Here the children communicate about events that occurred in the past, and there is the cognitive and linguistic freedom to anticipate and communicate about future occurrences.

Presupposition is a feature of communication that extends throughout one's life. Bates (1976*b*) describes presupposition at two levels. **Pragmatic presupposition** is defined as "conditions necessary for a sentence (or proposition) to be used appropriately in a given context" (p. 96, parentheses added). Subsuming pragmatic presupposition is **psychological presupposition,** which is the "use of an utterance (or other communicative signal) to comment upon information assumed to be shared by speaker and listener" (p. 97, parentheses added). More simply stated, presuppositional development means learning what needs or does not need to be said in a particular physical and social context so that communication is cooperative and effective. This means that one who is communicating cannot presume that what is seen, known, and felt is shared by one's conversational partner. This requires a subjective distancing of *I* and *you.*

Returning to the vignettes, let us explore how presuppositional abilities are evidenced. In Vignettes I through III, there is little separation of the *I* and *you.* Here, the youngsters are quite ego-involved in their communication. The children automatically presume that their interests are shared by their conversational partner. Vignette II can serve as an example of this. The context relates exclusively to objects and actions, which is an extension of the child's object-interests. Mother is primarily an agent for him. Perhaps the primary communicative paradigm here is the following: if child does or says *X,* mother will do *Y.* In Vignette IV, although there is a continuation of ego-interest, there is also some awareness of the perspective of the conversational partner (*Le's make dese*). Even the choice of pronouns (*my* and *I* in Vignette III) in contrast to *us* (*le's → let us* in Vignette IV) differs. Finally, in Vignette V, we witness a further decentration of *I* and *you* as the conversation takes on a more cooperative quality. The topic introduced by Child 1 is continued by Child 2. Questions are used to acknowledge that the listener has indeed understood the speaker's intended message. In contrast, in Vignette IV, the partners, while maintaining a joint topic (building with Legos), pursue the topic from their own perspectives (Child 1: *Le's make da airplane.* Child 2: *I know, le's make da jet.*). More will be said about presupposition later in this chapter.

As a child's cognitive, social, and linguistic abilities expand, communicative messages also become more precise and elaborate. In contrast, the developmentally young child's communication is quite cryptic, relying heavily on the physical context and shared knowlege in order to disambiguate the message. The nonverbal signals in Vignette I (i.e., looking and reaching) and the one word utterances accompanied by pointing and looking in Vignette II are examples of the potentially imprecise and cryptic quality of the young communicator's messages. Although the precision and elaborateness of the message increases during the preschool years (see Vignettes III and IV), due to the continued presuppositional nature of the child communication continues to rely heavily on context clues. This is illustrated in Vignette IV (i.e., *Yeah, le's make dese* while pointing to the lid of the box). One could validly argue that given the presence of shared visual information (i.e., the illustrations of various models on the lid of the Lego box) the use of the pronoun *dese* (for these) was a sufficient indexer. However, even in the absence of shared visual information, preschoolers' communication remains characteristically presuppositional in quality and somewhat imprecise in form.

By their early school years, children's communication is more elaborate in form and more precise in effectively communicating the intended messages. This is illustrated in Vignette V (i.e., *It's some kind of peace sign for the Vikings* while making a peace sign with two fingers). Although the form of the message is primarily linguistic, extralinguistic features, such as the peace sign, serve the function of adding emphasis or affect to the message.

Finally, as a child develops communicative competence, stylistic variation and the ability to comprehend and produce a variety of conversational postulates are evidenced. Because Vignettes I through V all take place in familiar and informal social situations, these two communication dimensions are not obvious. However, a brief description should suffice to introduce them as other dimensions on which the development of communication varies.

Just as people dress differently for different social situations, so do their communication styles vary in response to different social contexts. The perceived formality of the situation and the degree of speaker-listener familiarity are two major factors that potentially induce **stylistic variation** in one's communicative efforts. The most obvious influence is that of speaker-listener familiarity. As the degree of this familiarity decreases, the communicator, in order to be effective, must rely less on the presupposition of shared knowledge and attitudes. Consequently, the coding of the intended message must be more elaborate, precise, and self-monitored. The speaker must simultaneously think of both what the message is and how to precisely code it.

Rommetveit (1974) provides the following example of how shared information between speaker and listener influences the degree to which elaboration of the topic of the message is required. Two football fans are watching a televised game, during which a fantastic touchdown is made by player Bob Wilson. One fan immediately cries *Magnificent!* Since both watchers share the same information and attitude, the comment without any mention of the topic (the touchdown by Wilson) is sufficient. If, however, time passed and the two football fans met again, the comment alone would probably be insufficient to relate back to the topic of Wilson's touchdown. The speaker would then have to specify both the topic and the comment, as in *That play last week was magnificent!* Furthermore, if one of the football fans discussed the touchdown with a less familiar conversational partner, the topic of the touchdown might need to be expanded even further, as in *That touchdown that Bob Wilson made during the football game televised on Sunday, January 3rd, was magnificent!* As for the younger child, presuppositional constrains may mitigate against the child's awareness that the information contained in the topic of a sentence may not be shared by the unfamiliar listener. Therefore, statements similar to *That play was magnificent!* are sometimes offered to familiar and unfamiliar listeners alike.

Developmental changes in communication are also evidenced in the child's ability to comprehend and produce various **conversational postulates.** Originally introduced by Grice (1968) and discussed by Bates (1976*b*), conversational postulates are sets of assumptions about the nature of human discourse learned by speakers of a particular sociocultural group. According to Bates (1976*b*), these assumptions include the following:

1. Conversation is a cooperative process.
2. Speakers will tell each other the truth.
3. Only new and relevant information will be offered.
4. Only information that is sincerely desired will be requested.

However, violations of the above assumptions must also be learned by the child. Polite speech and indirect speech acts may violate the second and fourth assumptions, respectively. For example, Gordon and Lakoff (1971) suggest that the fourth assumption may be violated by indirect speech acts, as when *Do you know what time it is?* is asked when one is requesting information concerning the specific time. Clearly, the speaker does not sincerely want to know if the listener knows the time. Instead, the speaker wishes to make the direct request *Tell me the time.*

The development of an awareness of various conversational postulates continues through childhood and even into adulthood. Bates (1976*a* & *b*) found in a series of studies that certain polite forms, including indirect speech acts, are not acquired until the end of the Piagetian preoperational period of cognitive development. The development of polite forms will be discussed further in a later section of this chapter.

Thus far, this chapter has provided a brief sketch of how communication can vary as the child emerges into a competent communicator. Now let us turn to a somewhat more detailed account of the development of communication.

## COMMUNICATION DURING THE EARLY YEARS

Language is used as one means of expressing our thoughts, ideas, feelings, needs, and questions. The way in which we use language is dependent on many factors. First, usage requires at least a minimal degree of facility with the various aspects of language (i.e., syntax and semantics). However, competency with these aspects of language is not sufficient in and of itself to guarantee that an individual will be an effective communicator. Language usage requires that the individual perceive a need to give information, to express an idea, or to ask a question. This reflects a desire (or lack of desire) to interact with another human being. Furthermore, effective communication requires that an individual (both as speaker and listener) be able to take into account another person's perspective, as well as one's own. Without this ability, communication remains idiosyncratic, ambiguous, and ineffective.

Cognitive, social, emotional, and linguistic factors interact either to facilitate or to interfere with effective communication. Piaget (1955) has provided many insights into how the communicative functions of language differ between the cognitively mature individual and the developmentally young child. For the adult, language can serve to assert, to state objective facts, to convey and seek information, to express commands or desires, and to criticize or threaten (Piaget, 1955). In other words, language serves many functions. For the developmentally young child, communicative functions are somewhat restricted.

During the prelingual period of communication (from ten to fifteen months), children use gestures primarily to intentionally draw adults' attention to objects (proto-imperative) and to obtain adults' attention by showing, giving, or pointing to objects (proto-declarative). This perlocutionary stage certainly demonstrates the already social nature of the child, but it clearly is social only from the child's perspective. In other words, the child does not appear to be aware that the listener is anything more than an agent or object of the child's actions or needs. The very nature of the prelinguistic period of communication reflects the child's cognitive constraints, which in turn result in communication that is bound by both context and ego-orientation.

The illocutionary stage (from twelve to eighteen months) is marked by the emergence of the symbolic function. Linguistic symbols are now used to obtain adults' attention and to draw adults' attention to desired objects and events. However, this new symbolic form of communication suffers from the same functional limitations operating in the earlier developmental period. Communication continues to be oriented to the here-and-now, relies heavily on context clues for disambiguation, and is ego-centered.

Bloom and Lahey (1978) summarize the functions of early words and gestures as being primarily subjective in nature and cognitive in function. The cognitive function is described by Piaget (1955) and is nicely illustrated below:

> Ben (playing with large building blocks): "Dere . . . dere." (as he builds blocks). (Blocks fall down.) "Oops, down."

Here Ben's words lack real communicative intent. Instead, they serve as part of the action procedure of building and code the objects, actions, and events of the activity. Perhaps such early words actually guide the child's actions.

Halliday (1975) and Dore (1975) extend the description of the functions of early language to include interactional and personal functions, as well as speech acts that are affective and cognitive in nature. These early functions of language precede those that are more intentionally communicative (e.g., regulatory, instrumental).

The child's transition into the period of **preoperational thought** (from two to seven years) is characterized by three major developmental processes. The first is the move to distance one's self in time and space, thereby no longer being tied to the immediate, palpable environment. This process of spatial and temporal distancing is evidenced by the child's ability to talk about future events as well as past occurrences.

The preoperational period is also characterized by the development of presupposition, causing the child continually to make assumptions (often ill-founded) about shared information. There appears to be an inability to make the distinction between a personal perspective and a perspective of another person. The child does not differentiate viewpoints. This egocentric period of communication generally does not interfere with the informal discourse of everyday life, since the child remains at home for the most part, where familiar adults are able to disambiguate the frequently egocentric and idiosyncratic messages. However, merely observing the young child (from two to four years) trying to converse on the telephone demonstrates a virtual inability to take into account the listener's viewpoint. He talks about his actions and objects as though the listener shared his knowlege of present objects and events. The following brief telephone conversation between my son Benjamin (three years and two months old) and his grandmother illustrates the presuppositional nature of his thinking:

> "Hi Gramom, I ate all my food" (points to his empty bowl as if his grandmother could see). "I put it on (pointing to his sneakers) all by myself."

The period of egocentric communication is a fascinating one that, according to Piaget (1955), can be divided into three major categories:

1. **Repetition** (echolalia): This category of egocentric communication can be seen when the young child repeats words and syllables for the pleasure of talking. There is no apparent desire to communicate with others. The following is an example of repetition (Piaget, 1955, p. 35):

   > Jac says to Ez: "Look, Ez, your pants are showing."
   > Pie, who is in another part of the room, immediately repeats: "Look, my pants are showing and my shirt, too."

   While at first glance it appears that Pie engaged in social communication by processing and repeating valuable information, this is not the case; it was totally untrue that Pie's pants and shirt were showing. Pie repeated the sentence for the sheer pleasure of hearing himself talk.

2. **Monologue:** In this form of egocentric communication the child talks to herself about what she is doing. She appears to be practicing using language or thinking aloud. Once again, she is not apparently interested in communicating with anyone. The following are examples of monologues (Piaget, 1955, p. 37 and p. 242):

   > Lev sits down at his table alone: "I want to do that drawing, there . . . I want to draw something, I do. I shall need a big piece of paper to do that."

   > Geo talking to himself as he draws: "First I shall do the fingers, so as to make another round."

   In general, monologue serves no social function. Its function is one of accompanying, reinforcing, or supplementing action.

3. **Collective monologue:** The collective monologue occurs when two or more children are engaged in an activity either together or in close proximity. Language is directed to another child; at first this may appear to be

social communication. However, as can be seen in the following examples, the speaker is not concerned with whether the listener ever receives or undertstands the message. The other child who is present acts only as a stimulus for language.

> Charlie (at a table with his friend building a Lego construction): "Before that's finished, put it . . . on your . . . Where can I put this?" (doesn't look up at his friend for an answer, but continues to build).

> Charlie (continuing to build a Lego house): "Oops—now where's the window?" (doesn't wait for an answer). "This one doesn't go."

In the above episodes, Charlie engages in what at first glance appears to be listener-oriented communication. Twice he asks his friend questions (*Where can I put this?* and *Now where's the window?*). However, in neither case does he wait for an answer. His questioning did not have the intent of securing an answer, but rather served to guide his own actions. In fact, the attention of his friend was not even solicited prior to the asking of the questions.

In this context, we can recall Vignette IV presented earlier in this chapter (the three children are discussing what to make out of Lego blocks). There is little to suggest that that interaction is anything other than a collective monologue. There is no evidence that any of the speakers is concerned with whether the listener ever receives or understands the message.

The third major process of the preoperational period is the expansion of the functions of language. In addition to the personal, affective, and cognitive functions of language, there are also instrumental and regulatory functions. Halliday (1975) describes these functions as communication forms that intentionally serve to satisfy the child's material needs (instrumental) and to regulate the behavior of others (regulatory). The prototypes of these functions have their roots in the sensorimotor period of development.

Additional early communicative functions have been described by Moerk (1976). These include imitation; requesting information; responding to a question; describing objects, events, acts, and plans; demanding; requesting; labeling; denying; affirming; and demonstrating lack of understanding. The expansion of communicative functions reflects the child's growing understanding of the things that can be done with words.

## COMMUNICATION DURING THE SCHOOL YEARS

As the child enters school (at about five years), his use of language reflects a growing awareness of the various perspectives of the listener. According to Piaget, this "social" quality of language marks it as truly communicative. The five categories described below are examples of communication that is increasingly listener-oriented.

1. **Adapted information.** Here the speaker has the desire to tell the listener something that may interest the latter. In other words, the speaker is taking into account the interests and perspectives of the listener, instead of only talking about and to himself (collective monologue). The following example illustrates how the speaker is concerned with effectively offering information to the listener (Piaget, 1955, p. 42):

> Lev is helping Geo to play Lotto: "I think that goes here." (Geo points to a duplicate card).
> Lev: "If you lose one, there will still be one left."

2. **Criticism.** Criticism is another social function of language in which the view of the listener is taken into account. It is a separate category from that of adapted information because its messages are affective rather than cognitive. "Their function is not to convey thoughts, but to satisfy non-intellectual instincts of pugnacity, pride, emulation, etc." (Piaget, 1955, p. 48). In the following examples, the distinction between adapted information and criticism is evident (Piaget, 1955, p. 48 and p. 245):

> Lev: ". . . That's not fair. Pooh! That's no good . . ."

> Lev: "I can do much more than Bur?"

3. **Commands, requests, and threats.** For the young child, both egocentric and most socialized speech have the function of assisting action. Commands and requests, as illustrated below, all involve the function of assisting work and play, but are also directed at the other's assistance (Piaget, 1955, p. 49 and p. 246):

> Lev: "The yellow paint, please. I should like some water."

> To Bur: "Give me your pencil."

4. **Questions.** Those questions of a child that require an answer are considered to be a subcategory of socialized speech. These are social questions as differentiated from egocentric questions (collective monologue) and are marked by the child's pausing and awaiting an answer. A child's social questioning is a spontaneous search for information (Piaget, 1955). The following examples provided by Piaget (1955, p. 241 and p. 243) are illustrative of social questioning:

> Rio brings some paper cigarettes. He distributes them.
> Lev asks for some: "How about me?"

> Mlle. L. "Now you must write."
> Lev: "Write what?"

5. **Answers.** The responses of a child that are answers to direct questions or commands constitute the final subcategory of socialized speech. In order for answers to be considered socialized, they must resemble the question. The answers must show that the child has listened to the question, has thought about it, and has chosen to respond. This is in contrast to ego-

centric answers (collective monologue), which have nothing whatsoever to do with the questions or commands. The following examples provided by Piaget (1955, p. 50) illustrate socialized answers:

> To the question: "What colour is that?"
> Lev: "Brownish yellow."

> To the question: "Will you give it (the ticket) back to me?"
> Lev answers: "No, I don't need it. I'm in the boat."

As the child develops socially, cognitively, and linguistically, the relationship between egocentric and social communication reverses in proportion. For example, between the ages of six and eight the child begins to recognize that different perspectives exist. He understands that others may see, feel, and think differently than himself. However, because of continuing cognitive and linguistic constraints, the child may have difficulty representing the other person's viewpoint. As a result, his communicative efforts will continue to be somewhat inaccurate unless both speaker and listener coincidentally share the same perspective.

This gradual move from egocentric to social communication can be seen from the following task involving referential communication. Referential communication, that is, talking about objects and events that are present, is probably the earliest function of communication. However, when someone must communicate about objects that are present and a visual barrier is placed between the listener and speaker, the speaker must take into account what the speaker can and cannot see. In other words, the speaker must be aware that the listener may have a different visual perspective, and be able to represent or communicate the listener's perspective.

In a block-building task, where two youngsters are provided with duplicate sets of blocks and a visual barrier separating them, the speaker is requested to tell the listener how to make a configuration just like his. Younger children (three to five years) are not aware that the listener may have a different visual perspective. This can be seen by the following communicative attempt.

> There's two blocks on the bottom and one on the top. Two on the bottom and one on the top. There's four on the bottom and one on the top. Then there's two stacked up on . . . There's one and there's another one stacked up and one in the middle.

This message provided by the speaker to the listener is both egocentric and cryptic. It is as though the speaker coded the message for herself only, not taking into account the listener's needs. The speaker never identified which block she was referring to, which was critical information because each of the six blocks had a different geometric drawing on it. The presumption the speaker is making is *I know what block I'm referring to, therefore, so must you.*

Egocentric communication is not only characteristic of the speaker. The listener as well acts as though she understands the speaker even though the message provided by the speaker is insufficient, ambiguous, or in conflict with the listener's perceptions. In the referential communication task described above, the listener never questioned the speaker as to what block she was identifying, the left to right positioning of the blocks, and so on. Instead, the listener proceeded to use the visual information available, operating on the assumption that her knowledge, choices, and perspectives were the correct and only ones.

In contrast to the egocentric child, we see the child who is aware that there is another perspective, but is not fully able to communicate that perspective to the listener. The following example illustrates the child at this period. Once again, the task is to communicate in such a way so the listener can build a block configuration that is identical to that of the speaker.

> Get the one with the circle. Get the diamond. Put it about an inch away from it. Then get the, uh, six-pointed star. Put it on top of the other two. Get the circle with the dot in the middle. Put it about one-quarter inch away from the other blocks that you just built and put on top of that one, the block with an *X*. Then the other one that you built put, the . . . get the last one, the one with the circle with the *X* in the middle and connect the other one on top of the other one—on the top of this one, that you just built.

Note in this episode that the speaker does not assume that the listener knows what block he is referring to. Instead he names each intended block for the listener. However, there is still difficulty in representing critical communicative information to the listener. Pronouns are sometimes used that either ambiguously refer to previously specified objects (*Put it about an inch away from it.*) or do not refer back to previously identified objects ( . . . *connect the other one on top of the other one—on the top of this one, that you just built.*) However, there are examples of the speaker using pronouns that unambiguously relate to previously specified referents (*Then get the, uh, six-pointed star. Put it on top of the other two.*) The transitional speaker is also aware that the listener needs information about positioning and distance (*on top of, one-quarter inch away*), but does not always communicate this information to the listener. Finally, it is not until the last period of development that the speaker communicates such critical information as the left or right orientation from the listener's reference point.

The final move away from egocentric thinking and communication occurs between eight and twelve years of age. This developmental period is characterized by recursiveness in thinking, meaning that the individual begins to think about thinking, and language becomes an object of both actions and thoughts. The child thinks about what others see, feel, and think and is able to coordinate her perspective with that of others. As a result of this cognitive ability, the child's spoken messages are elaborate, precise, and accurate. A last example illustrates this communicative accuracy in the block-building task.

> Uh, three blocks are in a row, together, they're touching, touching each other. An um, the *X* is on the left, the six-pointed star, with the dot in the middle is in the middle, and the diamond on the right side. On top of

the six-pointed star with a dot is the circle with the *X*. (pause) On top
of the diamond is the circle. (pause) On top of the circle with the *X* and the
circle is the circle with the dot.

In contrast to the two previous speakers, this one provides accurate information
concerning the intended block, its positioning, and the left or right orientation. In
addition, the speaker occasionally pauses, demonstrating an awareness that the
listener needs time to carry out the directions just given. Communciation at this
stage is viewed not only as an information-giving process but also as a social and
cooperative interaction.

Since communication involves both a speaker and a listener who are interacting, it is insufficient to simply analyze their roles independently. Instead, we
must ask the questions: What does the listener do when information provided is
either insufficient or ambiguous? How, then, does the speaker respond to feedback from the listener? Karabenick and Miller (1977) studied the interaction of
speaker and listener in a referential communication task. They found that there is
an increase between the ages of five and seven in the asking of questions by the
listener concerning inadequate messages. However, they also found evidence suggesting that listeners confirm messages that are either ambiguous or lack critical
information. Speakers attempted to answer 91% of the listeners' questions but
provided additional information only 41% of the time. This data suggests that,
while improving with age, both speakers and listeners by the age of seven had still
not completely developed the necessary communicative skills, which include the
accurate use of listener feedback. These results are supported by the earlier works
of Glucksberg and Krauss (1967), Alvay (1968), Meissner (1975), Dittman (1972),
and Bearison and Levey (1977).

Before leaving this section on the development of communication, we must
emphasize that referential communication is only one form of communication.
Language is used for other functions, including the later-appearing functions of
"requesting an action, requesting permission, warning, inviting or promising"
(Bloom & Lahey, 1978, p. 211). Another function is that of persuasion. Language
can be used not only to provide information about objects, events, or relationships, but also to influence another person's point of view or position on a particular topic. This function of language is an important social tool and has been traditionally ignored.

As for referential communication, the development of persuasion reflects the
child's emerging social and cognitive abilities. At first, the young persuader is
handicapped in providing convincing arguments by her self-embeddedness, or
egocentrism. Given a situation in which a young child tries to persuade an adult to
do something that the older person might not ordinarily do, the child does not go
beyond simple pleas and descriptions of why the desired event is important (*I
want to play longer because it is fun.*). It is not until the youngster can coordinate
her thinking with the thinking, attitudes, or values of the listener that she is able to
effectively use persuasion as a communicative tool. Contrast the following per-

suasive argument used by a twelve-year-old youngster with that of the younger child mentioned above. The twelve-year-old is trying to convince her science teacher to allow the class to have additional free time for informal chat: *If we have more time to talk, we will be more alert for the science lesson.* Here the youngster is able to coordinate her inclinations (to prolong the free time) with the attitudes of the science teacher (an alert youngster can more readily benefit from a science lesson).

To summarize thus far, as the child's cognitive, linguistic, and social abilities develop, we see a concomitant sophistication and variety in communication. This is evidenced in the interaction between the speaker and the listener as they become more capable of providing adequate messages, of giving feedback when messages are either ambiguous or lack critical information, and of effectively utilizing feedback.

## STYLISTIC VARIATION

Embedded in various social situations are differing expectations or norms about how one behaves. Included in these normative patterns are expectations of how language is to be used and by whom. Bryen, Hartman, and Tait (1978, p. 181) have noted that each society has behavioral expectations depending on a person's age level. These societal expectations cover dress codes and use of alcohol and cigarettes, as well as speech and language styles.

> A little girl wearing makeup and a middle-aged woman wearing pigtails and hair ribbons would cause raised eyebrows. . . . Similarly, certain speech and language patterns are acceptable in children, but not in adults and vice-versa. Words that are taboo for children are acceptable for adults in certain situations (our infamous four-letter words), and words forbidden to adults (*horsie, doo-doo*) are expected from children.

As the child matures cognitively and socially, he becomes more and more aware of these social expectations. This awareness increases as the youngster ventures away from the home and is influenced by varying social groups. He learns "who can say what, in what way, where and when, by what means, and to whom" (Hymes, 1971, p. 15). He learns that colloquialisms and language patterns that are socially stigmatized are acceptable in familiar and informal contexts but not in more formal situations. Similarly, he learns that highly formal styles of speaking are inappropriate in familiar and informal conversational contexts. However, Labov (1966) argues that use of stylistic variation is neither fully appreciated nor mastered until late adolescence.

The range of mastered linguistic styles is not dependent solely on age. McDavid (1973) indicates that region is also a significant factor, with Southerners (particularly educated Southerners) having command of a wider range of styles than either Northerners or Westerners. Sex is another variable affecting the range of styles available. Labov (1966) in New York City; Shuy, Wolfram, and Riley (1968) in Detroit; and Trudgill (1972) in Norway found that women are more sensitive to the social appropriateness of certain language patterns in that they use stigmatized language patterns less frequently than men, particularly in formal situations. (See Transcripts 21 and 22 in the appendix of this book.)

The ability to switch linguistic styles according to perceived differences in social expectations appears to be linked to at least two factors—one primarily cognitive and the other social. Making allowances for the listener's perspective (including knowledge, attitudes, and values) is a cognitive process that only gradually emerges as the child develops. This decentration process, which has already been described, is a crucial factor influencing stylistic variation. Without this ability, the speaker will be unable to satisfactorily make use of clues from the social context regarding culturally expected styles of interaction. Therefore, an inability to use a variety of linguistic forms to express intended content will likely reduce the speaker's communicative effectiveness. The interaction of form (the how of communication) and content (the what of communication) is a necessary one if we are to effectively learn how to do things with words.

Cognitive and linguistic flexibility is a necessary but not sufficient condition for achieving a wide range of stylistic variation. Exposure and sensitivity to different social contexts are also critical, so that feedback from a variety of listeners can help the speaker to begin to formulate hypotheses about how language works in different contexts. Simple exposure to different social contexts is not enough in itself to further this task. The speaker must be motivated to influence the listener(s) in a given context; otherwise stylistic accommodation will seem to be unnecessary. The corollary to this motivational variable is the notion that the speaker *can* influence members of a particular social group. Without this real or perceived condition, the speaker will see no reason for accommodating her linguistic style in the direction of the cultural and communicative practices of that group. This important social factor may be the major reason why certain minority groups (e.g., blacks and Chicanos) "fail" to adequately learn the language style of the dominant culture in America. It may also help to explain why certain institutionalized populations (e.g., the emotionally disturbed and mentally retarded) rarely learn to effectively communicate (Bryen, 1980).

## CONVERSATIONAL POSTULATES

As the child's experience in using language to achieve certain social and material ends grows, the child begins to adjust his language style to include polite forms and indirect requests. The use of these social conventions begins at about the age of three and continues throughout adulthood. For example, Bates (1976*a*) studied children's development of *polite forms* when trying to achieve certain desired ma-

terial ends. Her findings, based on a study of sixty Italian preschool children between the ages of three and seven, suggest that children at three years of age can
correctly judge the appropriateness of certain polite forms, such as the presence or
absence of *please* and a soft intonational pattern. However, at this age, children
are rarely capable of changing their original requests (e.g., *Give me a piece
of candy*) to a more polite form (*I would like a piece of candy* or *May I have
some candy?*). Not until children are five and a half to six years old are they capable of accurately judging and using complex polite forms, such as conditional
verbs (e.g., *I would like* versus *I want*). Bates concluded that the ability to
use and to reason about polite forms continues to develop beyond the preschool
years.

This finding should not be surprising to parents or educators working with developmentally young children. Numerous times, children say to one another
(about a desired object) *Gimme it.* Patiently we then make the request *How about
saying that nicer?* What generally follows from quite young children is a softer intonational pattern accompanying the words *Please, gimme it.* What we are suggesting to the children is not that the intended content of the message be changed,
but rather that the linguistic form be changed, that is, from an imperative to a declarative (*I want/would like it*) or to an interrogative form (*Can I/may I have it?*).
However, it is just this interaction between content and form that creates communication problems for young children.

Why do young children have difficulty using and reasoning about polite forms?
R. Lakoff (1973) suggests it is because young children have recently learned certain conversational postulates such as efficiency, economy, and informativeness
and must now violate these postulates in order to be polite. Being polite means (1)
not offending, (2) giving options, and (3) making the listener feel good. As we analyze the following forms of the same request, we see how the polite forms have the
potential to violate certain more fundamental conversational postulates.

| Imperative | | Polite forms |
|---|---|---|
| *Give me the ball.* | *I want the ball.* | *Can I have the ball?* |
| + efficiency | ? efficiency | ? efficiency |
| + economy | − economy | − economy |
| + informational | ? informational | − informational |
| − don't impose | ? don't impose | + don't impose |
| − give options | ? give options | + give options |
| − make listener feel good | ? make listener feel good | + make listener feel good |

As we move from less to more polite forms (from left to right above), we are likely
to sacrifice economy, efficiency, and informativeness in favor of factors related to
politeness. Since the child spends the early years learning how to communicate
economically and informatively (i.e., through gestures and one-word utterances),
it is not surprising that it is so difficult for her to later subordinate these basic rules
to a new set of conversational rules. Bates (1976b, pp. 318–26) provides some very
interesting insights into just how politeness is acquired.

## DISCOURSE

The child learns that there are rules for combining words into meaningful sentences and, in the same way, must learn that sentences within a topical episode should be connected and relevant to one another. The development of **discourse** reflects this growing realization that sentences and their elements should comprise a cohesive structure. Clark and Clark (1977) use the term **cooperative principle** to express the tacit rules which govern connected speech. Included in the cooperative principle are rules governing the use of pronouns, conjunctions, and adverbs. One rule, for example, asserts that pronouns should be used only when their referents are clear to the listener. This pertains to phrases within sentences as well as intersentential propositions. The following example illustrates a violation of the cooperative principle as it relates to pronouns.

Carol and Sue went to the store. She bought candy with the money her grandmother gave her.

Ambiguity exists in the above episode because the pronouns *she* and *her* (in the second sentence) do not clearly specify whether reference is being made to *Carol* or *Sue*. As a result, the conditions of the cooperative principle have not been met.

The cooperative principle is equally violated in the following sentences:

**(1)** *I like cookies, but my dog is sick.*

**(2)** *I like cookies, but I want to eat them.*

How has the cooperative principle been violated above? According to Lakoff (1971), one does not use *but* either to cojoin two propositions that are not related as in sentence **(1)** or with two propositions that are quite compatible as in sentence **(2)**.

The cooperative principle extends beyond the use of particular word classes such as pronouns and conjunctions. It includes the general notion that later sentences should be linked topically to earlier ones. Consider the following sentences:

Robert and Joseph went to the beach. She cried all night long. The ticket cost fifty cents.

Our reading of this paragraph probably leaves us with a sense of discomfort, because expectations of how sentences are generally linked together have been violated. After reading the first sentence, we would expect the second sentence to contain further information about either *Robert* or *Joseph* (the topic of the sentence) or about going to the beach (the comment of the sentence). Instead, the second sentence refers to some female (dog?, child?, baby?) crying all night.

The cooperative principle not only encompasses sentences linked together in discourse by the same person, but also covers sentences in a conversation between two persons. Consider the following dialogue:

Person 1:   "I have to go to the store."
Person 2:   "Did you see the ball game last night?"

We can argue that, in fact, a dialogue has not taken place, because Person 2 switches topics without even confirming that the statement made by Person 1 has been recognized and understood. Consequently, the discourse rule that the statement made by Person 2 should be relevant and linked to the statement (or question) made by Person 1 has not been followed. This rule is in effect until both conversational partners agree (at least tacitly) to a switch in topics.

The development of rules and conventions for discourse begins as early as two years or age (Bloom, Rocissano, & Hood, 1976) and continues well into the early school years (Maratsos, 1974; Bates, 1976*b* ). This development takes place in the areas of reciprocity and cohesiveness of discourse (Keenan, 1974; Bloom, Rocissano & Hood, 1976) the use of specific pronouns (Maratsos, 1974; Chipman & deDardel, 1974), the use of definite and indefinite articles (Maratsos, 1974), and conjunctions and adverbs (Bates, 1976*b* ).

Knowledge of discourse is extremely critical for adequate functioning in the classroom. When children begin school, they are confronted by an instructional language style or code that makes many assumptions about their knowledge of how language is connected. These assumptions are reflected in the teacher's use of language to the students (see Chapter 10) and in the nature of the reading materials presented (see Chapter 8).

## CONCLUDING REMARKS

Learning to communicate effectively in different social contexts is a process that begins before the child learns to talk and continues well into adulthood. It includes diverse aspects, such as a growing mastery of a large repertoire of verbal and nonverbal signals, presupposition based on shared information, building an adequate model of the listener, the use of conversational postulates, broadening one's linguistic style, and learning about the structure of discourse. In essence, learning to communicate is learning to "make meaningful things happen" with language (Bates, 1976*b*, p. 354).

The following inquiries should further your understanding of the development of communicative abilities. These inquiries are designed to study various aspects of communication, as well as the varying roles of the speaker and listener. The reader is also referred to Bates (1976*b* ); Wood (1976); Cazden, John, and Hymes (1972); Halliday (1977); and G. Lakoff (1972) for a more in-depth analysis of the development of communication.

_____                **INQUIRY 3.1**                _____

The language of preschoolers is to a large extent egocentric in nature. Unless the children coincidentally happen to share the same perspective much of the language used will serve nonsocial functions (e.g., pleasure in talking reinforces or supplements action). In contrast, as the child reaches school age, the proportion of social to egocentric communication increases. Social communication is characterized by occurrences of providing information that is adapted to the listener, criticizing, commanding and requesting, asking questions and waiting for the answer, and answering questions.

**OBJECTIVES**   The objectives of this inquiry are to:

1. Analyze the differences in communication between preschool children and school-aged children.
2. Analyze what preschoolers talk about in contrast to what school-aged children discuss.

**PROCEDURES**   Observe two preschoolers (ages from three to five) and two school-aged youngsters (ages from seven to ten) in a familiar and informal context. This can occur in a preschool classroom in the doll or block corner, during free-play time in school, or at home during play. You should function as an observer rather than as a participant. For each of the two pairs of youngsters, you should obtain approximately fifty sentences. Tape-record all interactions for later transcription.

**REPORT**   Include the following in your report:

1. A brief description of the two pairs of children, including their ages.
2. A brief description of the context in which the interaction took place.
3. A transcript of the communication occurring between each pair of youngsters using the format below.
4. The percentages of social and egocentric speech used by each child.

| Text and context | Communication used[a] | Basis for judgment |
|---|:---:|:---:|
| 1. Child 1 (playing with blocks): "Is it big yet? It's big like a house." | CM | Never waits for an answer |
| 2. Child 2 (reading a book): "It's big like a house." | R | Is not even building with blocks |

[a] Code:   R = Repetitions
       M = Monologue
   CM = Collective monologue
     Q = Questions
     A = Answers
     C = Criticism
     I = Adapted information
     D = Demands, commands, orders, etc.
   MR = Motor responses, e.g. builds a tower with blocks
     O = Other

In addition, address yourself to the following questions:

1. What were the differences between how the younger children communicated and how the older children communicated? Refer to your transcription for examples.
2. Was there a difference in what the younger and the older children talked about? Describe, including such factors as time (past, present, or future) and topics.

**EVALUATION**   Did this inquiry develop the specified objectives? If so, how? If not, why? How could the effectiveness of this inquiry be increased?

_____                      **INQUIRY 3.2**                      _____

In order to be an effective communicator, one must not only have competency in the use of various linguistic structures, adequate vocabulary, and related concepts, but one must also be able to take into account the "knowledge" of the listener and any feedback from the listener. Therefore, the language of the speaker must be accurate, precise, and descriptive of events as they actually occur in time and space. This skill, while critical at all times, becomes even more so when extralinguistic elements, such as gestural or visual cues, are absent. Then, the precision, elaborateness, and accuracy of the linguistic information given by the speaker become crucial.

**OBJECTIVES**   The objectives of this inquiry are to:

1. Explore the necessity for the use of expanded, precise, and accurate language when the speaker cannot rely on extralinguistic cues.
2. Explore the relationship between "knowing" and "communicating."
3. Analyze the effects of listener feedback on the speaker.
4. Analyze how communicative competence varies with age.

**PROCEDURES**   Select two pairs of children, one pair preferably younger (ages from five to six) and one pair older (ages from eight to ten). Provide two identical sets of blocks (six to eight blocks in each set), which differ in shape, size, and color; or shape, size, and texture; or shape, color, and texture. Seat the first pair of children at a table in such a way that they each have access to one set of blocks, and so that the blocks are out of the range of each other's vision. Figure 3.1 indicates the setting.

Build a configuration with one child's blocks in two stages, that is, arrange three blocks first and three later. Have the child whose blocks are being used for the examiner's construction give directions to the other child (the listener) with the objective being that the listener will be able to construct an identical configuration without seeing the original one.

Tape-record the speaker's verbal directions to the listener. Also, as the speaker

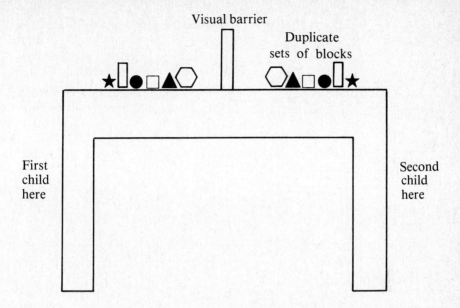

FIGURE 3.1   Setting for the Block-building Task

gives directions, use the "Referential Communication Checklist" shown in Table 3.1 to check off the type of information the child gives. For example, if the child says *Place the blue block next to the red one,* you would check off for items (1.) name—*block,* (2.) color—blue, and (3.) position—next to.

Once the task is completed, remove the visual barrier and let the two children compare their configurations. Question both the listener and the speaker to determine what information was missing, if there was, indeed, a discrepancy in configurations.

Finally, you have some evidence of the kinds of information the speaker spontaneously gives. Probe the speaker, again using the checklist, to determine what the child actually knows. For example, put a large square block next to a small square block and ask the child to point to the large square block (name, size, shape).

Repeat the entire procedure with the second pair of children.

**REPORT**   Include the following in your report:

1. The ages of the two pairs of children participating in the activity.
2. The unedited transcript of the communicative interaction.
3. The "Referential Communication Checklist" with data concerning the information the speaker spontaneously gave and what information the speaker actually knew.

TABLE 3.1   Referential Communication Checklist

| Information | Speaker Spontaneously Communicated | Speaker Knows (Determined through Probes) |
|---|---|---|
| 1. Name of object: | | |
| block | _____ | _____ |
| ball | _____ | _____ |
| 2. Color of object | | |
| red | _____ | _____ |
| blue | _____ | _____ |
| yellow | _____ | _____ |
| green | _____ | _____ |
| white | _____ | _____ |
| black | _____ | _____ |
| 3. Shape of object: | | |
| square | _____ | _____ |
| circle | _____ | _____ |
| round one | _____ | _____ |
| rectangle | _____ | _____ |
| half-circle | _____ | _____ |
| triangle | _____ | _____ |
| oblong | _____ | _____ |
| diamond | _____ | _____ |
| 4. Size of object: | | |
| large | _____ | _____ |
| small | _____ | _____ |
| biggest | _____ | _____ |
| smallest | _____ | _____ |
| bigger | _____ | _____ |
| smaller | _____ | _____ |
| 5. Position: | | |
| next to/beside | _____ | _____ |
| in front of | _____ | _____ |
| in back of/behind | _____ | _____ |
| to left of (mirrored) | _____ | _____ |
| to right of (mirrored) | _____ | _____ |
| to left of | _____ | _____ |
| to right of | _____ | _____ |
| on top of | _____ | _____ |
| beneath | _____ | _____ |
| toward window/ blackboard | _____ | _____ |

TABLE 3.1   Referential Communication Checklist (*Continued*)

6. Texture/structure:
   hard     _____     _____
   soft     _____     _____
   rough    _____     _____
   smooth   _____     _____
   spongy   _____     _____
   wooden   _____     _____
   paper    _____     _____
   cloth    _____     _____
7. Spatial relationship:
   near     _____     _____
   far away _____     _____
   ½-inch apart _____     _____

In addition, address yourself to the following questions:

1. Analyze the accuracy, precision, and specificity of language used by the speaker to communicate the critical information to the listener. For example, did the child use pronouns for which the listener had no specific referent? Be specific and refer back to the transcript and the checklist.
2. Analyze the discrepancy, if any, that existed between what the speaker told the listener and what the speaker appeared to know. Speculate why this discrepancy exists.
3. Describe how communication varied with the age of the speaker. Be specific.
4. Did the speaker seem to be aware of the quantity and quality of information the listener required to complete the task? Explain.
5. Did the speaker utilize feedback from the listener? If so, how did the speaker modify the original message?
6. Discuss this statement: When extralinguistic cues, such as pointing, gesturing, and so on, are minimal, the linguistic and cognitive demands made of the speaker are increased.

**EVALUATION**   Did this inquiry develop the specified objectives? If so, how? If not, why? How could the effectiveness of this inquiry be increased?

_____     **INQUIRY 3.3**     _____

In order to utilize language competency for the purpose of communication, the listener must process with accuracy and precision the expanded language in discourse. In other words, it is not enough to say that the child can comprehend isolated sentences of various levels of syntactical and semantic complexity. The listener must be able to comprehend the meaning of expanded language as it occurs on an ongoing basis (i.e., discourse). This is especially true in the school milieu, where the child spends a great proportion of the instructional day in the role of the listener.

**OBJECTIVES**   The objectives of this inquiry are to:

1. Explore the various cognitive and linguistic demands made on the listener during the processing of ongoing language when gestural or visual cues are absent.
2. Explore how communication is affected by the developmental level of the child.

**PROCEDURES**   Select two children, preferably one younger (ages four to seven) and one older (ages eight to ten). Administer the following activity, "Making a Movie" (Lopez, 1975) to each child individually. (As you become familiar with this activity, it can be done with a group of children.) The directions and materials needed for this activity are as follows:

MATERIALS.

1. Two pieces of construction paper or oak tag, approximately 8 by 10 inches. Each paper should be divided into eight sections, numbered consecutively from one to eight to represent the eight scenes.
2. One box of crayons in assorted colors.
3. The script for "Mary Martian Comes To Earth" (or Mark, depending on the listener's sex).

SETTING AND INSTRUCTIONS TO THE NARRATOR. The narrator and the child sit at a table facing each other at a comfortable distance, such that the child can clearly hear the narrator. The narrator's task is to read each scene to the child so that the child can pictorially produce the movie. The narrator's script follows.

DIRECTIONS AND SCRIPT FOR THE MOVIE "MARY MARTIAN COMES TO EARTH." Say to the child: "You and I are going to make a movie. I'm going to read the script for the movie, and in order for the movie to come out, you have to listen carefully and draw exactly what I say. I'll read each scene to you, and you draw each scene on the paper where I show you." Each scene should correspond to the appropriate sequential block on the child's paper.

### Scene I

"Hi, I'm Mary Martian, from Mars. As you can see, I'm a little purple girl with red eyes, an egg-shaped head, and pointed ears. My two little pigtails point up because of the gravity."

### Scene II

"My planet is Mars. It is round, and big, and red. It has blue rivers and brown mountains. That's where I live."

### Scene III

"This is my green flying saucer; got it for my birthday. It is the shape of your kites and has three little green circles on it. It also has two antennae for directions."

### Scene IV

"It can fly very fast and blinks a red light at the tail as it zooms through the sky."

### Scene V

"Through a little window at the top I can see your Earth planet with green trees, flowers, birds flying around, and blue oceans."

### Scene VI

"I can also see your pretty sky with a big, round, smiling yellow sun and blue clouds. Hey, I think I can also see a rainbow forming out there! Oh, boy, everything is so beautiful on your planet!"

### Scene VII

"Mars-O-My! I have been so happy looking at all your lovely things, that I forgot to check my gas-o-meter, and I'm running out of gas! I better zoom back home!"

### Scene VIII

"Good-bye, my friend! It was nice talking to you. Maybe one day you can come visit with me. So long,... see you in our next movie!" Zooooooooooom!

Upon completion of this activity, analyze the children's performance using their drawings. For example, absence of color, shape, and position in the drawings may indicate that the children are not processing expanded noun phrases.

**REPORT**   Include the following in your report:

1. The ages of the children participating in this activity.
2. The drawings of the movie produced by the children.

In addition, address yourself to the following questions:

1. Describe each child's receptive communicative ability as demonstrated by performance on this task. Analyze the kinds of comprehension errors, if any, made by each child. This is reflected by the pictorial portrayal of the script. For example, were there errors with the expanded noun

phrase, errors of position, errors of coordination, or errors in relating pronouns to their previously specified referent?

2. How did the listener's communication vary with developmental age? Was egocentricism evident? Give examples and explain.
3. Discuss this statement: When extralinguistic cues such as pointing or gesturing are minimal, the linguistic and cognitive demands made of the listener are increased.

**EVALUATION**   Did this inquiry develop the specified objectives? If so, how? If not, why? How could the effectiveness of this inquiry be increased?

----                          **INQUIRY 3.4**                          ----

Egocentric communication is not only a characteristic of the young speaker. Young children are frequently egocentric listeners. They may confirm messages that are either ambiguous or lack critical information. They may not ask questions of the speaker that might aid them in recoding the message to provide more accurate and adequate information. They may give no feedback at all.

**OBJECTIVES**   The objectives of this inquiry are to:

1. Observe the behaviors of the listener in a communicative task, that is, what kinds of feedback the listener provides the speaker.
2. Analyze what the listener does when the message provided either lacks critical information or is ambiguous.
3. Compare listener feedback from younger communicators and older communicators.

**PROCEDURES**   Select two pairs of youngsters, preferably one pair younger (ages five to six) and one pair older (seven to nine). Utilize the block-building task described in Inquiry 3.2. Observe and note all listener feedback both verbal and nonverbal. Also, tape-record the communicative task for later transcription.

**REPORT**   Include the following in your report:

1. The ages of the two pairs of children participating in the block-building activity.
2. The transcript of the communication that occurred between the listener and the speaker. Include any nonverbal feedback that you noted during your observation.

In addition, address yourself to the following questions:

1. What kinds of feedback did the listener provide the speaker? Did the listener confirm the adequacy of the message? If so, how?

2. When the speaker's message was either lacking in critical information or ambiguous, what, if any, feedback did the listener provide?
3. Describe any differences, with respect to age, concerning how listener feedback was used.
4. Evaluate the following statement: Communication is a *cooperative* process between listener and speaker.

**EVALUATION**   Did this inquiry develop the specified objectives? If so, how? If not, why? How could the effectiveness of this inquiry be increased?

_____              **INQUIRY 3.5**              _____

Imprecise and cryptic language is characteristic of the young child. This unelaborated form of language is not just a manifestation of limited vocabulary and restricted syntactic options. These factors are certainly related to the phenomenon of young children's ineffectual communicative abilities. However, they do not totally explain it. Instead, we can look to Piaget's concept of egocentricism, that is, the inability to think about and gain useful insights from what another person thinks, feels, knows, or sees.

**OBJECTIVES**   The objectives of this inquiry are to:

1. Analyze communicative ability as the ability to recode a message for someone else, taking into account what that person knows.
2. Investigate how development affects the ability to think about thinking, therefore increasing one's ability to effectively communicate.

**PROCEDURES**[1]   Select three youngsters, one younger (between the ages of six and eight), one older (between the ages of ten and twelve), and one teenager. Have each of the youngsters participate independently in the task of developing a shopping list. Ask each youngster to give you two shopping lists—one for himself and one for an unknown person. Tape-record both shopping lists. After each youngster completes the task, read the second list back to the child, asking what other information the unknown person might need to have to get the exact kind of items the child wants (e.g., brand name, flavor, size).

**REPORT**   Include the following in your report:

1. The ages of the youngsters who participated in the task.
2. The transcript of the tape.

In addition, address yourself to the following questions:

1. How did the shopping list prepared for the youngster differ from the one prepared for an unknown person?

2. What differences did you see between the younger and older children's ability to think about what the unknown person needed to know?
3. When you probed concerning the youngster's second shopping list, what kinds of additional information, if any, were provided? Were there obvious age-related differences?

**EVALUATION**    Did this inquiry develop the specified objectives? If so, how? If not, why? How could the effectiveness of this inquiry be increased?

_____                  **INQUIRY 3.6**                   _____

Persuasive communicative skills change qualitatively as the child develops cognitively. Not until the child reaches the late concrete operations–early formal operations period (ten to twelve years of age) is the youngster able to coordinate thinking with the thinking and attitudes of others. It is this recursiveness of thinking (i.e., thinking about thinking) that frees youngsters from using pleas as their primary arguments and allows for more sophisticated persuasive arguments.

**OBJECTIVES**    The objectives of this inquiry are to:

1. Analyze persuasive communication as the ability to adjust one's arguments to the thinking, feelings, and attitudes of the listener.
2. Investigate how development (as measured by age) affects the quality of persuasive communication.

**PROCEDURES**    Select three youngsters—one between the ages of six and eight, one between eight and ten, and one between ten and twelve. Have each of the youngsters participate in the following two activities. Using a puppet, say the following to each youngster separately:

### Activity I

"Pretend that this puppet is your mother. You have just found a lost kitten and you want to bring it home, but you know that your mother does not want to have a kitten as a pet. Convince your mother to allow you to keep the kitten. Use whatever and as many arguments as possible to convince her to allow you to keep the kitten."

### Activity II

"Pretend this puppet is your teacher. She has given you a lot of homework to do tonight, but your father is taking you to the movies this evening. You know that you can't do the homework *and* go to the movies tonight. Try to convince your teacher to give you less homework tonight so that you can go to the movies. Use as many arguments as possible to convince her to give you less homework."

Tape-record all persuasive arguments for later transcription.

**REPORT**   Include the following in your report:

1. The ages of the youngsters who participated in the activities.
2. The transcript of the tape.

In addition, address yourself to the following questions:

1. What do you consider to be the characteristics of an effective persuasive argument? How does taking into account the listener's knowledge, attitudes, and feelings affect the quality of a persuasive argument?
2. How does age (development) affect the quality and quantity of persuasive abilities? Describe, using examples from your transcript as illustrations.

**EVALUATION**   Did this inquiry develop the specified objectives? If so, how? If not, why? How could the effectiveness of this inquiry be increased?

----------                         **INQUIRY 3.7**                         ----------

The development of conversational postulates, such as the use of polite forms, increases as the child develops several syntactic options (imperatives versus interrogatives). But more important is the child's growing awareness of the social appropriateness of certain linguistic forms in particular social contexts.

**OBJECTIVES**   The objectives of this inquiry are to:

1. Analyze the production and comprehension of polite forms as one type of conversational postulate.
2. Investigate how children of various ages demonstrate awareness of the social appropriateness of certain linguistic forms.

**PROCEDURES**[2]   Select three children—one between the ages of three and four years, one between four and six, and one six to seven. Work with one child at a time, completing the entire activity with all three. First, introduce the child to a woman puppet, "Ms. Fine," who owns a large bowl of candy placed before her and visible to the child. Say to the child:

"If you ask Ms. Fine for a piece of candy, she will give you one."

Wait for the child to make the request. Then pretend to whisper with the puppet and say:

"Ms. Fine wants to give you a piece of candy, but she likes children to ask very, very nicely. Could you ask her once again even nicer?"

After the child has requested the candy a second time, give the child a piece of candy. Then say to the child:

"You are going to pretend to be Ms. Fine. You are going to decide who asks most nicely for candy."

Present two puppets who take turns making requests, as follows:

| **Puppet 1** | **Puppet 2** |
|---|---|
| Pair 1: *I want a piece of candy.* | *I would like a piece of candy.* |
| Pair 2: *Can I have a piece of candy?* | *I want a piece of candy.* |
| Pair 3: *Please, can I have a piece of candy?* | *Can I have a piece of candy?* |
| Pair 4: *Gimme some candy, please.* | *I want some candy, please.* |

After each pair of requests, ask the child, "Who asked the nicest?" After each decision, ask the child, "Why was he nicer? What did he say that was better?" Tape-record all activities with each of the three children to be used for subsequent transcription.

**REPORT**   Include the following in your report:

1. The ages of the children who participated in the activities.
2. The transcript of the tape-recorded activities.

In addition, address yourself to the following questions:

1. Describe how the youngsters requested candy. Was there a change in the politeness of their latter request from their original one? How does age relate to their understanding of the conversational postulate politeness?
2. Was there an age-dependent difference in how the children understood various requests? How did their ability to understand polite requests relate to their ability to produce polite requests?
3. How were the children able to justify why one request was "nicer" than the other one. Were there age-dependent differences in their ability to justify or explain their judgment concerning the niceness of a request? How did the justifications relate to their ability to produce and understand polite request forms?

**EVALUATION**   Did this inquiry develop the specified objectives? If so, how? If not, why? How could the effectiveness of this inquiry be increased?

### NOTES

1. Based on Elasser and John-Steiner (1977).
2. Based on Bates (1976*a* ).

# 4

# The Acquisition
# of Language

By the time most children reach school age their knowledge of their native language(s) is quite substantial. In fact, it is quite astounding how much language learning takes place during the very early and preschool years. The following interaction between Joel (four years and four months) and David (five years and six months) should demonstrate the level of phonological, syntactic/semantic, and pragmatic knowledge attained by the time children reach school age.[1]

(The boys were seated at the kitchen table of their home and involved in their first attempt at playing dominoes.)

1. David (D) (shouting): "Did you do that?"
2. Joel (J) (shouting back): "Wha did you do that for?"
3. D (smiling and pleased with himself): "Heller, how's that for a match?"
4. J (exasperated, puts hands in air): "I don't have any."
5. D: "No, you're not s'posed to. I can do it better . . . All right Joel let me see—you need either a five or a four."
6. J (in a loud whine): "I can do it!"
7. D (getting impatient and speaking in a high pitch and rapidly): "Put it anywhere you want—anywhere you want. . . . Good, now I'm going to beat him."

That both boys already show a great amount of linguistic knowledge can be seen even from this short interaction. They demonstrate the basics of effective communication (e.g., turn-taking, choosing words that take into account the physical context). Their syntax is well formed and varied (e.g., use of declarative, negative, and interrogative sentence types; use of the grammatical morphemes *a, or,* and *an*). Phonologically, the segmental phonemes are well developed, and the suprasegmental features, such as pitch and intonation, indicate knowledge of the "melody" of English.

Although language acquisition does continue after the age of six, the basic syntactic, semantic, and phonological structures have already been acquired by this age. This chapter provides an overview of language acquisition. First, prelinguistic correlates of language are discussed, followed by the development of syntax and semantics through the elementary school years.

## COGNITIVE CORRELATES OF LANGUAGE

We have already mentioned in Chapter 2 that much of the structure of language has its roots in the prelinguistic period (between birth and eighteen months). At first glance this may appear to be an odd statement. However, given the facts that language is a symbol-system and that language and communication reflect the notion of causality (i.e., what I say about something will affect something or someone), much cognitive development must occur prior to the onset of language. Cognitive psychologists (e.g., Piaget, 1952; Sinclair, 1970) and more recently developmental psycholinguists (e.g., Bloom, 1970, 1973; Brown, 1973a; Slobin, 1973) have recognized that there are certain cognitive antecedents of language. This is not a surprising conclusion in light of the fact that language is a symbol system. In order to be able to utilize such a system, the child must have previously developed certain necessary cognitive abilities, such as the ability to represent $X$ with $Y$.

One of these cognitive abilities, as described by Piaget (1952), is the development of the **object concept.** In order to use the linguistic symbol *ball,* or any symbol representing the concept "ball," the child must first understand that the object concept "ball" is permanent in its existence, regardless of its presence or absence from view or changes in actions, locations, or attributes of ball. The development of the object concept begins at birth and is completed roughly between eighteen and twenty-four months of age. (For a more detailed analysis of the development of the object concept, interested readers should consult Piaget, 1952; Morehead & Ingram, 1973.) Further discussion of the object concept can be found in Chapters 6 and 10.

In addition to recognizing the permanence of objects, the child must know that $X$ can stand for $Y$. This ability is known as **representation.** It is critical for language because all linguistic symbols represent or stand for not just one object such as a ball, but for all objects that can be classified as "ball." At first the symbol is tied to the object or to the action involved with the object; however, eventually the symbol must be freed from the significant, that is, the actual object or event. True representation only occurs when the symbol and the significant are differentiated, and therefore $X$ can stand for $Y$. The development of representational abilities can be witnessed in the child's interaction with objects and culminates with the appearance of symbolic play.

In Chapter 1, language was partly defined as being capable of representing—or more likely growing out of—one's understanding of the world. Therefore, we must look to prelinguistic indicators of the child's growing understanding of the world. For example, before the child uses the basic semantic relation agent + object or agent + action or action + object, the child must first recognize that he is a separate entity from the objects in his environment, that objects exist beyond one's actions, and that actions can be initiated by others (i.e., separation of the child and actions). Similarly, before the child can use *more* to represent the recurrence of actions and objects, he must first understand that objects are more or less permanent in time and space, that quantity is characteristic of most objects, and that actions can be continued. Therefore, the content of what is eventually coded symbolically in language has its roots in the prelinguistic, sensorimotor stage of development. It is during this period that the child begins to develop a practical knowledge of the physical and social world.

Another aspect of the definition of language in Chapter 1 maintains that language is a social code. This means that during the sensorimotor period, the child must learn to not only view himself as separate from his environment but must also come to coordinate previously separate schema,[2] such as seeing and grasping, vocalizing and hearing, so that he can begin to reconstruct that which he sees and hears in his environment. This development of **imitation** enables the child to move from exploratory interactions with objects (e.g., sucking, patting, and mouthing) to socially determined interactions with objects. Similarly, the development of imitation facilitates the move from undifferentiated vocalizations to the acquisition of the sounds specific to the particular linguistic community.

It is important to note at this point that imitation is not seen here as simply a passive phenomenon, as is maintained by behavioral psychologists. Imitation is not the passive one-to-one copying of an external stimulus. Rather imitation, as used here, is an active process of **reconstructing** (Piaget, 1962) that which exists outside the child. The development of both gestural and vocal imitation begins with uncoordinated schema that are exploratory and assimilatory in nature (i.e., vocalizing, imitating sounds that are familiar and self-initiated) and evolves to imitation that represents the coordination of schema (e.g., hearing and vocalizing), that is social in nature (i.e., imitating unfamiliar sounds and actions), and that accommodates schema to the external world. For a further discussion of imitation, see Chapters 6 and 10.

Finally, in tracing the development of communication, we can again look to the sensorimotor period for its roots. The structure of prelinguistic communication has already been described in Chapters 2 and 3. Therefore, it is only necessary to describe here the basis for communication as it relates to the child's general cognitive development. According to Piaget (Ginsburg & Opper, 1969), Stage IV of the sensorimotor period (eight to twelve months) marks the beginnings of intentional behavior—a necessary condition for communication. At this time, the infant uses previously developed schema to obtain desired ends. For example, Ginsburg & Opper (1969) cite the case in which Piaget used a pillow to block his son's approach to a matchbox. The child first struck the pillow, knocking it aside, then he grasped the box. The use of the familiar schema of striking, previously an end in itself, now had a new end, that of obtaining a desired object.

Later, in Stage V (twelve to eighteen months), the child is no longer constrained to using old, previously developed schema to obtain desired ends. In contrast to Stage IV, Stage V includes the emergence of the capacity for inventing new means to obtain desired ends. Rather than merely applying previously acquired schema, such as striking the pillow, the child begins to use objects as instruments (new means) to obtain desired objects. For example, a stick is now used to obtain an object out of the child's reach. Similarly, the child begins to view other people as *agents* capable of securing desired objects or causing events. We see the emergence of the following means-to-ends relationships:

| **Means** | **Ends** |
|---|---|
| $X_1$ objects | $Y_1$ objects and events |
| $X_2$ people | $Y_2$ people's attention |

Now that objects ($X_1$) can be used as instruments for obtaining desired objects and events ($Y_1$) and people's attention ($Y_2$) and people ($X_2$) can be used as agents to obtain desired objects and events ($Y_1$), we have the basis for intentional communication.

To summarize thus far, given the nature of language and communication, we can look to certain cognitive structures that emerge during the sensorimotor period as being a set of precursors, or at least correlates, of later linguistic behavior. However, just how these early cognitive structures correlate with or direct the course of linguistic development continues to be debated (see Corrigan, 1978; Ingram, 1976a; Sinclair, 1969, 1970, 1971; Huttenlocher, 1974; and Schlesinger, 1977 for further discussion of the role of early cognitive development in language acquisition). Since there continues to exist some uncertainty concerning the exact relationship between cognitive structures emerging during the sensorimotor period and the early acquisition of language, Table 4.1 presents a *tentative* sketch of the emergence of various cognitive, phonological, and syntactic/semantic structures during the first two years of life. Inquiries 4.1 and 4.2 are designed to further explore the relationship between the emergence of certain sensorimotor cognitive structures and the acquisition of language.

## SEMANTIC/SYNTACTIC DEVELOPMENT

Linguists, psycholinguists, psychologists, and many parents are constantly amazed by the similarities that are demonstrated in the course of semantic/syntactic development by children coming from very different situations. This phenomenon, coupled with the rapidity with which language develops, has made the study of language acquisition truly fascinating.

TABLE 4.1  Sensorimotor Period

| Cognitive Structures | Age | Phonological Aspects | Syntactic/Semantic Correlates |
| --- | --- | --- | --- |
| I. **Reflexive State** <br> a. Child is fused with environment <br> b. Lacks coordination <br> c. Imitation not present <br> d. Sucking (reflexive—S-R behavior; some differentiation of sucking reflexes) | Birth to 1 month | *Crying:* first two or three weeks undifferentiated cries (alike in response to all stimuli). Entire body used in crying. Expression is innate—no awareness on child's part. Vocalization results from air expelled from lungs passing between tense vocal cords. At end of first two or three weeks, manner of crying more directly related to nature of stimuli (hunger, cold, wet, pain, etc.). Due to muscle-pattern sets, internal states stimulate different sounds in crying. | |
| II. **Primary Circular Reactions** <br> a. Coordination of actions (e.g., hearing and seeing) <br> b. Attempts to repeat an action over and over again <br> c. Imitation sporadic and restrained to familiar behaviors (mostly vocal and self-initiated) | 1–4 months | Differentiated crying up to about six to seven weeks, still essentially reflexive. Hearing is not necessary. *Babbling:* sounds uttered at random—by chance some sounds may be repeated, most aren't—vowels usually precede consonants. A variety of /a/ sounds repeated at length with variations in | Precursor to attributes of action and object. Lack of differentiation of: <br> a. Self and environment <br> b. Action and object |

99

TABLE 4.1 (Continued)

| Cognitive Structures | Age | Phonological Aspects | Syntactic/Semantic Correlates |
|---|---|---|---|
| | | pitch and loudness are among first produced. Then labial consonants (/p/, /b/), gutterals (/g/), dentals (/e/), and nasals (/n/). Children younger than three months vocalize back consonantlike sounds such as /k/, /g/, and /x/ and vowellike sounds such as /i/ and /u/. In babbling period, more sounds are added; sounds move forward in the case of consonants and move backward in the case of vowels. | |
| III. **Secondary Circular Reactions** | 4–8 months | *Babbling:* from a wealth of vocalizations to concentration on a few sounds. *Lalling:* repetition of heard sounds and combinations. Association of hearing and sound production. Learns to imitate own sounds in preparation for imitation of sounds others produce. While they are unintentional, use of vo- | Early differentiation of: |
| a. Separates self from the environment | | | a. Agent and action |
| b. Further coordination of actions (vision and prehension, vision and hearing) | | | b. Action and object |
| c. Begins to act on objects and attends to the effects of action (causality) | | | |

calizations takes on practical aspects: attract attention, accompany, accept, and refuse motor acts, etc.

*Specific sounds:*
1. Predominately vowellike sounds
2. Front vowels 92% of total
3. Some back vowels (/o/, /ou/)

d. Beginning of the object concept (drops objects and watches them fall)
e. Imitation of familiar actions that can be monitored auditorily and/or visually (other-initiated)

8–12 months

Further differentiation of:
a. Agent and action
b. Action and object

Agent is differentiated into self and others

Early preconcept of:
c. Location
d. Future

*Echolalia:* imitation of sounds produced by self, recognized, produced by others. No actual comprehension of sounds imitated. Imitates on selective basis (whatever pleases). Vocalization while playing.

*Specific sounds:*
1. Vowel types are /I/ and /ʌ/
2. Back vowels appear
3. Glottal and velar sounds frequent
4. Appearance of dental and labial consonants

IV. **Coordination of Action Schema**
a. Action schema are freed from old content (are generalized)
b. Actions coordinated in novel ways
c. Purposeful actions
d. Actions are anticipatory
e. Further development of object concept (actively looks for an object)
f. Signifier and significant are fused (occurrence of one depends on the occurrence of the other)
g. Imitates actions that are unfamiliar but perceptually monitored

TABLE 4.1 (Continued)

| Cognitive Structures | Age | Phonological Aspects | Syntactic/Semantic Correlates |
|---|---|---|---|
| **V. Tertiary Circular Reaction**<br>a. Emphasis on the novel<br>b. Interest in discovering attributes of objects<br>c. Self and others as recipients of actions<br>d. Coordination of object and people schemas | 12–18 months | First words monosyllabic or duplicated disyllabic (e.g., *da-da*, *ma-ma*).<br>*Specific sounds:*<br>1. Consonants more frequent than vowels<br>2. Nasal/oral distinction<br>3. Consonant used in initial position more frequently.<br>Vocalizations have communicative intent. | a. Modification<br>b. Differentiation of recipient into self and others<br>c. Recurrence<br>d. Nonexistence<br>e. Attribution<br>f. Precursor to questioning<br>g. Can detach concept (word) from object or event (significant)<br>h. Agent is natural |
| **VI. Invention of New Means**<br>a. Thought freed from action; representation—symbolic behavior<br>b. Object permanence<br>c. Deferred imitation (can imitate behavior without model being present)<br>d. One object can stand for another (symbolic) | 18–24 months | (Meaningful expressive language) *two to three word utterances*<br>*Specific sounds:*<br>1. More front than back vowels<br>2. Instability of voicing<br>3. Rare use of medial and final consonants | a. Beginnings of temporality (past)<br>b. Can manipulate grammatical structures<br>c. Language can be displaced (context-free) |

**SINGLE-WORD UTTERANCES**   We have already suggested that the child's construction of reality begins during the sensorimotor period and reaches a new plane of representation at the end of this period, which is marked by the emergence of language. By this time, the child has acquired a basic practical knowledge of actions, agents, objects, location, the structure of immediate time and space, causality, and recurrence—all of which will soon be encoded linguistically. However, initially the child's single-word utterances are tied to or are a part of the child's actions. This can be seen as the child pushes an object and refers to the object using a single-word utterance. When her actions stop, so does her use of language.

During the single-word utterance stage two language classes of such utterances appear to emerge: (1) those semantic notions referring to relations among objects, actions, and events **(function words)**, and (2) those semantic notions naming actual objects, persons, actions, and so on **(substantives)**. Bloom (1973) argues that function words occur earlier than substantives because the former are not dependent on the fully developed object concept.

Although the form, or structure, of all single-word utterances is exactly the same, that is, one word at a time, the semantic notions encoded by them vary considerably, as illustrated by the following:

| Semantic notions (functional) | Examples |
|---|---|
| 1. Vocatives, such as greeting and announcing | *mama, baby* |
| 2. Existence | *there, cookie* |
| 3. Negation | *no* |
| 4. Disappearance | *allgone* |
| 5. Recurrence | *more, juice* |
| 6. Cessation | *stop* |
| 7. Nonexistence | *no* |
| 8. Possession | *shoe, mama* |

| Semantic notions (substantive) | Examples |
|---|---|
| 1. Agent of action | *Daddy* |
| 2. Action | *push* |
| 3. Object of action | *truck* |
| 4. Location | *there* |

There is some disagreement concerning the intent of these single-word utterances. Some researchers believe that the single words used by the young child are propositionally simple, that is, that they do not represent the propositional content of a complete sentence. Their position is that when the child says *push* as her mother pushes a truck across the room, the single word *push* does not represent the whole proposition *Mommy pushes the truck* (agent + action + object), but simply the single concept "push." Others, such as Bloom (1973), suggest that these single words are functionally complex, that is, that the same words are used for different communicative functions. Given this perspective, the word *Mommy* can represent an agent of an action, a possessor, or disappearance, depending upon the specific context in which the utterance is made. Finally, McNeill (1970) proposes that single-word utterances are holophrastic, meaning that each single word represents the propositional content of an entire sentence (e.g., *milk* represents the proposition *I want more milk*). It is clearly beyond the scope and intent of this chapter to explicate the conceptual and empirical evidence for each of these three positions. It is sufficient to say here that adults, and mothers in particular, respond to children's single-word utterances as though they represented a complete, propositionally complex sentence.

The context in which single-word utterances are used is quite restricted at this stage of language development. The child refers to objects, actions, and agents only when these are present. She names objects and actions as she acts on them. Interestingly, the child talks about objects on which she can act, such as shoes and chairs, but not about objects that she cannot act on or change (Nelson, 1973). Similarly, the child's comprehension of language is contextually bound at this stage, in that she appears to understand only language referring to present objects and events. Therefore, single-word utterances are not truly symbolic in nature, for they are tied to here-and-now objects, actions, and relationships rather than being capable of displacement in time and space.

In addition to differing from those of adults with respect to their exclusive here and now quality, many of the single words used by the young child represent semantic boundaries larger than those of adults (overinclusion) or semantic boundaries more restricted than those of adults (underinclusion). In overinclusion, the child uses one word for several classes of referents that are clearly differentiated through adults' eyes. For example, the child may refer to all four-legged animals, including lions and bears, as *dog*. In this case, *dog* is marked by the features [+animate, +four-legged] and therefore logically includes dogs, lions, bears, and perhaps even humans crawling on all fours. Because the semantic features associated with the word *dog* have not been further differentiated to include such things as domestication, the child overextends the use of the word *dog*. Brown (1973a) provides another example of overinclusion at the two-word utterance stage. His subject Eve said *Eat sweater*. To adults *eat* and *sweater* do not share the semantic feature [+edible]. However, in Eve's experience sweaters, like food, could be put in her mouth and chewed, and the feature [+edible] was likely to be defined by her by the actions of mouthing and chewing, but not ingesting. In fact, many of the words overextended by the child can be attributed to the child's developing (yet somewhat undifferentiated) conception of the physical and social world.

It is clear that both semantic overinclusion and underinclusion occur in children's single-word productions (Bloom, 1973; Brown, 1970, 1973a). However, they are not as readily apparent in children's comprehension of language. Huttenlocher (1974) suggests that there is little evidence for overinclusion in comprehension. This may be due to the fact that much of the natural language directed to very young children is accompanied by gestures used to specify the intended referent. Therefore, the child has two sources of input for comprehension—potentially ambiguous language and usually unambiguous gestures.

To summarize thus far, there has been significant interest in the stage of single-word usage resulting in major advancements in our understanding of the form and function of these utterances. However, considerable numbers of questions remain unanswered. For example, how are the semantic notions acquired? Are they the result of the child's earlier action-based knowledge of objects and events as Piaget (1952) and Nelson (1971) suggest? Or are they a function of static perceptual input to the child, as proposed by Clark (1973)? Also, if the child is already using agents, actions, and objects in single-word utterances, why does she not combine them into two- or three-word utterances, such as agent + action or agent + action + locative? Is the absence of combinational speech due to memory restrictions, cognitive constraints, or communicative demands (see Bloom, 1973 for a discussion of this issue)? These questions are just two of the many unresolved issues that relate to the period of single-word utterances.

**COMBINATIONAL SPEECH**   The use of combinational speech marks the beginning of the interaction of syntax and semantics. While single-word utterances continue to be used by the child, the changing form and function of combinational speech marks a major developmental milestone. The development of combinational speech has been described by Roger Brown (1973*a*) as occurring in five continuous but ordinal stages; it is Brown's model that will be used here. Early Stage I (approximately eighteen to twenty-four months) is characterized by the development of the basic semantic relations. Two-word utterances appear during this stage and include the combining of semantic notions present in the single-word period (e.g., location, action) and the emergence of new semantic relations. Table 4.2 presents the semantic relations that appear during early Stage I. It should be noted that the meanings expressed in early Stage I are still largely dependent on the context. This can be easily seen when a young child utters words like *Mommy sock*. Without the use of contextual clues, it is difficult to determine if the child means *Mommy put on the sock* (agent + action + object) or *It is Mommy's sock* (possessor and object possessed).

As the child moves into Stage I, his language is somewhat freed from his actions. He no longer talks about objects only when he acts on them. However, the child continues to talk predominantly about the here and now. The semantic boundaries of many words are still not in direct accord with those of adults. Therefore, we continue to see the overextension of words, though to a lesser degree than during the period of single-word utterances.

During late Stage I, we find the addition of three more basic semantic relations: (1) dative (*Give Mommy*), (2) experiencer and state, as in the following:

$$\left\{ \begin{array}{l} doggie \\ Mother \\ me \end{array} \right. + \left. \begin{array}{l} need \\ hear \\ want \end{array} \right\}$$

TABLE 4.2    Basic Semantic Relations: Early Stage I

| **Semantic Relations** | | |
|---|---|---|
| 1. Nomination | Calling attention to the refer-ent $X$ | *this* + $X^a$<br>*that* + $X^a$<br>*see* + $X$<br>*here/there* + $X^a$ |
| 2. Recurrence | Comments on or requests the recurrence of a thing, person, or process ($X$) | *more* + $X$ |
| 3. Nonexistence | Either the absolute nonexistence of $X$ or the temporary nonexistence of $X$. | *allgone* + $X$<br>*no more* + $X$ |
| 4. Agent and action | Comment on the agent (usually animate) performing an action | *Mommy go*<br>*me push*<br>*car go* |
| 5. Action and object | Someone or something suffering a change of state or receiving an action | *push truck*<br>*cut meat* |
| 6. Agent and object | Relationship between the agent of an action and the object of the action | *Mommy sock*<br>*Benji truck* |
| 7. Action and locative | Place or locus of an action | $sit \begin{Bmatrix} chair \\ here \\ there \end{Bmatrix}$ |
| 8. Entity and locative | Relationship between a thing (or person) having a distinct existence and its location | *ball chair*<br>*Mommy home* |
| 9. Possessor and possession | Alienable or unalienable relationship between an object and the possessor of the object.[b] | *Mommy sock*<br>*dog tail* |
| 10. Entity and attribute | Specifies some attribute of an entity | *ball dirty*<br>*big doll* |

Adapted from Brown (1973a, pp. 189–98).

[a] *This/that* and *here/there* do not at this stage refer to location or distance.

[b] Alienable possession means the relationship between external objects and the possessor (e.g., *Mommy sock*). Inalienable possession refers to a permanent part-whole relationship (e.g., *Dog tail, Mommy nose*) (Brown, 1973a, p. 196).

and (3) instrumental (*knife cut*). In addition, the child begins to use longer utterances combining more than one basic semantic relation, such as the following:

Agent + action + object: *Me push truck.*
Agent + action + locative: *Truck go chair.*
Action + dative + object: *Give Jonnie truck.*
Action + object + locative: *Push truck chair.*
Agent + action + object + locative: *Me push truck there.*
Action + possession + locative: *Sit Mommy chair.*

Language used during this stage reflects the expansion of the NP (e.g., *Daddy pipe allgone; See dirty hands*). We also see the appearance of various sentence types, such as the following:

Negation: *He no hit you.*
Yes/no questions: *See dirty hand?*
Wh- questions: *Where daddy go? What that?*
Imperative: (You) *give me cookie.*

Also during Stage I, we witness the development of pronouns. According to Brown (1973*a*), the most commonly used pronouns are *I, you, me,* and *that/this.* Pronominal usage represents the following semantic roles:

*I, you, me* as agent or person affected
*It, this/that* as object of action or as an entity
*My* as possessor

Therefore, the semantic distinction [± animate] is appropriately marked—*I, me, you* $\longrightarrow$ [+ animate]; *it, that* $\longrightarrow$ [− animate]. It is not clear whether the child, at Stage I, has made the semantic distinctions [± singular] $\longrightarrow$ *I* versus *we;* [± male] $\longrightarrow$ *he* versus *she,* [± nominative case] $\rightarrow$ *he* versus *him;* or [± distance] $\longrightarrow$ *this* versus *that* or *here* versus *there.* It is clear, however, that it is not until much later that the child begins to make the semantic distinction [± speaker's reference point] as when *this* refers to the close proximity of an object in relation to the speaker's reference point and not the listener's.

What is primarily missing from the language of Stage I is the use of the grammatical morphemes, such as auxiliary verbs, prepositions, and inflectional endings. The appearance of these grammatical features marks the transition into Stage II.

**THE DEVELOPMENT OF GRAMMATICAL MORPHEMES** Once the basic semantic relations have been acquired during Stage I, meaning is modulated by the use of grammatical morphemes. These morphemes, while frequently redundant, further differentiate such aspects as time, containment (*in*), support (*on*), and number. However, it should be noted that semantic intent is not dependent on the appearance of these morphemes and is, in fact, signalled prior to their emergence (e.g., past $\longrightarrow$ *Yesterday, I play ball;* plurality $\longrightarrow$ *I want more cookie*).

The approximate order of acquisition of fourteen of these grammatical morphemes has been identified by Brown (1973*a*) and his colleagues and is presented in Table 4.3. Although Stage II is characterized by the emergence of the grammatical morphemes, the development of these linguistic features is not completed until after Stage V. In fact, even after a particular morpheme, such as the plural $-s$ marker, first appears, a considerable amount of time passes before it is reliably found in the obligatory contexts of a sentence. However, it is this emergence of the grammatical morphemes that results in the child's language sounding more adultlike. Earlier phrase structure rules (PS rules), such as the following:

$$S \longrightarrow NP_1 \quad + V \quad + NP_2$$
$$\text{(agent)} \quad \text{(action)} \quad \text{(object)}$$
$$\textit{Boy hit ball}$$

$$NP \longrightarrow \left\{ \begin{array}{l} it \\ that/this \\ Noun \end{array} \right\} \quad VP \longrightarrow \left\{ \begin{array}{l} V \\ V + NP \end{array} \right\}$$

are now expanded to more complex PS rules, such as the following:

$$S \longrightarrow NP_1 \quad + is + V \quad + \textit{-ing} + NP_2$$
$$\text{(agent)} \quad \text{(action)} \quad \text{(object)}$$
$$\textit{The boy is hitting the ball.}$$

$$NP \longrightarrow \left\{ \begin{array}{l} that/this \\ Det + N \\ it \\ Noun \end{array} \right\} \quad VP \longrightarrow \left\{ \begin{array}{l} V \\ is + V + ing \\ is + V + ing + NP \end{array} \right\}$$

These more complex PS rules, although marking the same basic semantic relations that appeared in Stage I, characterize Stage II and continue to be added to through Stage V. The resultant increase in syntactic complexity is demonstrated by the fact that the mean length of utterance (MLU) increases from 1.75 at Stage I (with an upper range of 5) to 2.25 at Stage II (with an upper range of 7) to 4.00 at Stage V (with an upper range of 13) (Brown, 1973*a*).

**MODALITIES OF SIMPLE SENTENCES**    Stage III is distinguished by the refinement of the use of the major transformations of simple declarative sentences: *yes/no* questions, *wh-* questions, negatives, and imperatives. This is not to say that negation or interrogation are only now making their appearance, for we have already seen that negation was present prior to Stage I (e.g., *no*). Similarly,

*Stage 1 — word's meaning dependent on context*
*2 = used of grammatical morphemes*
*3 = use 109*
*neg... infinitive*
*wh ques*
*yes/no*
*ques.*

TABLE 4.3   The Acquisition of Fourteen Grammatical Morphemes

| Morpheme | Marks | Example |
|---|---|---|
| 1. *-ing* | Present progressive tense | *See Mommy rolling ball?* |
| 2. Preposition *in* | Containment | *baby in car* |
| 3. Preposition *on* | Support | *truck on chair* |
| 4. *-s* | Plurality | *dirty hands* |
| 5. Past irregular | Remote/immediate past | *went* |
| 6. *'s* | Possession | *Mommy's cup* |
| 7. *is* | Uncontractible copula | *I not. He is.* |
| 8. *a, the* | Indefinite/definite | *Here the book.* |
| 9. *-ed* | Past tense (regular) | *He goed.* |
| 10. *-s* | Third person regular | *She walks.* |
| 11. *has, says* | Third person irregular | *He has; Don says.* |
| 12. *have* | Uncontractible auxiliary | *I know he has.* |
| 13. *'s, 'm, 're* | Contractible copula | *You're here.* |
| 14. *'ve, 's, 'd* | Contractible auxiliary | *I've gone.* |

Based on Brown (1973*a*, pp. 259–74).

*wh-* questions and *yes/no* questions were present in a syntactically reduced form during Stage I (e.g., *What that?; Where ball?*).

For *yes/no* questions, we witness the following sequence of development:

1. S $\longrightarrow$ X *(yes/no )*
   Where *yes/no* questions are expressed by a rising intonational pattern associated with nouns and verbs (*X*). Examples: *More cookie? See car?*
2. S $\longrightarrow$ Q *(yes/no )*: $NP_1 + V + (NP_2)$
   Where there is no inversion of $NP_1$ with the auxiliary, because the auxiliary verb has not yet been acquired (see Table 4.3). Questioning is expressed through rising intonation. Examples: *You fix my truck? That cookie mine?*
3. S $\longrightarrow$ $NP_1 + Aux + V + (NP_2)$ $\Rightarrow$ $Aux + NP_1 + V + (NP_2)$
   Where the auxiliary is inverted with $NP_1$ and *do* is provided when necessary.

The development of *wh-*, or content, questions follows a similar course of development, but, in addition to syntactic constraints, there are very clear semantic ones. Besides learning the appropriate syntactic transformations, the child must learn what particular concepts each question form represents. Table 4.4 gives the conceptual basis of each *wh-* question form. The sequence of development of the *wh-* question forms presented in Table 4.4 recapitulates the order of appearance of the basic semantic relations in Stage I (one could also make a strong case for its reflecting earlier sensorimotor knowledge). For example, the early interest in objects and actions is now expressed by new forms, that is, *what?* questions. Simi-

TABLE 4.4   Conceptual Bases for *Wh-* Question Forms

| Conceptual Basis | Question Form | Examples |
|---|---|---|
| 1. Objects | *What + be* | *What that?* |
| 2. Action | *What + do* | *What Jon doing?* |
| 3. Location | *Where* | *Where truck?* |
| 4. Attribution | *What* | *What color that?* |
| 5. Persons | *Who* | *Who that lady?* |
| 6. Possession | *Whose* | *Whose car is that?* |
| 7. Selection | *Which* | *Which cookie I can have?* |
| 8. Time | *When* | *When Jon come home?* |
| 9. Manner | *How* | *How does it taste?* |
| 10. Cause-effect | *Why* | *Why I have to eat lunch first?* |

Adapted from Brown (1968; 1973*a*) and Ervin-Tripp (1970).

larly, the early interest in objects in space and the early emergence of locatives prior to Stage I is now expressed in the question form *where?* Therefore, the appearance of question forms such as *how?* and *why?* represents not just syntactic growth in the child but also major cognitive achievements. For *wh-* questions, we witness the following sequence of development as described by Klima and Bellugi-Klima (1971, pp. 421–23):

1.      $$S \longrightarrow Q: \left\{ \begin{array}{c} What \\ Where \end{array} \right\} + NP_1 + \left( \begin{array}{c} doing \\ go \end{array} \right)$$

Where *what* or *where* question forms introduce the sentence and $NP_1$ is not inverted with the verb or auxiliary. Examples: *What that? What cowboy doing? Where Kitty? Where horse go?*

2.      $$S \longrightarrow Q: \left\{ \begin{array}{c} What \\ Where \\ Why^3 \end{array} \right\} + NP_1 + (V) + (NP_2)$$

Examples: *Where baby Sarah rattle? What me think? Why you waking me up? Why not you have coffee?*

3. (early) $S \longrightarrow Q: Wh\text{-} + NP_1 + Aux + (V) + (NP_2)$
Where the auxiliary appears but is not inverted, there is no inversion of $NP_1$, and *do* is not present when obligatory. Examples: *What I did yesterday? Why I can't go out? How he can be a doctor? What you have?*

3. (late)  Where the auxiliary is appropriately inverted with $NP_1$. Examples: *Where is my cookie? What can I have? Why can't I go? Who is coming here?*

The development of *negation,* similar to that of interrogation, begins its course prior to Stage I (e.g., *no*) and continues through Stage V (*He shouldn't be eating*). The following is the sequence of development:

1. $\begin{Bmatrix} no \\ not \end{Bmatrix} + X$   *or*   $X + \begin{Bmatrix} no \\ not \end{Bmatrix}$

   Where the negative morpheme (*no* or *not*) is simply attached. It is not embedded within the sentence. Auxiliaries are not present. Examples: *Not go night-night. Not me go.*

2. $NP_1 + Neg + (V) + (NP_2)$

   Where Neg $\longrightarrow \begin{Bmatrix} not \\ no \\ V\ neg \end{Bmatrix}$ and V neg $\longrightarrow \begin{Bmatrix} can't \\ don't \end{Bmatrix}$

   Auxiliary and *not* are not used as separate morphemes. Examples: *Daddy can't go. Jonnie not my friend. He no play with me. Why he can't play?*

3. $NP_1 + Aux + Neg + (V) + (NP_2)$

   Where Aux $= \begin{Bmatrix} can \\ will \\ do \\ be \end{Bmatrix}$

   Examples: *I'm not your friend. Daddy can't go. Daddy can not go. I don't like that.*

To summarize thus far, by Stage III, where MLU is approximately 2.75 (with an upper range of 9), the child has acquired the basic semantic meanings and relations, has begun the development of grammatical morphemes to modulate meaning, and has begun to acquire the necessary syntactic transformations to relate negation and interrogation to the simple declarative sentence type. All of this language learning has usually occurred prior to the child's third birthday. All who observe this process unfold recognize this remarkable accomplishment. However, this does not mean that the learning of language is complete.

**EMBEDDING AND COORDINATION**   By approximately the age of three, the child can use a variety of simple sentences, such as the following:

**(1)**          *This is a truck.*

**(2)**          *Daddy bought the truck.*

**(3)**          *I like candy.*

**(4)**          *Candy tastes good.*

**(5)**          *John went to the store.*

**(6)**          *John bought some gum.*

**(7)**          *The cookie is good.*

**(8)**          *The cookie is not big.*

You will notice that each of the eight sentences above contains one proposition. The child's earlier sentences are characterized by a single proposition being contained within one sentence. However, as her language becomes more sophisticated, the child demonstrates the ability to include more than one proposition within a sentence. This process of either embedding one proposition within another or coordinating two propositions represents not only a linguistic achievement but a cognitive one as well. The child is now able to understand, and therefore encode linguistically, causal relationships, part-whole relationships, coordination, and logical relations.

Let us use the eight sentences presented above to see how more than one proposition can be represented in a sentence. Sentences **(1)** and **(2)** can take the following combined forms:

**(9)**                      *This is a truck and Daddy bought it.*

**(10)**                     *This is a truck that Daddy bought.*

In sentence **(9)**, sentences **(1)** and **(2)** are coordinated using the conjunction *and*. Each proposition in sentence **(9)** is given equal importance and is considered true; therefore, $p \cdot q$ is true ($p$ = true: *This is a truck;* $q$ = true: *Daddy bought the truck*). In contrast, sentence **(10)** does not maintain the equivalence of importance of propositions **(1)** and **(2)** even though $p$ and $q$ are both still true. What is important is *This is a truck,* and that *Daddy bought the truck* is only of secondary importance. Therefore, in sentence **(10)**, the clause *that Daddy bought* is subordinate to the proposition *This is a truck.*

Sentences **(3)** and **(4)** can take the following combined forms:

**(11)**                      *I like candy and it tastes good.*

**(12)**                      *I like candy because it tastes good.*

Sentence **(11)** is similar to sentence **(9)**; it gives equal importance to both propositions and shows the propositional relationship $p \cdot q$ is true. In contrast, sentence **(12)** shows a causal relationship between the two propositions with the first proposition occurring as a result of the second proposition.

There are still other relationships that can be represented by embedding or coordinating more than one proposition with another. For example, sentences **(5)** and **(6)** can take the following combined forms:

**(13)**            *John went to the store and bought some gum.*

**(14)**            *When John went to the store, he bought some gum.*

**(15)**            *Before John bought some gum, he went to the store.*

**(16)**            *After John went to the store, he bought some gum.*

The coordinating value of sentence **(13)** is evident as it is the same as that of sentences **(9)** and **(11)**. Sentences **(14)** through **(16)** use adverbial clauses (i.e., *When John went to the store, Before John bought some gum,* and *After John went to the store*) to join the two propositions in each sentence in time. However, in each sentence only one proposition is dominant. See if you can identify the dominant proposition in each of sentences **(14)** through **(16)**.

One last example should be sufficient to demonstrate the various ways in which more than one proposition can be joined or embedded within one sentence. Let us return to sentences **(7)** and **(8).** These two propositions together can take the following form:

**(17)**  *The cookie is good but it is not big.*

Sentence **(17)** conjoins the two propositions **(7)** and **(8)** and gives each of them equal prominence. However, there is a different propositional relationship being expressed. In sentences **(9)** and **(11)** we had the following propositional relationship between $p$ and $q$:

$$p = \text{true and } q = \text{true}$$
$$\text{therefore } p{\cdot}q = \textit{true}$$

In sentence **(17)** the following relationship between $p$ and $q$ is being expressed:

$$p = \text{true and } q = \text{not true}$$
$$\text{therefore } p, \text{ not } q = \text{true}$$

In summary, the abilities to conjoin two sentences and to embed one sentence within another mark the attainment of a sophisticated level of cognitive development that enables the child to map these cognitive abilities into complex linguistic structures. The child by the end of Stage V is no longer constrained to propositionally simple sentences. Table 4.5 summarizes the linguistic accomplishments occurring between Stages I and V.

## LATER LANGUAGE DEVELOPMENT

The elementary school years are marked by the continuation of language growth. This is due not only to increased experience, which results in new concepts to be encoded in language, but also to the child's further cognitive development. Therefore, language reflects the child's growing understandings of both the physical and social world.

As children move from preoperational thinking (ages of approximately two to seven) to concrete operations (from seven to eleven), they become capable of representing the world not only in relation to themselves (i.e., egocentricism) but also in relation to others' perspectives (i.e., decentration). In doing so, children must not only be aware that another perspective exists, but they must also perform certain mental operations in thinking about what the other person sees, knows, and feels. Decentration is further reflected in children's increasing freedom from the rather rigid attributional descriptions of objects and events that are characteristic of preoperational thought. When asked to draw quantitative conclusions about objects, as, for example, if asked which glass contains more water, the child no longer centers on one quantitative aspect (*taller/shorter* versus *thinner/fatter*) instead of coordinating both attributional dimensions in order to account for transformations in perceptual qualities. Therefore, when asked which of two differently shaped glasses has more water, the child no longer selects the tall, thin

TABLE 4.5   Summary of Linguistic Accomplishments: Stages I–V

| | Basic Semantic Relations | Grammatical Morphemes | Sentence Modalities | Embedding of One Sentence in Another | Coordination of Simple Sentences |
|---|---|---|---|---|---|
| Stage I: 18–28 mos. | Uses up to four-term semantic relations (e.g., agent + action + object + locative) | | $\text{Neg} \rightarrow \begin{Bmatrix} no \\ not \end{Bmatrix} + X$ <br> $Q_{y/n} \rightarrow X$ + rise in intonation <br> $Q_{wh} \rightarrow \begin{Bmatrix} what \\ where \end{Bmatrix} + X$ | | |
| Stage II: 22–34 mos. | Uses up to five-term semantic relations (e.g., agent + action + dative + recurrence + object) | -ing <br> in <br> on <br> plural -s | (same as above but with expanded NP or VP) | | |
| Stage III: 24–38 mos. | Uses up to five-term semantic relations | possessive -s <br> uncontractible copula | $\text{Neg} \rightarrow NP_1 + \text{Neg} + (V) + (NP_2)$ <br> $Q_{y/n} \rightarrow NP_1 + V + (NP_2)$ + rise in intonation <br> $Q_{wh} \rightarrow \begin{Bmatrix} where \\ what \\ why \\ why\ not \end{Bmatrix} \begin{aligned} &+ NP_1 + \\ &(V) + \\ &(NP_2) + \\ &\text{rise in intonation} \end{aligned}$ | | |

Stage IV:
26–42 mos.

Uses five-term semantic relations

articles
third person regular
past irregular

(same as above)

Stage V:
28–48 mos.

Uses five-term semantic relations and embeds

Past regular
uncontractible auxiliary
contractible copula
third person irregular
contractible auxiliary

$$\text{Neg} \rightarrow NP_1 + Aux + Neg + (V) + (NP_2)$$
$$Q_{y/n} \rightarrow NP_1 + Aux + V + (NP_2)$$
$$Q_{wh} \rightarrow \left\{\begin{array}{l} what \\ where \\ whose \end{array}\right\} + NP_1 + Aux + V + NP_2$$
$$Q_{y/n} \rightarrow Aux + NP_1 + V + (NP_2)$$
$$Q_{wh} \rightarrow wh + Aux + NP_1 + (V) + (NP_2)$$

Embeds
1. Object NP
2. Indirect question
3. Relative clauses

Coordination of sentences and propositional relations

glass over the short, fat one, because he is now able to mentally coordinate the two attributional dimensions of height and thickness and reach the conclusion that both glasses hold the same quantity of water.

This cognitive development is manifested in language in a variety of ways. Semantically, new features are added that demonstrate the child's ability to coordinate perspectives, such as [±speaker as a reference point]. Webb and Abrahamson (1976) demonstrate this latter semantic differentiation in children's use of *this* and *that*. By the age of two most children in their study could be credited with the [+demonstrative] feature. By four years of age, the children seemed to control the features [+demonstrative] and [±far]. However, children of this age group did not have control of the necessary feature [+speaker as a reference point] when using *this* and *that* but rather used themselves [+ego] as the reference point. This phenomenon of egocentrism is one of the predominant characteristics of the preoperational child. Not until the children reached the age of seven or more did they incorporate all three features, [+demonstrative, ±far, +speaker as a reference point], necessary for the accurate production and comprehension of *this* and *that*.

The use of mental operations, which is characteristic of the period of concrete operations, accounts for several other advancements in the child's language abilities. Consider, for example, the child's growing comprehension of pronouns. A pronoun can make reference to a noun occurring in the same sentence, as in the sentence *Kangaroos carry their young in their pouches.* In this sentence, it is clearly evident that the referent of the possessive pronoun *their* is *Kangaroos*. Retaining the referent across sentence boundaries presents greater cognitive demands. Take, for example, the following sentences:

**(18)** *Galileo, a defender of Copernicus, established the fact that the earth revolved around the sun.*

**(19)** *Born in 1564, he began to be inquisitive at an early age.*

The child must not only comprehend sentence **(18)**, which is both semantically and syntactically complex, but must also establish that the pronoun *he* [+animate, +topic] in sentence **(19)** does not refer to the *sun* [−animate] nor to *Copernicus* [−topic], but to *Galileo* [+animate, +topic].

A more complex level of pronominal processing that occurs more frequently in written than in spoken language is the case where a clause, not a single word, is the referent of a subsequent pronoun. For example:

**(20)** *Ptolemy believed that the earth is the center of the universe.*

**(21)** *According to his argument, this meant that it was a stationary sphere.*

Examining these sentences makes apparent the level of cognitive demands required for accurate comprehension. In sentence **(21)**, the child must identify the referent of *his* as *Ptolemy*, of *this* as the *earth is the center of the universe*, and of *it* as the *earth*. The accurate processing of pronouns in these situations requires the ability to hold more than one element simultaneously in mind in order to perform the necessary operations to establish the correct relationship between the pronouns and their preceding referents. Once again, the ability to hold more than one dimension in mind and to coordinate them is characteristic of the concrete operations period.

This ability is of added importance in the face of the cognitive and linguistic demands of a typical elementary classroom. The language of education is generally of an order of abstractness and complexity that differs from that of the language of everyday social intercourse. The teacher, in giving directions or in presenting information to the class, may very likely use language that requires that the student identify the referents of pronouns appearing previously in the same sentence or in a preceding sentence.

A few other linguistic aspects highlight the continuing development of syntax and semantics during the elementary years. Syntactically, the child's level of development is quite complex even before she reaches school age. However, according to Baldie (1976), it is not until they reach a mean chronological age of 7;6–7;11 that 80% of the children sampled can produce sentences reflecting the passive voice (e.g., *The house was painted by the man*). Hayhurst (1967) suggests that the development of the passive transformation continues until the age of nine.

Similarly, C. Chomsky (1969), in studying language development during the elementary school years, has demonstrated that language continues to evolve during this period. In one such study, Chomsky tested to see how children differentiated *ask/tell* constructions. She presented *ask/tell* constructions of three different levels of difficulty. In the first level, all that the children had to do was to rework the clause into a question, as can be seen below (Chomsky, 1969, p. 47):

### Level I
*Ask Laura what color this is.*
*Ask Laura what you should feed the doll.*

In the second level, the children must supply more information and cannot rely simply on the principle of reworking the clause into a question as in Level I (Chomsky, 1969, p. 47).

### Level II
*Ask Laura her last name.*
*Ask Laura the color of this book.*

Finally, in Level III, the subject of the clause is omitted and therefore must be supplied when the appropriate question is generated (Chomsky, 1969, p. 47).

### Level III
*Ask Laura what to feed the doll.*
*Ask Laura what to put back next.*

In testing children from five to ten years of age, Chomsky found the following pattern of development:

**Stage I**    *Ask* is interpreted as *tell*.

**Stage II**   Successful in Level I, but unsuccessful in Levels II and III.

**Stage III**  Successful in Levels I and II, but unsuccessful in Level III.

**Stage IV**   Responded to Level III *ask* questions by asking questions, but assigned the wrong subject to the question.

**Stage V**    Successful at all Levels.

On the basis of this and other data, C. Chomsky rightfully concluded that semantic/syntactic acquisition continues at least to the age of nine or ten. This demonstrates that the elementary years are productive years for language development.

The preceding section on syntactic/semantic development is just an introductory sketch; further inquiry into child language is necessary to truly understand this remarkable process. The following inquiries are designed to meet this need by sampling several aspects of development. In addition, the reader is referred to Brown (1973*a* ), Moore (1973), Menyuk (1971), and C. Chomsky (1969) for a more extended analysis of language acquisition in children.

———————            **INQUIRY 4.1**            ———————

Both the theories of cognitive development and language acquisition in normal children (Piaget, 1963, 1967; Sinclair, 1970) and applied research in the language of the profoundly retarded (Kahn, 1975) have demonstrated a strong relationship existing between cognitive abilities and the development of meaningful language. One of these abilities is the symbolic use of objects.

**OBJECTIVES**   The objectives of this inquiry are to:

1. Explore what a prelingual child does when given familiar objects to manipulate.
2. Analyze the child's cognitive readiness to use meaningful language.

**PROCEDURES**[4]   Select a child who appears to use no meaningful language. Place the first group of four items from the twelve objects listed in Table 4.6 on the floor in front of the child and bring his attention to them in an enticing manner. Carefully observe exactly what the child does to and with each object. Specific notation of the child's behavior should be recorded in the designated column of the form in Table 4.7 (examples of behaviors at each level are presented in Table 4.6).

Determine the predominance of sensorimotor exploration, self-utilization, or play application, and check the appropriate column(s). Sinclair (1970) reports that children of this age level often engage in an organized series of activities in which they may intersperse self-utilization (Level 2) with play application (Level 3).

TABLE 4.6   Example Items and Behavior Patterns at the Sensorimotor, Self-Utilization, and Play Application Levels

| Object | Level 1 | Level 2 | Level 3 |
|---|---|---|---|
| Doll | Sucking; pulling on its move-able parts and playing with them. | Rocking and holding it in his arms. | Putting the doll to sleep on the floor and covering it with a Kleenex. Having the doll roll the ball or use the spoon. |
| Ball | Squeezing, chewing sucking it; accidentally kicking or knocking it with no purpose in mind. | Bouncing or rolling it in self-play. | Kicking, rolling, or throwing it to the observer or the doll in gamelike interaction. |
| Spoon | Banging, sucking, or throwing it. | Placing it in his mouth as if eating. | Feeding the doll or observer with it. |
| Box of Kleenex | Chewing, crumpling, ripping it in shreds; sucking on box and getting it all wet. | Pretending to blow his nose. | Blowing the doll's nose and then throwing it away; covering the sleeping doll with it. |
| Plastic phone | Sucking, banging, throwing it; playing with dial; chewing on the cord. | Placing some part of the phone to his ear; babbling into it; dialing and saying "Hello." | Dialing a "ding-a-ling" and having the doll answer by putting receiver to doll's ear. |

119

TABLE 4.6  (*Continued*)

| Object | Level 1 | Level 2 | Level 3 |
|---|---|---|---|
| Doll hat | Sucking, stretching, folding it. | Trying to put the hat on his own head. | Dressing the doll. |
| Wash cloth | Sucking, stretching, feeling it. | Rubbing it over his face as if scrubbing it or using it on the phone or mirror. | Washing the doll's face; having the doll wash the other items with it. |
| Hand mirror | Grasping, sucking, and banging it; reflecting image. | Holding it up to his face for careful look at himself. | Holding it up to the doll's face so she can look at herself. |
| Toothbrush | Stroking the brush part; banging it. | Placing it to his teeth in brushing position. | Holding it to the doll's teeth. |
| Cup with juice | Grabbing, spilling, banging it. | Drinking from it. | Giving the doll a drink from it. |
| Hair brush | Banging, stroking, dropping it. | Brushinglike gestures with his own hair. | Brushinglike gestures with the doll's or observer's hair. |
| Small pillow | Squeezing, punching, mouthing it. | Pretending to sleep on it. | Putting the doll to sleep on it. |

From Chappel, G. E., and Johnson, G. A. Evaluation of cognitive behavior in the young nonverbal child. *Language, Speech and Hearing Services in the Schools*, 1976, *1*, 17–24. Used with permission of the authors.

TABLE 4.7   Record Form for Observations

| Object | Verbal Directive | Level of Development 1 | 2 | 3 | Comments on Observations |
|---|---|---|---|---|---|
| Doll | Make Dolly sleep on floor. | | | | |
| Ball | Throw ball to Dolly. | | | | |
| Spoon | Feed Dolly with spoon. | | | | |
| Box of Kleenex | Blow Dolly's nose with Kleenex. | | | | |
| Plastic phone | Make Dolly talk on phone. | | | | |
| Doll hat | Put Dolly's hat on her head. | | | | |
| Wash cloth | Wash Dolly's face with wash cloth. | | | | |
| Hand mirror | Show Dolly her face in mirror. | | | | |
| Toothbrush | Brush Dolly's teeth with toothbrush. | | | | |
| Cup with juice | Give Dolly drink in cup. | | | | |
| Hair brush | Brush Dolly's hair with brush. | | | | |
| Small pillow | Make Dolly sleep on pillow. | | | | |

From Chappel, G. E., and Johnson, G. A. Evaluation of cognitive behavior in the young nonverbal child. *Language, Speech and Hearing Services in the Schools*, 1976, *1*, 17–24. Used with permission of the authors.

Symbolic play behavior (as evidenced in Level 3) may be seen as a cognitive prerequisite of language development. Although the child may portray some overlapping behaviors among the three levels, one pattern should emerge to demonstrate a prevailing degree or level of advancement. For any given item where several levels are displayed, credit the highest level.

If the child did not spontaneously interact with any of the four items, hand each of the previously unexplored objects to the child, one at a time, and encourage the child to interact with them. Encourage him to look at each item. Observe his manipulatory behavior. Interject the verbal directives listed for the items in Table 4.7 and witness their effect or lack of it.

Repeat the above procedure for the next group of four items, advancing into subsequent groups as long as the child remains interested; discontinue and return later if there is dwindling interest.

**REPORT**   Include the following in your report:

1. Descriptive information concerning the child.
2. A profile of the child's level of development in object manipulation/symbolic representation (Table 4.7).

In addition, address yourself to the following questions:

1. Describe the child's general developmental status in this form of representational competence (object use).
2. On the basis of your findings, what do you consider to be the child's readiness for learning language?

**EVALUATION**   Did this inquiry develop the specified objectives? If so, how? If not, why? How could the effectiveness of this inquiry be increased?

<hr>

## INQUIRY 4.2

In addition to the development of symbolic use of objects, the development of object permanence and vocal imitation appear to be related to the emergence of the symbolic function, which includes language (Piaget, 1962; Bates, 1974; Bloom, 1973). This relationship has been studied in normal youngsters and in profoundly retarded children (Kahn, 1975) and adolescents (Capuzzi, 1978).

**OBJECTIVES**   The objectives of this inquiry are to:

1. Explore two of the cognitive precursors to language (i.e., object permanence, vocal imitation).
2. Assess the cognitive readiness of a child for the development of meaningful, expressive language.

**PROCEDURES**   Select an individual who appears to use no meaningful expressive language. Identify the area(s) of object permanence and/or imitation and assess the child's development within the cognitive area(s). Use as a prototype the developmental stages and activities (as well as others) presented in Tables 4.8 and 4.9. Before engaging in this inquiry you should refer to Piaget (1952) or Uzgiris and Hunt (1975) in order to become familiar with the bases for these tasks.

**REPORT**   Include the following in your report:

1. Descriptive information on the individual being assessed.
2. A profile (results) of the individual's developmental status in the area(s) of object permanence and/or imitation.
3. Your assessment procedures and developed forms.

TABLE 4.8   Object Permanence

| Stage | Activity/Object | Response |
|---|---|---|
| 1. Visual pursuit of slowly moving objects<br>  a. horizontal<br>  b. Vertical<br>  c. Disappearing | a. Select objects of interest to child.<br>b. List them.<br>c. Move them slowly in front of child and observe. | + eyes follow<br>0 eyes fixate but don't follow<br>− no response (N.R.) |
| (Rationale: coordination of movement and form) | | |
| 2. Finds objects that are partially hidden (visually displaced) | a. Select objects of interest.<br>b. List objects.<br>c. Partially hide each object and observe (make certain child is watching). | + searches<br>0 cries<br>− loses interest |
| 3. Finds objects that are totally hidden (one screen visibly displaced) | a. Select objects of interest.<br>b. List objects.<br>c. Hide object behind or under a screen (e.g., pillow) while child watches you.<br>d. Observe child. | + searches and finds<br>0 cries<br>− loses interest |
| (Rationale: coordination of vision and action) | | |
| 4. Finds objects totally hidden (several screens visibly displaced) | a. Select objects.<br>b. List objects.<br>c. Child watches as you hide objects first under one screen then under another one.<br>d. Observe child. | + searches and finds<br>0 looks under screen where last hidden<br>− loses interest |
| 5. Finds objects totally hidden (invisible displacement under one screen) | a. Select objects and list them.<br>b. Child watches object hidden in hand and invisibly displaced under one screen.<br>c. Observe child. | + searches and finds<br>0 looks in hand and loses interest<br>− loses interest |

TABLE 4.8   (*Continued*)

| Stage | Activity/Object | Response |
|---|---|---|
| (Rationale: holds image in mind) | | |
| 6. Finds invisibly dis-placed objects (several screens) | a. Select objects and list them. | + searches and finds |
| | | 0 searches under screen |
| | b. Child watches object hidden in hand and invisibly displaced under several screens. | where last found |
| | | V looks in hand and |
| | | loses interest |
| | | − loses interest |
| | c. Observe child. | |
| (Rationale: can hold image of object in mind, object no longer fused with the context or action) | | |

In addition, address yourself to the following questions:

1. What is the child's general developmental status in the above cognitive abilities?
2. On the basis of your assessment, what do you consider to be the implications for cognitive and language development? Explain.

**EVALUATION**   Did this inquiry develop the specified objectives? If so, how? If not, why? How could the effectiveness of this inquiry be increased?

———————                        **INQUIRY 4.3**                        ———————

Around the age of nine months the infant begins to show signs of understanding language. However, it is not clear just what the very young child is comprehending. Is it the symbol system itself? Is it the context in which language is being used? Or is it a combination of these two?

**OBJECTIVES**   The objectives of this inquiry are to:

1. Study the early receptive language development of the young child.
2. Analyze the relative contributions of context and linguistic symbols to the child's comprehension of language.

**PROCEDURES**   Select a young child (nine months to two years old) who (1) appears to demonstrate the cognitive precursors to language (this may require some cognitive assessments) and (2) appears to have *some* receptive or expressive language (this may be tentatively identified by information obtained from the parent). Using Table 4.10 as a format, explore the individual's development of receptive language.

TABLE 4.9   Vocal Imitation

| Stage | Activity | Response |
|---|---|---|
| 1. Vocalizes other than crying | a. Engage child in physical stimulation (e.g., "rough housing," rolling on bed, tickling, tossing).<br>b. Record sounds made and context in which sounds were made. | |
| (Rationale: importance of vocalization for subsequent speech development, need to know sounds familiar to child) | | |
| 2. Responds to familiar sounds, self-initiated | a. Select appropriate context.<br>b. Child vocalizes; adult imitates, child responds.<br>c. Observe; record sounds and context. | + correct imitation<br>0 approximation<br>− N.R. |
| (Rationale: beginnings of coordination of vocalization and hearing necessary for later vocal imitation) | | |
| 3. Imitation of familiar sounds, model-initiated | a. Select familiar sounds and context.<br>b. List sounds.<br>c. Model sounds and observe responses. | + correct imitation<br>a approximation<br>0 observes<br>− N.R. |
| (Rationale: necessary for imitation of unfamiliar sounds) | | |
| 4. Imitation of familiar words, model-initiated | a. Observe and list words that child spontaneously uses.<br>b. In appropriate context, model word.<br>c. Observe child's response. | + correct imitation<br>a approximation<br>0 observes<br>− N.R. |
| 5. Imitation of new sounds | a. Select sound not produced by child and easy to produce (e.g., vowels, labial consonants).<br>b. List sounds.<br>c. Model sounds and observe child's response. | + correct imitation<br>a approximation<br>f familiar<br>0 observes<br>− N.R. |

TABLE 4.9   (*Continued*)

| Stage | Activity | Response |
|---|---|---|
|  | d. Record sounds produced if other than those modeled. |  |
| 6. Imitation of new words | a. Select words not produced that child shows nonverbal knowledge of and that involve easily articulated sounds. | + correct imitation<br>a approximation<br>f familiar<br>0 observes<br>− N.R. |
|  | b. List words. |  |
|  | c. Model words and observe. |  |
|  | d. Record child's imitation if it is not an exact imitation of model. |  |
| 7. Deferred imitation | a. List words child imitates but does not spontaneously produce. | + correct imitation<br>a approximation |
|  | b. Observe in other settings. |  |

(Rationale: already can remember sounds, has mental image of sounds and words)

**REPORT**   Include the following in your report:

1. Descriptive information on the individual being assessed.
2. A profile of the individual's developmental status in early receptive language acquisition.
3. Your assessment procedures and developed forms.

In addition, address yourself to the following questions:

1. What is the child's general developmental status in the area of receptive language? Describe.
2. On the basis of your evaluation, what do you consider to be the relative contributions of context and linguistic symbols to the child's comprehension of language?

**EVALUATION**   Did this inquiry develop the specified objectives? If so, how? If not, why? How could the effectiveness of this inquiry be increased?

TABLE 4.10    Early Language Comprehension

| Stage | Activities | Responses |
|---|---|---|
| 1. Understands simple language that is context-related.<br>  a. Onomatopeia (symbol)<br>  b. Signs | a. Select contexts of commonly occurring activities and make a list.<br>b. Present simple words or phrases related to the context (e.g., kitchen—"Want to eat?" or door—"bye-bye").<br>c. Observe and note responses. | Describe child's responses. |
| 2. Understands simple language. | Same procedures as above, but not in the context that activity usually occurs (e.g., kitchen—"Want to go bye-bye?" or living room—"Want to eat?"). | Describe child's responses. |

----------     **INQUIRY 4.4**     ----------

At approximately one year of age, most children begin to talk, using one-word utterances. The first words the child uses generally refer to objects, actions, and relations in the immediate environment. In fact, it has been argued that the first words the child produces are tied to an action upon an object.

**OBJECTIVES**    The objectives of this inquiry are to:

1. Study the early expressive language development of the child.
2. Analyze the various contexts in which language is used.

**PROCEDURES**    Select a young child between the ages of twelve and twenty-four months who is beginning to produce language. Observe the child in a setting that is familiar to her (e.g., the kitchen or playroom at home). Observe the child in a situation in which she is interacting spontaneously with her parent or caretaker. Function as an observer rather than a participant. Only if it is impossible to arrange such a situation should you interact directly with the child. (If you are the adult interactor in this inquiry, you might find it helpful to use Table 4.11 as a guideline for your interactions.)

TABLE 4.11   Early Expressive Language

| Stage | Activities | Responses |
|---|---|---|
| 1. Spontaneous one- or two-word utterances | a. Observe child manipulating objects or engaging in an activity.<br>b. Record spontaneous verbalizations. | Note any meaningful language and the context in which it occurs (intent). |
| 2. Elicited one- or two-word utterances (names of persons, objects) | a. While child is engaged in play, say "What's this?"<br>b. Note response.<br>c. If child does not answer, ask "Is this a ball?" or "Is this Dave?"<br>d. Note response. | |
| 3. Elicited one- or two-word utterances (describing actions) | a. While child is engaged in object or person play, say "What's (name) doing?"<br>b. Note response.<br>c. If child does not answer, ask "Is (name) pushing?"<br>d. Note response. | |
| 4. Elicited relational terms (e.g., "more," "allgone," "up," etc.) | (Procedures as above) | |

Tape-record the interaction for later transcription. Continue your observation until approximately fifty separate utterances have been collected.

**REPORT**   Include the following in your report:

1. The age of the child.
2. Brief descriptions of the child, the person interacting with the child, and the context in which the interaction took place.
3. A complete transcript of the interaction, using the following format:

> Mother:   "You want some juice?" (points to the refrigerator). (Child gives no response.)

>Mother (opens refrigerator and points to a bottle of juice): "Want some juice?"
>
>Child: "No juice."

In addition, address yourself to the following questions:

1. What semantic notions were used by the child (e.g., actions, recurrence, negation)? Describe.
2. Using your transcript of the language used and the context in which it was used, evaluate this statement: Children talk about those aspects of the world they can act or operate on, neglecting those that they cannot. Support your evaluation with examples.
3. Were the utterances used by the child simple in their underlying structure or did they appear to represent the proposition of a whole sentence (e.g., *more* ⟶ *I want more juice*). Explain your position using actual examples and context clues.
4. Were there any instances of semantic overinclusion or underinclusion? If so, how does semantic features analysis account for them?

**EVALUATION**   Did this inquiry develop the specified objectives? If so, how? If not, why? How could the effectiveness of this inquiry be increased?

## INQUIRY 4.5

By the latter part of Stage I and the early part of Stage II (Brown, 1973*a*), the child has acquired the basic semantic meanings and relations. In addition, he is beginning to acquire the grammatical morphemes that modulate meaning.

**OBJECTIVES**   The objectives of this inquiry are to:

1. Analyze the basic semantic relations occurring during early Stage II.
2. Identify the grammatical morphemes present in the child's language.

**PROCEDURES**   Select a child between the ages of eighteen months and three years. Observe the child in a setting that is familiar to him (e.g., kitchen or playroom of his home). Observe the child in a situation in which he is interacting spontaneously with his parent or caretaker. Function as an observer rather than a participant. Continue your observation until fifty separate units of utterance have been collected. Tape-record the interaction for later transcription.

**REPORT**   Include the following in your report:

1. The age of the child.
2. Brief descriptions of the child, the person interacting with the child, and the context in which the interaction took place.
3. A transcript of the interaction, using the format shown in Inquiry 4.4.

In addition, address yourself to the following questions:

1. What semantic relations were used by the child? Examples:

   > *It mine.* (possession)
   > *I cleaning the stick.* (agent + action + object)
   > *Right there.* (location)

2. Which grammatical morphemes were used by the child and which were not used? Examples:

   **Used**

   | | |
   |---|---|
   | *Somebody walked up.* | (past regular *-ed*) |
   | *A monter.* | (article *a*) |

   **Not used**

   | | |
   |---|---|
   | *It good.* | (contractible copula *is*) |
   | *Somebody baby.* | (possessive *'s*) |

3. Were the grammatical morphemes reliably used by the child? In other words, were they used 100% of the time in obligatory contexts? Explain and give examples.

**EVALUATION**   Did this inquiry develop the specified objectives? If so, how? If not, why? How could the effectiveness of this inquiry be increased?

---

## INQUIRY 4.6

During Stage I, children begin to use interrogation and negation in addition to simple declarative sentences. However, Brown (1973*a*) suggests that at Stage III modalities of simple sentences appear.

**OBJECTIVES**   The objectives of this inquiry are to:

1. Analyze the development of interrogative and negative forms in a young child's speech.
2. Describe the PS rules of the young child's forms in relation to those of adults.

**PROCEDURES**   Select a child between the ages of eighteen months and three years. Observe the child in a setting that is familiar to her (e.g., kitchen or playroom at home. Observe the interaction of the child with her parent, caretaker, or sibling. Function as an observer rather than a participant. Continue your observation until fifty separate units of utterance have been collected. Tape-record the interaction for later transcription.

**REPORT**   Include the following in your report:

1. The age of the child.
2. Brief descriptions of the child, the person interacting with the child, and the context in which the interaction took place.
3. A transcript of the interaction using the format in Inquiry 4.4.

In addition, address yourself to the following questions:

1. How would you describe the development of interrogative and negative forms in the child that you observed?
2. Diagram the PS rules underlying the interrogative and negative forms used by the child. Examples:

> *Go out?*
> *Mommy, you play?*
> $Q \; yes/no \longrightarrow$ (NP) + VP + intonation
> Examples:
>> *Where bed?*
>> *Where ball?*
>> *What that?*
> $Q_{wh} \longrightarrow$ *Wh-* + NP + intonation
> where *Wh* $\longrightarrow \left\{ \begin{array}{c} what \\ where \end{array} \right\}$, NP $\longrightarrow \left\{ \begin{array}{c} N \\ that \end{array} \right\}$.

3. Compare the PS rules used by the child to those of adult interrogative and negative forms. (See pp. 108–111.)
4. How does context influence the child's use of interrogative, declarative, and negative sentence types? Use examples from your transcript.

**EVALUATION**   Did this inquiry develop the specified objectives? If so, how? If not, why? How could the effectiveness of this inquiry be increased?

───────────             **INQUIRY 4.7**             ───────────

Inquiry 2.7 explored the relationship between semantic features and selection restrictions. As a child develops linguistically, the use of semantic features and knowledge of syntax becomes more in accord with adult grammar.

**OBJECTIVES**   The objectives of this inquiry are to:

1. Investigate the semantic/syntactic competency of children of various developmental levels.
2. Relate this competency to the children's ability to justify or explicate their tacit linguistic knowledge.

**PROCEDURES**   Select two children, one younger (between the ages of three and five) and one older (between the ages of six and eight). Follow the procedures outlined in Inquiry 2.7.

**REPORT**   Include the following in your inquiry report:

1. The ages of the two children to whom you presented the task.
2. A transcript of the children's judgments, justifications, and corrections for each of the ten sentences.

In addition, address yourself to the following questions:

1. Was there an age-dependent difference in the judgments of the grammaticalness of the sentences? Explain.
2. Was there an age-dependent difference in the strategies used to justify or explain judgments? Explain.
3. Was there an age-dependent difference in the way the children corrected the anomalous sentences? Explain.

**EVALUATION**   Did this inquiry develop the specified objectives? If so, how? If not, why? How could the effectiveness of this inquiry be increased?

---

**INQUIRY 4.8**                         _____

As was mentioned in Inquiry 2.8, by the age of four or five most children have mastered the rules governing the use of the basic grammatical morphemes.

**OBJECTIVES**   The objectives of this inquiry are to:

1. Analyze the children's production of selected grammatical morphemes using previously unlearned words.
2. Analyze the children's production of selected grammatical morphemes using familiar words.

**PROCEDURES**   Select two children, one younger (between the ages of three and five) and one older (between the ages of six and eight). Follow the procedures described in Inquiry 2.8 with each child.

**REPORT**   Include the following in your report:

1. The ages of the children to whom the task was presented.
2. The exact responses that each child made for each of the picture stories.

In addition, address yourself to the following questions:

1. Did the children differ in their ability to generate the appropriate grammatical morpheme? For example, in the picture story about more than

one *gid,* did the children generate the plural morpheme, and, if so, was it the appropriate phonetic realization of the morpheme? Explain.

2. What was the relationship between the children's performances on the novel versus the familiar word situations? Were there age-related differences?

**EVALUATION**   Did this inquiry develop the specified objectives? If so, how? If not, why? How could the effectiveness of this inquiry be increased?

                              **INQUIRY 4.9**

In Chapter 2, we explored the structure of various sentences. This includes phrase structure rules (PS rules) and transformational rules (T rules). One T rule that may be acquired later than others is the passive transformation, which is symbolized as follows:

$$S \longrightarrow NP_1 + V + NP_2 \Rightarrow NP_2 + Aux + V + (en) + by + NP_1$$

Young children who have not yet acquired this rule may use word order as the only strategy for processing passive sentences and subsequently misunderstand the meaning of such sentences, as when *The boy was hit by the girl* is processed as *The boy hit the girl.*

**OBJECTIVES**   The objectives of this inquiry are to:

1. Analyze the age-dependent differences in ability to comprehend passive versus active sentences.
2. Analyze the age-dependent differences in ability to imitate passive versus active sentences.

**PROCEDURES**   Select two children, one younger (between the ages of three and five) and one older (between the ages of six and eight). Follow the procedures described in Inquiry 2.9.

**REPORT**   Include the following in your report:

1. The ages of the children to whom you presented the task.
2. Transcripts of the children's exact repetitions of the stimulus sentences and your notes as to whether their picture selections were correct or not.

In addition, address yourself to the following questions:

1. What was the relationship between the children's accuracy in imitating the stimulus sentences and their accuracy in selecting the correct picture? Did the relationship vary with age?

2. Did the active or the passive sentences present greater difficulty and were there age-related differences? Explain.

**EVALUATION**   Did this inquiry develop the specified objectives? If so, how? If not, why? How could the effectiveness of this inquiry be increased?

_____                **INQUIRY 4.10**                _____

One of the functions of grammatical morphemes such as *and, then, but not,* and *or* is to coordinate more than one proposition in a complex sentence. When the coordination of two propositions in a complex sentence occurs, each proposition is afforded equal importance. However, depending on the grammatical morpheme coordinating the propositions, the following logical propositions can result:

1. $p$ = true, $q$ = true
   therefore $p \cdot q$ = true
2. $p$ = true, $q$ = not true
   therefore $p$, but not $q$ = true
3. $p$ = true or $q$ = true
   therefore $p$ or $q$ = true

**OBJECTIVES**   The objectives of this inquiry are to:

1. Analyze how complex coordinated sentences are processed at different ages.
2. Explicate the underlying meanings of specific grammatical morphemes used to coordinate two propositions.

**PROCEDURES**   Select two children, one younger (between the ages of three and five) and one older (between the ages of six and eight). Follow the procedures described in Inquiry 2.10.

**REPORT**   Include the following in your report:

1. The ages of the children who participated in the task.
2. Transcripts of each child's repetitions of the stimulus sentences and your notes as to whether the children correctly or incorrectly performed the tasks.

In addition, address yourself to the following questions:

1. What is the relationship between each child's repetition of the stimulus sentences and performance on the task? Analyze errors made on each of the two tasks and any discrepancies between the repetitions of the sentences and the performance of the commands. Did the children's performance vary with their ages? How?

2. What syntactic structures affected the children's performance on the tasks (e.g., sentence length, type of grammatical morpheme used)?
3. How do each of these grammatical morphemes affect the coordination of the two propositions of each sentence?

**EVALUATION** Did this inquiry develop the specified objectives? If so, how? If not, why? How could the effectiveness of this inquiry be increased?

_____ **INQUIRY 4.11** _____

The use of complex sentences enables the child to express causal relationships between two propositions (e.g., *She is proud because she learned how to ride her bike*), to coordinate propositions (e.g., *The boy went to the store and bought some candy*), to link propositions in time (e.g., *Before it rained, they went out*), and so on. However, the use of complex sentences does not emerge until rather late in the child's language development.

**OBJECTIVES** The objectives of this inquiry are to:

1. Study the effects of age on the use of complex sentences.
2. Analyze the types of complex sentences used by children.

**PROCEDURES** Select two children, one younger (between two and three and a half years old) and one older (between four and six years). Observe each child in a setting that is familiar (e.g., home or school classroom). Observe the interaction of each child with a parent, caretaker, sibling, or classmate. Function as an observer rather than a participant. Continue observing until fifty separate sentences have been collected from each child. Tape-record the interaction for later transcription.

**REPORT** Include the following in your report:

1. The ages of the children you observed.
2. Brief descriptions of the children, the persons interacting with the children, and the context in which the interactions took place.
3. A transcript of the interactions using the format in Inquiry 4.4.

In addition, address yourself to the following questions:

1. Did the ability to use complex sentences vary with age? Describe and give examples.
2. What kinds of complex sentences were used by each of the children (e.g., coordination, adverbial clauses, causal relations)? Describe and give examples.
3. Did the kinds of complex sentences used vary with age? Describe.

**EVALUATION** Did this inquiry develop the specified objectives? If so, how? If not, why? How could the effectiveness of this inquiry be increased?

## INQUIRY 4.12

One of the later developments of language use occurring during the elementary years is the differentiation between *ask* and *tell*. The later development of this differentiation demonstrates that syntactic/semantic structures continue to develop during the elementary years (C. Chomsky, 1969).

**OBJECTIVES**   The objectives of this inquiry are to:

1. Identify how *ask/tell* sentences are understood by children.
2. Analyze how age affects the processing of *ask/tell* sentences.

**PROCEDURES**[5]   Select two children, one younger (between four and six years old) and one older (between eight and ten years old). For each of the children, have a friend join in the task. The friend is the person to be addressed. Using the following groups of sentences and a blue book, a puppet, and some clay, say to the first child:

"I'm going to have you ask or tell your friend (*name*) some things about the objects here. You say to (*friend's name*) what I tell you to say."

### Level I

1. Tell _____ what color this is. (point to blue book)
2. Tell _____ what you should feed the puppet. (point to puppet)
3. Ask _____ what you can make with the clay. (point to the clay)
4. Ask _____ what the puppet's name is. (point to puppet)

### Level II

1. Ask _____ her last name.
2. Ask _____ the color of this book. (point to book)
3. Tell _____ the name of the puppet.

### Level III

1. Ask _____ what to feed the puppet.
2. Ask _____ what to make with the clay.
3. Tell _____ what to call the puppet.
4. Tell _____ what to put away first.

Once you have finished with the first child and friend, repeat the procedures with the second child and friend. Tape-record the entire activity.

**REPORT**   Include the following in your report:

1. The ages of the children who participated in the task.
2. The transcripts of the children's responses.

In addition, address yourself to the following questions:

1. Were there differences in the ways the children processed *ask* and *tell* sentences? Describe.
2. Were there age-related differences in the ways the children processed *ask* and *tell* sentences? Describe.
3. How did the children's performances vary depending on the level of the sentences?
4. Why do you suppose *tell* sentences are easier to process than *ask* sentences?

**EVALUATION**    Did this inquiry develop the specified objectives? If so, how? If not, why? How could the effectiveness of this inquiry be increased?

### NOTES

1. Sample obtained by Susan Weiner and used with her permission.
2. Schema is defined as an elementary structure (e.g., sucking, grasping).
3. During period 2, *why* is used as *what*.
4. Adapted from Chappell and Johnson (1976).
5. This inquiry is based on work by C. Chomsky (1969).

# 5

# The Development of Phonology

From birth onward the child begins to experiment with the sounds of language. In fact, one can argue that the birth cry itself is the first milestone in the child's acquisition of phonology. However, it is not until about seven or eight years of age that the major developmental aspects of phonology are mastered. Ingram (1976*b* ) suggests that not until the period of the formal operations (twelve to sixteen years) is the process of phonological development truly completed. The purpose of this chapter, then, is to provide an overview of the acquisition of phonology.

## PRELINGUISTIC VOCALIZATIONS

Prior to the production of the first word, which normally occurs before the first birthday, the infant spends much of her waking time experimenting with the sounds of language. However, this period of experimentation is considered to be prelinguistic because the sounds that the infant makes are not yet associated with meaning.

**EARLY VOCALIZATIONS**   The vocalizations made by the infant in the first month are cries. Unlike later crying, the crying of the newborn is reflexive and is due merely to the inhalation and exhalation of air. Crying during the latter part of the first month and after is differentiated in response to various stimuli (e.g., wetness, hunger, illness) (Berry & Eisenson, 1956). These cries now vary in length, pitch, and volume and are no longer produced by reflexive inhalation and exhalation.

Sometime between one and three months, the crying gives way to other forms of vocalization. These early noncrying vocalizations, usually accompanying a period of satisfaction, are called **cooing.** Cooing is essentially vowellike in form; and the earliest vowel sounds are front, such as /ɛ/ as in *bet* and /i/ as in *beat,* and middle, such as /ʌ/ as in *but* (Irwin, 1948). Back consonantlike sounds, such as /k/, /g/, and /x/, and specific fricative sounds are also produced during this early period, although vowels exceed consonants in frequency (Irwin, 1946, 1947).

It should be noted, however, that infant sounds differ from the phonemes of speech produced by adults. These differences, according to Stark (1978), are reflected in voicing, breath control, pitch, and so on. Stark suggests that these phonological differences are due to two limitations: (1) the infant's vocal tract is different in shape and size in comparison to that of adults, and (2) the infant is unable to fully control the major articulators—the tongue, lips, and jaws.

As early as three months of age, the infant shows some phonological perception. Discrimination occurs between certain vowellike sounds (Eisenberg, 1969), between acoustic cues for segmental and intonational stimuli (Eimas et al., 1971), and between the rising and falling intonational contour of a syllable (Tonkova-Yampol' Skaya, 1973). The early perception of certain phonological features is demonstrated at about three months by the social behavior of smiling in response to the mother's voice (Lewis, 1963).

During the early part of this prelinguistic period, at about one month, the child is unaware of her own vocalizations. In other words, there is a lack of coordination between the schema of hearing and vocalizing. This lack of coordination gradually gives way to the ability to coordinate hearing and vocalizing and can be noted in the infant's sporadic attempts at imitation. However, imitation is restrained to sounds that are already familiar to the infant and initiated by her.

**INCREASED VOCALIZATION**   During the period from three to six months there is an increase in the variety of sounds produced. Additional consonantal sounds, such as /p/, /b/, and /d/, emerge (Irwin, 1947) along with nasal sounds. The area of articulation moves forward in the case of consonants and backward in the case of vowels. The repetitive chaining of sounds (e.g., *ba-ba-ba*), which is characteristic of the babbling period, first appears, and differentially produced sounds take on signal value for the caretaker (Tonkova-Yampol'Skaya, 1973).

Perceptually, the infant shows continued discrimination of speech sounds during this period (Moffett, 1971) and is beginning to localize the source of sounds by turning her head to the source of human voices (Lenneberg, 1967). There is the further development of imitation, characterized by the child's imitation of his own sounds (coordination of hearing and vocalization). This period of self-imitation may be viewed as a preparatory period for imitating unfamiliar sounds produced by others.

**BABBLING**   The babbling period from six to nine months is characterized by the move away from the vocalization of many nonnative speech-sounds to the concentration on a few native-language speech-sounds. In other words, the child is beginning to produce those speech-sounds that are unique to her language community (McNeill, 1970; Wier, 1966). Repetition of syllables, such as *ma-ma-ma,* is now accompanied by distinctive intonational patterns. There is a continuation of predominantly vowellike sounds; however, consonants increase in their frequency of production, with the appearance of the new sounds /g/, /m/, /n/, /l/, and /v/ (Pierce, 1974).

Accompanying the increase in productive abilities, there is marked growth in the young child's perceptual abilities during this period. In addition to the ability to locate sounds, the child demonstrates discrimination between speech and non-speech sounds (Kagan & Lewis, 1965). Speech perception increases rapidly, as is evidenced by the child's ability to discriminate between the presence and absence of consonants and between voiced and voiceless consonants. Further discriminatory ability is demonstrated by the child's recognizing her mother's voice as distinctive from that of a stranger (Tulkin, 1971). Self-monitoring of sound productions begins (Lenneberg et al., 1969), and this may explain why nonnative sounds begin to drop out of the child's vocal repertoire.

**ECHOLALIA**   In contrast to the babbling period, during the period from nine to twelve months the repetition of syllable chains begins to decrease. Additional speech-sounds are acquired, including back vowels (Irwin, 1948) and consonants, such as /h/, /p/, /m/, /j/, and /g/ (Pierce, 1974). The echolalic, or echolike, nature of this period is a result of further coordination of the hearing and vocal schema and of the ability to imitate novel actions and sounds. This imitation covers not only the segmental speech-sounds but also the suprasegmental feature of intonation.

Vocalization takes on new functions, as well as a new form, during this period. It retains the function of pure self-stimulation or sound play and also now accompanies and reinforces the child's actions on objects. In addition, the child's vocalizations take on the practical function of attracting adult attention. Old means, that is, vocalizations, now take on the new ends of serving as communicative vehicles.

## PRELINGUISTIC TO LINGUISTIC SPEECH

During the period from twelve to twenty-four months, speech-sounds, which were previously unattached to meaning, become phonemic with the onset of the first words. In other words, during the prelinguistic period, even though the sounds /p/ and /b/, for example, were used in such repetitive chains as *ba-ba-ba* and *pu-pu-pu*, they did not mark the minimal meaning distinctions characteristic of phonemes. Now, however, /p/ and /b/ are used differently to signal distinctions in meaning (e.g., *pat* versus *bat*). There is, however, some similarity in the form of the speech-sounds produced during the prelinguistic period and those used during this period. For example, the repetitive quality of the babbling period continues as the first words emerge. Reduplicated syllables, such as *da-da* and *ma-ma,* continue to be produced, along with monosyllabic words. The phonological structure of the first words is comprised of either the consonant and vowel (CV) and CVC combinations of most monosyllabic words or the CVCV and CVCVC combinations of disyllabic words. The occurrence of consonants becomes more frequent than that of vowels. Schwartz et al. (1980) describe the reduplication of syllables in children's early words. Reduplication consists of child's productions of adult equivalents (e.g. *bye bye* [dɛdɛ] ), reduplications of adult nonreduplicated syllables (e.g. *water* [wɔwɔ] ) and reduplications of monosyllablic adult equivalents (e.g. *ball* [bʌbə] ) (Schwartz et al., 1980, pp. 75–76). The role of syllabic reduplication may be a transitional one, facilitating the phonological acquisition of multisyllabic words. This hypothesis is shared by Schwartz et al. (1980) and Smith (1973).

One of the interesting aspects of this period of phonological development is the use of advanced forms (the term was coined by Moskowitz, 1970, and described in Ingram, 1976*b* ). Ingram (1976*b*, p. 12) describes the characteristics of these forms:

> These are pronunciations of words that are better or more advanced than their later productions. Moskowitz has noted that Hildegard Leopold pronounced the word *pretty* rather well for several months (e.g., 0:10 [prəti]; 0:11 [prIti]; 1:1 [prIti], [prəti]; 1:4 [pwIti], [pəti], [pyIti]). The next few months it stabilized to [bIdi] and remained so for quite a while.

It appears that at first the advanced forms were imitations of the adult model, but pronunciation eventually gave way to consistent phonological rules or processes, which generally characterizes the youngster's speech.

The perception of speech is less well studied and explicated than is speech production. However, the few studies that are available suggest that between the ages of one and seven the child's perception of adult speech continues to improve (Templin, 1957; Edwards, 1974) and that perception is continually more advanced than production (Smith, 1973; Templin, 1957). This advancement of perception over production is made evident when one repeats back to a child as young as twenty-four months his spontaneous vocalizations and he attempts to disconfirm them, as in the following:

> Child:   "Dat *geen* car."
> Mother:  "It's geen?"
> Child:   "No! It not geen, it *geen!*"

## PHONOLOGICAL DEVELOPMENT OF THE SPEAKING CHILD

Ingram (1976*b* ) describes the phonological development of the period from two to four years on two levels: (1) the phonetic level and (2) the use of phonological processes to simplify speech. By age four, according to Menyuk (1971), the following consonants have been mastered: /b/, /m/, /n/, /f/, /w/, /h/, /p/, /d/, /g/, /k/, /j/, and /l/. Although their mastery is not evidenced in all word positions (i.e., initial, medial, and final), their intelligibility is at a fairly high level. In addition to these individual speech sounds, the following initial consonant clusters are reported by Templin (1957) to be mastered by age four: /sm-/, /sn-/, /sp-/, /st-/, /tw-/, /bk-/, /kw-/, /pl-/, /pr-/, /br-/, /tr-/, /dr-/, /kl-/ and /kr-/.

The misarticulation of words, which is characteristic of the normally dysfluent speech of this age level, is described as being the result of phonological processes used by the child to simplify speech. These phonological processes are neither random nor simply distortions, substitutions, deletions, or additions, as was once thought. Instead, one can argue that these processes represent phonological rules characteristic of particular developmental periods. Ingram (1974, 1976*b* ) provides a rather detailed account of some of these phonological processes; several examples based on his work are as follows (Ingram, 1976*b*, p. 15):

### Syllabic Structure Processes

1. Reduction of consonant clusters. Examples:

$$step \longrightarrow [d\varepsilon p]$$
$$green \longrightarrow [geen]$$

2. Deletion of unstressed syllables. Examples:

$$banana \longrightarrow [n\ae na]$$
$$remember \longrightarrow [member]$$

### Assimilatory Processes

1. Devoicing of final consonants. Examples:

$$bed \longrightarrow [b\varepsilon t]$$
$$big \longrightarrow [bIk]$$

2. Velar assimilation. Examples:

$$duck \longrightarrow [g\textschwa k]$$
$$tongue \longrightarrow [g\textschwa\eng]$$

### Substitution Processes

1. Stopping—fricatives are replaced with a stop consonant. Examples:

$$soup \longrightarrow [dup]$$
$$thank \longrightarrow [tank]$$

2. Vocalization—the replacement of a syllabic consonant with a vowel. Examples:

$$apple \longrightarrow [\ae po]$$
$$flower \longrightarrow [fawo]$$

**PHONETIC MASTERY**   During the years from four to seven, we witness two major phenomena in the child's speech. First, there is a decrease in the phonological processes used to simplify speech (Ingram, 1976b). Second, the mastery of speech-sounds is completed. In addition to the vowels, which, in general, have been mastered by age four, and the consonants already acquired as described above, the following consonants are added to the child's phonetic inventory: /t/, /v/, /s/, /z/, /ʃ/, /ʒ/, /tʃ/, /r/, /dz/, /θ/, and /ð/ (Menyuk, 1971). Finally, the mastery of approximately fifty clusters by age seven fills out the phonetic inventory of the English language.

**PHONOLOGICAL MASTERY** Although traditionally it was thought that the development of phonology is generally completed by approximately seven years of age, investigations by Ingram (1976b), Atkinson-King (1973), and Schane (1973), among others, have demonstrated that phonological development continues well into the teens. For example, further development of the suprasegmentals, such as stress, pitch, and intonational patterns, occurs. This can be seen as the child begins to use contrastive stress as a feature for differentiating compound nouns such as *greenhouse* and *blackboard* from noun phrases such as *green house* and *black board* (Ingram, 1976; Atkinson-King, 1973). Similarly, the ability to think about one's phonological knowledge aids the child in learning to spell complex words. It is one thing to pronounce words in natural ongoing speech and quite another to apply this tacit knowledge of speech to the abstract and analytic process of spelling. This ability, while beginning before the age of twelve, continues well beyond it (Ingram, 1976b).

## CONCLUDING REMARKS

The preceding discussion has centered on providing an overview of the development of phonology. However, there is much that is still unknown about phonological development, such as the course of development of the suprasegmental features and perceptual development during the preschool years. Our knowledge of the sequence of development of the speech-sounds is rather complete, but this is just a small aspect of the process of phonological development.

The following inquiries are designed to further explore the phonological development of children. Each inquiry focuses on a different aspect of phonological development.

## INQUIRY 5.1

The form and function of the child's prelinguistic vocalizations are quite different from those of the period of linguistic development. Prelinguistic vocalizations have not yet acquired meaning, and therefore their function may not yet be that of communication.

**OBJECTIVES**   The objectives of this inquiry are to:

1. Analyze the form of the vocalizations produced by a prelinguistic child.
2. Analyze the function of the vocalizations produced by a prelinguistic child.

**PROCEDURES**   Select an infant younger than one year old who has not begun to say her first words (this may be ascertained by talking with the infant's parent or caretaker). Observe the infant in several familiar, informal contexts (e.g., bath-time, while diaper is being changed, playing on floor at home). For some of these observations, the infant should be interacting with a familiar adult. For at least one observation, the infant should be interacting with objects. You should function as an observer rather than a participant. Tape-record all vocalizations and note the context in which they occurred and their apparent functions. Continue observing and tape-recording until you have collected approximately fifty vocalizations.

**REPORT**   Include the following in your report:

1. The age of the child.
2. A transcript of the tape, including the context in which vocalizations occurred and the apparent functions of these vocalizations.

In addition, address yourself to the following questions:

1. What was the form of the vocalizations (e.g., vowel sounds, cries, gurgles)?
2. What were the apparent functions of these vocalizations (e.g., cries signaled discomfort, coos when satisfied, vowel sounds accompanying play with objects)?
3. How, if at all, did the context affect the quantity, form, and function of these vocalizations?

**EVALUATION**   Did this inquiry develop the specified objectives? If so, how? If not, why? How could the effectiveness of this inquiry be increased?

---

## INQUIRY 5.2

Most researchers studying the development of phonology agree that perception precedes the production of speech-sounds. Adults who informally interact with young children act as though the advancement of perception over production was the case.

**OBJECTIVES**   The objectives of this inquiry are to:

1. Analyze the relationship between the young child's dysfluent productions and his perception of speech-sounds.
2. Speculate on why the discrepancy between perception and production exists.

**PROCEDURES**   Interact with a young child between the ages of two and three and a half years. As you interact, you will probably note some words that are "misarticulated" in comparison with the adult forms. When this occurs, repeat back to the child his pronunciation of the word, using the word in its intended context as follows:

Child:   "I wan some doup." (meaning *soup*).
Adult:   "You want some doup?"

Observe the child's responses to your repetitions of his pronunciations. Continue this procedure until you have had the chance to repeat several of the child's mispronounced words. Tape-record the entire interaction.

**REPORT**   Include the following in your report:

1. The age of the child with whom you interacted.
2. A description of the context in which the interaction took place.
3. An exact as possible transcript of the tape-recorded interaction.

In addition, address yourself to the following questions:

1. How did the child react to your repetitions of his mispronunciations? Describe.
2. What clues does this provide concerning the relationship between speech perception and production?

**EVALUATION**   Did this inquiry develop the specified objectives? If so, how? If not, why? How could the effectiveness of this inquiry be increased?

_____   **INQUIRY 5.3**   _____

One of the major phonological processes used by the young child to simplify speech affects the structure of syllables. This process of syllabic simplification is responsible for the childlike character of young children's speech. In describing some of the phonological processes used by young children, Ingram (1976*b*, p. 15) identifies the following syllabic processes:

1. Deletion of final consonant. Examples:

$$out \longrightarrow [æw]$$
$$bike \longrightarrow [bay]$$

2. Reduction of consonant clusters. Examples:

$$floor \longrightarrow [f\eth r]$$
$$step \longrightarrow [dep]$$

3. Deletion of unstressed syllables. Examples:

$$banana \longrightarrow [n\ae na]$$
$$remember \longrightarrow [member]$$

4. Reduplication. Examples:

$$rabbit \longrightarrow [w\ae \ w\ae]$$

**OBJECTIVES**   The objectives of this inquiry are to:

1. Analyze the phonological processes affecting the syllabic structures of words.
2. Speculate about why these processes occur with young children.

**PROCEDURES**   Select a child between the ages of two and a half and three and a half years. Observe the child in a familiar, informal context as she is interacting with a familiar person (e.g., parent, caretaker, sibling). You should function as an observer rather than a participant. Tape-record and observe the interaction until you have collected approximately fifty sentences from the child.

**REPORT**   Include the following in your report:

1. Brief descriptions of the child, the person with whom she is interacting, and the context in which the interaction took place.
2. A transcript of the taped observation.

In addition, address yourself to the following questions:

1. Describe how particular phonological processes affected the syllabic structure of the words used by the child. Include examples of such words and describe the specific processes resulting in structural change.
2. What functions do these phonological processes serve in the young child's acquisition of the speech-sounds of her language?

**EVALUATION**   Did this inquiry develop the specified objectives? If so, how? If not, why? How could the effectiveness of this inquiry be increased?

————————                    **INQUIRY 5.4**                    ————————

Not until he reaches the age of seven or eight does the child complete developing the phonetic repertoire of his native language. This includes the mastery of the

speech-sounds (i.e., vowels, semivowels, consonants, and c▯
positions of a word (i.e., initial, medial, and final).

**OBJECTIVES**   The objectives of this inquiry are to:

1. Analyze the child's discrimination and articulation of
   minimal word-pair paradigm.
2. Study the effects of age on the child's ability to discrii▯ ▯▯▯▯ and articulate word-pairs that differ in one phoneme.

**PROCEDURES**   Select two children, one younger (from four to six years old)
and one older (from seven to nine years old). Following the procedures described
in Inquiry 2.12, administer the tasks to each child independently.

**REPORT**   Include the following in your report:

1. The ages of the children who participated in the tasks.
2. The word-pair lists you developed, with the phonological feature that
   each word-pair measures.
3. An exact transcript of the articulation task and the same/different judgments of the discrimination task.

In addition, address yourself to the following questions:

1. What were the types of errors, if any, that the child made on the discrimination task? For example, were they errors involved in voicing (e.g.,
   *tuck/tug*)? Errors discriminating sounds in the final, medial, or initial position of words? Errors involving place of articulation (e.g. *meat/neat*)?
   Describe.
2. What were the types of errors, if any, that the child made on the articulation task? Use the same criteria as for the discrimination task to analyze
   the errors.
3. Describe the relationship between the child's performances on the discrimination task and the articulation task. Were the errors similar in both
   the receptive and productive tasks?
4. What age-related differences did you note on both the discrimination and
   the articulation tasks?

**EVALUATION**   Did this inquiry develop the specified objectives? If so, how? If
not, why? How could the effectiveness of this inquiry be increased?

# 6

# Perspectives on
# the Acquisition
# of Language

Although how the young child acquires language continues to be a controversial issue among psychologists, linguists, anthropologists, and, more recently, psycholinguists, it is quite astounding how uniform are our intuitions concerning how language is acquired. For example, when graduate students were asked "How did you learn language?" one key factor that was consistently cited was imitation. Less constant in their appearance, yet rather frequent, were the following explanations: listening and interacting with others, innate capacity to learn language, and associating sounds with objects.

Similarly, in response to "What was the role of your parent(s) or caretaker in your language learning?" the functions of reinforcer, corrector, model, teacher, and prompter were consistently attributed to the parent. Listener and stimulator were also viewed as important parental roles, although clearly subordinate to the first set of functions.

If these responses of graduate students were, in fact, correct, there would be little need for a chapter such as this. However, the acquisition of language represents a complex set of interrelated factors, with those factors cited above constituting a rather incomplete, or perhaps even a self-contradictory, model. The purpose of this chaper, then, is to explore the two basic questions just raised: (1) How is language acquired? and (2) What are the various roles played by the caretaker and the child in the acquisition process?

## THREE MAJOR PERSPECTIVES

Each of the three major perspectives on the acquisition of language represents some very basic assumptions concerning the nature of language. Most notable among the theories of language development are those espoused by behaviorists, nativists, and, more recently, cognitive psycholinguists. The focus of this section is on these three perspectives, exploring the assumptions of these models concerning the nature of language and the nature of the human organism.

**BEHAVIORISTIC PERSPECTIVE**　Although the behavioristic perspective has been modified during the years since B. F. Skinner's publication in 1957 of the landmark *Verbal Behavior,* its basic premises and assumptions remain intact. For the behaviorist, the human organism is psychologically empty and is a rather passive, inactive transducer of information. It is important to qualify the terms passive and inactive in this context, for passivity and inactivity do not presume total lack of action on the part of the organism. To the contrary, the response of the organism to external stimuli is of prime importance to the behavioral perspective. Inactivity (although *reactivity* may be a more accurate term) connotes the lack of purposeful self-initiation on the part of the individual rather than the absence of activity. However, all behavior, hence all activity, is seen as a direct result of a stimulus.

Assumptions about the a priori psychological structures of the human organism are deemed unwarranted because all organisms, while varying in their physiological make-up, start out psychologically the same. Differences in behavior are accounted for by differences in experiences, thus elevating the role of the environment to paramount importance. Control by the environment is critical in the shaping of behavior, whereby **differential reinforcement** for successive approximations of a desired behavior is used until that behavior is achieved. The emphasis is on the active role of external forces, relegating the child to the role of reactor.

According to Skinner (1957), language is but a verbal behavior and as such is dependent on reinforcement and subject to extinction, maintenance, discrimination, and generalization. One can predict the occurrence of verbal behavior in the same way one can predict and control other less complex behaviors. It is important to keep in mind that Skinner states that all behavior is operant in nature and that one can tamper with the probability of the occurrence of a specific behavior by systematically manipulating reinforcers. In his view, a linguistic utterance is an operant response, as is flexing a muscle.

How, then, according to Skinner, does the learning of language occur? When the baby utters her first familiar sounds, these utterances are reinforced by the excited caretaker. This reinforcement can take the form of attending to the baby, soothing the baby, or providing the baby with a bottle. These are all examples of outside reinforcement. Later, the baby begins to self-reinforce when she hears what she says and recognizes its familiarity—an example of inner reinforcement (Skinner, 1957). When superficially observing a one-year-old child, we allow that Skinner's theory has a certain degree of surface validity. Such a child no longer produces speech-sounds that are not present in the child's speech community (extinction of nonreinforced behaviors) and does produce sounds like the syllables of her native language (reinforcement of successive approximations).

Somewhere between the ages of ten and twelve months, the child will probably say something that sounds like *dada* while in the presence of her father. When approximating the word *daddy,* the child is rewarded by social attention, being held, or simply the presence of the person. Skinner calls this kind of verbal response a **tact,** which generally has the function of naming or labeling objects or people that are in close proximity to the child. Later, however, the child may say *dada* when the father is not present and consequently will receive no reinforcement. Thus, the father becomes the discriminating stimulus for the word *dada.* As the child begins to develop a larger vocabulary, she learns tacts through verbal interactions, such as the following:

Child:   "What's that?"
Parent:   "It's a car."
Child (pointing to a wagon): "Is this a car?"
Parent: "No, that's a wagon."

According to Skinner, adjectives, such as colors, are similarly learned. The tact *red* is controlled by the color of red apples, red cars, and red dresses. Therefore, the utterance *red* is controlled by a "complex of stimuli including our memory of the object and a request to name its color (rather than its shape or size)" (Hilgard & Bower, 1975, pp. 233–34).

Another verbal function is operative when a child makes an utterance, such as *cookie,* in the absence of the object (or person), and the caretaker complies with the perceived request by producing the object. The reinforcement in this context is the actual object. Skinner has assigned the term **mand** to this verbal function. A third function is **echoic responses,** which are utterances that are strictly imitative. After the appearance of this function, the occurrence of mands and tacts can be facilitated, since the parent or caretaker no longer has to wait around for them to occur spontaneously.

The final verbal function that Skinner defines is the **autoclitic,** whereby each word acts as a stimulus for the next. This is apparent in such phrases as *bread and . . . , I was about to say . . . ,* and *I don't believe that . . . ,* (Skinner, 1957, p. 315). The ordering of words is another aspect of the autoclitic phenomenon—a phenomenon traditionally described by linguists as the learning of grammatical rules. Through conditioning, the child learns, for example, that a phrase such as *the lady's dog* indicates possession and that objects follow verbs or nouns syntactically. Skinner stresses the fact that the information about syntactic structures concerns the grammatical properties of words located within sentence frames. In the specific case of *the lady's dog,* the child can tact, or name, the objects and their relationship after learning the generalization of the possessive frame. Similar frames have to be learned for the positions of nouns, verbs, and adjectives (Hilgard & Bower, 1975); all of this is initially learned through the caretaker's reinforcement of the child's closer approximations to the desired grammatical usage.

Several other aspects of the behavioral interpretation of the language learning process are worth mentioning. Regarding the learning of the meaning of words, the process is seen as one of abstraction and association. A concept is first learned by abstracting common elements among referents, although it is not made clear just what principle is used to determine what elements or attributes should be attended to and abstracted (i.e., what are the commonalities). In learning the word *dog,* the child hears the word *dog* uttered in association with the referent "dog." Therefore, the child associates *dog* with the object "dog." She will hear the word *dog* in the presence of other instances of "dog" and will somehow abstract the similar attributes in each instance and associate these common attributes of "dog" with the word *dog.*

Clearly, if we accept this explanation, the learning of the meanings of words that stand for objects should be a long, tedious, and chancy proposition; this is not reflected in the data concerning vocabulary development and concept learning. This perspective on the learning of meaning is, nonetheless, extended by behaviorists to the learning of the meanings of internal states. Skinner believes that children learn about internal states when the community assigns a verbal label to a state at the time that critical stimuli are impinging on the child. For example, when a child is crying and holding her head, the adult might say *That's painful!* (Skinner, 1957, p. 157). Thus, the child learns the meaning of *painful* after some number of associations of the word with the hurting state and subsequently discriminates it from all other feeling words.

The comprehension of language is explained by Skinner (1957, p. 139) quite simply as understanding what someone is saying when we ourselves say it for the same reasons. Given this perspective, there is no real distinction between the comprehension and production of language. Skinner goes on to suggest that there is **contextual generalization** of the functions of the words filling slots in the grammatical frames that control the right interpretation of a sentence. This generalizing process purportedly enables the child to understand novel combinations and orderings of words.

To summarize thus far, the behavioristic perspective asserts the following concerning the nature of humans and language and the processes involved in language learning:

1. The organism is psychologically empty, and the environment is all important.
2. Language is merely another learned, observable behavior.
3. No distinction exists between speech and language.
4. No real distinction exists between the comprehension and production of language.
5. Meaning is the association of the word with its referent.
6. No distinction exists between thought and language. To know is largely to be able to talk (Skinner, 1957).
7. Learning language is largely contingent upon the processes of imitation, reinforcement, stimulus discrimination and generalization, and shaping.

8. Mastery of one's language is demonstrated through observable responses (i.e., speech production).

Before leaving the behavioristic perspective, we must briefly evaluate the adequacy of this model. First, and perhaps foremost, Skinner assumes that operant conditioning processes such as reinforcement are systematic and lawful. This is not so. Reinforcement is only systematically controlled under laboratory conditions; this can be readily verified by simply observing parent/child interactions. Furthermore, it is highly unlikely that children learn language only through meticulous care on the part of the adults who shape their verbal repertoires through systematic use of differential reinforcement (Chomsky, 1959). This argument against differential reinforcement will be further developed in the section of this chapter entitled "Interaction of the Child with the Environment."

Attempts to explain grammar and syntax by using the concept of the autoclitic function, an intraverbal operant, appear quite insufficient (Osgood, 1963). First, in our limited lifetime we can learn only a finite number of new associations or conditioned responses, even allowing for the effects of stimulus generalization (Deese, 1970). Second, the behavioral perspective fails to adequately explain the creative use of language and the generation and comprehension of novel utterances.

The behaviorists' heavy reliance on imitation as a language-learning requisite and process has been widely challenged. For example, Ramer (1976) argues that imitation cannot be considered a requisite for language acquisition since there is an observed wide range in children's use of imitation as a language-learning strategy. In fact, some (e.g., Menyuk, 1964) argue that children can only imitate those linguistic structures which they have already spontaneously produced.

Another criticism of the behavioristic perspective decries its lack of any real distinction between the comprehension and production of language. If comprehension does, in fact, precede production, "this makes Skinner's exclusive emphasis on speech production inadequate" (Bartel, 1967). Similarly, the lack of separation of language and thought has been almost universally refuted (see Sinclair, 1970; Nelson, 1974; Macnamara, 1972). Finally, the behaviorist perspective simply does not adequately account for the following empirically verified phenomena:

1. The uniformity of language acquisition throughout the human species.
2. The relative absence of reinforcement, positive or negative, of the linguistic form (speech or syntax) used by the child during early language acquisition.
3. The dropping of early correct forms in favor of incorrect, overregularized forms, such as *comed, goed,* and *foots.*
4. The child is exposed to a corpus of particular sentences, yet what she learns is not these particular sentences but the organizing principles or rules underlying them.
5. The short time in which the learning of language takes place.

**NATIVISTIC PERSPECTIVE** In direct contrast to the work of Skinner and the behaviorists is the work of such nativistic theorists as Noam Chomsky (1957, 1959, 1965), Eric Lenneberg (1967), and David McNeill (1966). Each of these theorists challenged the very basic assumptions espoused by the behavioristic model concerning the nature of the organism and the nature of language. For example, following Chomsky's (1965) lead, Lenneberg (1967) and McNeill (1970) proposed that, instead of the organism being psychologically empty, the human species is endowed with a species-specific, biological foundation of language. This biological foundation includes prior linguistic knowledge of "basic grammatical categories and relationships and the fact that sentences are represented on two levels—deep and surface structure" (Edmonds, 1976, p. 180).

Although the notion of a biological basis for language learning among humans appears to be a rather bold and extreme assumption, there exist several bases for this formulation. First, in the acquisition of language, there appears to be a built-in biological schedule of development. The onset of speech and language is regular, and the order of the developmental milestones is quite invariant. Regardless of whether the child is advanced or retarded, the developmental sequence is quite predictable. Furthermore, cross-cultural research on language development supports the uniformity of linguistic development. Some have argued that this regularity is intimately linked with central nervous system maturation and the establishment of hemispheric laterality.

The second source of support for the nativistic position is evidenced by the relative difficulty of suppressing the acquisition of language. Even in the face of rather dramatic handicaps (e.g., congenital blindness or deafness, parental neglect), if the child has some access to language, it is subsequently acquired.

A third source of support for this perspective can be derived from the linguistic analyses done of many different languages. It has been discovered that rather than there being fundamental differences among diverse languages, as one would expect from merely studying their surface structures, there are instead dramatic commonalities among languages. For example, all languages are rule-governed, with organizing principles of semantics, syntax, and phonology. Furthermore, all languages make a distinction between the subject and predicate of a sentence, permit the embedding of one proposition within another, express tense, and utilize various linguistic transformations. This notion of linguistic universals is seen as another support for a biological basis for language in humans.

The position that language is relatively independent of intelligence constituted an additional argument for a biological foundation. Lenneberg (1964) studied the intellectual and language development of eighty-four retarded people. He found that although their IQs deteriorated with increasing age, these people were in complete possession of basic language. While there were many cases of poor articulation and grammatical errors, basic language structures were intact.

The assumption of a species-specific basis for language is further reinforced by the fact that humans, and only humans, naturally acquire language. It must be noted, however, that the major formulations of the nativists predated the revolutionary work of the Gardners (1969, 1971, 1975), Premack (1970, 1971, 1972) and Fouts (1973, 1976) in teaching language to chimpanzees. Nevertheless, notwithstanding the debate on the capacity of chimpanzees to be taught language, there is little question that only humans *naturally acquire* language (a distinction is being made here concerning one's ability to acquire language rather than being taught a language).

Finally, indirect support for a biological basis for language comes from systematic analyses of the corpora of adult language. It was argued that if, in fact, adults do teach language to children, then the adult model must be an adequate one, that is, syntactically and semantically simple and well-formed. Instead, the opposite was found to be true. The typical adult model is complex and frequently occasioned with poorly constructed sentences, false starts, and ambiguous linguistic propositions. On the basis of these findings, it is argued that something other than the apparently complex, flawed adult model of language must be responsible for the child's ability to induce the regularity of linguistic structures. This ability is due to the language acquisition device, or LAD, which Chomsky, and later McNeill, described as an innate mechanism enabling humans to extract or induce the regularity from a corpus of language, therefore making them potentially meaningful users of language.

Just as the nativists' view of the human species is in direct opposition to that of the behaviorists, so is their view of the nature of language. Chomsky (1957, 1959) opposed the behavioristic model of language and language development represented primarily by Skinner. He asserted that language is not developed through stimulus-response, or S-R, associations as described by Skinner or the mediational S-R theories, such as that of Osgood (1963). He argued that a probabilistic Markovian model, whereby there are habitually established left-to-right relationships with the subsequent word determined by the immediately preceding one, was simply inadequate. His explanation was that a probabilistic model explains only surface associations and not the underlying rule system. Reinforcement does not occur for general grammatical rules, only for particular, individual utterances. Chomsky's second criticism of the behavioristic model was that the mere stringing together of words in an associative manner does not ensure that the string will, in fact, be a grammatical sentence. Chomsky also argued that the probabilistic model did not explain or account for the embedding of one sentence within another. In addition, Chomsky criticized Skinner's reinforcement theory by pointing out that negative reinforcement for an incorrect utterance does not necessarily reveal what is correct. Furthermore, language "errors" drawing negative reinforcement are not usually extinguished.

In refuting the behaviorists' model of language and language development, Chomsky posits a **transformational grammar** model of language with two levels—a surface and a deep structure. This two-level model was proposed to overcome some of the difficulties associated with a Markovian model and the phrase structure grammar, which only analyzed the actual utterance or surface structure of a sentence. In Chomsky's model, "sentences are represented at two levels—a deep structure which contains the semantic meaning and a surface structure which represents this meaning in sound patterns" (Edmonds, 1976, p. 170). The syntactic component ". . . must specify, for each sentence, a *deep structure* that determines its semantic interpretation and a *surface structure* that determines its phonetic interpretation" (Chomsky, 1965). The syntactic component, then, allows the correct pairing of meaning and sound and enables similar surface structures to have different meanings and vice versa. The conversion of a deep structure into a surface structure is accomplished through the use of a third component of Chomsky's model, transformational rules. Graphically, Chomsky's model of language can be represented by the following:

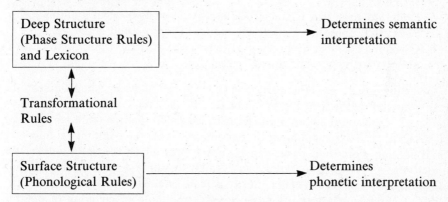

The transformational rules are more extensive than the phrase structure rules in that the former provide for embedded sentences, the meaningful similarity of the passive and active voice, and so on. Transformational rules convert one phrase structure into another by moving elements around, by adding, substituting, or deleting elements. As a result, an ambiguous sentence such as *I like her cooking* can be related to the underlying phrase structures of *I like what she cooks, I like the way she cooks,* and *I like the fact that she cooks.* Similarly, two different surface structures, such as *The boy hit the girl* and *The girl was hit by the boy,* can be shown to be derived from the same phrase structure. This transformational model of grammar attempts to account for all possible utterances of a language and to do so while reducing the number of rules necessary to write a complete grammar. The learning of this finite set of rules permits one to generate and comprehend a potentially infinite number of sentences never uttered or heard before. This results in language being depicted as a highly generative and creative process.

Chomsky's conceptualization of the nature of language stimulated renewed interest in the study of child language and language acquisition. This was so despite the fact that Chomsky's model is one of **competence**—adult competence—rather than of **performance**. In this competence model, the focus is the person's tacit knowledge of language. This is in contrast to a performance model, which focuses on how a person actually uses language.

From studies of children in various language communities, many of Chomsky's theoretical formulations received considerable support. Edmonds (1976, p. 179) summarizes this confirmation as follows:

1. Similar rules and developmental sequences were found in children from a variety of language communities.
2. Early language development was characterized as learning the rules of deep structure (e.g., noun, verb).
3. Children, in learning language, seem to be inducing the underlying latent structures of a language, not learning a collection of sentences.
4. Only developmentally later did transformational rules and more complex sentences appear.
5. Child language was characterized as having its own set of grammatical rules rather than being a linearly reduced form of adult language.
6. Given the existence of this child grammar, the generative and creative aspects of language were already present.

Given these findings, a theory of language acquisition was posited whereby the LAD was the mechanism for the induction of the latent structures underlying language. Exposure to an adult model is necessary so that the child has the data on which to test out his grammatical hypotheses. Thus, the adult model offers the child nothing more than particular examples from which the child induces the underlying rules. While imitation can account for some aspects of language acquisition, as a complete explanation it is seen as clearly inadequate (McNeill, 1966). A child simply does not produce exact imitations of the adult model, but rather selectively produces imitations that reflect the child's current grammatical system.

In summarizing Chomsky's transformational generative model of language, the following can be said:

1. The organism is psychologically active and creative.
2. The organism is biologically endowed with a language acquisition device (LAD), which provides the individual with generalized knowledge about language.
3. Language is a generative system characterized by two levels—a deep structure and a surface structure—with a transformation component relating the two levels.
4. A distinction is made between language (deep structure and transformational rules) and speech (phonological component).
5. A distinction is made between one's knowledge of language (competence) and one's use of language (performance).
6. A distinction is made between the comprehension and production of language.
7. Syntax is considered to be the basic component of language through which meaning and sound are paired.
8. Language is largely independent of thought.

9. The role of imitation and practice in the learning of language is quite minimal.
10. Although the child is exposed to particular sentences, what he learns is the grammatical rules underlying these sentences.
11. Child language is not simply a linearly reduced form of adult language but is characterized by a generative set of grammatical rules that are qualitatively different from those of adults.
12. Mastery of one's language is demonstrated both by one's use of language (performance) and by one's tacit knowledge of the grammaticality of language (competence).

There is little doubt that Chomsky revolutionized the field of language study, providing a rich paradigm from which to investigate child language. However, subsequent research and analysis have brought into question many of the basic formulations from which Chomsky's model is derived. To begin with, the primacy of syntax in Chomsky's theory of language has been challenged (e.g., Bloom, 1970, 1973; Brown, 1970, 1973*a*, 1973*b*). Rather than being interpretive as Chomsky suggested, it has been argued that semantics is, in fact, generative, as is shown graphically by the following (see Chafe, 1970, p. 19):

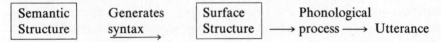

| Semantic | Generates | Surface | Phonological |
| Structure | syntax | Structure | ⟶ process ⟶ Utterance |

Therefore, semantics began to be viewed as having equal or primary importance (Lakoff, 1971; Chafe, 1970; Fillmore, 1968).

Second, the independence of language and thought was also questioned. Viewing language as a symbol system, several theorists saw a relationship between the emergence of certain semantic concepts in child language and particular cognitive attainments. The completion of the sensorimotor period (Piaget, 1952) can be closely related to the emergence of expressive language.

The nativistic perspective has also been challenged on the grounds that the adult role assigned by it is a rather benign and passive one in the acquisition of language. Research investigating mother-child interactions has revealed that the adult model is, in fact, a well-formed, syntactically and semantically simplified register of language. As a model for language learning, it is ideal in that it is rarely dysfluent, is slow in rate, and is attuned to informal teaching of a conversational style. Therefore, while the child continues to be an active participant in the learning of language, the adult is elevated in this opposing view from a passive role, as proposed by Chomsky, to being an equally active participant in the child's learning of language.

Further doubt has been cast on the nativists' declarations that language is a phenomenon that is uniquely human. As was mentioned previously, research conducted by the Gardners (1969, 1971, 1975), Premack (1970, 1971, 1972), and

Fouts (1973, 1976) on teaching language to chimpanzees revealed that chimps are apparently capable of some degree of linguistic functioning.

Chomsky's exclusive focus on competence to the exclusion of performance has been questioned. For example, Bloom (1970), in recording both the language used and the context in which it was used by three young children, revealed that the same utterance can have decidedly different meanings. *Mommy sock* in one context might mean "Mommy is putting on the sock" (agent + object); in another context it might mean "it is Mommy's sock" (possessor + possessed). Therefore, without studying language in actual use (performance), one could possibly develop an underestimated, and even distorted, view of children's language.

Finally, the construct of the LAD has been criticized. While there is little doubt that humans have a unique propensity for and ability to acquire language, it is less clear that this uniqueness lies solely in the particulars of linguistic knowledge specified by the LAD. Rather, human uniqueness may cover more qualities, extending to more general abilities to symbolize and to deal with complex concepts (a cognitive hypothesis). As Edmonds (1976, pp. 180–81) questions, "If all that is necessary for LAD to operate is exposure to language, why then doesn't language make an appearance earlier in the child's life . . . and how do we account for LAD's origins?"

The questions raised concerning the primacy of syntax in language and the assumptions on the acquisition of language resulted in a shift in theoretical focus. This paradigmatic shift resulted in theorists' beginning to reconceptualize the relation between language and cognition and to focus primarily on the semantic and pragmatic aspects of language. We now turn to this new perspective.

**SEMANTIC AND COGNITIVE PERSPECTIVE**    In reaction to what many theorists believed to be a "semantically empty" theory of language as proposed by Chomsky, the most recent theoretical perspective holds that semantics is the crucial component of language (Chafe, 1970; Bloom, 1970; Fillmore, 1968). According to most semantically oriented theorists, semantics is the representation of basic concepts about events and relationships in the world. These concepts, Chafe (1970, p. 74, parentheses added) has argued, are "real entities in people's minds and it is through language that they are symbolized by sounds (or manual signs or graphemes) so that they can be transmitted from the mind of one individual to that of another." Therefore, semantics is now seen as the generative component of language, rather than as an interpretive component as Chomsky asserted. While borrowing from Chomsky the concept of a two-level language system, theorists have reconceptualized the essence of the deep structure as being made up of semantic concepts that generate the surface structure through a process of symbolization and linearization (Chafe, 1970) or through transformational rules (Fillmore, 1968; Greenfield, Smith, & Laufer, 1972).

Semantic units such as agent, action, state, and experiencer are viewed as being conceptually more fundamental than syntactic units such as nouns and verbs, because the former are aspects of the environment apparently common to all humans. It is only through an abstraction process that one learns that either agent or experiencer can constitute the subjective noun phrase and that both action and state are represented by the syntactic unit verb.

To explicate observed linguistic uniformity across cultures, the nativists' position is that linguistic universals existing within LAD provide the only reasonable explanation for this phenomenon. Semantic theorists could not wholly accept this position. They recognized that common events and relationships exist in the environments of humans and consequently suggested that it is something in the environment common to all mankind or in the human genetic endowment, or both, that produces cross-cultural linguistic agreements (Chafe, 1970). Although they acknowledge the uniqueness of the human organism, they are neither willing to ascribe to humans a particular genetic language component, nor are they ready to accept a wholly nativistic view of language.

If one subscribes to the primacy of semantics in a theory of language, one is then confronted with the question of the origins of meaning. Neither the nativistic view, nor the behaviorally-oriented abstraction theory (see pp. 150–51) adequately account for the development of concepts and their subsequent mapping into semantic structures. The semantic features theory (Clark, 1973) provides another explanation. According to this theory, as we have already seen in Chapter 2, all referents can be defined by a set of universal semantic features, such as [± animate] or [± human]. The child learns the meaning of words by combining already established features. These features can be relational (e.g., location), functional (e.g., edibility), or perceptual (e.g., shape, color). However like the abstraction theory, the semantic features theory fails to identify the psychological principles determining what features are attended to and combined by the child.

Nelson (1973) criticized both the abstraction and semantic features theories on the basis of their exclusive reliance on analysis. She argued that identifying and abstracting common attributes or features of a given object or event require a highly analytic process, for which the young language-learning child may not be equipped.

In further attempts to explain the origins of meaning, many psycholinguists turned to Piaget's theory of cognitive development. The assumption here was that young children do not learn language and then apply it to situations, but rather first learn about situations and then apply that knowledge to language (Smith, 1977). In other words, in learning language, young children map concepts already developed nonlinguistically into language (Dale, 1976). Therefore, the development of basic cognitive structures precedes the development of corresponding linguistic structures, implying that thought is at least initially independent of language. These conclusions are clearly compatible with Piaget's early formulations concerning the relationship between language and cognition. He states that language does not cause cognitive development, rather language and cognition are processes maturing simultaneously in the young child. Thus, more complex use of language is but one aspect of the growing symbolic function (Piaget, 1974).

In Piaget's theory of the origins of intelligence, action is seen as the source of thought and meaning. During the sensorimotor period (birth to eighteen months), the infant actively learns to distinguish among various features in the environment. Objects that are similar come to be acted on in similar ways, and this activity on objects forms the concepts (or preconcepts) that are later mapped into language. In order to trace the origins of meaning, it is helpful to have some familiarity with the six stages of the sensorimotor period. The following sections summarize these stages. It should be noted that the six stages are invariantly ordered such that "each new stage in development incorporates previous stages" (Beard, 1969).

STAGE I. Throughout most of Stage I (birth to one month), the behavior of the infant is reflexive. At this point one sees such reflexes as sucking, grasping, crying, and movements of the arms, trunk, and head. The infant appears to make no distinction among objects, as it is observed that she sucks on all objects with which she has contact. Even at this stage the infant can be viewed as an active learner. We find that the infant actively searches for the mother's nipple, which is viewed as the first sign of the infant **accommodating** to the environment.

Important to Piaget's theory, and already manifested by Stage I behaviors, is the idea of **functional assimilation.** This is the tendency of the individual to exercise present schema, that is, the infant actively practices the schema she is learning. In Stage I, the infant practices the sucking reflex to make it function. Later, in the preoperational period (two to six years) the child is observed to exercise rather different schema. For instance, when the child practices newly acquired linguistic structures when alone, the process of functional assimilation is once again being evidenced.

During Stage I, the infant begins to learn a very primitive form of recognition called **recognitory assimilation.** Piaget (1967) cites an example of an infant sucking all objects until he is hungry. At that point the infant begins to perceive the differences between his mother's nipple and other objects. This experiential factor (i.e., any of a variety of visual, tactile, kinesthetic, and auditory experiences) is critical, for it helps the infant in developing discriminations, even the crudest. Piaget does not assume that the young infant has the innate ability to view self as separate from the environment; therefore, it is only through the active exploration of his world that the infant gradually achieves this differentiation.

STAGE II. During Stage II (one to four months), reflexive behaviors of Stage I are modified, and new behaviors begin to appear. **Primary circular reactions** are developed by which the infant tries to rediscover a behavior first performed by chance. "During this stage coordinations (of various schemas begin to) develop in the use of eyes. Also, coordination between hearing and vision is developed. The infant is observed moving his head toward the direction a sound is coming from" (Wadsworth, 1969, p. 32, parentheses added). The object concept is still quite underdeveloped; however, the beginnings of its development are indicated by the infant's attempts to visually follow the path of an object as it disappears from sight. As yet, objects have no reality of their own for the infant; they do not exist beyond the infant's perceptions. This is why the infant ceases to actively search for the object once it has left his view.

Primitive forms of imitation first appear during this stage in the form of vocal contagion and mutual imitation. In both of these activities, the infant appears to be practicing (functional assimilation) vocalizations, and this practice is aided by the caretaker, who stimulates the already existing schema.

STAGE III. Characteristic of Stage III (four to eight months) is the young infant's becoming more oriented to objects in the environment. She engages in a great deal of manipulation, coordinating visual and tactile schemes (Wadsworth, 1969). The infant has progressed to a level where actions are beginning to become intentional. This is seen when she tries to repeat an interesting event that was accidentally discovered.

Piaget describes abbreviated movements that show a fundamental precursor to **classification,** or meaning, which is interpreted to be the first approximation of thought. This is seen in Lucienne's first attempts to selectively act upon objects (Piaget, 1952, p. 186):

> At 0;6(12) Lucienne perceives from a distance two celluloid parrots attached to a chandelier and which she had sometimes had in her bassinet. As soon as she sees them, she definitely but briefly shakes her legs without trying to act upon them from a distance. . . .

Piaget interprets Lucienne's kicking when she perceives the parrots as being the first step toward "thinking the thought, 'That's the parrot, that's something to be swung.' " (Ginsburg & Opper, 1969, p. 47). Here one sees the beginning of the eventual mental representation of objects—a process critical to the emergence of language.

STAGE IV. At Stage IV (eight to twelve months), means and ends are still separate. For example, when a desired object (end) is out of the reach of the child, the presence of another object (means) is ignored while futile attempts to obtain the first object persist. The object concept has developed to the level where there is little subjectivity left. When an object vanishes from view, the infant will actively search for it. However, it should be noted that the object is still somewhat fused with the physical context, for active searching ceases if the object is not found where it was last seen. Imitation has progressed to the point where the child imitates new actions initiated by the model. However, imitation is only successful when the modeled action is similar to those actions already in the child's repertoire.

STAGE V. Several achievements occur during Stage V (twelve to eighteen months). First, the child begins to discover new means for obtaining desired ends.

Unlike the child at Stage IV, who does not use one object as a tool, or means, for obtaining another desired object, the child at Stage V discovers new means of attaining desired goals. Bates, Camaioni, and Volterra (1975) and Bates et al. (1977) observed at Stage V not only the emergence of nonsocial forms of tool use, such as using a cloth support to obtain an object, but also noted "two forms of social tool use (i.e., using an adult as a means to an object, using an object as a means to adult attention)" (Bates et al., 1977, p. 3). Here object schemes and people schemes become interrelated as the child uses one to obtain the other. As we have already learned, it is at this stage that intentional communication first makes its appearance as what Bates has termed the **protodeclarative** (using an object to get the attention of an adult) and the **protoimperative** (using the adult as an agent or a means to obtain a desired object).

Also at this stage, the child is continually experimenting with objects in his environment. Through this experimentation, the child gradually develops a practical understanding of both his physical and social world. For example, he is learning about the "resistance of certain objects and the existence of properties of the objects" (Beard, 1969, p. 45). Finally, both imitation and the object concept are becoming firmly established. The child is now capable of systematically imitating new models that are in his present environment, and the object is sought in terms of its displacements alone (Piaget & Inhelder, 1969).

STAGE VI. Stage VI (eighteen to twenty-four months) is the transition stage to the next period of cognitive development, the preoperational period, in which the child is able to use mental symbols and words to signify both present and absent objects. At Stage VI, the child can coordinate complex schemes, and the object concept is firmly established. The latter is demonstrated by the child's retrieval of an object that has been invisibly displaced; the object concept is no longer tied to its physical context. The attainment of the object concept implies that the object is permanent regardless of its presence or absence perceptually or the action placed upon it (Brown, 1973*a* ). The child now has mental images of objects, and these mental images serve as one symbolic form providing the basis for both language and more advanced intellectual operations (Sinclair, 1970). Whereas mental images are somewhat idiosyncratic in nature, words are conventional and can be combined to form sentences.

The emergence, at Stage VI, of deferred imitation (i.e., imitation of an action that is distanced in time and space) is another sign that the child can represent actions even though they are not present. It is at this developmental level that the child has formed an internal symbolic form by means of a visual or auditory image.

In even this brief description of the sensorimotor period, we find striking evidence that the origins of meaning as a precursor to language arise here. Certain cognitive readiness factors for language can be derived from Piaget's description of the six stages of sensorimotor development. First, in order to develop the intent to communicate, the child must first be able to separate herself from the environment and her actions. Without such a separation, why the need to communicate? Furthermore, without this cognitive differentiation, how can semantic units such as agent, action, and object evolve as intact semantic categories and as categories that can be combined in many ways (i.e., the generative aspect of language)? Second, the child must develop a permanent object concept in order to understand that her world is more or less stable. Without this stability, the words used to symbolize objects and events would similarly lack stability. Third, through active experimentation or play with objects, the child learns that objects can be acted upon differentially and that they have different properties and functions. As a result, objects take on different meanings, which are subsequently mapped onto different words. This is the essence of the basic semantic categories. Fourth, the child must learn about the nature and function of communication (the interrelationship of people schemes and object schemes), before the newly developed conventional symbols (i.e., words) can have a communicative function. Fifth, the child must learn the basis of symbolization, that is, that $Y$ can be represented by $X$. This symbolic process enables the child to separate the signifier (the word) from the significant (the object or event). It is from functional play to the emergence of early forms of symbolic play (e.g., a block can represent a truck) in Stage VI that we note the beginnings of representation and symbolism (Bates et al., 1977).

In discussing the relationship between the symbolic function (of which language, Piaget argues, is one form) and cognitive development, Sinclair (1970) differentiates the child's knowledge and actions into three categories that are related to Piagetian theory and are successively and hierarchically ordered. The first category consists of "those activities that can be interpreted as concerning knowledge about the objects themselves; the discovery of their properties" (Sinclair, 1970, p. 120). The second category is comprised of those activities which show organization of the objects (functional activity). Finally, the third category includes "acting as if," or the symbolic function. The establishment of the symbolic function requires the possession of a stable object concept, which includes a rudimentary knowledge of the core properties and results in the inclusion of all instances of $X$ while simultaneously excluding all instances of $Y$. Sinclair explains that the child does not necessarily need to use language before it can be claimed that she has attained the ability to symbolize. By watching the child's play one gains insight as to the level of sensorimotor activity. If the child shows that an object or event can be represented by something else, such behavior is a clear indication of symbolic functioning. For example, a child pushes a matchbox along a table and collides it with a salt shaker. This pretend play represents an actual incident that occurred the previous day—a car had crashed into a garage door. In this context, the child is engaging in deferred imitation to represent a situation observed the previous day. In fact, Piaget (1967, p. 91) states that "imitation is one of the links between sensorimotor behavior and representational behavior."

In discussing the symbolic function in relationship to language, Sinclair (1970) goes on to suggest that this general symbolic behavior precedes and is requisite to the emergence of language. Several reasons are assigned for this ordinality. First, words as symbols are more abstract and arbitrary than are objects acting as signifiers. Second, words cannot be chosen idiosyncratically as signifiers because words reflect socially defined conventions. Finally, although the child can link actions together in pretend play, they are not necessarily rule-governed as are words.

To summarize thus far, there is compelling empirical and logical support relating the emergence of language to sensorimotor development, especially in Stages V and VI (e.g., Bates, Camaioni, & Volterra, 1975; Bates et al., 1977; Edmonds, 1976; Bloom, 1970; Bowerman, 1973). However, a major question remains to be answered: How does the child's prelinguistic knowledge of objects, events, and relationships become mapped onto the conventional social symbols that are words? To gain some insight into this question, we turn to the role of the adult caretaker as the primary socializing agent. This is the focus of the following section.[1]

## INTERACTION OF THE CHILD WITH THE ENVIRONMENT

The semantic and cognitive perspective discussed in the preceding section emphasizes a complex interaction between the organism and the environment. The child is seen as active and purposeful, and the environment serves to either facilitate or depress the development of the child. The ongoing interaction of the child with the environment, which is frequently mediated by the primary caretaker(s), is the source of additional clues concerning the complex process of language acquisition.

Many analyses of mother-child[2] interactions in the 1970s provided added insight into the relationship between internal and external factors in language acquisition. Here, internal factors refer, but are not restricted, to the cognitive attainments described earlier, whereas external factors refer to the environment within which language acquisition occurs (Cross, 1977). Interpretations of the nature and extent of external factors influencing language acquisition vary depending on one's theoretical orientation. As previously discussed, from the nativistic perspective, the environment is quite benign, simply providing the child with a language model from which the child will somehow induce the underlying linguistic rules. In direct contrast, however, from the behavioristic perspective, the environment is of paramount importance in the learning of language.

Gleason (1977) modifies the nativists' position and accounts for the development of language through a triadic process. Within this process, there is a dynamic relationship among the child with ". . . appropriate neurological equipment in a state of readiness . . . an older person who engages in communicative interchanges with him and some objects in the real world as well" (Gleason, 1977, p. 200). Gleason further states that a large part of the language-learning process focuses on ". . . learning how to make conversation" (1977, p. 203). Gleason's view clearly represents an active child *and* an active environment interacting in both the physical and social world.

Similarly, Snow (1977*b*) proposes that three basic factors underlie language acquisition. These factors are an unknown component (possibly LAD), a cognitive component, and an interactive component between mother and child. Within this framework, internal and external factors are all catalysts of language acquisition. Cross (1977) also presents an interactive perspective; however, she speculates that the role of internal factors (e.g., cognition) outweighs the role of external factors. All three of these researchers, Gleason, Snow, and Cross, highlight the importance of the interaction between mother and child in the acquisition of language. It will be instructive, therefore, to further explicate this interaction.

One can argue that the roots of the mother-child interaction can be found in the development of **attachment behavior.** Initially, the mother responds to reflexive behaviors, such as sucking and rooting, which creates close proximity between her and her child (Stone & Chesney, 1978). With subsequent development, the infant is able to signal, albeit unintentionally, needs by smiling, cooing, crying, and clinging. The mother learns to read these unintentional signals and, in fact, frequently attributes intentional meaning to them. This interactional process is facilitated by the child's ability to send out clear signals and the mother's ability to interpret them. Faulty or inconsistent signaling, as has been reported in autistic babies, creates a faulty communicative system, which jeopardizes the formation of the attachment bond (Stone & Chesney, 1978), and may have deleterious effects on the child's acquisition of language.

Within this interactional framework, the foundations for communication are formed. The mother appears to be motivated both by her desire to understand her child and by her intent to be understood by him (Cross, 1977). Sylvester-Bradley and Trevarthen (1978) describe the interaction similarly, ascribing to the motivational forces in communicating a process of knowing or getting to know. We will next identify the specific processes or vehicles involved in the communicative phenomenon and the specific roles of the mother and child in this interactional process.

In the earliest stages, the communicative model includes tactile, visual, and linguistic modalities (Sachs, 1977). At this perlocutionary stage of development, interactions are social in nature. The infant's crying, vocalizations, and body movements are interpreted as intentional signals and elicit a searching for meaning as a response in the mother. Whether or not realization of the child's meaning is attained is influenced by both the quantity and the quality of the infant's signals and feedback (Buckhalt, Rutherford & Goldberg, 1978). During the first three months of life, the infant is receiving systematic responses to his developing signaling system that are strengthening the bond of attachment, encouraging his involvement in the communicative process, and providing a firm foundation for future language acquisition.

The mother's concern to involve the child in the communicative process has been discussed and studied by Snow (1977*a*). An emphasis on reciprocal activity

by mother and infant is revealed in what Snow terms a **conversational model.**
Snow based her work on a previously existing body of evidence that mothers
modify their speech when talking to their language-learning infants. She found,
however, that mothers began modifying their speech when their infants were only
five to seven months old (Stage III, according to Piaget), thus anticipating the linguistic needs of their children. These modifications appear to be attuned to the
child's growing interest in objects and activities outside the mother-infant dyad.
Even when the infant is as young as three months of age (Stage II), the mother
appears to promote what could be termed conversation by phrasing questions so
that any minimal response by the child, such as a smile, a laugh, a burp or a
sneeze, can be considered as a conversational reply (Snow, 1977a).

This process described by Snow encourages what Bruner (1975) calls turn-
taking. Bruner describes the mutual play between infant and mother as preparing
the child for later linguistic communication. Through mutual play, the infant
learns to role-shift from agent of action to recipient of action and learns that conversation requires taking turns. Bruner has identified certain behaviors of mothers
that facilitate this turn-taking, such as holding out a hand for an object so as to
make the baby the agent. He stresses that the mother's role as interpreter of the
child's intended meaning is crucial in confirming the child's hypotheses. Bates et
al. (1977) reinforce Bruner's observations by describing infants of about nine to
ten months of age who intentionally begin to share interesting objects and events
with familiar adults. "They begin to give and show toys, and somewhat later, to
point to objects and events out of reach while turning to look at the adult for confirmation" (Bates et al., 1977, p. 1). This pattern of sharing (and turn-taking) becomes a ritualized component of the mother-child interaction.

In addition to paving the way for communication, the mother also supplies a
linguistic environment that makes language quite accessible to the child. This linguistic register is quite different from the register used among linguistically competent adults. In fact, both Cross (1977) and Ferguson (1977) suggest that the
young child has access to a highly specialized speech register of the mother, who is
sensitive to the child's linguistic and cognitive capabilities. **Motherese** (Newport,
Gleitman, & Gleitman, 1977), or **baby talk register** (Brown, 1977), is characterized by language that is rarely dysfluent, is well-formed, clearly articulated, and
half as slow in rate as speech directed to adults (Phillips, 1973; Broen, 1972; Snow,
1972). Its phonological contours are heightened, and its pitch is higher (Garnica,
1977). It has been hypothesized that the slow, exaggerated contours and heightened pitch hold the child's attention and make the object or event focused upon
more salient. Not only is the mother's speech slower and more well-formed, but it
is also adjusted in complexity to the developmental level of the child. Syntactically, it is less complex, and the vocabulary is less varied and more concrete
(Phillips, 1973). In addition, semantic complexity is reduced, which suggests that
these utterances are much less cognitively complex (Baldwin & Baldwin, 1973).

As the young child's linguistic abilities evolve, the mother adjusts her input, increasing its complexity until the child is linguistically competent. What ap-

parently happens is that the mother's speech to the child is regulated by cues from the child. The cues may be receptive language cues (i.e., the child does or does not comprehend the mother's utterance), productive language cues (e.g., semantic units produced), interest cues, and so on. That maternal input is closely tailored to the child's linguistic requirements has been termed the **fine-tuning hypothesis** and has received considerable support from Pfuderer (1969), Cross (1977), Newport, Gleitman, and Gleitman (1977), and Snow (1977*b* ).

Another feature of baby talk register is the mother's use of repetitions. She may repeat the young child's cryptic utterances, or she may repeat her own utterances. In the former case, the mother's repetitions serve to confirm the child's communicative attempt and to facilitate the child's comprehension (Garnica, 1977). When the mother repeats the child's utterances with slight modifications and expansions, she is also providing additional linguistic information. Mothers frequently repeat their own utterances, as in the following case:

> Mother (points to the toy duck): "That's a duck. That's a duck. See the duck? Here's the duck." (Mother picks up the duck.)

Here, the mother's repetitions serve to highlight the focus of the conversation—by repeating the word *duck* four times in slightly different sentences. Since mother and child are focused on a shared object and since her repetitions make the word *duck* more salient, it is likely that this process is helping the child map his concept of duck onto the word *duck*.

In opposition to previously held beliefs, it is now thought that neither parental disapproval and correction of syntactic and speech errors nor selective reinforcement have much language-learning validity (Brown & Bellugi, 1964). Reinforcement is given for most of the child's communicative attempts, even when the utterances are structurally incorrect. Instead of directly correcting the child, which would interfere with the ongoing interaction, mothers correct by expanding or recasting the child's utterance (Nelson, Garskaddon, & Bonvillian, 1973). This process is illustrated by the following interchange:

> Child: "Pu pocke'."
> Mother: "Put it in my pocket?"

When direct correction does occur, it is when the child's utterances do not correspond with reality (Brown, 1973*b* ). For example, when the child sees a horse for the first time and points to it saying *doggie,* the mother will respond *That's not a dog, it's a horse.* The mother negates the child's proposition (*not a dog*), corrects it (*it's a horse*), but rarely, if ever, asks the child to confirm her correction. Nelson (1973), analyzing the relative absence of corrections in mother-child interactions, suggests that mothers who are more accepting of their children's speech and language may actually enhance their language development. Maternal acceptance encourages the child to interact linguistically, and in so doing the child gains practice and confidence in using language to affect his social world.

The mother's speech to her developing child is also characterized by a high frequency of interrogatives and declaratives, as opposed to imperatives. This may reflect the mother's view that language has an informational and social function rather than a regulatory one. In the case of interrogatives, mothers use them both for informational requests and for the social purpose of involving the child in the conversation. In asking questions that are frequently rhetorical, the mother is requesting that the child join the verbal interaction. The mother frequently invokes a conversational paradigm that places greater importance on the interaction itself than on the correctness of responses to her requests. This can be seen in the following interaction between mother and child:

> Mother (as she points to a ball):   "What's that?"
> (Child gives no response.)
> Mother (still pointing to the ball):   "Is it a ball?"
> Child:   "Ball."
> Mother:   "It's a ball."

Here, the mother initially requests information concerning the identity of the object, using a *wh-* question. However, when the child fails to respond, she changes her questioning strategy by reverting to a simpler question form, the *yes/no* question *Is it a ball?* She is reducing the linguistic demands placed on the child by providing the answer within the question itself. This step maximizes the child's opportunity to enter the conversation. When the child responds to the informational request by answering with the word *ball,* the mother continues the conversation by confirming the child's answer and by recasting it into a grammatically complete sentence. If the child would fail to respond even to the simpler question form, the mother would answer the question herself. Thus, she sacrifices the tutorial aspect of the interaction to keep the conversation going, even if it means providing the requested information herself.

The high frequency of declarative sentences used by the mother to the child reflects the mother's interest in coding for the child what is happening in the here and now. She seems to be especially attuned to the interests of the child as she refers to objects, people, and events in the child's environment on which the child's attention has focused. This results in a topical agreement in mother-child conversations, with the child frequently initiating the topics.

Not only is the mother apparently tuned to the child's interests in objects and events in the environment, but she is also sensitive to the child's growing linguistic and cognitive capabilities. She appears to be hypothesis-testing, confirming or disconfirming her hypotheses based on her child's verbal and nonverbal feedback. For example, for a long period early in the child's development, the mother talks only about the here and now, and her tense is exclusively the present one. At some point in time, she questions the child about an object, person, or event that is either elsewhere or that occurred in the recent past. If the child responds in a way that shows readiness, "thereness" or "pastness" will be included in the repertoire by the mother. If, however, the child does not display readiness, either by inattentiveness, lack of response, or inappropriate responses, the mother temporarily eliminates this conversational strategy.

To summarize thus far, the characteristics of baby talk register, or motherese, are such that they maximize the child's accessibility to language and encourage interaction between mother and child. Features of this register can be summarized as follows:

1. It is characterized by a high degree of responsiveness to infants' communicative signals, whether intentional or unintentional, verbal or nonverbal.
2. Conversational model is established early, stressing reciprocity and turn-taking. When their infants are three months of age, mothers are responding to physiological signals, such as burps, yawns, and sneezing, using these signals as "topics" of conversation.
3. When their infants are at earliest ages, mothers constantly talk about their inferred wishes, needs, and intentions.
4. As the child shows interest in objects and events (from twenty weeks on), there is a decline in the mother's references to the child alone and an increase in references to objects and other people.
5. Phonological features, such as higher pitch, slower pace, and exaggerated prosodic contours for segmentation, are used to make the mother's speech more accessible to the child.
6. A special lexicon characterized by phonological simplification is initally used, once again to make the mother's speech more accessible to the child. Examples: *doggie, nana* (banana), and *bye-bye* (go out).
7. The syntactic and semantic complexity is at a reduced level. When their children are approximately eighteen to thirty-six months old, mothers use a small set of semantic categories (i.e., agent, action, location, and possession).
8. There is considerable use of redundancy and repetition in the mother's linguistic input to the child.
9. A high proportion of interrogatives is used by the mother as a device for passing the turn to her young conversational partner.
10. Both mother and child discuss what is going on around them in the here and now. This is characterized by the use of present tense, gestures, encoding of their ongoing actions, and so on.
11. There is an almost one-to-one numerical ratio between the mother's utterances and those of her child, reflecting the turn-taking nature of their interactions.
12. In establishing conversational agreement, the mother follows the direction of the child's interest/topic.
13. Mothers neither correct their youngsters' grammatical mistakes nor praise their successes. Mothers do frequently correct violations of truth.

It appears, then, that a mother's primary motivation is to understand her child and to be understood by him.

**THE ROLE OF THE FATHER**   Before leaving the topic of the child and the environment, we must take note of the role of the father in the language-learning process. This is especially important given the changing male and female roles, whereby fathers and mothers are increasingly sharing child-rearing responsibilities. The question that arises is whether the father's speech also exhibits the kinds of accommodations to the child's language abilities just described. The findings of three studies analyzing the father's linguistic input to the child will be briefly discussed here.[3] Rebelsky and Hanks (1971) found that fathers spend little time interacting with their newborns (up to three months of age) and that fathers' linguistic input to their infants differs from that of the mothers. Fathers decreased their verbalizations to female infants as the children aged, but they increased their verbal interactions as their male infants matured.

Studying the characteristics of one father's speech to his three-year-old daughter, Giattino and Hogan (1975) found many similarities to that of the mother-daughter dyad. Like the mother's, the father's linguistic input is short and simple. The frequency of interrogative and declarative sentences is also comparable. However, unlike mothers' speech as reported by Snow (1972), Giattino and Hogan indicate that the father's speech contains very few instances of repetitions and expansions. Gleason (1975) also notes that while the father's speech contains many of the basic features of motherese, certain differences do exist. For example, fathers tend to use more imperatives and directives than do mothers, particularly when they address their sons. Furthermore, fathers appear to be less attuned to their children's speech. They misunderstand such speech more often and appear to be less involved in the speaker-listener role-changing aspects of the verbal interactions.

If fathers in general use many instances of imperatives and few instances of repetitions and expansions and if, more importantly, they are not as attuned to their children's speech as mothers are, could fathers' speech be viewed as a less effective model for language learning? In any family where the mother is the primary caregiver, the mother will no doubt be more attentive and responsive to the child as a result of increased familiarity and shared knowledge. The opposite might be true if fathers were the primary caregivers, suggesting that role differences rather than sex differences are operative.

As most fathers are secondary caregivers to their children, perhaps, as Chubrich (1975) suggests, the father's role is to provide a link between the child and the outside world. The father may facilitate the extension of the child's representations beyond the here and now. For example, not being home with the child during the day, and thus lacking shared knowledge, the father may ask the child what she did that day. In responding, the child would have to transcend the here and now and be more explicit about actions and events that occurred in the past. The mother, that is, the primary caregiver, may aid the child's communicative attempts in this situation by recasting and expanding any cryptic propositions, thus diminishing the child's burden of attempting to be understood. Therefore, the father may indeed play a complementary role in the language-learning process, encouraging the child to accommodate her language while she is simultaneously accommodated to by the primary caregiver.

## CONCLUDING REMARKS

Our understanding of the process of language acquisition has greatly increased, yet we are still far from having a complete picture of the process. There is little doubt that the child is an active participant in the language-learning process or that there is a strong relationship between language and cognition. The primary caregiver can no longer be relegated to a role of benign model. The importance of the communicative function as a foundation and precursor to language has been clearly documented (e.g., Bates et al., 1977). However, several important questions do remain. First, what is the precise relationship between language and cognition? Are cognitive developments, such as object permanence, causal prerequisites to language, or do they parallel language development, or do both of these share some underlying operative scheme (Bates et al., 1977)? What is the significance and role of the child's social development in facilitating language development? (See Bates, Camaioni, and Volterra, 1975, for a discussion of this question.) How is the child's nonlinguistic understanding of the world mapped onto conventional symbols that are rule-governed and generative? These issues are but a few of the unanswered questions concerning the complex process of language acquisition. The following inquiries are designed to further analyze the various perspectives presented in this chapter, primarily by studying interactions between the parent and child.

## INQUIRY 6.1

Imitation, differential reinforcement, and correction are considered by behaviorists to be the key factors in the learning of language. However, recent psycholinguistic and linguistic theory holds that none of these factors can adequately account for the child's acquisition of language.

**OBJECTIVES**   The objectives of this inquiry are to:

1. Describe the child's imitations and parental reinforcement and correction in a parent-child interaction.
2. Analyze the role played by each of the above factors in accounting for the acquisition of language in children.

**PROCEDURES**   Observe and tape-record a spontaneous language interaction between a parent and a young child (between the ages of twelve months and three years). The observation period can be quite brief (fifteen minutes). Without editing anything that either the child or the parent says, transcribe the language sample, including any nonverbal and contextual information.

**REPORT**   Include the following in your report:

1. A description of the setting where the activity took place.
2. The participant's age.
3. The unedited transcript of the tape with contextual notes.

In addition, address yourself to the following questions:

1. Did the child spontaneously imitate any of the parent's utterances? If so, describe the nature of the child's imitations (e.g., exact imitations, partial imitations).
2. Did the parent request or command the child to imitate any utterances or a specific word or phrase? If so, what did the child do in response to this request? Describe and provide examples.
3. Were there instances where the parent systematically reinforced a particular aspect of the child's communicative attempts (e.g., articulation, syntactic constructions, lexical items, truth statements)? Describe and illustrate.
4. What aspects of the language used by the child did the parent formally correct, if any? Did the parent correct faulty articulation, grammar, or violations of truth statements? Describe and analyze. What did the child do in response to any corrections made by the parent?
5. What do you see as the role of imitation, reinforcement and correction in the language-learning process?

**EVALUATION**   Did this inquiry develop the specified objectives? If so, how? If not, why? How could the effectiveness of this inquiry be increased?

---

### INQUIRY 6.2

The nativistic position was greatly enhanced by descriptions of the adult language model as being poorly formed, highly complex (syntactically and semantically), frequently ambiguous, and quickly paced. If this description of adult language is accurate, then it is hardly an adequte model for the learning of language. On the other hand, some researchers (e.g., Snow, 1972) argued that the language used by adults to children is significantly different from that used between two adult speakers. This baby talk register (Brown, 1977) is, in fact, a reasonable language-learning model.

**OBJECTIVES**   The objectives of this inquiry are to:

1. Describe the differences between language used by an adult to a young child and language being used in an adult-adult dyad.
2. Analyze the adequacy of each corpus as a model for language learning.

**PROCEDURES**   Observe and tape-record a spontaneous verbal interaction between a parent and young child (aged twelve to thirty-six months). This interaction can be quite brief (ten to fifteen minutes). Afterwards, ask the parent to tell you about the child and the interaction that took place. Tape-record this interaction (adult/adult dyad). Transcribe both taped interactions, including any nonverbal and contextual information.

**REPORT**   Include the following in your report:

1. A description of the setting in which the interactions took place.
2. The ages of the participants.
3. Transcripts of both interactions.

In addition, address yourself to the following questions:

1. What were the differences between the language used by the parent to the child and to you? Include such features as:
   a. Language complexity (e.g., MLU).
   b. Variety of vocabulary (e.g., type: token ratio).
   c. Well-formedness of the language.
   d. Pace of speech.
   e. Use of gestures.
2. What is the adequacy of each model for the process of language acquisition and why?

**EVALUATION**   Did this inquiry develop the specified objectives? If so, how? If not, why? How could the effectiveness of this inquiry be increased?

---

### INQUIRY 6.3

There is considerable support for the position that language abilities have their roots in the nonlinguistic, cognitive structures of the sensorimotor period (see Piaget, 1952; Sinclair, 1970; Bates, 1976*a*; 1976*b* ). This cognitive perspective focuses on the child's interactions with the physical environment and stresses semantic organization as the foundation of language.

**OBJECTIVES**   The objectives of this inquiry are to:

1. Study the cognitive abilities of a child who has begun to use language and of a child who is prelinguistic.

2. Speculate on the nature of the relationship between language and cognition.

**PROCEDURES**   Select two children, one who is prelinguistic and one who has just begun to use language. This information can generally be obtained from parents or by observing the child interacting with her parents. Assess each child's cognitive abilities, studying specifically the following: (1) use of objects, (2) object permanence, and (3) tool use. For assessing object use, refer to the procedures described in Inquiry 4.1. Refer to Inquiry 4.2 for the procedures used to study the child's development of the object concept. In order to assess the child's use of objects to obtain other objects (i.e., tool use), place a desired object out of the child's reach while placing another object, such as a stick or a pillow, which could be used to obtain the desired object, near the child. Observe and note what each child does in attempting to obtain the desired object.

**REPORT**   Include the following in your report:

1. Brief descriptions of the children and the context in which the activities took place.
2. A detailed description of each child's performance on each of the cognitive tasks.

In addition, address yourself to the following questions:

1. What were the differences between the prelinguistic and the linguistic child in their performance on the cognitive tasks presented?
2. What do you view as the nature of the relationship between language and cognition?
3. Evaluate this statement: Cognitive abilities, as demonstrated by the completion of the sensorimotor period, are necessary but not sufficient conditions for the acquisition of language.

**EVALUATION**   Did this inquiry develop the specified objectives? If so, how? If not, why? How could the effectiveness of this inquiry be increased?

———————                         **INQUIRY 6.4**                         ———————

It can hardly be denied that parents are usually the child's first teachers of language, whether the teaching role is considered a benign one (the nativistic position), a superordinate one (the behavioristic view), or an interactive, facilitative one (the semantic/cognitive perspective). However, during parent-child interactions, what are the various functions of the parent's linguistic input to the child? Are they primarily tutorial, social-interactive, or regulatory?

**OBJECTIVES**   The objectives of this inquiry are to:

1. Describe the various functions of parental linguistic input to the child.
2. Speculate on the role of the parent as a teacher of language.

**PROCEDURES** Observe and tape-record a spontaneous language interaction between a parent and a young child (between the ages of twelve and thirty-six months). This observation can be quite brief (ten to fifteen minutes). Transcribe the taped language interaction, including any nonverbal and contextual information. Using the categories outlined below (Mazur, Holzman, & Ferrier 1976, pp. 4–6), analyze the communicative functions of the parent's linguistic input to the child.

### Communicative Functions

1. *Social Functions*
   a. Phatic: Utterances whose primary function is to initiate or maintain an interaction that is warm in tone, soothing. Focus is on the channel of communication rather than on the message. Included are utterances to comfort the child, vacuous statements or questions, responses to the child's vocalizations, and utterances pretending to speak for the child.
   b. Expressive: Utterances whose primary function is to express the mother's sincere feeling for, attitude to, or evaluation of a person, situation, activity, or object.

   Examples: *My goodness!*
   *Good show.* (indicating approval)
   *You could have done a better job.* (indicating disapproval)

2. *Regulatory Function*
   a. Directive: Utterances whose function is to influence or direct the child's behavior. Includes both commands and suggestions, as well as those utterances that the mother uses while helping the child carry out the desired behavior.
   Examples: Command: *No!* (when child reaches for electric cord)
   Suggestion: *You can play with the bunny instead.*
   Transitional: *Lift up your arm.* (mother lifts it)

3. *Tutorial Functions*
   a. Performative: Utterance that signals or accompanies mother's actions directed toward the child. Verbal components of an ongoing action.
   Examples: Noncontentives: *Upsydaisy.* (as child is picked up)
   Descriptive: *Get the mouth.* (as she washes it)
   Activity boundary: *Now.* (as she lifts child)

b. Report: Utterance that conveys (or requests) information but does not
gloss the mother's actions. May include reference to past
or future events, description of objects or persons or of attributes
of the child. May be a statement or question.

Examples: Future event: *After mommy has lunch we'll go out.*
Description: *That's part of the blender.*

c. Tutorial Speech: Utterance designed to directly teach the child something
related to performance of a motor, social, or language
function.

Examples: *Can you say "pretty baby"?*
*Wave bye-bye to grandmom.*
*Here's the way it goes.*

**REPORT**   Include the following in your report:

1. Brief descriptions of parent and child and the context in which the interaction took place.
2. The transcript of the parent-child interaction, coded using the communicative categories described above.
3. A table, such as the following, illustrating the percentage of the total parent linguistic input represented by each communicative category.

| Function | % |
|---|---|
| Social | |
| Phatic | 13 |
| Expressive | 16 |
| Regulatory | |
| Directive | 6 |
| Tutorial | |
| Performative | 20 |
| Report | 32 |
| Tutorial Speech | 8 |
| Others | 5 |

In addition, address yourself to the following questions:

1. What were the various communicative functions represented by the parent's linguistic input to the child?
2. On the basis of this interaction, how do you define the parent's role as a
teacher of language?

**EVALUATION**   Did this inquiry develop the specified objectives? If so, how? If
not, why? How could the effectiveness of this inquiry be increased?

## INQUIRY 6.5

The interaction between parent and child has been viewed from different perspectives and has generated several hypotheses relating it to the child's acquisition of language. Cross (1977) presents three hypotheses:

1. The indifferent hypothesis: The adult's linguistic input is unfavorable to the child's task of acquiring langauge.
2. The fine-tuning hypothesis: The adult's linguistic input to the child is closely tailored to the child's linguistic requirements.
3. The multi-factor hypothesis: Since the adult's speech is shaped by a multiplicity of purposes, it is not perfectly tuned at any level.

**OBJECTIVES**   The objectives of this inquiry are to:

1. Observe and analyze the interaction between a parent and a young child.
2. Analyze the parent's linguistic input to the child on the basis of the hypotheses identified above.

**PROCEDURES**   Observe and tape-record a spontaneous language interaction between a parent and a young child (aged twelve to thirty-six months). This observation can be quite brief (ten to fifteen minutes). Transcribe the taped language interaction, including any nonverbal and contextual information.

**REPORT**   Include the following in your report:

1. Brief descriptions of the parent and child and of the context in which the interaction took place.
2. A transcript of the taped interaction.

In addition, address yourself to the following questions:

1. What was the relationship between the parent's syntactic complexity (e.g., MLU) and that of the child?
2. What was the relationship between the parent's semantic complexity (e.g., agent + action + object) and that of the child?
3. What topics of conversation did the parent initiate and what topics did the child initiate? Describe the match or mismatch between the two.
4. What discourse strategies did the parent use in talking to the child (e.g., reference to the child versus reference to the outside world, reference to the here and now versus reference to the past or future)?
5. On the basis of this interaction, which of the three hypotheses identified above best describes the parent's input to the child? Provide a rationale for your choice.

**EVALUATION**   Did the inquiry develop the specified objectives? If so, how? If not, why? How could the effectiveness of this inquiry be increased?

## NOTES

1. A portion of this section is adapted from A. Coren, Analysis of videotaped mother-child interaction. Unpublished paper, Temple University, 1979. Used with the permission of the author.
2. Since most research focuses on the mother as the primary caretaker, the word mother is used here instead of the more general term caretaker. Research addressing the role of the father will also be cited and so indicated.
3. Information on father-child interactions is based on R. Y. Milhalisin, Father and son: an analysis of father's speech to his two-year-old son. Unpublished paper, Temple University, 1978. Used with the permission of the author.

# 7

# Dialect Variation

That languages, as conventional symbol systems, vary is a compelling linguistic reality. All that you need to do is to travel to a foreign, non-English-speaking country for the phenomenon of language variation to become obvious. You will note differences in the melody of the language, differences in the speech-sounds, or segmental phonemes, differences in lexicon and grammar, and perhaps even differences in the communicative style. What is less obvious is the language variation occurring within a particular language and among individual speakers of a language community. Casual observations indicate that no two persons speak exactly alike. In fact, one can reasonably argue that each person speaks an individual dialect, an **idiolect,** which simultaneously reflects the uniqueness of the person's language and the commonalities shared with other speakers of the particular language. Similarly, within a particular language, one will also find group-based language variation in which certain divergent linguistic features differentiate varieties of the same language. Language varieties resulting from sociocultural rather than individual differences are called **dialects.** A dialect of any language shares sufficient linguistic features with that language so as to permit speakers of both to be mutually understood. However, it is sufficiently different from the standard form to be considered a separate and distinct entity (Buchanan, 1963). Like languages, dialects of the same language may differ from each other in pronunciation, grammar, lexicon, and communicative style.

The relationship among idiolects, dialects, and a language is graphically illustrated in Figure 7.1. Note that in the cases of the idiolect and dialect, the majority of the variance is included within the main language. This allows for communication among all members of the language community. However, there is some degree of both individual and group distinctiveness resulting in the uniqueness of

This chapter is based in part on the book *Variant English* by D. N. Bryen, C. Hartman, and P. E. Tait. Columbus, Ohio: Charles E. Merrill. Used with the permission of the publisher.

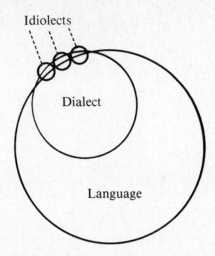

Idiolects

Dialect

Language

FIGURE 7.1    Relationship among Idiolects, a Dialect, and a Language

the individual speaker and the dialect group. If for any number of reasons two dialects become so different over time that communication between members of the two dialect groups is precluded, they no longer are dialects of the same language, having evolved into two distinct languages. This process of linguistic evolution is illustrated in Figure 7.2 and is represented by the present existence of French and Spanish as two separate languages, whereas historically they were once dialects of the same language.

Language variation can be viewed as the result of a psychological process (idiolects) or from a historical perspective; however, the focus of this chapter is on the language variation resulting from sociocultural differences in America. A further purpose of this chapter is to examine how these dialect differences affect the school experiences of the many youngsters who speak a less prestigious dialect of English. The term **variant English** will be used throughout this chapter when referring to the major dialects of English. Other terms, such as nonstandard or substandard English and, more recently, black English, have been used in the past to describe essentially the same dialect difference. However, in agreement with Bryen, Hartman, and Tait (1978, p. v), these terms are avoided here for several important reasons:

> First, dialect variation in America is not a racial issue and it is not isolated to Blacks in America. We reject the term non-standard because "standardness" is a situational phenomenon—standard English in one situation would not be considered the standard in another. Second, we have rejected the term non-standard because of the frequent (and erroneous) myths and negative attitudes associated with a dialect so termed.

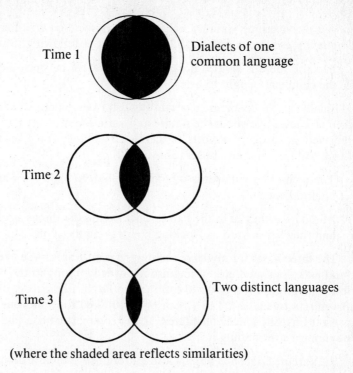

(where the shaded area reflects similarities)

FIGURE 7.2   Evolution of Two Dialects into Two Distinct Languages

In contrast, the term variant English reflects the realities of language. Language does vary, resulting in sociocultural language variants. These variants of English are the concern of this chapter.

## MYTHS CONCERNING VARIANT ENGLISH

The dialect of variant English, primarily spoken by many working-class blacks in the North but also found among working-class whites and blacks in the South, has been continually the subject of many erroneous beliefs. These myths evolved from racially based notions of physiological and genetic differences, illustrated by the following (Gonzales, 1972, p. 10):

> Slovenly and careless of speech, these Gullahs seized upon peasant English used by some of the early settlers and by the white settlers . . . wrapped their clumsy tongues about it as well as they could and enriched with certain expressive African words, it issued through their flat noses and thick lips.

Myths concerning variant English also have socio-environmental origins (albeit frequently erroneous ones) as illustrated by the following (Shuy, 1972, p. 201):

> Because there is no real honest communication between parent and child, the child isn't taught to listen.

Finally, myths concerning variant English have sometimes evolved due to a real lack of knowledge about the nature and variation of language. This ignorance is reflected in teachers' reports concerning the language problems presented by black children in their classes (Shuy, 1970, pp. 123, 124):

> These children cut words off: could would be *'ould* . . . too their *l*'s were often missing.

> I think that they're in the habit of not saying the things as clearly as we do and they say a word as "looking" by leaving the *g* off.

The three bases for myths concerning variant English (i.e., genetic factors, cultural pathology, and lack of linguistic knowledge) support the belief that this dialect is an inferior, bastardized form of the English language, if a language at all. Bryen, Hartman, and Tait (1978, p. 3) outlined the following six beliefs about variant English, which constituted, and to some extent continue to constitute, the mythology surrounding it.

1. Variant English is linguistically inferior to standard English.
2. Due to their dialect, speakers of variant English are deficient in their cognitive development.
3. Speakers of variant English are delayed in their acquisition of language.
4. Variant English usage is a result of certain genetic characteristics.
5. Poor environmental conditions have produced the language deficiencies of speakers of variant English.
6. There is one white standard English dialect, which is correct, and one black variant English, which is incorrect.

Culminating in the mid-1960s, controversy over the cause and nature of dialect variation resolved into two opposing views. On the one hand, psychologists and educators who had contact with black and working-class children but little background in sociology and language either tacitly or explicitly accepted the assumptions about variant English listed above. This acceptance led to a position often called the **verbal deficit hypothesis,** which is summarized by Dale (1972, p. 249):

> Because Negro children from the ghetto hear very little language, much of it ill-formed, they are impoverished in their means of verbal expression and reception. They cannot formulate complete sentences; they speak in "giant-words." They do not know the names of common objects, they lack crucial concepts, and they cannot produce or comprehend logical statements. Sometimes they are even reported to have no language at all.

In order to remediate these perceived verbal deficits, language programs were developed (e.g., *DISTAR Language* by Engelmann & Osborn, 1970), compensatory education programs, such as Head Start, emerged, and a disproportionately high percentage of black youngsters were enrolled in special education classes and speech therapy (Weintraub, 1971; Mercer, 1972; Dillard, 1972).

During this same period, some linguists and sociolinguists, such as William Labov, Roger Shuy, Roger Fasold, and William Wolfram, began to compile compelling evidence that all dialects are well-formed, highly developed language systems. Their research findings were primarily responsible for dispelling the previously listed myths about variant English. In studies of specific linguistic features of variant English (especially of what is called black English) and how these features diverge from standard English, several basic observations were made. First, it became evident that the differences between the two dialects are consistent and systematic. Pronunciation and syntactic differences were not random errors as previously thought but were instead highly structured and rule-governed. Second, research conducted by Moore (1968) and Labov (1967) provided strong evidence that children acquire the linguistic rules of their dialect at the same pace as the standard dialect is acquired by the middle-class children studied by Brown, Cazden, and Bellugi-Klima (1971). Third, Labov (1973; 1975) and others provided additional support for the view that all dialects are effective tools for communicating to other native speakers of the dialect. These findings refuted the myths that variant English is linguistically inferior to standard English and that speakers of variant English are delayed in their acquisition of language.

Research into the relationship between thought and language also contributed to the dispelling of myths concerning variant English. Originally, behaviorally based conceptions about language fostered the belief that language is an exact manifestation of thought, that is, the two are equivalent processes. Therefore, if certain agreed-upon linguistic structures are absent, that provides direct evidence for the corollary absence of certain concepts. For example, Bereiter and Engelmann (1966) concluded that variant dialect speakers who did not use the *if-then* construction failed to understand the logical concept of conditionality. However, Bereiter and Engelmann failed to recognize that different languages and different dialects have different ways of expressing logical notions. Similarly, although there is a strong relationship between language and thinking, there is not a one-to-one correspondence between words and concepts. This fact about the nature of language went unrecognized by proponents of the verbal deficit hypothesis. Finally, as indicated by Wolfram and Fasold (1974, p. 5):

> There is nothing inherent in a given language variety that will interfere with the development of the ability to reason.... All language varieties are equally capable of use in reason, abstracting, and hypothesizing.

That speakers of variant dialects are cognitively and linguistically deficient was sometimes explained on the basis of beliefs of either physical or social pathology.

However, it must be noted that there is no evidence that dialect differences can be attributed to physiological differences, except in cases of cerebral palsy or brain damage. Dialects, like languages, have social, historical, and regional origins; they do not have a physiological basis such as that described by verbal deprivationalists. The impact of the social pathology explanation was also weakened by the appearance in the literature of observations of children from variant-speaking homes. Instead of describing these children as receiving little sustained verbal interaction in the home, Horner and Gussow (1972) and Labov (1973) reported that children were receiving enormous amounts of verbal interaction with both adults and peers. While it is quite possible that the functions of language may vary among sociocultural groups, there is little reasonable evidence for the view that speakers of variant English experience linguistic deprivation during the language-learning period.

Despite the rather compelling findings presented by linguists and sociolinguists that no dialect is less systematic or less logical than another, there is a widespread belief that standard English is correct and variant English is incorrect. How can we account for this? This belief most likely has grown out of a sociopolitical framework rather than a linguistic context. The favoring of one dialect over another is in reality the favoring of one social group over a less prestigious one. The dialect of the most prestigious (and powerful) group is considered to be the most reputable dialect and acquires "the status of being the correct dialect. The lower the social status of a group, the more incorrect their dialect will be considered" (Bryen, Hartman, & Tait, 1978, p. 4). For example, black English, the dialect spoken by many urban blacks, has been widely devalued. Although there is no linguistic basis for this devaluation, sociopolitical factors have been pervasive. Ford et al. (1976) suggest that blacks historically have been assigned the greatest cultural deficit of all races. As an example, they quote an assertion made by the influential historian Toynbee in 1947 that "the black races alone have not contributed positively to any civilization as yet" (Ford et al., 1976, p. 6). Such negative attitudes toward blacks have been carried over to their dialect as well.

It is not surprising that sociopolitical factors cause many variant dialects to be devalued and viewed as incorrect. However, as Hall (1972) argues, "correctness" only means social acceptability. It does not correspond to the linguistic findings concerning the nature and structure of variant English.

To conclude this section, let us look again at the sixth myth:

> There is one white standard English, which is correct, and one black variant English, which is incorrect.

There are two fundamental misconceptions in this statement. First, the notion of a categorical differentiation between standard English and variant English is faulty. Such a dichotomous situation does not exist. Different dialects should more realistically be viewed as falling along a continuum ranging from hypothetically pure standard English (closest to formal, written language) to hypothetically pure variant English (which is presented later in Tables 7.2 through 7.4). The language used by any speaker of American English falls somewhere along this continuum, ranging from predominant use of standard English features to frequent use of variant English features.

The second misconception embedded in the statement above is that there is one black dialect known as variant or black English and one white dialect known as standard English. Not all white youngsters speak one dialect, and not all black youngsters speak one dialect. This categorical misperception can lead to racially based assumptions regarding language. It is true that many working-class black urban youngsters speak a dialect containing many features of variant English; however, it is equally true that many Southern, and even Northern, working-class whites share many of the same variant linguistic features. Although most middle-class whites speak a dialect of English characterized by a predominant use of standard English features, so do most middle-class blacks.

Dialect variation is a complex, interactional phenomenon influenced by various sociocultural factors, including ethnicity, social class, and region (see Bryen, Hartman, & Tait, 1978, pp. 156–97 for a further analysis of these influences). It cannot be dichotomized along racial lines.

## SOCIOCULTURAL FUNCTIONS OF DIALECTS

Each culture develops a language or dialect to meet its specific needs. These needs relate to the values, physical necessities, social and esthetic factors, and climatic and technological demands of that society. By their very nature all languages are equally suited to the cultures to which they belong, and, as cultural needs change (e.g., new technological advances), so do languages. It is equally true that a given language or dialect may not be adequate for the needs of another culture. For example, the Eskimo language has approximately forty different words representing different states of snow. This does not make the Eskimo language more generally precise than English. Rather it reflects the Eskimo's cultural need to be sensitive to different states of snow for fishing, hunting, and general physical survival. Similarly, Dale (1972, p. 205) notes that "many languages do not have a word equivalent to the English word atom." This fact does not undermine the adequacy of any of those languages, rather it underscores their relevancy to the needs of their particular cultures. Culturally-based linguistic differences are not limited to lexicon but extend to grammatic categories as well (e.g., presence or absence of the definite and indefinite). (For a contrasting view of the relationship between language, thought, and culture, the reader is referred to Whorf, 1956.)

In addition to serving the relevant needs of a culture, language has the function of cultural preservation (Sapir, 1970). Language and dialects have a community or cultural maintenance function, serving to include members of the particular community (**inclusionary function**) while simultaneously excluding those who are not members of the community (**exclusionary function**). Interaction and communication continually take place among members of a community. The motivation toward more effective communication among community members compels people toward linguistic similarity.

Given the culture-preserving function of language, let us consider the case for the existence of a variant dialect called black English. Labov (1971) has suggested, rightfully so, that most linguistic features of black English are found in other variant dialects in America, particularly in southern regional dialects. Therefore, if linguistic features are the sole criterion for viewing black English as a distinctive dialect, the case is not strong at all. However, Falk (1973) suggests an additional criterion. The question of whether or not a black English dialect exists should not be decided solely on linguistic distinctiveness, but rather, he argues, this issue "depends on . . . personal, psychological, and sociological factors" (Falk, 1973, p. 209). Black English may serve the sociocultural role of promoting cultural solidarity. By the addition of this sociocultural criterion, the case for a distinct dialect called black English is clearly strengthened. It is further strengthened by observing the communicative style of many urban black youths. While having their roots in the slave period where they were socially adapted to the plight of slaves (Kochman, 1972, p. 241), communicative acts such as " 'rapping,' 'shucking,' . . . and 'sounding' " continue today. Table 7.1 gives brief descriptions of these and other verbal games.

In summary, a dialect cannot be studied solely on the distinctiveness of its phonological and grammatical features. It is also necessary to consider the sociocultural function it serves.


## LINGUISTIC FEATURES OF VARIANT ENGLISH

Variant English differs from hypothetically pure standard English on the basis of phonological and syntactic features. Vocabulary differences are also present; however, Labov (1971) argues that these vocabulary differences are not socially significant. The question of whether or not semantic differences exist between these two English dialects remains unanswered, although it is mostly agreed that linguistic differences appear only in surface structures rather than in deep structures where the semantic component of language is generated. Communicative styles that have emerged in black urban communities are also viewed as a feature differentiating black English from other English dialects. These expressive styles are described at length by Brown (1972), Kochman (1972), Smith (1972), and Foster (1974).

Most recent research has focused on particular syntactic and phonological differences; therefore, it is in these areas that the greatest knowledge has been accumulated. It should be noted, however, that some of the linguistic features presented here have been only tentatively described, while others have yet to be studied. This status reflects the somewhat embryonic stage of the study of variant dialects in America.

TABLE 7.1   Communicative Acts in an Inner City—Chicago Sample
(Kochman, 1972)

| Name of Verbal Behavior | Function of Verbal Behavior | Examples |
|---|---|---|
| "rapping" (p. 243) | "used . . . to create a favorable impression and be persuasive at the same time . . ." (p. 243) | "Baby, I sho' dig your mellow action." (p. 244) |
| "shucking or jiving" (p. 253) | manipulative deception | "It was a jive tip." (Brown, 1965, p. 142) |
| "copping a plea" (p. 255) | "to beg, plead for mercy" (p. 255) | "The night before my hearing, I decided to make a prayer. It had to be on my knees, cause if I was gonna cop a plea to God, I couldn't play it cheap." (Thomas, 1967, p. 316) |
| "signifying" (p. 258) | insulting the listener directly | "Boy, you so black, you sweat super Perma-lube oil." (p. 259) |
| "playing the dozens" (p. 258) | insulting the opponent via his or her family, usually his or her mother | "Yo mama so bowleg-ged, she looks like the bite out of a donut." (p. 261) |
| "sounding" (p. 258) | general term for the game of insult | (See examples of signifying and playing the dozens.) |
| "running it down" (p. 254) | used to "communicate information in the form of an explanation, narrative, giving advice and the like" (p. 254) | "If I saw him hanging out with cats I knew were weak, who might be using drugs . . . I'd run it down to him." (Brown, 1965, p. 390) |
| "gripping" (p. 254) | "the talk or facial expression which accompanies a partial loss of face or self-possession" (p. 254) | An example would be a display of fear, which is looked at with contempt. |

Presented in Tables 7.2 through 7.4 are approximately forty linguistic features that have been characterized as part of variant English. These features are categorized into phonological, morphological, and syntactic patterns. The linguistic environment affecting each feature is described, and examples of the divergence from standard English are given.

Several important observations can be made from the features listed in Tables 7.2 through 7.4. First, nearly half of the features that differentiate standard from variant English are phonological in nature. Also, several of the morphological features, such as the deletion of the -ed past tense markers, appear to have a phonological basis. Given this, one can legitimately argue that pronunciation constitutes the majority of the variation between standard and variant English. This contention can be further supported by additional phonological features that are not presented in the tables. For example, vowel variations have also been studied, and it has been shown that certain words that are contrastive in standard English are pronounced (and perhaps heard) similarly in variant English. An example of this vowel feature is as follows:

$$oil = all \longrightarrow toil = tall$$

There is also some variation in stress or accent in variant English, yielding pronunciation differences such as the following (Fasold & Wolfram, 1970, p. 57):

| Standard English | Variant English |
|---|---|
| police | pólice |
| hotél | hótel |
| Julý | Júly |

These differences appear to be isolated to certain words, but since they are socially significant they are therefore worth mentioning.

The nature and frequency of the variation in linguistic features make up the linguistic variables that differentiate standard and variant English dialects. However, the social significance of this variability is equally important to consider. Not all of the phonological divergences are socially stigmatizing, for example, the -r and -l reduction or the merging of -e- and -i- occurring prenasally. Other phonological features, such as consonant cluster simplification and variants of the *th* sounds, occur with relatively high frequency and are socially stigmatizing (Wolfram, 1970). Because of the social significance of such features, it is likely that a person may be classified as a variant English speaker for merely using one such feature even if the remainder of his speech is standard.

An additional observation concerning the features distinguishing variant and standard English relates to the extent of their occurrence. For example, in standard English the short *e* to *i* prenasal feature also occurs, but the extent of its occurrence is restricted to one particular linguistic environment, within an unstressed syllable. Similarly, consonant cluster simplification is also a linguistic reality in standard English, occurring when the cluster precedes a word beginning with a consonant, as in *He lef' the ball*. In variant English, consonant clus-

TABLE 7.2  Summary of Phonological Features in Variant English

| Feature | Linguistic Environment | Standard English | Variant English |
|---------|------------------------|------------------|-----------------|
| *th* | voiced, initial position | *them* | *dem* |
| *th* | unvoiced, initial position | *think* | *tink* |
| *th* | voiced, medial position | *mother* | *moder* |
| *th* | unvoiced, medial position | *nothing* | *nofing* |
| *th* | voiced, final position | *breathe* | *breave* |
| *th* | unvoiced, final position | *bath* | *baf* |
| *th* (nasal) | position post nasal | *month* | *mont* or *mon'* |
| *r* | vowel plus *r* yielding *er* sound | *first* *sister* | *fuhst* *sistuh* |
| *r* | postvocalic not yielding *er* sound | *car* *hard* | *cauh* *hauhd* |
| *l* | postvocalic preconsonantal | *help* *hail the* | *he'p* *hai' de* |
| *l* | postvocalic, prepausal | *Don't fall!* | *Don't fa'!* |
| short *e-i* | prenasal | *pen* *went* | *pin* *wint* |
| *ing* | final position, unstressed syllable | *singing* *something* | *singin* *somefin* |
| consonant cluster | both unvoiced, final position | *left* *must* | *lef'* *mus'* |
| consonant cluster | both voiced, final position | *bend* *blamed* | *ben'* *blame'* |
| initial syllable | unstressed | *about* *suppose* | *'bout* *'pose* |
| *t* and *d* | postvocalic, preconsonantal between words | *let me* *bed broke* | *le' me* *be' broke* |
| *t* and *d* | final position, postvocalic, prepausal | *Have a seat.* | *Have a sea'.* |
| *t* and *d* | final position of an unstressed syllable | *waited* *bandit* | *waite'* *bandi'* |
| indefinite article *a* | preceding a word beginning with a vowel | *an apple* | *a apple* |

From Bryen, D.N., Hartman, C., and Tait, P.E. *Variant English: An introduction to language variation.* Columbus, Ohio: Charles E. Merrill, 1978, p. 248. Used with the permission of the publisher.

TABLE 7.3   Summary of Morphological Features in Variant English

| Feature | Linguistic Context | Standard English | Variant English |
|---|---|---|---|
| plural marker deletion | regular nouns | *beds* | *bed'* |
| plural marker addition | irregular nouns | *feet* *women* | *feets* *womens* |
| reflexive pronoun | third person, singular | *himself* | *hisse'f* |
| reflexive pronoun | third person, plural | *themselves* | *deiuhse'ves* |
| possessive pronoun | first person, singular | *mine* | *mines* |
| possessive markers -s, -z, or -iz | | *boy's hat* | *boy' hat* |
| noun-verb agreement (-s, -z, or -iz) | third person, singular | *he runs* | *he run'* |
| noun-verb agreement (have, say, do) | third person, singular | *Mary has* | *Mary have* |
| past tense marker (-t, -z, -id) | phonological rules applied | *waited* *walked* *played ball* | *waite'* *walk'* *play' ball* |
| noun-verb agreement (was) | past tense | *you were* *they were* | *you was* *dey was* |

From Bryen, D.N., Hartman, C., and Tait, P.E. *Variant English: An introduction to language variation.* Columbus, Ohio: Charles E. Merrill, 1978, p. 249. Used with the permission of the publisher.

ter simplification is extended to a larger set of linguistic environments, such as postvocalic and preconsonantal (*I lef' i'*). Extension to a wider range of linguistic environments in variant English is seen with *t* and *d* deletions as well. These instances of extension are further support for replacing the dichotomous difference approach as a description of the differences between standard and variant English with a position viewing these differences along a continuum, which takes into account frequency, extent, and social significance of the variant features.

Let us turn briefly to the morphological and syntactic differences presented in Tables 7.3 and 7.4. Just as the phonological features have been discussed with respect to frequency, extent, and social significance, so too can the morphological and syntactic features. Certain features, such as variations in the pluralization of nouns, occur relatively infrequently. This is also true of the syntactic feature of embedded direct questions (*I wonder if he can come* ⟶ *I wonduh can he come*). In contrast, variant features affecting noun-verb agreement (*He comes* ⟶ *he come*) and multiple negation (*He doesn't like anyone* ⟶ *He don't like no one*) occur relatively frequently. This frequency of occurrence acts in concert with the social significance of the particular variant feature and affects our "categorical"

TABLE 7.4 Summary of Syntactic Features in Variant English

| Feature | Linguistic Context | Standard English | Variant English |
|---------|-------------------|------------------|-----------------|
| auxiliary verb deletion | contracted in standard English | *I'll see you there.* | *I' see you deuhe.* |
| *is, are* deletion | contracted in standard English | *She's sweeping. He's tall.* | *She' sweepin. He ta'.* |
| deletion of inversion of auxiliary verbs and copulas | direct question *yes/no* | *Do you swim?* | *'You swim?* |
| deletion of inverted auxiliary verbs and copulas | direct *wh-* question | *Who do you want?* | *Who you want?* |
| negation of *to be, to have* | present tense | *I'm not ready.* | *I ain't ready.* |
| negation of *to do* | past tense | *We didn't go.* | *We ain't go.* |
| multiple negation, indefinite before main verb | must negate indefinite; may negate main verb | *Nothing is ready.* | *Nofin is ready* or *Nofin ain't ready.* |
| multiple negation, indefinite after main verb | must negate main verb and indefinite | *He doesn't like anyone.* | *He don't like no one.* |
| embedded direct question | replace with direct question construction | *I wonder if the mail came.* | *I wonduh, di' de mai' come.* |
| conditional *if-then* deletion | conditionality expressed by word order only | *If he dies, I'll be sad.* | *He die', I' be sa'.* |
| nominative pronoun addition | follows the subject immediately | *My sister is pretty.* | *My sistuh, she' pretty.* |
| existential *it* | existential pronoun *there* | *There is smog today.* | *I' smog today.* |

From Bryen, D.N., Hartman, C., and Tait, P.E. *Variant English: An introduction to language variation.* Columbus, Ohio: Charles E. Merrill, 1978, p. 250. Used with the permission of the publisher.

perceptions concerning whether or not a person is a variant English speaker. Wolfram (1970, p. 259) has identified the following grammatical features as being of high social significance:

1. Third person singular -*s* (*He go'*).
2. Multiple negation (*didn't do nothin*).
3. Possessive *'s* (*man' hat*).
4. Invariant *be* (*He be home*).
5. Copula absence (*She' nice*).
6. Existential *it* (*It was a whole lot of people*).

The social significance of these features is an attitudinal reality despite the observation that these features range in occurrence from infrequent to highly frequent.

Again, the extension of particular grammatical features in variant English undermines the dichotomous view of differences existing between standard and variant English. For example, Bryen, Hartman, and Tait (1978) suggest that variant pronouns, such as *hisse'f* (*himself*), *dieuhse'ves* (*themselves*), and *mines* (*mine*) reflect not a qualitative divergence from pronominal usage in standard English but rather an extension and regularization of standard English pronouns. Similarly, it is quite apparent that the deletion of auxiliary verbs and copulas when forming direct questions is not restricted to variant English. Deletion of these features occurs quite frequently in standard English as well (e.g., *You finished?*). The important difference is that this deletion occurs more frequently in variant English, in a wider range of linguistic environments and in a wider range of social contexts (both formal and informal situations).

To summarize, the features of variant English presented in this section not only contrast to those of standard English, they also vary in their frequency and social significance. The extent of the variance from standard English and the frequency of its occurrence are what influences our perceptions concerning where a person falls along the variant to standard English continuum. The educational implications of this linguistic variance are of critical importance and are considered in the following section.

## EDUCATIONAL IMPLICATIONS OF DIALECT VARIATION

Lack of understanding of language in general and of dialect variations in particular has led to a number of educational problems. First, and perhaps foremost, of these has been the negative attitudes held by teachers toward both the speaker and the speech of variant English. It is not unusual for teachers, for whom standard English is the primary dialect, to judge a socially less prestigious dialect as "incorrect." (This misconception has already been discussed as the first myth about variant English.) Teachers' misconceptions about the nature of language are evident from the following teacher reports concerning the language of their variant-speaking students (Shuy, 1970, p. 124):

"Their grammar problems are many. They use *dis* for *this.*"

"I think that they are in the habit of not saying the things as clearly as we do and they say a word as 'looking' by leaving the *g* off."

In the first of these statements, the teacher's confusion of pronunciation features and grammatical constructions is obvious, and confusion between written language (i.e., graphemes) and spoken language (phonemes) is evident in the second.

Misconceptions about how dialects are similar and how they vary are evident in the following two teacher reports (Shuy, 1970, p. 123):

"The biggest problem that I've had so far is 'I'm gonna.' "

"When I say 'Where can I get a pencil?' they will answer, 'Here it goes.' It's hard for them to say 'Here it is.' "

In the first statement, the teacher erroneously attributed the intentive construction *I'm gonna* only to speakers of variant English, failing to recognize that this feature is also present in standard English. In contrast, the teacher who made the second statement does not recognize that several different lexical items can represent the same phenomenon (i.e., *is* and *goes*) and that lexical variation is one way in which dialects do vary.

These misconceptions about language and dialect variations are not confined to teachers' reports concerning their students' language "problems." Negative attitudes affect teacher-student interactions in the classroom. Teacher's remarks, such as *I don't understand what you are saying* or *Speak more clearly* or *Don't say that as dat, it's that* are not unusual. Comments such as these are likely to result in potentially troublesome teacher-student relationships. The teacher may devalue the child's language, and this devaluation may lead to a spread effect and a self-fulfilling prophecy concerning both the child's linguistic abilities and cognitive capabilities. This problem is especially likely if the teacher subscribes to the second myth described earlier. Also, children who are frequently confronted by negative feedback from teachers concerning their communicative efforts are likely to view the classroom environment as an essentially hostile one. As a result, these youngsters may feel that the safest course is to use a minimum of language in the classroom. Their exercising this option is likely to reinforce another commonly held misconception about the linguistic abilities of speakers of variant English, that is, that these youngsters are close to nonverbal (another aspect of the verbal deficit hypothesis).

It is therefore essential that all educators have an accurate knowledge of the phonological, grammatical, lexical, and communicative features characteristic of the dialect varieties of English, for each educator is a potential teacher of variant-speaking students (Ford et al., 1976). Without this knowledge, negative attitudes will continue to produce troublesome classroom interactions, lowered teacher expectations, and even misdiagnoses concerning language, reading, and writing deviations.

**DIAGNOSIS OF LANGUAGE AND COGNITIVE PROBLEMS**   Without an accurate knowledge of the phonological, grammatical, lexical, and communicative characteristics of variant English, teachers are likely to make faulty educational diagnoses and instructional decisions concerning many youngsters. This is especially true in light of the fact that most standardized achievement, aptitude, and diagnostic tests are both language mediated and based on standard English (see Bryen, Hartman, & Tait, 1978 and Wolfram & Fasold, 1974 for a further discussion of test bias). Even informal educational judgments and decisions may be erroneously influenced by misconceptions about the nature of variant English, since conscious and unconscious notions about what a person is like are frequently based on one's reactions to the way a person talks. These misconceptions may lead not only to inaccurate judgments and diagnoses, but also to faulty instructional practices. Dillard (1972, p. 312, parentheses added) describes this problem as it relates to instructors' mistaken notions concerning pronunciation differences:

> Pronunciation problems of Black children have motivated some of the greatest pedagogical blunders of all. Speech correctionists, mistaking pronunciation patterns of . . . (variant English) for genuine deficiencies . . . have extended their own practices to areas in which they are not applicable. Black children who already do so quite well are "taught" to make sounds like "oom" in weekly practice sessions.

Similar confusions have arisen in the areas of auditory discrimination (Politzer, 1971; Bryen, 1976), grammatical abilities (Waddell & Cahoon, 1970; Bereiter & Engelmann, 1966), and communicative style (Foster, 1974).

Teachers may make erroneous evaluations of a child's cognitive abilities and disabilities as a result of their lack of knowledge of variant English. Bryen, Hartman, and Tait (1978, p. 17) provide the following transcript to illustrate how faulty judgments concerning the concepts of plurality, temporality, possession, negation, and conditionality might be made:

> I ain' nevuh gonna trus' her agin wif my chilren. Las' night dey almos' kill' deyselve when she was 'pose to be watchin' dem. My two kid mean too much to me. My kid' lives mo' impo'tan' dan anytin to me. 'Sump'n happen to dem, I nevuh fo'give myself.

Someone unfamiliar with this dialect is likely to conclude that the speaker has problems understanding the concept of negation due to the use of double negatives (*ain' nevuh*) and lacks conditional logic due to the absence of the *if-then* construction (*Sump'n happen to dem, I nevuh fo'give myself*). The absence of the plural, past tense, and possessive markers may lead to the false assumption that these concepts are not possessed.

Informal discussions with educators reinforce the conclusion that faulty decisions are being made concerning the cognitive abilities of variant English–speaking students. Teachers fail to recognize that the possession of basic concepts is not dependent on the expression of these concepts via standard English linguistic structures.

**READING AND VARIANT ENGLISH** Since reading is essentially a language-based process, it is not surprising that problems exist in the instruction of reading with youngsters who speak a variant dialect. Shuy (1975), for example, found that teachers do confuse dialect differences with reading errors. Their confusion is likely to be the result of two basic shortcomings—a lack of knowledge concerning variant English and a misperception about the reading process itself. Traditionally, reading has been viewed either as a visually-based process (e.g., Orton, 1925; 1937) or as a speech-based process (e.g., Downing, 1973; Elkonin, 1973; Mattingly, 1972; Savin, 1972). Those who emphasize the role of speech in the reading process argue that learning to read is essentially establishing the phonetic or sound representations of the printed symbols (i.e., establishing a phoneme-grapheme relationship). (See Chapter 8 for a further discussion of this approach to reading.) However, a number of psychologists (e.g., Smith, 1971; Vellutino, 1977) argue persuasively that it is unlikely that one can derive meaning from printed symbols if they are only mediated through speech, that is, pronunciation. These psychologists instead suggest that reading is a cognitive and linguistic process, whereby the meaning of a word is triggered by its spelling and the grammatical context of the sentence.

Due to the phonological features of variant English, the letter-sound correspondences are slightly different for the variant speaker than for the standard English speaker. Therefore, written passages are likely to be pronounced differently when they are orally read. For example, consider the following written passage:

> The boy walked around the corner to the store. He had two dimes to buy two balls.

A speaker of variant English might read this passage orally in the following manner:

> *De boy walk 'roun' de couhnuh to de stouh. He ha' two dime' to buy two ba'.*

Some of the orally read deviations in pronunciation, such as *de* and *stouh,* are likely to be ignored, because they are seen as unimportant in comprehending the printed passage. Others, such as reading *walk* for *walked* (pronounced *wakt*) and *dime* for *dimes,* might be judged as reading errors. Variant English phonological differences (e.g., simplification of certain consonant clusters, such as *-kt* in *wakt* yielding *walk*) and morphological features (e.g., plural *-s* deletion) result in these oral deviations from the printed text. These oral deviations may lead the teacher to the following faulty assumption: If the child does not pronounce *ed* and *s,* then she is not comprehending the meanings of pastness and plurality symbolized by these two visual configurations.

In reality, the child reading in the manner indicated above has actually accomplished the task demanded of her. She has comprehended the visual code and has orally read it using her own linguistic system. One might understandably ask why the child assumes that *ed* and *s* have no spoken counterpart. According to Bryen, Hartman, and Tait (1978, p. 20), "all children learn quickly that a one-to-one correspondence rarely exists between letters and sounds." Such words as *know, though, straight,* and *two* illustrate this point. The variant English speaker has also learned that *walk* and *walked* are homonyms, that is, while they are pronounced the same, they vary in meaning. Homonyms occur in variant, as well as in standard, English. What creates confusion is that most teachers are familiar with homonyms of standard English, shown below, but not with those of variant English.

1. *to, two, too*
2. *cents, sense*
3. *meat, meet*
4. *knew, new*
5. *him, hymn*
6. *seem, seam*
7. *so, sew*
8. *their, there*

Only a teacher familiar with the characteristics of variant English would be able to recognize that *walk* and *walked* are homonyms to a variant English speaker. Knowledge of the linguistic features of variant English and of the processes involved in reading should minimize the mistaking of reading deviations for reading errors.

As a result of existing dialect differences and their possible interference with the process of reading, several instructional alternatives have been suggested. The search for other approaches to the teaching of reading was hastened in the early 1970s when research uncovered evidence of dialect interference when speakers of variant English faced the task of reading standard English texts. (See Hooper & Powell, 1971; Jones, 1973; Osser, Wang, & Zaid, 1969; Ames, Rosen, & Olson, 1971; Bartel & Axelrod, 1973; Rosen & Ames, 1972.)

In response to these findings and in recognition of the existence of variant English, several linguists (e.g., Baratz, 1969a; 1969b; 1970; Fasold & Shuy, 1970) suggested that dialect-based readers be developed to be used for beginning reading instruction. The rationale behind this suggested approach is that the divergence between standard and variant English is large enough to warrant the use of separate reading materials. In this way, variant English–speaking children are not faced with learning to decode a written language system that is poorly matched with the sounds and grammatical constructions of their spoken language system. This position, while logical, has been criticized at several levels. For example, Venezky and Chapman (1973) and Somerville (1975) criticized those who opposed the use of traditional orthography, arguing that the orthographical system presently used puts speakers of variant English at no greater disadvantage than standard dialect speakers. Somerville (1975, p. 255) noted that "all children, regardless of native dialect, are expected to learn words that are not spelled phonetically." Extending this logic, the same point can be made against those (e.g., Stewart, 1969) who propose maintaining the standard spelling but representing variant grammatical constructions in the printed text. Their rationale is that there is a greater mismatch between the linguistic code of printed materials and spoken variant English than between the former and spoken standard English. There is no doubt that spoken variant English differs from the linguistic code represented in printed standard English. There is also little doubt that spoken standard English differs from the written linguistic code. Written language, in general, is a more formal, less contextually-bound linguistic register. The question that does remain is whether or not the differences between written standard English and spoken variant English are great enough to impede the variant speaker from learning to read.

A second major objection to reading materials written in variant English comes not from linguists or reading specialists, but from educational consumers in the black community. Hoover (1975) has shown that while spoken black English is highly valued by many in the black community, black parents do not want their children to learn to read materials written in black English. Instead, they want their children to receive reading instruction in standard black English, which is characterized by standard grammatical patterns combined with the phonological features of black English, such as intonation and pronunciation (Ford et al., 1976).

Another approach to the teaching of reading advocated by some linguists and educators is that of dialect reading of existing standard English materials. Somewhat more responsive to recommendations coming from the black community (Hoover, 1975), this approach calls for speakers of variant English to be taught using existing standard English texts, but to be guided or encouraged to translate the printed symbols into their spoken linguistic system. This translation includes variant pronunciation, grammatical constructions, and even lexical items. In support of this approach to the teaching of reading, Goodman (1968) found that only fluent readers demonstrate dialect translations while reading orally. He argued that an "actual translation process will begin to emerge in which the dialect of the material is translated into the dialect of the reader" (Goodman, 1968, p. 43), if less emphasis is placed on specific sound-symbol deviations.

If educators are to help guide children in translating the linguistic code of the written material into the spoken dialect, they must be aware of the mismatches existing between the two. This is true whether the reader speaks a standard or a variant dialect. For a standard dialect, most educators are already familiar with the various matches and mismatches existing between the two linguistic codes. They know that written standard English deviates to a certain extent from spoken standard English with respect to function, contextual abstractness, and style

(Goodman & Goodman, 1977). The dialect of standard written materials also deviates from spoken variant English, yet without knowledge of variant English the educator is probably unfamiliar with these deviations. For example, the letter-sound correspondences are slightly different for the variant dialect speaker than for the standard dialect speaker. If educators are to guide children in using these correspondences as one reading strategy, they must be aware of these differences. Several of these variant letter-sound correspondences appear in Table 7.5.

While being aware of the differences of the two language systems and recognizing that reading is not a speech process, educators should encourage readers to translate from the dialect of the written materials to the readers' dialect. Knowledge of the phonological and grammatical rules of variant English may enable educators to do this and may minimize the likelihood of their confusing dialect translations with reading errors. For example, knowledge of the consonant simplification feature (see Table 7.3) may enable the educator to recognize that when a child reads *walked* (pronounced *wakt*) as *walk* (pronounced *wak*) he is treating the two words as homonyms. The child thus does recognize the difference in meaning between the two words that are spoken the same. The educator may determine that the meanings are successfully differentiated by asking comprehension questions. Variant phonological features are responsible for many hom-

TABLE 7.5   Letter-sound Correspondences in Standard and Variant English

| Letters | Sounds in Standard English | Sounds in Variant English |
|---|---|---|
| s | /z/ as in *Mary's balloon* | φ as in *Mary' balloon* |
|  | /s/ as in *three cents* | φ as in *tree cint'* |
| th | /th/ as in *thin* | /t/ as *tin* |
|  | /th/ as in *death* | /f/ as *deaf* |
|  | /th/ as in *the* | /d/ as *de* |
|  | /th/ as in *brother* | /v/ as in *brovuh* or *d* as in *broduh* |
|  | /th/ as in *bathe* | /v/ as in *bave* |
| -ng | /ŋ/ as in *doing, singing* | /n/ as in *doin, singin* |
| -e + n | /i/ as in *open* | /i/ as in *open* |
|  | /e/ as in *pen* | /i/ as in *pin* |
| -er | /er/ as in *runner, father* | /uh/ as in *runnuh* and *faduh* |
| -st | /st/ as in *rest, mist* | /s/ as in *res', mis'* |
| -sed | /zd/ as in *raised* | /z/ as in *raise'* |
| -ked | /kt/ as in *walked* | /k/ as in *walk'* |
| -ned | /nd/ as in *stoned* | /n/ as in *stone'* |
| -r | /r/ as in *star* | /uh/ as in *stauh* |
| -ll | /l/ as in *toll* | φ as in *to'* |

From Bryen, D.N., Hartman, C., and Tait, P.E. *Variant English: An introduction to language variation.* Columbus, Ohio: Charles E. Merrill, 1978, p. 205. Used with the permission of the publisher.

TABLE 7.6   Some Homonyms in Variant English

| Feature | Examples |
|---|---|
| Vowel variations | *pin = pen* |
| | *boil = ball* |
| | *beer = bear* |
| *th-* sounds | *then = den* |
| | *through = true* |
| | *clothe = clove* |
| | *Ruth = roof* |
| *l* deletions | *fault = fought* |
| | *toll = toe* |
| *r* deletions | *shore = show* |
| | *tore = toe* |
| Consonant cluster simplification | *mist = miss* |
| | *missed = miss* |
| | *an = and* |
| | *blamed = blame* |
| *-t* and *-d* deletions | *state = stay* |
| | *fad = fat* |
| | *road = row* |
| Third person noun-verb agreement | *runs = run* |

onyms in variant English with which many educators may be unfamiliar. Several of these homonyms are presented in Table 7.6.

To summarize, it is suggested here that there is nothing inherent in the reading materials themselves to place the speaker of variant English at a greater disadvantage in learning to read than a speaker of standard English. What is being argued here is that the reading instruction given by educators who are unfamiliar with variant English may be the critical problem. Misguided "corrections" and undue emphasis given to the role of speech in determining the meaning of the printed word may lead the student to the conclusion that reading is an arbitrary process bearing little relationship to familiar spoken language.

**WRITING AND VARIANT ENGLISH**   Writing, like reading, is a language-related process, and consequently dialect translations also occur in it. This is especially true of the mechanics of writing (i.e., spelling, grammar, and usage). It should be noted that speaking a variant dialect should not interfere with the ability to produce a good written composition characterized by a controlling idea, coherence and unity of content, and adequate organization and sequencing of ideas. However, deviations in spelling, grammar, and usage as results of variant phonological, grammatical, and stylistic features are to be expected.

Spelling, for example, may be especially difficult for variant English speakers if they do not have a knowledgeable educator who can guide them in making the relationship between the spoken word and its conventional standardized graphic representation. In both standard and variant English, a one-to-one correspondence between the phoneme (sound) and the grapheme (written symbol) does not exist. Therefore, learning to spell should not be inherently more difficult for the speaker of a variant dialect. When learning to spell, all youngsters will attempt to accomplish the spelling of words by imposing a letter-sound relationship even when this strategy alone is insufficient. As a result, spelling errors such as *sine* for *sign* and *new* for *knew* commonly occur. However, these errors usually arouse little concern because it is apparent that they are the result of attempts to derive the spelling from its spoken counterpart. In these cases, youngsters need to be taught that the spelling system is more than a written representation of how words are pronounced.

Consider, on the other hand, the variant English speaker who makes the following spelling errors: *skits* for *skirts, saw* for *sore, tes* for *test,* and *goin* for *going.* Without a knowledge of the phonological features of variant English, a teacher may conclude that these spelling attempts represent seemingly unsystematic errors rather than dialect-based sound-letter correspondences. Therefore, educators, who have a knowledge of variant phonological features, recognize the many homonyms in variant English, and realize that letter-sound relationships are not always reliable clues to spelling, should be able to guide variant-speaking youngsters in learning how to spell. (See Bryen, Hartman, & Tait, 1978, pp. 215–18 for further discussion of spelling.)

The mechanics of writing also include writing grammatically "correct" sentences. Bryen, Hartman, and Tait (1978, p. 218) suggest that, because speakers of variant English may use divergent syntactic and morphological features in their spoken language, "they may be excessively penalized when they use these same structures in their writing." Analyzing the writing of black urban youngsters, Ross (1976) and Bryen, Hartman, and Tait (1978) identified several features of variant English frequently occurring in their writing. These features are presented in Table 7.7. In informal writing, such as letters to friends, these dialect-based grammatical features should cause no problems. However, as students become more aware of situational appropriateness, they should be guided to switch to a more formal, standard code of writing. This process should present no inherent problem since learning to write entails the usage of a more formal, deliberate, and somewhat constrained style of language. Fortunately, as Goodman and Goodman (1977, p. 322) note, "written language can be polished and perfected before it is read." (Unlike spoken language, which is temporal, written language is spatial and allows deliberate monitoring.) Therefore, the variant English speaker can be deliberately sensitized to include in writings the more formal and standard grammatical features.

To summarize, there may be some interference by variant features when youngsters who speak a variant dialect begin to learn written language. However, this interference should only affect the mechanical aspects of writing, such as

TABLE 7.7   Dialect-based Grammatical Interference in Writing

| Feature | Written Response |
|---|---|
| Zero copula | *She a nice person.* |
| Subject-verb agreement | *She have a pleasant smile.* |
| Absence of plural marker | *The feeling of other people . . .* |
| Absence of past tense marker | *They offer me . . .* |
| Absence of possessive marker | *This is Joan coat.* |
| *If* construction | *I ask him was he hungry.* |
| Pronominal predicate markers | *The man who had a fight, he . . .* |

From Bryen, D.N., Hartman, C., and Tait, P.E. *Variant English: An introduction to language variation.* Columbus, Ohio: Charles E. Merrill, 1978, p. 219. Used with the permission of the publisher.

spelling and grammar. With proper guidance by someone who understands both the characteristics of variant English and that spelling is more than a simple sound-symbol relationship, learning to use the conventional spelling system of English should present no greater problem to the speaker of variant English than it does to the speaker of standard English. Similarly, guiding the variant dialect speaker to incorporate standard grammar and usage in his written language should present no inherent difficulty. All children learning to write must realize that it is a slightly different and more formal register of language—one that requires a shift of consciousness from an "immediate audience that shares the learner's experiences and frame of reference (including linguistic style) to a larger, abstract, and unfamiliar audience" (Elasser & John-Steiner, 1977, p. 358, parentheses added).

## TEACHING STANDARD ENGLISH

A recurring question is that of whether or not the schools should be responsible for teaching standard English to speakers of a variant dialect. Although it is beyond the scope of this chapter to explicate all of the issues surrounding this controversy, several critical ones should be highlighted.

If some of the myths concerning the linguistic inferiority of variant English have been dispelled here, then it is not necessary to even consider calls for the eradication of variant English and its replacement by standard English. Similarly, if the position is correct that speaking a variant dialect should present no inherent problems in learning to read and write, then there is little instructional support for the teaching of standard English to variant speakers. The only remaining rationale for teaching standard English comes from neither a linguistic nor an educational perspective but rather from a sociopolitical one. Several linguists have argued that variant English is an adequate linguistic system, but is socially stigmatizing. Therefore, its use may lead to poorer school, job, and career opportunities. There is some support for this view. For example, Shuy (1972) and Johnson

(1971) demonstrate that teachers have negative attitudes toward variant English. Such negative attitudes may result in lower teacher expectations concerning the capabilities of variant-speaking youngsters. To compound the problem of negative attitudes, Shuy, Baratz, and Wolfram (1969), Williams and Whitehead (1971), and Velletutti (1971) found that the use of a variant dialect is one of the most telling and stereotyping clues to an individual's racial or social origins. Therefore, as Bryen, Hartman, and Tait (1978) suggest, teacher expectations may be further influenced by latent or manifest prejudices toward particular social or racial groups. Shuy, Baratz, and Wolfram (1969) and Caselli (1970) identify the same attitudinal problems affecting employment opportunities.

On the basis of these findings, one could logically argue that social and political benefits are accrued by students who are taught standard English as a second dialect. However, several cautionary comments must be made regarding such an argument. First, is the basis for negative attitudes toward speakers of a variant dialect linguistic in nature or sociocultural? If the basis is sociocultural prejudice, then removing the symptom (i.e., the variant language features) should do little to change these prejudices. If, on the other hand, the origins of these negative attitudes are linguistic, then two options exist: (1) provide educators and employers with information about the nature and significance of dialect variation or (2) teach standard English to speakers of variant English. One may argue that the first option is utopian, unrealistic, or even un-American. However, the second approach, that of teaching for bidialectism, may be equally unrealistic. Results of studies documenting attempts to teach standard English as a second dialect do not show much promise (see Lin, 1965; Rystrom, 1969; 1970; Gladney, 1968; Kievman, 1969). Dialects and languages are resilient to change because they are cultural institutions. They are reflections of cultural loyalty and are carriers of communal traditions. Consequently, the time and effort required to teach standard English may be prodigious, and the results may be quite negligible.

In summary, whether we choose to teach standard English as a second dialect or accept variant dialects as just another aspect of the richness of cultural diversity, our decisions must be based on knowledge not myth. Therefore, understanding the nature and defining features of variant dialects is critical. The following inquiries are designed to provide a deeper understanding of variant English.

_____                    **INQUIRY 7.1**                    _____

Dialect variation is influenced by the geographical region in which a person is raised. Regional variations in dialect may include differences in lexicon (vocabulary), phonology (speech-sounds, stress, and intonation), and grammar.

**OBJECTIVE**   The objective of this inquiry is to study how geographical region is likely to affect dialect variation.

**PROCEDURES**   Select two youngsters of approximately the same age who were raised in two different geographical regions (e.g., Southern and Mid-Atlantic). Present each of the children individually with the following sentences to imitate.

**(1)**  *She walked along the street.*

**(2)**  *I asked him if he was hungry.*

**(3)**  *She runs two miles every day.*

**(4)**  *I will never do anything bad.*

**(5)**  *John wants an apple to eat.*

**(6)**  *His shirts are always good looking on him.*

**(7)**  *The man said, "This car is mine and that car is yours.*

**(8)**  *He doesn't like anyone but himself.*

**(9)**  *If you hit me, I'll tell my brother.*

**(10)**  *There is always a lot of traffic during rush hour.*

Tape-record their imitations and transcribe the recording, attempting to represent accurately pronunciation, vocabulary, and grammar.

**REPORT**   Include the following in your report:

1. Brief descriptions of the two children, including the geographical region in which they were raised.
2. Transcripts of their imitations of the stimulus sentences.

In addition, address yourself to the following questions:

1. What phonological differences, if any, were evident in the two children's imitations? (Use Table 7.2 as a guide.)
2. What lexical or grammatical differences, if any, were noticeable in the two children's imitations? (Use Tables 7.3 and 7.4 as guides.)
3. What linguistic features are most likely to differentiate the two speakers? Consider the issues of presence, frequency, and social significance of particular variant features.
4. Which of the two children do you consider to be a speaker of standard English and why?

**EVALUATION**   Did this inquiry develop the specified objectives? If so, how? If not, why? How could the effectiveness of this inquiry be increased?

———————                **INQUIRY 7.2**                ———————

Sociocultural group membership influences where an individual falls on the standard–variant English continuum. This refers to one's ethnic as well as socioeconomic class membership. Because social class and ethnicity are often closely interrelated, it is difficult to study each of these influences independently.

**OBJECTIVES**   The objectives of this inquiry are to:

1. Analyze how sociocultural group membership influences dialect variation.
2. Identify the linguistic features that differentiate two speakers who are members of different sociocultural groups.

**PROCEDURES**   Select two youngsters of approximately the same age who are members of different sociocultural groups. Your determination of sociocultural group membership should take into account both ethnicity and social class. Follow the procedures described in Inquiry 7.1.

**REPORT**   Include the following in your report:

1. Brief descriptions of the two children, including their sociocultural group membership (e.g., black, urban, middle-class).
2. Transcripts of their imitations of the stimulus sentences.

In addition, address yourself to the following questions:

1. What phonological differences, if any, were evident in the two youngsters' sentence imitations? (See Table 7.2.)
2. What lexical or grammatical differences, if any, were noticeable in the two children's imitations of the stimulus sentences? (Tables 7.3 and 7.4 can be used as guides.)
3. What linguistic (i.e., phonological, lexical, grammatical) features most obviously differentiated the two speakers?
4. On the basis of the presence or absence of particular variant English features, where do each of the two youngsters fall on the standard–variant English continuum? In arriving at your decision, take into account the frequency, nature, and social significance of the variant linguistic features.

**EVALUATION**   Did this inquiry develop the specified objectives? If so, how? If not, why? How could the effectiveness of this inquiry be increased?

_____                       **INQUIRY 7.3**                       _____

Interindividual variation in language is influenced by both regional and sociocultural factors. Another influence on language is the social context of the interaction. This factor influences how language varies for the same individual (i.e., intraindividual variation) in different social contexts. In learning language, all youngsters learn that certain linguistic features that are appropriate in one context may be socially stigmatized in a less familiar, more formal context. The more formal the context is, the more likely it is that individuals will monitor their speech, replacing socially stigmatizing features with more standard, prestigious forms. The ability to adapt one's language to the perceived social requirements of the situation is referred to as stylistic variation. Variant English speakers, especially adolescents and women (Labov, 1966; Wolfram & Fasold, 1974), engage in stylistic variation by increased movement of their language towards the standard end of the standard–variant English continuum as they perceive the social context to be more formal and less familiar.

**OBJECTIVES**   The objectives of this inquiry are to:

1. Observe intraindividual variation in language, given various social contexts.
2. Study the influence of the social context on the presence of variant English features.

**PROCEDURES**   Select an adolescent youngster who speaks variant English to interact in two social situations: (1) a discussion with you (more formal, less familiar) and (2) a spontaneous discussion with a peer (less formal, more familiar). Tape-record the interactions occurring in both social contexts to be transcribed at a later time.

**REPORT**   Include the following in your report:

1. Brief descriptions of the adolescent and the two social contexts.
2. Transcripts of the two interactions.

In addition, address yourself to the following questions:

1. What was the difference, if any, in the presence of variant English phonological features in each of the two social contexts?
2. What was the difference, if any, in the presence of variant English grammatical features?
3. In what ways might the social context influence where a person falls on the standard–variant English continuum? In addressing this question, consider the particular features, their frequency, and social significance.

**EVALUATION**   Did the inquiry develop the specified objectives? If so, how? If not, why? How could the effectiveness of this inquiry be increased?

<hr>

## INQUIRY 7.4

<hr>

Speakers of variant English frequently exhibit dialect translations when they read materials written in standard English. Goodman (1968) suggests that these dialect translations are not reading errors, as was previously thought, but rather translations of the dialect of the written material into the dialect of the speaker. This translation phenomenon is a sign that the process of reading has been accomplished.

**OBJECTIVES**   The objectives of the inquiry are to:

1. Analyze the difference between dialect translations and true oral reading errors.
2. Analyze the relationship between dialect translations in oral reading and reading comprehension.

**PROCEDURES**   Identify two children who are variant English speakers and who have begun the reading process. It is preferable to have these children reading at different levels. Select several reading passages at the appropriate reading level for each child. Have the children independently read the passages out loud. Tape-record each of the children as they read and follow their reading with comprehension questions. Transcribe the recordings and analyze whether deviations from the printed passage represent dialect translations or reading errors. Reading errors are noted by placing an *X* on them and dialect translations are circled. The following is an example of a reading passage and analyses (Bryen, Hartman, & Tait, 1978, p. 210):

### Reading Passage

It was a fine day to be in the park. Two boys went there early to see the animals. But first they played ball with another boy. Then they took a long ride in a small boat. At last they went to a big building, which was called the zoo. But it was not open. So they did not see any of the animals that day.

### Student 1

It was a fine day to be in the park. Two boys (wint)(dere) early to see the animals. But first (dey)(play) ball (wif)(nother) boy. (Den)(dey) took a long ride in a small boat. At (las)(dey)(wint) to a big buildin which was called the zoo. But it was not open. So (dey) did not see any of the animals (dat) day.

### Student 2

It was a fu🗙ey day to be in the park. Two boys w🗙t th🗙e early to see the animals. But first (dey) played ball (wif) a🗙y boy. D🗙t (dey) took a ride in a small boat. At last (dey) wa🗙ed to a big bu🗙ny which (were) called the zoo. But it was not open. So d🗙t did not see any of the animals (dat) day.

**REPORT**   Include the following in your report:

1. A brief description of each child, including age and approximate reading level.
2. A transcript of each child's oral reading, with your analysis differentiating dialect translations from reading errors.
3. The comprehension questions you presented to each child and the responses to these questions.

In addition, address yourself to the following questions:

1. What evidence was there for the presence of dialect translations versus true reading errors? How did you decide that deviations from the printed page were dialect translations versus reading errors?
2. What was the relationship between each child's oral reading ability and reading comprehension?
3. How do dialect translations in oral reading affect reading comprehension?

**EVALUATION**   Did this inquiry develop the specified objectives? If so, how? If not, why? How could the effectiveness of this inquiry be increased?

——————   INQUIRY 7.5   ——————

Dialect differences not only may affect oral reading, but may influence certain aspects of writing. For example, variant phonological features may result in variations in spelling, because the sound-symbol relationship differs from that in standard English. Similarly, variant morphological and syntactic features may also be manifested in written language.

**OBJECTIVES**   The objectives of this inquiry are to:

1. Analyze how variant phonological features affect spelling.
2. Analyze how variant morphological features affect the grammar of written language.

**PROCEDURES**   Select four third- or fourth-grade youngsters, two who speak standard English and two who speak variant English. Using the stimulus sentences presented in Inquiry 7.1, dictate them to each youngster individually. The child's task is to write each of the dictated sentences. After all four children have completed the dictation task, analyze their written responses. In doing so, note deviations in punctuation and capitalization, as well as in spelling and grammar.

**REPORT**   Include the following in your report:

1. A brief description of each youngster, including age and primary dialect spoken.
2. The written sentences that were dictated by the examiner.

3. Your analysis of all errors of spelling, punctuation, grammar, and so on.

In addition, address yourself to the following questions:

1. What differences, if any, were there among the error patterns of the four students?
2. What evidence did you find, if any, of dialect-based spelling errors? How did you arrive at the decision that the spelling errors were dialect-based?
3. What evidence did you find, if any, of dialect-based grammatical deviations? How did you arrive at the decision that these were dialect-based?
4. Evaluate this statement: A speaker of variant English faces no inherently greater disadvantage in learning to write than a speaker of standard English faces.

**EVALUATION**   Did this inquiry develop the specified objectives? If so, how? If not, why? How could the effectiveness of this inquiry be increased?

---                              **INQUIRY 7.6**                              ---

It has been suggested that speakers of variant English are overly penalized for utilizing variant features in their written language. One reason for this overpenalization may be that confusion exists concerning the difference between a mechanically correct written composition and a logical, well-developed, and coherent written composition. The position taken here is that speakers of variant English should have no greater difficulty learning to write a logical, well-developed, and coherent written composition than do speakers of standard English. Problems may arise, however, when speakers of variant English are expected to write a mechanically correct composition, that is, one which stresses standard grammar and usage.

**OBJECTIVES**   The objectives of this inquiry are to:

1. Analyze the difference between a logical, well-developed, and coherent written composition and a mechanically correct one.
2. Analyze how speaking a variant dialect may affect writing a composition.

**PROCEDURES**   Select two adolescents who have developed writing skills, one who speaks variant English and one who speaks a standard dialect. Choose an interesting topic or theme and have each student write a brief composition. Topics such as the value of gangs or solving family problems are usually of high interest. Analyze each of the compositions, utilizing two general criteria: (1) quality of the composition, including the identification of the theme and the coherency of the thematic development and (2) the mechanical correctness of the composition.

**REPORT**   Include the following in your report:

1. Brief descriptions of the two youngsters, including their ages and the dialect primarily spoken by each.
2. Both of the written compositions.

In addition, address yourself to the following questions:

1. What differences were demonstrated between the ability to write a well-developed written composition and a mechanically correct one?
2. What evidence did you find, if any, of dialect-based "errors" in spelling, grammar, or usage? How did you arrive at the decision that these mechanical "errors" were dialect-based?
3. Evaluate this statement: A speaker of variant English faces no inherently greater disadvantage in producing written language than a speaker of standard English faces.

**EVALUATION**   Did this inquiry develop the specified objectives? If so, how? If not, why? How could the effectiveness of this inquiry be increased?

## INQUIRY 7.7

The formality of the context affects intraindividual variation regarding the presence of variant, less prestigious features. Clearly, people are more conscious of their language when they are reading and even more so when they are writing than when informally speaking. For this reason, reading and writing situations are considered more formal than speaking situations. Therefore, one is likely to find fewer features of variant English in reading and writing contexts than in speaking ones.

**OBJECTIVES**   The objectives of this inquiry are to:

1. Compare the presence of variant English features in three contexts: speaking, reading, and writing.
2. Evaluate the relationship between speaking a variant dialect and being literate in standard English.

**PROCEDURES**   Identify two youngsters between the ages of ten and sixteen who are considered to be speakers of variant English. Each of these youngsters should participate in three language contexts: (1) spoken interaction, (2) oral reading, and (3) writing a brief composition. For the spoken language context, have the two youngsters discuss a topic of common interest. Tape-record their discussion, transcribe it, and then analyze the transcripts, considering the presence or absence of variant English phonological, morphological, and syntactic features. For the reading context, follow the procedures described in Inquiry 7.4. For the written language context, follow the procedures outlined in Inquiry 7.6.

**REPORT**   Include the following in your report:

1. Brief descriptions of the two youngsters, including their ages and reading levels.
2. The transcripts of the spoken language interactions, the reading passages used, and the transcripts of the oral readings.
3. The written compositions.

In addition, address yourself to the following questions:

1. What evidence was there for the presence of variant English features in each of the three language contexts?
2. How does the formality of the context affect the presence of variant English features?
3. Evaluate the commonly held belief that, in order to learn to read and write, one needs to speak standard English.

**EVALUATION**   Did this inquiry develop the specified objectives? If so, how? If not, why? How could the effectiveness of this inquiry be increased?

# 8

# Language and Reading: A Multidimensional Model

... to completely analyze what we do when we read would almost be the acme of a psychologist's achievements, for it would be to describe very many of the most intricate workings of the human mind, as well as to unravel the tangled story of the most remarkable specific performance that civilization has learned in all its history. [Huey, 1968, p. 6]

What is reading? You could try to answer this question through introspection while you are reading. For example, you could try the following exercise (Gibson & Levin, 1975, p. 460):

Read the following sentence and consider, as best you can, the skills and knowledge activated by your mind in its attempt to read: "Scholars have often wondered whether the concept palingenesis is related to the meta-theory of developmental psychology."

So, you have read the sentence. Or perhaps, did you just skim it to see if it was really worth reading? Maybe you decided its content was so uninteresting or its level of difficulty so demanding that it was not worth the effort of a detailed analysis. True, it is not an especially creative or poetic product. However, the potential utility of such a sentence, containing an unfamiliar word, is that it may have rendered the reading process less automatic and perhaps made you more conscious of the strategies you use while reading.

Let us assume that you were sufficiently interested in the sentence and in this introspective exercise to fully apply the powers of your brain to reading the sentence. Perhaps, your experience was similar to that described by Levin (Gibson & Levin, 1975, p. 460):

This chapter was written by Cheryl W. Hartman.

211

My initial and vivid reaction to this sentence was that I did not know the meaning of the word *palingenesis,* and how central to understanding the sentence was this particular word. The sentence concerned a concept, so that *palingenesis* was in effect the "semantic headword" of the whole sentence. Is this the developmental psychological shibboleth "ontogeny recapitulates phylogeny?" *Palingenesis* is a noun, a concept functioning as the object of the preposition *of;* the phrase is adjectival, modifying *concept.* Were this prolonged discourse, my impulse would have been to read further giving the sentence the reading I assumed. If the succeeding text made sense, I am not sure that I would have looked up *palingenesis.* It would depend on what I was reading for in the time I had, etc. On the other hand, I am interested in philology—word origins—enjoy and collect dictionaries, so that unless I was skimming the text or under some pressure of time, I would likely look up the word, even in discourse.

Levin in this passage describes consciously applying his knowledge of language while reading the given sentence, especially while attempting to identify the meaning of the word *palingenesis.* After applying his existing knowledge to the task of comprehending the sentence and, in particular, the word *palingenesis,* Levin does eventually consult the dictionary to look up the meaning of this unknown word. He discusses the process of determining on the basis of context the appropriate meaning of this word; indeed, his first guess had been accurate. The dictionary confirmed his hypothesis that *palingenesis* does refer to the concept of an individual's development (i.e., ontogeny) recapitulating the development of the species (i.e., phylogeny). Levin also mentions his use of the dictionary to find out how to pronounce *palingenesis.*

Is this what reading is? Is it associating sounds with letters, identifying words, and processing sentences?

**READING**   As indicated in the quote that opened this chapter, "to completely analyze what we do when we read would almost be the acme of a psychologist's achievements" (Huey, 1968, p. 6). In this chapter, reading is analyzed from the viewpoint of linguistics, which one could consider to be a branch of psychology in view of Chomsky's proposal that language is a "mirror of mind" (1972, p. x).

Applying the analytic tools developed in the study of language to explore the nature of reading is not a revolutionary method of responding to this challenge. One of the leading figures in American linguistics, Leonard Bloomfield (1942, p. 125), sought to elucidate the process of reading by viewing it through the microscope of linguistic "facts." In an article entitled "Linguistics and Reading," Bloomfield (1942, p. 183) offered the following description of reading:

When a literate adult reads, he passes his eyes rapidly over the printed text, and, scarcely noticing the individual words or letters, grasps the content of what he has read. This appears plainly in the fact that we do not often notice the misprints on the page we are reading ... the child ... stumbles along and spells out the word and in the end fails to grasp the content of what he has read. ... The trouble with the child, however, is simply that he lacks the long practice which enables the adult to read rapidly; the child puzzles out the words so slowly that he has forgotten the beginning of the sentence before he reaches the end; consequently he cannot grasp the content ... the adult reads silently; since he does not utter any speech-sounds, he concludes that speech-sounds play no part in the process of reading and that the printed marks lead directly to "ideas." Nothing could be further from the truth. The child does his first reading out loud. Then, under the instruction or example of his elders, he economizes by reading in a whisper. Soon he reduces this to scarcely audible movements of speech, later these become entirely inaudible.

Here Bloomfield is describing a mystery that remains elusive to educators and researchers: how does the young child progress from being a nonreader to a proficient adult reader? Whether or not one agrees with Bloomfield's description of the adult versus the child reader, his work in the realm of using linguistics as the key to unlocking the mystery of the reading process was important.

Many developmental models of reading, attempting to resolve the mystery of how we learn to read, have suggested that the child progresses from mastering the smallest units first (i.e., letters) to mastering larger and larger units sequentially (i.e., words, then sentences, and, finally, entire passages or discourse). The organization of this chapter may seem on the surface to endorse such a developmental model, in that letter processing is discussed first, word identification second, sentence comprehension third, and discourse analysis last. Such an organization was selected, however, to reflect a historical trend in linguistic theories of reading—the shift from analyzing reading at an atomic level (i.e., the level of letters) to analyzing it at increasingly broader levels. This chapter's organization was not conceived as an endorsement of the view that reading developmentally proceeds through the four distinct steps mentioned above. In fact, it is suggested within this chapter that to some extent all of these process levels supplement and interact with one another from the earliest stages of learning to read.

## LETTER PROCESSING

Let us begin at the beginning, when the child is first confronted with the task of making sense of the visual stimuli called letters. Put your mind in reverse and travel back in time; remember the experience of encountering seemingly meaningless, confusing configurations.

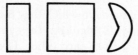

What is your reaction to the above configuration? Perhaps one of the first bits of information you would like to know is the function of this configuration. Is it to test your copying ability; must you reproduce these figures? Is it a design to admire? Just as learning the function of oral language is one of the earliest aspects of language to be acquired by children (see Chapter 2), so might the early learning of the function of printed symbols be necessary if reading is to be mastered.

Suppose you are told that the above sequence of symbols represents your name. If written on a drawing you have completed, it communicates the message that the drawing is yours. Click! Reading has meaning. Reading is an act of communication. You look for ways to apply this newly acquired knowledge about the function of written symbols. You find a drawing just created by your best friend, Mary. Yes, there it is—a sequence of written symbols on the bottom of the drawing, which you infer to be a representation of your friend's name. You seek out your friend and she confirms your hypothesis—that is how to write her name. Is this how reading began for you? Or, was it more like the following?

You are told and accept as incontrovertible that it is important to learn to identify the name of each of the following symbols:

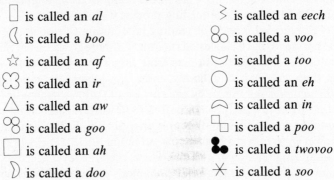

| ☐ is called an *al* | ⧁ is called an *eech* |
| ⟨ is called a *boo* | ⧀ is called a *voo* |
| ☆ is called an *af* | ⌣ is called a *too* |
| ⽕ is called an *ir* | ○ is called an *eh* |
| △ is called an *aw* | ⌢ is called an *in* |
| ⧂ is called a *goo* | ⅃ is called a *poo* |
| ☐ is called an *ah* | ⋮ is called a *twovoo* |
| ⟩ is called a *doo* | ✳ is called a *soo* |

Whether in the context of learning to read and write personal names or in the context of drills or games or by watching a lively television program, you do gradually learn to discriminate the symbols from each other and to call each one by its right name. How has this been achieved? By identifying the features that characterize each form as being different from the other forms? Perhaps you learned to categorize the forms, according to their **distinctive features.**

As described in Chapter 2, some linguists propose that we learn to identify phonemes, which involves categorization, on the basis of their distinctive features. Thus, we learn to distinguish a /t/ from a /d/ by learning that /d/ sounds have a quality (voicing) that /t/ sounds do not have. Similarly, research supports the contention that children learn to categorize letters on the basis of their distinctive features (Gibson & Levin, 1975). For example, children learn that the letters *b* and *d* differ visually in the direction in which they face. In the same way, you have just learned that directionality distinguishes the symbols called *boo, doo, in,* and *too* (i.e., ⟨, ⟩, ⌢, and ⌣) from each other. Directionality is one distinctive feature that the beginning reader uses in discriminating and identifying letters.

Once you have learned the distinctive features of the various written symbols, what is next? You will be escorted through a Bloomfieldian approach to learning to read. First, however, an introduction to Bloomfield's theory of reading is in order.

In his theory of reading, Bloomfield (Bloomfield & Barnhart, 1961) views letters as instructions that direct the reader to produce sounds in a particular order. Obeying these instructions is reading. According to this linguist, "in order to read alphabetic writing one must have an ingrained habit of producing the phonemes of one's language when one sees the written marks which conventionally represent these phonemes" (Bloomfield & Barnhart, 1961, p. 10).

Bloomfield's emphasis on the importance of learning to produce sounds in response to letters is especially evident in his statements that "if a child has not learned to utter the speech sounds of our language, the only sensible course is to postpone reading until he has learned to speak" and that "a person who cannot produce these sounds cannot get the message of a piece of alphabetic writing" (Bloomfield & Barnhart, 1961, p. 27). This perspective on reading is also evident in the quote from Bloomfield (1942) presented earlier in the chapter, describing the child as, first, learning to read aloud and, only later, as an adult, learning to suppress these vocalizations.

Next we will look at how Bloomfield's theory might be translated into practice. This simulation is based on the Bloomfield and Barnhart (1961) text, which is entitled *Let's Read: A Linguistic Approach*.

Assuming that you have mastered the visual discrimination of the written forms presented previously and that you can produce the sounds of English, you are now ready to learn to read, to associate certain sounds with these forms. In the first step, you are presented with a sequence of the forms, ⬜ ⬜ ⟩ , and asked to say their names (*al, ah,* and *doo*). Next, you are told: "Now we have spelled the word. Now we are going to read it. This word is *lad.* Read it: *lad*" (Bloomfield & Barnhart, 1961, p. 41). This procedure is repeated with ☆ ⬜ ⟩ or /*fad*/. You are taught to distinguish between these two words, so that you can consistently identify ⬜ ⬜ ⟩ as /*lad*/ and ☆ ⬜ ⟩ as /*fad*/. Gradually, you learn other words like: ⟨ ⬜ ⟩ or /*bad*/, ⟩ ⬜ ⟩ or /*had*/, ⟩ ⬜ ⟩ or /*dad*/, and ⬜ ⬜ ⟩ or /*pad*/. Once these words have been overlearned, so that identifying them is an ingrained habit, you are presented such words as: ✶ ⬜ ⌣ or /*cat*/, ⬚ ⬜ ⌣ or /*rat*/, ⬚ ⬜ ⌣ or /*vat*/, and ⟩ ⬜ ⌣ or /*hat*/. Eventually, you learn other vowel sounds (e.g., those corresponding to the symbols ◯ and △, called *eh* and *aw* respectively):

$$⟨ ◯ ⌣ = /bet/ \qquad ⬚ △ ⌣ = /got/$$

$$● ◯ ⌣ = /wet/ \qquad ⬚ △ ⌣ = /pot/$$

$$⌢ ◯ ⌣ = /net/ \qquad ⌢ △ ⌣ = /not/$$

Bloomfield's pedagogical method is called the inductive method, that is, you are presented with many examples of rules from which you must induce the letter-sound generalizations. Bloomfield criticized the phonics method popular in the 1940s. This utilized the deductive method of teaching letter-to-sound rules directly to children, who were then supposed to apply these rules while reading. In fact, one of the motivations underlying Bloomfield's commitment to improving the teaching of reading was his dismay at the method by which his own son was being taught in school: the letter *c* stands for /*cuh*/, the *a* stands for the short *a* sound /æ/, the letter *t* says /*tuh*/ and so on. Appalled at this unnatural and linguistically naive attempt to teach children to associate letters with isolated phonemes, which cannot be uttered as separate entities, for the most part, Bloomfield devised his teaching method, which relies on inducing letter-sound correspondences from lists of whole words and nonsense syllables. Bloomfield viewed this as a more natural way of learning to read.

In illustration of Bloomfield's notion of induction, you have probably, by now, induced enough knowledge about the form-sound correspondence rules to be able to recode the following sequences of forms into their appropriate phonemic counterparts:

Check your pronunciation of these "words" with the correct ones.[1] If your pronunciations match those given, you have learned to read, according to Bloomfield and Barnhart (1961). In this view, there is no need to discuss any aspect of reading other than letter processing or, in this simulation, form processing. First, you learn to discriminate the marks on the paper from each other. Next, you learn to associate these marks with particular sounds—you link up your visual categories with your auditory categories. Once this is done, you have learned to read.

In this simulation of a Bloomfieldian approach to learning to read, your knowledge of the form-sound correspondences is tested using nonsense syllables to prevent you from relying on any semantic clues, in accordance with the testing procedures in the Bloomfield and Barnhart (1961) text. Overall, Bloomfield places very little emphasis on the role of meaning in teaching a child to read. In fact, he feels that concern with meaning can actually be harmful to the beginning reader, that exclusive attention should be paid to letter-sound relationships, not to extraneous issues like meaning (Bloomfield & Barnhart, 1961, p. 42).

Reading is so familiar to us that we are likely to forget how difficult it is for the beginner. The child has so hard a time forming a connection between visual marks and speech sounds that he cannot attend to the meaning of what he reads. We must help him to establish this connection, and we must not bother him, for the present, with anything else. We can best help him by giving him the most suitable words to read ... without regard to their meanings. The child will get the meanings only when he has solved the mechanical problem of reading.

Certainly, Bloomfield (1942, p. 184) considers the acquisition of meaning to be the goal of reading, for he does state: "The only practical value of responding correctly to the letters of the alphabet lies in the messages which reach us through the written or printed page." However, meaning is viewed as the product of reading, which must not be confused with the mechanical process of learning to read. Once one has mastered the habit of associating letters with sounds, one can then "listen" (Bloomfield, 1942, p. 184) to these spoken sounds. The assumption is that one can thus comprehend the written message by applying the same skills involved in listening to oral language.

If letter-sound (or what have also been called grapheme-phoneme) correspondences were wholly predictable, perhaps Bloomfield's inductive method of teaching reading and his downplaying of reading as a meaningful act of communication would be uncontestably successful. However, to use the Bloomfield and Barnhart (1961, p. 26) terminology, there are many "irregular spellings."

In the Bloomfield and Barnhart (1961) text, the teaching of "irregular" words is delayed until after the "regular" ones have been overlearned. The first thirty-six lessons are devoted to teaching regular letter-sound correspondences. Each letter is taught as representing only one sound. The vowels represent their "short" rather than their "long" (Bloomfield & Barnhart, 1961, p. 57) sounds (the latter are considered irregular, that is, *a* in *cat* has a regular pronunciation, but is irregularly pronounced in *late*). The consonants each represent only one sound (e.g., *b* as in *bad, c* as in *can, g* as in *get* or *fig,* etc.). (This strategy is reflected in the preceding simulation of a Bloomfieldian reading curriculum. All words presented have regular one-to-one form-sound correspondences.)

In lessons 37 through 71 of the Bloomfield and Barnhart text, regular letter-sound relationships continue to be taught. Thus, the letter *s* always represents the /s/ sound as in *sit, us, cats, fits, it's, let's,* and *books.* In this section of the text, however, the regular sounds of certain letter combinations are introduced: *ng* as in *sing, nk* as in *sink, sh* as in *shed, ch* as in *chin, th* as in *thin, wh* as in *when, ck* as in *back, tch* as in *catch,* and *qu* as in *quit.* At this point, children have to learn to revise their notion that single letters always map onto single phonemes. They must replace this with the concept that more than one letter can represent a single sound. Furthermore, children learn that one letter can sometimes represent more than one sound, as does *x* in *ax* (pronounced /aks/). In lessons 72 through 97, children are taught the regular sounds of vowel combinations (e.g., *ee, ea, ai, ay, oa,* and *oo*) whose regular sounds are the "long" vowel sounds. Again, they learn that more than one letter can represent a single sound.

In summary, lessons 1 through 97 of the Bloomfield and Barnhart (1961, p. 206) text are designed to teach the student "the basic habit of reading (the same letters mean the same sounds)." It is mindboggling to think of how many words cannot be read using this "basic habit of reading"! The rest of the text is devoted to teaching such "irregularities" as when the /z/ sound is represented by the letter *s*, when the *th* pattern represents the voiced /th/ sound, when the *ed* pattern represents the /t/ or /d/ sounds as in some past tense suffixes, and so on.

Suppose that after ninety-seven lessons in reading regular words and nonsense syllables, you were to encounter the following sequences of forms:

You might wonder if these are nonsense syllables designed to test your knowledge of form-sound correspondences. With Bloomfield's system, this would be a possibility. As you are not taught that the aim in reading is to acquire meaning, you would not realize that letter-sound correspondence rules are quite unpredictable and that they must be used in conjunction with other clues, such as semantic information about what types of words exist in one's language, during the process of word identification.

In conclusion, if taught by Bloomfield's methodology, children learn that reading is a mechanical process of associating certain letters with particular sounds and that the identification of meaningful words is an incidental by-product of setting this mechanical process in motion. When children, finally, are confronted with "irregular" words, they must discard this view of reading. At this point, even Bloomfield and Barnhart (1961) admit that reading must be reconceptualized as the process of meaningful word identification, if children's reading ability is to progress.

## WORD IDENTIFICATION

Let us now shift our attention to the view that reading involves meaningful word identification. This concept of reading does not necessarily contradict the one that reading involves letter processing. Word identification can be viewed as incorporating letter processing and going beyond this level of analysis. Learning letter-sound associations can be seen as a subcomponent of learning to identify words.

In the early part of this chapter, you were urged not to conclude simplistically that letter processing precedes word identification developmentally. In fact, Levin and Watson (1963) have conducted research the results of which suggest that from the outset the beginning reader should be taught to think of reading as being more complex than the learning of invariant letter-sound correspondences. Beginning readers seem to fare better if they acquire early the mental attitude that letter-sound correspondences are only moderately predictable and must be used together with other clues—clues derived from viewing reading as involving meaningful word identification.

Let us consider this position as it applies to the simulation of learning to read. Suppose that you learned from the start to expect that all sequences of forms (e.g., □ □ ⟩ ) represent meaningful words. Furthermore, suppose that you were taught early to expect irregularities in the form-sound correspondences. Perhaps the process of identifying the irregular words, such as ⟨□□, □□, □◡, □℅⟩, □⌘ and □△ ⌘ , would have been a bit easier if you were expecting meaningfulness and some spelling irregularities (although there still may not be sufficient clues to definitively identify these words).

Venezky is a linguist who has extensively studied letter-sound relationships and who espouses the view that the primary function of these correspondences is "to facilitate the development of word recognition" (1976, p. 22). He rejects the notion that spellings can be treated strictly as instructions for producing sequences of phonemes. According to Venezky (1976, p. 7), "from the writing-to-speech definition of spelling comes a purblind concentration on oral reading, enunciation and meaningless syllables." He proposes that our spelling system is "more complex than an irregular letter-to-sound system" (1970, p. 16).

Venezky (1970) directly criticizes Bloomfield for asserting that writing is simply an imperfect image of speech. Perhaps Bloomfield's limited perspective on the nature of our spelling system can, at least in part, be attributed to his revulsion toward the study of meaning, which he felt should be excluded from the rigorous science of linguistics. Such a stance may have prevented him from considering the view espoused by other linguists (e.g., Edgerton, 1941; Hockett, 1958; Venezky, 1970) that "the complexities of English spelling cannot be accounted for completely on the assumption that the system is phonemic with irregularities. . . . It is necessary to assume that the system is partly phonemic and partly morphemic" (Hockett, 1958, p. 542). These linguists propose that the spelling system is designed to capture both the semantic and the auditory characteristics of words.

In what sense does semantics influence spelling? One way, which was noted as long ago as 1617 by Hume (1865), is the use of spelling to distinguish between homonyms, words that sound the same but that have different meanings (e.g., *seem* and *seam, sum* and *some,* and *to, two,* and *too*). If our spelling system were purely alphabetic (designed to represent sounds), homonyms would all be spelled identically, and we would not have the visual cues to mark their semantic differences. Inherent in this view of our spelling system is the assumption that we learn to directly relate the visual configurations of words (i.e., their spelling) to their meaning, thus acquiring spelling-to-meaning associations in addition to the spelling-to-sound correspondences that may have been learned. The likelihood that we form direct links between some word spellings and their meanings without first decoding the letters to sounds is demonstrated by the interference we experience while reading a sentence such as *The none tolled hymn she had scene a pare of bear feat in hour rheum* (Smith, 1971, p. 72). If words were identified strictly by first associating sounds with letters, then in "listening" to the sounds (as held by Bloomfield), we should experience no interference in identifying the meanings of the words in this sentence. Yet most readers find that this sentence does resist smooth, immediate comprehension, because of the spelling-to-meaning associations that are triggered.

Therefore, spelling-to-sound correspondence will not suffice in making the correct meaning of homonymous words available to the reader. Reliance on direct spelling-to-meaning associations is critical to the identification of the meaning of such words. In what other ways do the meanings of words influence the spelling system?

Next, let us consider the fact that many times the sounds one should associate with given letters are not evident unless meaning is first taken into consideration. One way in which meaning clues help us to determine which sounds correspond to which letters is via the rule that letter-sound correspondences occur only within morpheme boundaries, not across morpheme boundaries. For example, the *ph* letter pattern corresponds to the /f/ sound within morpheme boundaries, as in *phase, sphere,* and *phone,* but represents the two sounds regularly associated with the individual letters *p* and *h* when the pattern is split between separate morphemes, as in *uphill, topheavy,* and *shepherd.*

C. Chomsky (1970) points out that our spelling system often captures the similarity in the meaning of words that sound entirely different from each other. This tendency of English spelling to preserve morphemic identity in spite of phonemic differences is also noted by Francis (1958), an early critic of the Bloomfieldian approach to our spelling system. This aspect of English orthography is evident in such word families as *bomb* and *bombardier; sign, signature,* and *significant; paradigm* and *paradigmatic;* and so on. This characteristic of spelling is also reflected in the written representations of such markers as the past tense *-ed* suffix and the possessive *'s* suffix, the invariant spellings of which reflect their unchanging semantic roles, in spite of the varying pronunciations that occur (e.g., *rained, started,* and *popped; Mary's, George's, Pat's,* and *Bob's*).

Most educators, unlike Bloomfield but like Durkin (1972), who has written texts on phonics and the teaching of reading, recognize that semantic clues must be used together with letter-sound correspondences if the child is to have even a fighting chance at deciphering a new written word. For this reason, these educators stress the importance of using reading materials that contain words falling within a child's oral language vocabulary. Unless the child knows the meaning of the spoken word that is represented by the unfamiliar visual configuration, it will be difficult for the child to successfully apply letter-sound generalizations to that unknown written word.

Other aspects of the spelling system are overlooked by Bloomfield, as Venezky (1970) indicates. For one, there are rather arbitrary orthographic rules that one must learn. As they are defined by Gibson and Levin (1975, pp. 172–73), *"orthographic rules* govern what sequence of letters and groups of letters may be put together to form words." For example, the reason that certain words end with a so-called silent *e* is because there is an orthographic rule prohibiting words to end with the letter *v.* If you were to run across a word like *kov,* you would notice immediately that something is wrong, even though you might not be able to consciously state the rule about words not ending in *v.* An orthographic rule of which you may be more consciously aware is the one dictating that the letter *q* must be followed by the letter *u.*

Another aspect of the spelling system that is bypassed by Bloomfield is the effect of syntax. Like semantic variables, syntactic factors also influence word identification. Knowing its syntactic role is, at times, critical in establishing the pronunciation of a written word. For example, syntactic knowledge enables one to disambiguate such homographs as *pérmit* (the noun) and *permít* (the verb), *cónduct* (the noun) and *condúct* (the verb), and *désert* (the noun) and *desért* (the verb). Unless one knows the syntactic functions of these written words, one cannot correctly identify and pronounce them. When reading these words, one places the main stress on the first syllable if the word is a noun, on the second syllable if it is a verb. Thus, spelling-to-sound correspondences are affected by syntactic factors.

Another syntactic influence on spelling-to-sound correspondences occurs in the case of the *th* spelling unit. As Venezky (1970, p. 44) indicates, the initial *th* corresponds to the unvoiced /*th*/ sound in "contentives" such as *thermometer, thimble,* and *thumb,* and to the voiced /*th*/ sound in "functors," such as *the, thus,* and *then.* Some linguists call functors structure words, since their primary function is to indicate the syntactic role of the structures in which they occur. While one may not consciously rely on the knowledge that the initial *th* in contentives is unvoiced and the initial *th* in functors is voiced, this syntactic factor is a reliable predictor of the sounds one should associate with the initial *th* pattern.

Analyses of the orthographic system have led to the conclusion that word identification is facilitated if the reader realizes that the following factors influence the spelling system: (1) letter-sound correspondences, (2) orthographic rules rendering only certain letter sequences permissible, (3) semantic influences, and (4) syntactic factors. This conclusion implies a view of reading that has already been suggested—that reading involves more than letter processing, more than associating sounds with letters.

As indicated earlier, semantic interpretations suggest that reading must extend, at least, to the level of meaningful word identification. However, if reading were just the process of identifying isolated words on word lists, only limited semantic clues and no syntactic clues would be provided to facilitate the process of word identification. In sentences, words are governed by semantic constraints that indicate which words can be combined meaningfully. Also, only in sentences do words fulfill syntactic functions. If semantic and syntactic clues do aid in the process of word recognition, children should learn to read more efficiently if words are presented in the context of sentences, rather than as isolated entities in word lists.

## SENTENCE COMPREHENSION

According to Stauffer (1969), letter processing, word identification, and sentence comprehension are interdependent. The first two aspects are only meaningful when embedded within the context of sentence comprehension. Consistent with this view of reading, Stauffer (1969, p. 252) specifically avers that "skill and efficiency in the use of language-content clues for word-recognition purposes are attained only through constant, diligent effort. Therefore, the directive to 'read to the end of the sentence' is only a crude beginning." He goes on to say that children must learn to use "language-context clues" from the very start of their learning-to-read program.

The following exercise has been designed to illustrate how the clues available in a sentence can facilitate word identification. This will be accomplished by having you compare the tasks of identifying the irregular words presented earlier in isolation as a list and of reading them below in the context of sentences. To simulate the situation of knowing all of the words of a sentence except one new word whose identification might be facilitated by relying on the cues available in the sentence, the unknown words have been embedded within sentences that are printed in familiar written English. Taking advantage of the linguistic clues available, try to identify the unknown words:

(1)        *The* ⟨☐☐⟩ *bounced down the street.*

(2)        *You are driving me up a* ♣☐☐.

(3)        ♣☐∽ *do you want for dinner?*

(4)        *The clown made the child* ☐☐∞⟩.

(5)        ♣☐☎ *are you going tonight for dinner?*

(6)        *The bumper sticker read:* ☐△∞ *it or leave it.*

Certainly, these sentences provide more clues to aid you in your efforts at word identification than were available when the words were presented in a list. Syntactic clues do not exist in word lists; more definitive semantic information is offered in the context of sentences.

Only general semantic information about what words exist in the English language can be used as a guideline when reading isolated words. Spoken words occurring in isolation are ambiguous carriers of meaning, and so are written words. For example, suppose that when it was presented in isolation you were able to identify ⟨☐☐⟩ as the counterpart of the spoken word usually spelled as *ball*. You would still not know whether ⟨☐☐⟩ referred to a round sphere or to a dance. You would only have been able to associate the written word with its spoken realization. Is this reading? It is not, according to Lefevre (1964, p. 5), who views such reading as "word calling."

Lefevre (1964) expresses dismay about the reputation that linguistics has acquired through Bloomfield's work. In the preface of his book *Linguistics and the Teaching of Reading* (1964, p. vii), Lefevre asserts that "no one can get meaning from the printed page without taking in whole language patterns at the sentence level, because these are the minimal meaning-bearing structures of most written communication." Thus, Lefevre, like Stauffer, proposes that reading extends not only beyond letter processing, but also beyond identifying individual words to the level of sentence comprehension and that this happens right at the initial stage of learning to read.

This view of written communication is similar to Bransford and McCarrell's (1974) position regarding oral communication. They contend that the route to comprehension is not paved by identifying isolated words. In fact, they propose that "even isolated words are understood to have propositional or sentential content. For example, the utterance 'paper' is understood to mean 'there is a paper,' 'I want some paper,' 'it's made of paper,' etc. . . . If someone utters a single word and one cannot understand its propositional significance (e.g., someone runs into your office and yells 'paper'), one will be puzzled by this act" (Bransford & McCarrell, 1974, p. 190).

What evidence is there in studies of reading to indicate that learning to read is facilitated when sentences are presented rather than isolated words? Goodman (1969) in a study of first, second, and third graders compared their ability to read words in isolation as opposed to in the context of sentences. He found that on the average 62% of words that were miscalled when they were presented in list form could be read correctly by first graders when they were presented in the context of sentences. This percentage increased to 75% for second graders and to 82% for third graders. The conclusion is that even first graders take advantage of the language clues available in sentences. This research on oral reading indicates that word recognition is, in fact, made easier when words are encountered in the context of sentences rather than in isolation. This supports Stauffer's (1969) and Lefevre's (1964) view of reading.

Consistent with his position that sentence comprehension is of paramount importance, Lefevre (1964, p. 5) places the bulk of the blame for reading problems on "poor sentence-sense, demonstrated in word calling, or in reading various nonstructural fragments of language patterns as units." Being even more specific, this linguist-educator describes the poor reader as follows (Lefevre, 1964, p. 23):

> Lacking a sure grasp of the printed sentence as the common building block of the paragraph and of the more extended forms of written discourse, the crippled reader cannot comprehend what he "reads" as organized, coherent form. Instead, he tends to register only arbitrary, random elements, and even to miss important language structures altogether in the material the writer sets before him. He sees a subject without its verb, a verb without its subject; combines the subjects with the wrong verbs and verbs with the wrong subjects . . .

Lefevre (1964) proposes that producing exact word-for-word renditions while reading aloud is less critical than using appropriate intonation, which is considered an important indicator of a reader's ability to identify the meaning and syntactic structure of a sentence. He stresses the need to learn to use the following clues to a sentence's structure and meaning: (1) word order, (2) structure words, or Venezky's (1970) "functors" (i.e., noun markers such as *a, the, some,* and *any;* verb markers such as *is* and *have;* phrase markers or prepositions; clause markers such as *if, because,* and *that;* question markers such as *who, why,* and *when*), and (3) word form changes (i.e., grammatical inflections such as plurals, verb tense markers, etc.).

Psycholinguists Clark and Clark (1977), in their discussion of the strategies listeners may rely on for identifying the syntactic structure of spoken sentences, also mention the types of clues described by Lefevre (1964) as important to the reader of written language. Let us examine the strategies they outline as possible steps that lead toward comprehension.

STRATEGY 1. As described by Clark and Clark (1977 p. 59), this strategy is cited as having been first proposed by Kimball (1973): "Whenever you find a function word, begin a new constituent larger than one word." Or more specifically: "Whenever you find a determiner (*a, an, the*) or quantifier (*some, all, many, two, six,* etc.), begin a new noun phrase. Whenever you find an auxiliary verb with tense (*is, are, was, were, have, can, could,* etc.), begin a new verb phrase . . ." (p. 59). This strategy encompasses Lefevre's (1964) proposal that function (i.e., structure) words are useful clues for identifying the structure and meaning of sentences.

STRATEGY 2. "After identifying the beginning of a constituent, look for content words appropriate to that type of constituent" (Clark & Clark, 1977, p. 61). This strategy somewhat overlaps the first one in that it also involves using function or structure words. However, they are now signals regarding the types of content words that might comprise the subsequent constituent phrase. For example, after encountering the word *the,* one anticipates a noun, which completes the noun phrase (e.g., *the appropriate mental strategy* or *the big dog*). Or, after encountering the tensed auxiliary verb *would,* one looks for a main verb to complete the verb phrase (e.g., *would be frequently used* or *would have been hit*).

STRATEGY 3. "Use affixes to help decide whether a content word is a noun, verb, adjective or adverb" (Clark & Clark, 1977, p. 63). This strategy encompasses Lefevre's (1964) observation that word-form changes (e.g., pluralization or tense marking) are important clues regarding sentence structure. For example, the knowledge that only nouns are pluralized can be used as a clue to identify the nouns in the noun phrases of a sentence. By way of further illustrating the utility of structure words and affixes, consider the following verse of Lewis Carroll's "Jabberwocky."

> 'Twas brillig and the slithy toves
> Did gyre and gimble in the wabe;
> All mimsy were the borogroves,
> And the mome raths outgrabe.

Do the structure words and affixes help you to identify the grammatical functions of the nonsense words? Is *brillig* a noun, verb, adjective, or adverb? How do you know? Is *tove* a noun, verb, adjective, or adverb? What clues can you use to determine its syntactic classification?

The strategies described by Clark and Clark (1977) presume that, as we listen, we activate hypotheses about the syntactic structures we expect to hear. We expect grammatically acceptable sentences. Thus, when we hear a structure word, we anticipate that it is beginning the type of syntactic structure usually started by such a word (Strategy 1). For example, when we hear the determiner *the* in the verse above, we anticipate that it is beginning a noun phrase. Therefore, we listen for a noun to follow and complete the noun phrase (Strategy 2). Listening carefully, we seek confirmation of our hypothesis. Does a noun follow?

If we apply our knowledge of affixes, specifically, the knowledge that nouns can often be converted to adjectives through a transformation that inserts the affix *-y,* we might guess that *slithy* is an adjective derived by such a transformation. Thus, we have used our syntactic knowledge to reject the hypothesis that the next word after *the* might be a noun and we entertain the possibility that *slithy* is an adjective (Strategy 3). Therefore, we must still search for a noun to complete the noun phrase. (Strategy 2 must still be in operation since its expectation has not yet been fulfilled.)

Next, we encounter the word *toves,* which seemingly has a plural affix. We identify it as a noun by applying Strategy 3, since we know that only nouns can be pluralized. Our noun phrase is complete; therefore, we expect the beginning of a new phrase, perhaps a verb phrase. Lefevre (1964) in his chapter on word order discusses this type of syntactic knowledge—learning to anticipate sentences consisting of a noun phrase followed by a verb phrase. Such a hypothesis has not been identified as a strategy by Clark and Clark (1977), but it certainly seems feasible that listeners might through syntactic knowledge arrive at such an expectation. Indeed, the next word in the verse is an auxiliary verb (*did*), which marks the beginning of a verb phrase.

Lefevre's (1964) concept of the reader and Clark and Clark's (1977) description of the listener are very similar to Goodman and Goodman's (1977, p. 323) view of "receptive language users" (a term that encompasses readers *and* listeners). They describe the comprehension process as follows (Goodman & Goodman, 1977, pp. 323–24):

> ... through strategies of predicting, sampling, and confirming, receptive language users can leap toward meaning with partial processing of input ... continuous monitoring of subsequent input and meaning for confirmation and consistency. Many miscues reflect readers' abilities to liberate themselves from detailed attention to print as they leap toward meaning. Consequently, they reverse, substitute, insert, omit, rearrange, paraphrase and transform. ... In both reading and listening, prediction is at least as important as perception.

Goodman and Goodman (1977, p. 317) carefully analyze the types of errors, or "miscues," made by children at all levels of reading. Using these miscues as a "window on the reading processes" (Goodman & Goodman, 1977, p. 319), they found that, beginning as early as the first grade, children usually make miscues that reflect their use of syntactic and semantic predictions in attempts to construct the meaning of the writer. To illustrate this point, Goodman and Goodman (1977) present a nine-year-old girl's miscue and subsequent self-correction, which resulted from her use of syntactic strategies while reading. When presented with the text "Then he was afraid that she would fall off," this girl read aloud, *Then he was afraid that the—that she would fall off*" (Goodman & Goodman, 1977, p. 325). Using the syntactic strategy of predicting that a noun phrase beginning with *the* will follow the complementizer *that,* this young reader substituted *the* for *she.* However, apparently as her eyes read on, our reader realized that she had made a mistake, since *the* should not be followed by *would.* Using Clark and Clark's (1977) Strategy 1, she predicts that a noun will follow *the* before a verb phrase can begin. Therefore, the nine-year-old reader backtracks and corrects her substitution, reading *that she* instead of the erroneous *that the.*

Goodman and Goodman (1977) thus provide some evidence to support the position held by Lefevre (1964) and Clark and Clark (1977) that receptive language users do apply their syntactic competence while reading. Another source of support for this view of the reader comes from studies of eye-voice span. Eye-voice span refers to the number of words that the eye can process ahead of what is being read aloud. As Smith (1971, p. 196) explains, ". . . the skilled reader's eye usually runs four or five words ahead of his voice when he is reading aloud." One could turn out the lights while someone is reading aloud, and note how many words the reader can recall beyond the point reached when the lights went out. As Smith (1971, p. 196) indicates, it is especially noteworthy that

> . . . the span tends to extend to a phrase boundary, to a significant point in the structure of a sentence. If the phrase that the reader happens to be reading ends three words after the light goes out, he will probably only be able to cite those three words in the dark, but if the phrase ends just one or two words later and the following phrase extends to no more than six words from the point at which illumination is removed then the eye-voice span may well extend to six words . . . the size of the eye-voice span is not so much determined by the number of words as by the structure of the passage being read.

Thus, to derive meaning from sentences, readers do seem to analyze the syntactic structure of the sentences.

Goodman and Goodman's (1977) research on oral reading suggests that semantic, as well as syntactic, knowledge is applied by the reader. They found that miscues creating semantically anomalous sentences were usually corrected by the children themselves, in the same way that syntactically incorrect miscues result in self-corrections. Let us now consider the types of semantic strategies that might be employed during the comprehension process, that is, the types of semantic predictions one might make while listening or reading.

Clark and Clark (1977) incorporate within their model of the listener strategies that involve applying semantic knowledge to the task of comprehension. One such strategy is credited to Bever (1970), who has observed that most English sentences have the order agent+action+object, as in *Mary hugged George.* Bever proposes that the listener learns to expect such sequences—tends to expect the first noun phrase to fulfill the semantic role of agent and the verb phrase to consist of an action verb and an object. This strategy has been found to lead young children to misinterpret passive sentences (e.g., *George was hugged by Mary* might be misinterpreted as *George hugged Mary*). These children seemingly have not learned to modify a semantic prediction on the basis of such syntactic information as is provided by a passive transformation (e.g., *was hugged by*) (Fraser, Bellugi, & Brown, 1963).

Another semantic strategy is suggested by Clark and Clark (1977) on the basis of their observation that events are usually described in the order they occur. They describe this strategy as follows (Clark & Clark, 1977, p. 78): "Look for the first of two clauses to describe the first of two events, and the second clause the second event, unless they are marked otherwise." To illustrate this, decide which of the following two sentences better matches your expectations:

**(7)**          *After he fell, he decided to quit skiing forever.*

**(8)**          *He decided to quit skiing forever, after he fell.*

According to Clark and Clark (1977), the sentence **(7)** better reflects what the listener expects, since the first clause describes the chronologically first event. Clark (1971) found that young children rely heavily on this strategy.

Another semantic strategy proposed by Clark and Clark (1977) is the tendency to look for words, phrases, and clauses that fit the semantic requirements underlying each word that is heard. For example, "*put* requires . . . an agent, an object, and a location. *Tall* requires . . . an object with height . . . *Quickly* requires an action of movement. *In* requires . . . an object and a container" (Clark & Clark, 1977, p. 76). Thus, if we hear the adverb *quickly* at the beginning of a sentence, we anticipate a verb such as *ran* rather than a verb such as *slept.*

To recapitulate, according to Goodman and Goodman (1977), Bever (1970), and Clark and Clark (1977), the receptive language user (the reader or listener) anticipates grammatical and meaningful sentences. This application of syntactic and semantic knowledge facilitates word recognition. Levin (Gibson & Levin, 1975, p. 460) describes deploying knowledge of both syntax (i.e., that *palingenesis* is a noun) and semantics (i.e., knowledge of the semantic constraints associated with a "meta-theory of developmental psychology") in his attempt at identifying the word *palingenesis.* In fact, Levin was able to successfully predict the meaning of this word and, thereby, to comprehend the sentence. This is the goal of applying one's syntactic and semantic knowledge—sentence comprehension. However, is this the complete story of reading?

## DISCOURSE ANALYSIS

Try reading the following sentence (Smith, 1971, p. 196):

> We gave her dog biscuits because she said animals were fed better than humans.

Do you find that when reading this sentence your intonation first reflects an assumption that biscuits are being given to a dog, which you must correct when you read the second clause in the sentence indicating that a female person has been given dog biscuits? If so, you are experiencing the potential ambiguity inherent in many isolated sentences (just as isolated words tend to be ambiguous in meaning). Let us imagine that you encounter the above sentence at the end of the following paragraph, instead of in isolation:

> Mary is such a chronic complainer about food, we decided to shut her up once and for all. We bought her some dog food although she owns no dog. It came in handy, however, the next day. When we gave her the dog food, she was quite puzzled. We provided her with the following explanation: We gave her dog biscuits because she said animals were fed better than humans.

Do you find that when read within the context of this discourse, the previously confusing sentence is more readily understood?

Goodman and Goodman (1977) have found that just as words are more easily read in sentences, so are sentences more easily read when embedded within connected discourse. They herald the current trend toward viewing reading as the processing of "full, natural linguistic text" (Goodman & Goodman, 1977, p. 330). This trend pervades many areas of psycholinguistic research, as noted by Kintsch (1974, p. 2):

> Psycholinguistics is changing its character.... The 1950's were still dominated by the nonsense syllables ... the 1960's were characterized by the use of word lists, while the present decade is witnessing a shift to even more complex learning materials. At present, we have reached a point where lists of sentences are being substituted for word lists.... Hopefully, this will not be the endpoint of this development, and we shall soon see psychologists handle effectively the problems posed by the analysis of connected texts.

Indeed, more and more researchers are viewing reading as the comprehension of connected texts, or what some refer to as **discourse.** This is a welcome change since reading in reality does usually involve connected discourse, as does natural listening.

There are rules governing the discourse level of language, just as there are rules about grammaticalness at the sentence level. Consider the grammaticalness of the following paragraph:

> Bob and Jane went to the store. It barked all night long. He swam there and she flew high in the sky.

What basic rule does this paragraph violate? In the terminology of Clark and Clark (1977, pp. 72–73), it violates the "cooperative principle," which refers to the rule that sentences within connected discourse should, in fact, be connected and relevant to one another. This principle encompasses another rule regarding pronominalization—that pronouns should be used only when their referents are clear to the reader or listener. In an attempt to apply the cooperative principle, most readers of the above paragraph assume that the sentences following *Bob and Jane went to the store* are relevant to this statement and that they refer to *Bob, Jane,* the act of going, or *the store.*

Evidence of the operation of this cooperative principle during a listening comprehension task is provided in research by Bransford and McCarrell (1974). The following paragraph was read to subjects who were told that the topic of discourse was "Watching a peace march from the fortieth floor" (Bransford & McCarrell, 1974, p. 207):

> The view was breathtaking. From the window one could see the crowd below. Everything looked extremely small from such a distance, but the colorful costumes could still be seen. Everyone seemed to be moving in one direction in an orderly fashion and there seemed to be little children as well as adults. The landing was gentle and luckily the atmosphere was such that no special suits had to be worn. At first there was a great deal of activity. Later, when the speeches started, the crowd quieted down. The man with the television camera took many shots of the setting and the crowd. Everyone was very friendly and seemed to be glad when the music started.

The listeners expressed confusion over the sentence within the paragraph about a landing. This confusion did not arise when listeners were told that the passage referred to a space project, because the cooperative principle was not violated in that case.

If the cooperative principle is satisfied, the discourse can be described as having cohesion (Grimes, 1975). Without cohesion, a text is not a meaningful unit and, therefore, cannot be considered as discourse. A sentence by definition must be grammatical, and so must discourse by definition have cohesion (Halliday & Hasan, 1976).

Having knowledge of the cohesive requirement for discourse facilitates the process of comprehension. We, thus, know to expect pronouns to have referents specified within the passage we are reading. Furthermore, we expect sentences to be related to one another within a paragraph, and we assume that paragraphs within a larger discourse unit will be related to each other. In other words, the strategies derived from expectations of cohesion can be applied not only to discourse longer than individual sentences, but also to discourse longer than a single paragraph. Indeed, a connected text may have cohesion and, thus, satisfy the cooperative principle at the level of the several paragraphs, even though the individual component paragraphs making up the larger discourse unit do not necessarily satisfy the cohesion requirement when considered separately from their context.

Just as isolated words and isolated sentences are often ambiguous carriers of meaning, so can single paragraphs be ambiguous out of context.

The previously described experiment by Bransford and McCarrell (1974) illustrates how much easier it is to process paragraphs that are embedded within a meaningful context. Consider the following paragraph developed by Bransford and Johnson (1972, p. 722):

> The procedure is actually quite simple. First you arrange things into different groups. . . . Of course one pile may be sufficient depending on how much there is to do. If you have to go somewhere else due to lack of facilities that is the next step, otherwise you are pretty well set. . . . At first the whole procedure will seem complicated. Soon however, it will become just another facet of life. It is difficult to foresee any end to the necessity for this task in the immediate future, but then one never can tell. After the procedure is completed one arranges the material into different groups again. Then they can be put into their appropriate places. Eventually they will be used once more and the whole cycle will then have to be repeated. However, that is a part of life.

Most readers find this passage difficult to comprehend and recall unless it is encountered within some meaningful context. For example, reread the paragraph, assuming that it has been written by your mother in a letter, in which she explicitly explains that she is describing the unavoidable, never-ending chore of washing clothes. This experiment by Bransford and McCarrell (1974) supports the conclusion reached by Goodman and Goodman (1977, p. 330) from their studies of reading, that is, "sentences are easier than words, paragraphs easier than sentences, pages easier than paragraphs and stories easier than pages."

Does *this* capture the whole story of reading? It does not, according to Goodman and Goodman (1977). In their description of their theory of reading, these researchers indicate that the reader's whole range of "experiences, values, conceptual structures . . . dialects and life styles are integral to the process" (Goodman & Goodman, 1977, p. 324) of reading. In this statement, Goodman and Goodman (1977) are asserting that even entire discourses are not completely independent units of meaning, uninfluenced by any other factors. Entire discourse units are always embedded within a broader context. The reader's comprehension of discourse is inevitably influenced by personal background and characteristics.

This author vividly recalls the experience of her first college-level course in biology. Having attended a high school in South America, which was especially weak in the sciences, the experience was a traumatic one. This author remembers not only having difficulty with the new vocabulary being used, but also being consciously aware of an inability to distinguish the important information from the trivia. The structure of the class presentations was elusive, unless the professor was exceedingly explicit about the relationship between the main ideas presented and the supporting data. It is fascinating to go back in a mental time-machine and to compare the experience of this first course with biology courses taken later. Indeed , if you are contending with a book about language for the first time, your experience of reading this book may be very similar to this author's recollection of that first biology course. Any time one braves the frontier of a new field of study, one can appreciate the role that background knowledge plays in facilitating the comprehension of discourse.

Anderson et al. (1977, p. 367) refer to the reader's experiential background as "frameworks for comprehending discourse." They summarize their main thesis as "the meaning of communication depends in a fundamental way on a person's knowledge of the world" (Anderson et al., 1977, p. 368). These researchers developed an interesting method of studying the effects of the reader's experiential background on comprehension. They presented a potentially ambiguous paragraph to two groups of students—physical education students and music education students. The paragraph developed for their study is presented here (Anderson et al., 1977, p. 372):

> Rocky slowly got up from the mat, planning his escape. He hesitated a moment and thought. Things were not going well. What bothered him most was being held, especially since the charge against him had been weak. He considered his present situation. The lock that held him was strong but he thought he could break it. He knew, however, that his timing would have to be perfect. Rocky was aware that it was because of his early roughness that he had been penalized so severely—much too severely from his point of view. The situation was becoming frustrating; the pressure had been grinding on him for too long. He was being ridden unmercifully. Rocky was getting angry now. He felt he was ready to make his move. He knew that his success or failure would depend on what he did in the next few seconds.

The students in the study were asked to respond to comprehension questions of the following kind, for which there are two possible correct answers, depending on which of two interpretations the reader imposed on the paragraph (Anderson et al., 1977, p. 372):

> How had Rocky been punished for his aggressiveness?
> A. He had been demoted to the "B" team.
> B. His opponent had been given points.
> C. He lost his privileges for the weekend.
> D. He had been arrested and imprisoned.

Which of the multiple-choice answers did you choose? If you interpreted the paragraph as describing a wrestling match (as did the physical education students), you selected answer B. If you interpreted the passage as depicting a prisoner planning a jail break (as did the music education students), you chose answer D. Thus, the study provides evidence that students' experiential backgrounds influence their reading comprehension.

Russell Stauffer, the author of *Directing Reading Maturity As a Cognitive Pro-*

*cess* (1969), proposes that the influence of the child's "framework for comprehending discourse" (Anderson et al., 1977, p. 367) is of paramount importance
and must be taken into consideration by teachers. He stresses how vital it is to
prepare children for reading particular passages by setting in motion the appropriate expectations or predictions, that is, activating a "purpose" (Stauffer, 1969,
p. 43) for reading. In Stauffer's (1969, pp. 43–44) words:

> The reading-thinking process begins in the mind of the reader as he experi-
> ences a state of doubt or curiosity about what he knows or does not know,
> and what he thinks will or will not happen or be reported. . . . When pupils
> have become involved in the dynamics of a purpose-setting session, the self-
> commitment on an intellectual as well as an emotional level has tremendous
> motivating force. The power of this force . . . compels and sustains the
> reader until an answer is found. . . . He is out to prove himself right or wrong
> . . . the reading climate. . . . Its tempo is geared to the finding of answers and
> to the proving or disproving of conjectures. He will want to move forward to
> test his ideas, to seek, to reconstruct, to reflect and to prove.

Stauffer (1969, p. 45), in his directive to the teacher to act as an "agitator" of
purposes for reading within students, is embracing a particular view of reading
that "begins in the mind of the reader" (Stauffer, 1969, p. 43). For the reader
brings to the page certain predictions, whether these are conscious or subcon-
scious purposes for reading. Thus, a context exists in the mind of the reader,
which guides the process of comprehending written discourse. This mental context is determined by the reader's conceptual level, interests, background knowledge, and the teacher's ability to agitate in the reader's mind appropriate questions and expectations.

In summary, Goodman and Goodman (1977), Anderson et al. (1977), and
Stauffer (1969) suggest a model of reading in which written discourse is considered context-dependent, in that discourse comprehension is influenced by the
reader's experiential background. This model suggests another strategy that may
be employed during the comprehension process—the strategy of activating the
part of one's background knowledge that is relevant to the discourse being read. If
one integrates this perspective with the earlier descriptions of the processes involved in reading, one might construct a model of reading such that letters are
viewed as embedded within words, words are integral parts of sentences, sentences comprise the larger units of meaning, or discourse, and discourse units are
themselves influenced by the broader context of the reader's framework for comprehension. In this model of reading, letter processing, word identification, sentence comprehension, and discourse analysis are viewed as subsystems of each
other. These interrelationships are depicted in Figure 8.1.

This model of reading can be seen as having a biological analogue in that cells
comprise tissues, tissues make up organs, organs function within systems, and
systems serve the entire organism, which itself cannot be understood unless con-

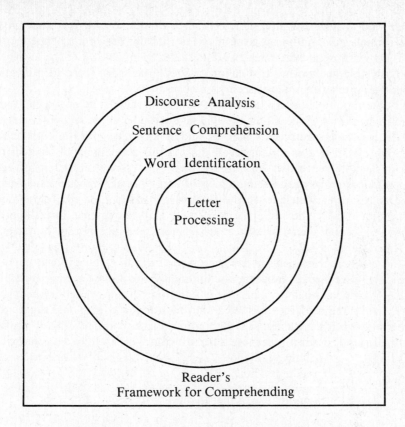

FIGURE 8.1   Multidimensional Model of Reading

sidered within the broader context of its environment. The biological processes that exist at the various levels of organization are each influenced by the broader context in which they operate.

What is reading? The chapter began with this question. To be defined as discourse, this chapter should have cohesion. To be cohesive, must the chapter answer its initial question? Various attempts at providing answers have ranged from the Bloomfield and Barnhart (1961, p. 206) concept of the "basic habit of reading," where letter processing was the only aspect of reading to be described, to the final model presented here, in which reading is viewed as highly complex and multidimensional. Does this historical progression reflect the developmental stages of a child learning to read? This is not so, for Goodman and Goodman (1977) found that even first graders apply their language and experiential background to the task of deriving meaning from written discourse. Thus, from the earliest stages of reading, children engage in strategies appropriate for processing connected discourse. Do you recall the child described at the beginning of the chapter who sought to confirm her hypothesis that the marks written on her friend's drawing communicated the message that the drawing belonged to her friend? Right from its beginnings, reading seems to involve all of the levels that have been described within this chapter: letter processing, word identification, sentence comprehension, and discourse analysis.

This description of reading leaves unresolved the mystery of how a child masters its complexities. If the simple developmental model of the sequential mastering of letters, then words, next sentences, and, finally, discourse is not applicable, then what model is appropriate for describing the developmental changes that occur during the process of learning to read? Are some strategies involved in reading (i.e., certain letter-to-sound clues, certain types of syntactic and semantic strategies, certain discourse-level rules) acquired later than others? The model of reading developed within this chapter should spark an interest in tackling the mystery of learning to read from an angle different than that typically pursued—a multidimensional angle.

In this chapter, brief mention has been made regarding how different views of the reading process might translate into different views of the teaching of reading. The major emphasis has been on theory construction rather than on pedagogy. Consequently, the reader is urged to go beyond the few educational suggestions, primarily drawn from Stauffer's (1969) approach to teaching reading, to consider further the implications for teaching inherent within this multidimensional model of reading.

## INQUIRY 8.1

Phonics, according to Durkin (1972), is the study of the relationship between phonology and orthography—phonology being the study of the speech-sound system of a language and orthography being the study of the curves and lines used to communicate graphically (i.e., the writing system). Bloomfield and Barnhart (1961, p. 206) propose that learning how speech-sounds map onto letters is the totality of learning the "basic habit of reading." As Venezky (1970) indicates, the English spelling system cannot be fully explained through phonics. Other factors, in addition to speech, have influenced our spelling system. Our spelling system has such complexity that most educators agree that letter-sound correspondences tell only part of the story and must be used in conjunction with other clues (syntactic and/or semantic) when one is learning to identify unknown words.

As Bloomfield and Barnhart (1961) recognize and as Venezky (1970) clearly describes, the twenty-six individual letters of the alphabet are not the sole functioning spelling units in the English spelling system. There are other spelling units that consist of more than one letter (e.g., *th, sh, ch,* and *tch*). Therefore, in this inquiry we refer to spelling units, rather than to letters.

A spelling unit does not map neatly and consistently onto one and only one phoneme. The sound or sounds associated with a particular spelling unit depends on such factors as (1) semantic factors such as morpheme boundaries (e.g., *ph* is pronounced */f/* only when both the *p* and *h* fall within the same morpheme, as in *graphic* versus *uphill*), (2) syntactic factors such as parts of speech (words spelled identically have different pronunciations if they belong to different parts of speech: the noun *désert* versus the verb *desért*), (3) position in the word (i.e., whether the spelling unit occupies initial, medial, or final position, for example, *gh* in *ghetto* versus *gh* in *aghast* versus *gh* in *tough*), and (4) the preceding and following letters (e.g., the letters *c* and *g*, when followed by the letter *e*, correspond to the */s/* and */j/* sounds, as in *cent* and *gent*).

Some spelling units have other functions than carrying information about the pronunciation of words. For example, the final silent *e* can serve the function of preserving arbitrary orthographic rules (e.g., words should not end in a *v* or *u*, hence, *love* and *blue*). Other so-called silent letters may mark the similarity in the meanings of words that have varying pronunciations (e.g., the final *b* in *bomb* captures its semantic relationship to *bombardier* and *bombard*, and the silent *g* in *sign* plays a similar role with *signature*, and *signify*).

**OBJECTIVES** The objectives of this inquiry are to:

1. Develop an appreciation for the complexity of the English spelling system.
2. Explore the role played by letter-sound correspondences in learning to identify unknown words.
3. Critically analyze the Bloomfield and Barnhart approach to beginning reading.

**PROCEDURES** Venezky (1970) identifies the following as the major consonant spelling units: *b, c, ch, d, f, g, gh, h, j, k, l, m, n, p, ph, q, r, rh, s, sh, t, th, u* (as in *quack*), *v, w, y, z, ck, dg, tch, wh,* and *x*. Some of these spelling units are single letters; some consist of as many as three letters. To complete this inquiry, first identify all of the consonantal speech-sounds associated with ten of the consonant spelling units. Depending on which consonantal spelling units you choose to analyze, you may have more than one sound associated with each spelling unit. For example, *f* only has one corresponding speech sound (with the exception of the preposition *of*). On the other hand, this is not the case for the *gh* spelling unit (see Table 8.1). For each speech-sound associated with each spelling unit, identify any factors that influence the association. Also indicate for each spelling unit whether or not it ever functions as a silent marker. For those spelling units that are sometimes silent identify: (a) the factors that influence when they are silent and (b) the function that they play. Table 8.1 provides an example of how a spelling unit can be analyzed according to these procedures. Follow this format when presenting your analyses.

TABLE 8.1   The Spelling Unit *gh*

| The speech-sound correspondents of the spelling unit *gh* | | |
| Speech sounds | Examples | Relevant factors influencing the spelling unit–speech sound relationships |
| --- | --- | --- |
| /g/ | *ghost* *aghast* | The *gh* unit corresponds to the /g/ phoneme when it is word initial (e.g., *ghost*) and word medial (e.g., *aghast*), except when the *gh* is silent (see below). |
| /f/ | *enough* | The *gh* unit corresponds to the /f/ phoneme when it is word final (e.g., *tough*), except when the *gh* is silent (see below). |

| *gh* as a silent marker | | |
| Examples | Functions of the silent marker *gh* | Relevant factors influencing when the *gh* unit is silent |
| --- | --- | --- |
| *right* *sigh* | It marks the preceding *i* as corresponding to the long *i* sound. | This occurs when the *gh* unit follows the letter *i* and is word medial (*right*) or word final (*sigh*). |
| *bough* *dough* | It marks the preceding *ou* spelling unit as corresponding to the long /o/ sound. | This occurs when the *gh* unit follows the *ou* spelling unit and is word final. |
| *bought* *fought* | It marks the preceding *ou* spelling unit as corresponding to the /aw/ sound. | This occurs when the *gh* unit follows the *ou* spelling unit, is word medial, and precedes the letter *t*. |

**REPORT**   Submit your analyses of the ten consonantal spelling units, following the procedures outlined. Be sure to provide examples throughout your analyses. Be as clear and specific as possible.

In addition, address yourself to the following questions:

1. Your analysis could be viewed as an explication of the rules governing a part of the English spelling system. Do you think children learn these kinds of rules when learning to read? Why or why not? Do these rules play any role in the process of learning to read? Explain.
2. When instructing reading, how could you apply your knowledge about the functions of the various spelling units to facilitate children's attempts to learn? For example, how might you help children induce these rules?
3. Do you think it is important to guide children so that they do learn these rules?
4. Now that you have explored in some depth the complexity of the English

spelling system, do you agree with Bloomfield and Barnhart (1961) that children should only be exposed to certain simple letter-sound correspondences at the outset of reading? *Or,* should children learn from the start that the English spelling system is complex? Do you agree with Bloomfield and Barnhart (1961) that introducing the concept of reading for meaning only confuses the beginning reader? Explain.

**EVALUATION**   Did this inquiry develop the specific objectives? If so, how? If not, why? How could the effectiveness of this inquiry be increased?

_____          **INQUIRY 8.2**          _____

Clark and Clark (1977) identify syntactic strategies that may play a role in listening comprehension. Similarly, Lefevre (1964) proposes that syntactic knowledge plays an important role in reading comprehension. He emphasizes the importance of sentence comprehension and contends that, in order to successfully comprehend written sentences, children must learn to rely on syntactic knowledge about: (1) word order, (2) structure words, and (3) grammatical inflections. Consistent with his emphasis on sentence comprehension, Lefevre (1964) feels that it is more important to read aloud using the appropriate intonation and pausing, than to render precise word-for-word oral reading renditions.

**OBJECTIVES**   The objectives of this inquiry are to:

1. Observe and analyze the role of syntactic knowledge in reading.
2. Utilize intonation and pausing as clues to gauge the extent to which a child is identifying the syntactic structure of a sentence.
3. Explore the extent to which reading differences among children may be due to "sentence-sense" (Lefevre, 1964, p. 5), that is, their ability to use syntactic knowledge while reading to identify the structure of sentences.

**PROCEDURES**   Select two children who read at least at the fourth-grade level but vary in reading ability (either from different grades or from the same grade but reading at different levels). Present each child with Story 1 (see below) and say:

> I would like you to read this very short story. When you have finished reading it to yourself, try to answer the questions that you will find at the bottom of the page.

Once each child has answered the comprehension questions, ask each one separately to read the story aloud. Do not let the children hear each other reading. Tape-record each child's oral reading. Listen to the tapes to analyze the students' intonation and pauses.

Allow at least one day to pass, then present each child with Story 2 and say:

This time I want you to try to read a story that is written in a strange language. Try to understand the story as best you can, although there will be many strange words to read. When you have finished reading to yourself, try to answer the questions that you will find at the bottom of the page.

Do not allow the students to refer back to Story 1. Repeat the procedure described for Story 1, taping each child's oral reading separately. The two stories are as follows:

### Story 1

A boy was eating his soup. Suddenly a friend tossed some ice in his soup. "Why did you toss ice in my hot soup?" the boy asked the friend. "I'm terribly sorry," the friend answered. "I thought you liked ice in your soup. Do you eat your soup hot?"

### Questions

1. What did the friend toss in the boy's soup?
2. What did the boy ask the friend?
3. Was the friend sorry?
4. How does the boy like to eat his soup?

### Story 2[2]

A marlup was poving his kump. Parmily a narg horped some whev in his kump. "Why did vump horp whev in my frinkle kump?" the marlup jufd the narg. "Er'm muvvily trungy," the narg grupped. "Er heshed vump norpled whev in your kump. Do vump pove your kump frinkle?"

### Questions

1. What did the narg horp in the marlup's kump?
2. What did the marlup juf the narg?
3. Was the narg trungy?
4. How does the marlup norple to pove his kump?

**REPORT**   In addition to submitting the children's answers to the comprehension questions and descriptions of their reading levels (as identified by their teachers), address yourself to the following questions:

1. What type of syntactic knowledge did the children need to apply in order to answer the comprehension questions for Stories 1 and 2? For example, what knowledge is necessary about word order (e.g., rules governing the order of adjectives and nouns within noun phrases), structure words (e.g., rules governing what kinds of structures begin with the structure word *the*), and grammatical inflections (e.g., rules about what kinds of words can be pluralized)?
2. Semantic clues are obviously missing from Story 2, which is designed to test children's use of purely syntactic strategies while reading. Did either

of the children manage to answer any of the comprehension questions for Story 2? If so, which questions were answered correctly and what type of syntactic knowledge was apparently used? Was the student reading at a higher level more successful in relying on strictly syntactic clues?

3. How did the students' performance on the comprehension questions for Story 2 compare with their performance on the comprehension questions for Story 1? In answering the questions for Story 1, do you think the students relied strictly on their syntactic knowledge about word order, structure words, and grammatical inflections? In other words, did they rely purely on the kinds of syntactic strategies described by Clark and Clark (1977)? Explain. If not, what other types of strategies (i.e., what other clues) did they rely on for replying to the comprehension questions?

4. Do you agree with Lefevre (1964) that intonation and pausing are important clues to how well a reader comprehends a sentence? How did the two students' use of intonation and pausing differ, if at all? Did the students' use of intonation and pausing differ when reading Story 2 versus Story 1? If so, how?

**EVALUATION**   Did this inquiry develop the specific objectives? If so, how? If not, why? How could the effectiveness of this inquiry be increased?

## INQUIRY 8.3

Goodman and Goodman (1977) conducted extensive studies of students' oral reading behavior. They feel that such studies provide a "window on the reading processes" (Goodman & Goodman, 1977, p. 319). They analyze children's observable attempts at word identification while reading connected discourse aloud. By taping the oral readings, transcribing them, and studying them, Goodman and Goodman (1977) have been able to gain insight into the types of strategies children use while reading, for example, their attempts at using letter-sound correspondences and their application of syntactic and semantic knowledge to predict upcoming words and to correct their miscues (i.e., their substitutions, insertions, word order changes, and deletions). They conclude that miscues and self-corrections are very revealing reflections of the students' active attempts to construct meaning while reading. Rather than viewing miscues simply as errors, Goodman and Goodman (1977) analyze them from the positive perspective of what they reveal about the strategies children apply in order to comprehend written language.

**OBJECTIVES**   The objectives of this inquiry are to:

1. Observe the reading process in action during an oral reading task.
2. Observe and analyze the kinds of miscues and self-corrections children make while reading aloud in order to determine the influence of letter-

sound correspondences and syntactic and semantic clues on attempts to read connected discourse.

3. Compare students' word identification skills when words are presented in isolation with such skills when words are presented in the context of connected discourse.

**PROCEDURE**   Select a student who reads at least at the third-grade level but not above the sixth-grade level. Administer the word recognition test, consisting of the list of sixty individual words shown below. Present these words in isolation, one at a time, by using two index cards. Line up the cards one above the other, so that the top card is just above the first word and the bottom card is just below it, covering the second word on the list, as follows:

Once the child has tried to read the first word and is ready to move on, lower the bottom card to reveal the second word and cover the third word, and lower the top card so that it now covers the first word. Repeat this procedure for each word on the list. Do not dwell too long on each word. Look for signs that the child is ready to move on to the next word.

Tape-record the student's word identification attempts during this task. If all the words are identified correctly, however, the task is too easy for the student. Therefore, you should select another student. If the first student can only read ten or fewer words from the list, the task is too difficult for the child. Again, select a different student.

### WORD RECOGNITION LIST

| | | |
|---|---|---|
| ahead | dependent | meant |
| alive | discern | motion |
| aware | dictionary | narrow |
| assigned | examine | often |
| activities | education | outside |
| bares | excited | possible |
| beginning | focuses | pattern |
| brain | gaze | pedal |
| consider | however | panic |
| confidence | interpret | pilot |
| canvas | intently | reading |
| continue | lens | root |
| countryside | looms | rather |

| | | |
|---|---|---|
| renewed | surge | transmitted |
| riddle | symbols | trail |
| reminds | stern | twisted |
| redefining | straighten | understand |
| received | travels | vacation |
| sixty | there | word |
| sidewalk | tremendous | yourself |

Once you have found a student reading at an appropriate level for this inquiry, you are ready to follow the word recognition part of the inquiry with the discourse reading task. Present the young reader with the written discourse given below. This passage was used by Turner (1979) in a study of the miscues and self-corrections of fifth-grade students. Instruct your student to read the passage aloud. Do not allow the student to read the passage silently first, as this would contaminate the "window" through which you are peering at the reading process. Tape-record the student's oral reading. Do not coach or instruct the student in any way during the procedure, except to provide encouraging looks or comments to proceed reading.

### Reading: What Is It?[3]

Reading. What is it? In the beginning the word came from an Anglo-Saxon word, "raeden." In Old English the word meant to discern, to interpret. The word "riddle" also came from this root word.

We often consider "reading" in a rather narrow way, thinking only of "interpreting" meanings assigned to written symbols. Most of our formal education, that which takes place in school, is dependent upon reading. However, it is possible to look at the meaning of reading through a wider lens. Let's consider reading to be what you do when you tune yourself in to the activities of the world.

Reading. What is it? The eye focuses, becomes aware of a pattern. The pattern is transmitted to the brain. Then the brain says, "Got it. Move on."

Reading. The car you're riding in travels down the road at sixty miles an hour. A yellow and black sign looms ahead with the letters "CAUTION." The driver's foot comes off the gas pedal and in the same motion goes to the brakes.

Reading. You are excited. It's the first day of a vacation and you are in a hurry to get outside. It's great to be alive! You start to rush out of the front door. Your mother is standing nearby. Something about her stern look reminds you that you forgot to straighten your room. You stop.

Reading. You are walking along the street. There's a dog on the sidewalk ahead. You must pass it. Its tail is not moving. The dog bares his teeth. You cross to the other side of the street.

Reading. You gaze at it. The colors seem to jump at you from the canvas. The twisted shapes take on meaning. The feelings the artist had come through to you—"Tremendous!" you say to yourself.

Reading. You look intently at the map. The train hurries through the countryside. You turn to your friend and say as you point to the map, "We should be about here."

Reading. For a moment you feel a surge of panic. You examine the trail closely. You are certain that you are not lost, but. . . . Then you notice a familiar cut on a tree which says to you, "This is the trail."

Reading. What is it? It is interpreting the meaning of what you see, hear and feel. The pilot who says to the tower, "I read you loud and clear," is saying, "I received the message; I understand."

A check in your dictionary will show that there are many ways of redefining reading. Maybe it would be wise to go back to the Anglo-Saxon root word and say, "Reading is interpreting the riddles of life."

**REPORT**    Submit your transcripts of the student's oral readings of the isolated words and the connected discourse. Make an accurate record of all words and all false starts, where only sounds may have been uttered (e.g., *s . s . sixty*). Mark where major pauses occur during the oral reading of the connected discourse using dots (e.g., *s . . . s . . . sixty*).

In addition, address yourself to the following questions:

1. What types of strategies did the student use in attempting to identify the unknown words during the word recognition task? Did the student try to associate sounds with letters? Were attempts that resulted in nonsense words self-corrected to yield meaningful words?
2. Analyzing the miscues and self-corrections, what types of strategies were used during the discourse reading task? Reread this chapter to refresh your memory about the types of letter-sound generalizations and syntactic and semantic strategies that could play a role during the reading of discourse.
3. How did the student's reading of the isolated words compare with the reading of the same words in the context of the discourse?
4. On the basis of the observations made during this inquiry, do you agree with Goodman and Goodman's (1977, p. 330) conclusion that "sentences are easier than words, paragraphs easier than sentences, pages easier than paragraphs"? Do you agree with the following description of the reading process proposed by Goodman and Goodman (1977, pp. 323–24)?

> . . . through strategies of predicting, sampling and confirming receptive language users can leap toward meaning with partial processing of input . . . continuous monitoring of subsequent input and meaning for confirmation and consistency. Many miscues reflect readers' abilities to liberate themselves from detailed attention to print as they leap toward meaning. Consequently, they reverse, substitute, insert, omit, rearrange, paraphrase and transform. . . . In both reading and listening, prediction is at least as important as perception.

**EVALUATION** Did this inquiry develop the specific objectives? If so, how? If not, why? How could the effectiveness of this inquiry be increased?

_____ **INQUIRY 8.4** _____

Bransford, Barclay, and Franks (1972), Goodman and Goodman (1977), and Clark and Clark (1977) view comprehension as extending beyond the level of sentence perception to the level of discourse analysis. Discourse comprehension is characterized as involving the ability to identify the relationships that connect the sentences and paragraphs into a cohesive, meaningful unit—an ability that requires being able to process more information than is available in the separate sentences.

Although comprehension studies have typically used auditory input and adult subjects, Blachowicz (1977–1978; 1978–1979) conducted studies of reading comprehension that revealed that children as young as seven are capable of making inferences that link the sentences comprising a short paragraph into a meaningful unit. These inferences involved "semantic constructivity . . . integration of information in a text with one's world knowledge (Blachowicz, 1978–1979, p. 169). This inquiry is designed using procedures similar to those of Blachowicz (1978–1979).

**OBJECTIVES** The objectives of this inquiry are to:

1. Explore the types of inferential skills involved in deriving information from short, cohesive discourse units.
2. Compare the discourse comprehension skills of children who vary in their reading ability.
3. Explore the validity of a multidimensional model of reading.

**PROCEDURES** Select two children who read at different levels, but at about the second-grade level. Ask each child separately to read aloud to you the mini-stories given below. This will give you an indication of the children's ability to identify the words comprising the mini-stories. If either child makes more than five reading errors (i.e., is apparently unable to identify the meaning of more than five words), select a different child. The mini-stories are as follows:

### Story One[4]
The birds sat on the branch.
A hawk flew over it.
The birds were robins.

### Story Two
Two ducks sat on a log.
A fish swam under it.
The fish was a goldfish.

### Story Three

Two bugs sat on the grass under a flower.
A butterfly sat on the flower.
It was a pretty rose.

### Story Four

Two cats slept in a basket.
A bird in a cage hung over them.
The bird was a parrot.

### Story Five

A baby sat on a swing.
A bug flew under her.
The bug was a bee.

When the children have finished reading, instruct them to circle the true statements on the Discourse Comprehension Test, and to draw a line through the false statements. Ask each child to repeat the instructions, to make sure that they have been understood. The children may refer back to the original stories, since this is a test of comprehension, not of memory. The children should complete this test independently of each other and of you.

The comprehension test includes literally true statements (LTS) that involve no inference (e.g., *The birds sat on the branch*); literally false statements (LFS) that involve no inference (e.g., *The birds sat on the ground*); true inferential statements of Level I (TIS-I) that involve simple inferences made by correctly identifying the referent of a pronoun (e.g., *A hawk flew over the branch*); false inferential statements of Level I (FIS-I) (e.g., *A hawk flew over the log*); true inferential statements of Level II (TIS-II) that involve more complex inferences made by applying one's knowledge of the spatial relations of objects in the world (e.g., *A hawk flew over the birds*); true inferential statements of Level III (TIS-III) that involve still more complex inferences made by applying one's knowledge of spatial relations and one's logical skills (e.g., *A hawk flew over the robins*—a conclusion one could logically reach by knowing the hawk flew over the birds and that the birds were robins); and false inferential statements of Level III (FIS-III) (e.g., *The robins flew over the hawk*). The statements have been coded so that you can tally the number of correctly identified statements. Summarize each student's results as follows:

Student #＿＿＿          Reading level ＿＿＿
Number of correctly identified literal statements ＿＿＿
Number of correctly identified inferential–Level I statements ＿＿＿
Number of correctly identified inferential–Level II statements ＿＿＿
Number of correctly identified inferential–Level III statements ＿＿＿

## Discourse Comprehension Test

### Story One

1. A hawk flew over the branch.     (TIS-I)
2. The birds sat on the ground.     (LFS)
3. A hawk flew under the birds.     (FIS-II)
4. The birds sat on the branch.     (LTS)
5. A hawk flew over the birds.     (TIS-II)
6. The robins flew over the hawk.     (FIS-III)
7. A hawk flew over the log.     (FIS-II)
8. A hawk flew over the robins.     (TIS-III)

### Story Two

9. A fish swam under a log.     (TIS-I)
10. Two ducks swam under a fish.     (FIS-II)
11. The fish was a minnow.     (LFS)
12. The fish was a goldfish.     (LTS)
13. A fish swam under a butterfly.     (FIS-I)
14. There were two goldfish.     (FIS-III )
15. A goldfish swam under two ducks.     (TIS-III)
16. A fish swam under two ducks.     (TIS-II)

### Story Three

17. A butterfly sat under two bugs.     (FIS-II)
18. A butterfly sat on a flower.     (LTS)
19. The grass was a rose.     (FIS-I)
20. A butterfly sat next to a flower.     (LFS)
21. Two bugs sat under a butterfly.     (TIS-II)
22. Two bugs sat under a rose.     (TIS-III)
23. There were two roses.     (FIS-III)
24. The flower was a rose.     (TIS-I)

### Story Four

25. Two cats slept in a cage.     (LFS)
26. There were two birds.     (FIS-III)
27. The bird was a parrot.     (LTS)
28. A bird in a cage hung over two cats.     (TIS-I)
29. A bird in a cage sat next to a basket.     (FIS-II)
30. A parrot in a cage hung over a basket.     (TIS-III)
31. A bird in a cage hung over a basket.     (TIS-II)
32. A bird in a cage hung over a butterfly.     (FIS-I)

## Story Five

33. The baby was a girl.          (TIS-I)
34. The bug was a girl bug.       (FIS-I)
35. A baby sat on a swing.        (LTS)
36. A bug flew under the swing.     (TIS-II)
37. A bug sat on the swing.       (LFS)
38. A bug flew over the swing.      (FIS-II)
39. A bee flew under a swing.     (TIS-III)
40. A baby was under a tree.      (FIS-III)

**REPORT**   Present the results of the comprehension test for each student and the student's reading level (as reported to you by the student's teacher).

In addition, address yourself to the following questions:

1. Was each student capable of drawing inferences that linked the sentences into cohesive discourse units? What types of inferences were most successfully made: Level I, Level II, or Level III? Why do you think those inferences were easiest?
2. Compare the students' performances on the comprehension test. Was the better student more capable of drawing inferences? If so, what types of inferences were easier for this student?
3. On the basis of your observations in this inquiry, do you feel the multidimensional model of reading described at the end of this chapter is valid? That is, does reading transcend sentence comprehension, extending to the level of discourse analysis, and does discourse analysis  require the application of the reader's knowledge of the world? Explain and defend your position.

**EVALUATION**   Did this inquiry develop the specific objectives? If so, how? If not, why? How could the effectiveness of this inquiry be increased?

## NOTES

1. The sequences of symbols represent: /tat/, /cad/, /neb/, /bot/, /pov/, and /heg/.
2. Story and questions developed by Goodman (1968).
3. From M. S. Johnson, R. A. Kress, J. D. McNeill, E. B. Black, and M. H. Black, *Kings and things* (Level 5) Reading Experience and Development Series. Cincinnati, Ohio: American Book Company, 1968, pp. 300–301. Reprinted with permission of D.C. Heath and Co.
4. This story is from Blachowicz (1978–1979, p. 171).

# 9

# Assessing Language and Communication

The scope and emphasis of this chapter derive from the positions that the assessment of language and communication is embedded in one's view of the nature of language itself and also that, whereas teachers may need to be familiar with commercially available standardized tests, the strength of any assessment depends on the teacher's ability to construct and sensibly utilize nonstandard informal measures of language. Following a model for the assessment of language, including its nature and purposes, available standardized tests are briefly summarized. This is followed by a somewhat detailed description of informal nonstandardized procedures for assessing language, communication, and metalinguistic knowledge. Where feasible, brief cases are presented to illustrate the actual use of these procedures. However, two cautions must be given at this point. First, this chapter on assessment is meant to be introductory. Its intent is to *familiarize* the reader with the issues, nature, and scope of language assessment rather than to provide the necessary skills to become a fully competent language diagnostician. Second, the assessment procedures presented in this chapter are meant to be suggestive, *not* exhaustive, of the ways by which useful information can be obtained.

## DEVELOPING A MODEL FOR ASSESSMENT

Before we can determine the need for language intervention or the focus of intervention, we must perform a comprehensive assessment of language structure and use. Our approach to language assessment must reflect a model of language that takes into account several considerations, ranging from the purposes of the assessment to one's conceptualization of the very nature of language.

Part of this chapter also appears in A. Gerber and D. N. Bryen, *Language and learning disabilities.* Baltimore: University Park Press, 1981.

The purpose of assessment is to provide information concerning a particular skill, body of knowledge, or ability so that decisions can be made concerning whether or not intervention is called for and, if so, what should be the focus of the intervention. In order to make such decisions, we must use much more than simply a set of scores or data. What is also needed is a way of organizing, or making sense of, the data so that they have meaning. This requires the use of a model of language—a model incorporating such factors as the nature of language, the role of language and the sequence of language development. Without such a model, our attempts at interpretation of the particulars of a language assessment will be futile ones. Also, differences in one's view of language may in fact result in very different interpretations of the assessment information, yielding very different decisions concerning the need for and nature of language intervention.

How specifically does a particular model of language affect the assessment of language? Let us briefly return to our definition of the nature of language as given in Chapters 1 and 2. You recall that language is defined there as a rule-governed symbol system that is capable of representing or coding one's understanding of the world. Given this definition of language, our assessment of language cannot merely be concerned with measuring vocabulary or the mean length of utterance (MLU). We are also bound to be interested in other questions, such as: (1) What linguistic rules are part of the speaker's repertoire? (2) How do these linguistic rules compare to those of speakers of similar age and language community? (3) In what ways do these linguistic rules compare to those used by a competent language user? and (4) In what ways does deviation in the rules used by a speaker demonstrate knowledge of language? When we specify that language is composed of symbols that code one's understanding of the world, we imply that we are interested in seeking information concerning both an individual's nonlinguistic knowledge of social and physical events and ability to use conventional symbols to represent and communicate this knowledge.

In Chapter 1, it was also stated that language is a generative system. If we accept this view of language, we are concerned not only with what linguistic rules an individual has acquired, but how flexible is the use of these rules. Assessment questions growing out of this concern are as follows: (1) Can the child produce and comprehend utterances that were never heard or spoken before (given that the concepts and vocabulary are familiar)? and (2) Are the child's syntactic options restricted and stereotypic or does the child have versatility in the use of linguistic structures?

It was also specified that language is a social and conventional code and that one learns the particular language of one's speech community. If we accept this characteristic of language, then we must recognize both language and dialect variation. We cannot simply ask if the child has learned the structures of standard English, but must also ask if the child has mastered the specific language of his speech community. This question has very important implications for both assessment and intervention, and, furthermore, forces us to view deviation in a broader sense—not simply as a sign of deficiency. Whether this recognition of language variation entails developing separate tests, separate scoring procedures, or broadened interpretation strategies, the sociocultural role of language should be neither underestimated nor translated into a monocultural phenomenon.

In addition, a model of language must include the communicative functions. The implication of this should be quite clear; that is, language must be assessed in its social context. When assessing language, we cannot rely exclusively on structured tasks, such as elicited imitation paradigms, object manipulation tasks, or picture identification. This is not to say that these do not provide important information about a child's knowledge of language. However, it is equally important to question how a child uses this knowledge in various social contexts. A related concern is how various social contexts affect the cognitive and communicative demands placed on the child. If we accept that language is used in social contexts and, furthermore, that social contexts vary with respect to familiarity (i.e., shared knowledge), formality, and purpose, then we must assess not only the child, but also the social context itself. This is especially important when we study the language used in school classrooms for the purposes of instruction. We cannot assume that a match exists between the linguistic code the child uses in familiar, less formal, and interpersonally motivated contexts and the linguistic code used for instruction. This aspect of our model of language broadens the focus of assessment efforts to include not just the child, but the child's teachers and even the instructional materials. (See Chapter 10 for further discussion of the instructional code.)

To be in line with the statement earlier in this book that communication is not restricted to the use of spoken language, an adequate assessment of language must include the child's ability to comprehend and produce other communicative signals. These communicative signals include gestures, facial expression, prosodic features, eye contact, and so on.

Finally, all languages are acquired through a series of developmental phases, and a model of assessment must take account of this factor on at least two levels—content and process. At the content level, consideration of this factor must yield an assessment model that is not based on the assumption that child language (or deviant language, for that matter) is simply a quantitatively and linearly reduced picture of adult language. Sufficient evidence favors the position that linguistic rules governing child language are qualitatively different from those governing adult language. Furthermore, if assessment information is to have any relevance to decisions concerning intervention, then the content of assessment strategies must reflect the developmental sequence inherent in normal acquisition of language. Without this developmental perspective, the results of an assessment effort will provide little insight into what aspects of language the child has already mastered and what aspects remain undeveloped.

The second level of a developmental assessment model relates to assumptions concerning process, that is, how language is learned. To clarify this somewhat, we can draw an analogy between the content level and the scope and sequence of the educational curriculum. In contrast, the process level is more analogous to teaching methodology in educational curriculum. Although there is not complete consensus among psychologists and psycholinguists concerning how language is learned, there is increasing evidence concerning, for example, the relationship between language and cognition. This evidence should guide assessment efforts, especially in the area of understanding the why of language problems. This perspective also broadens the evaluative strategies that are to be employed, so that we should assess not only language structures and functions, but also related cognitive abilities, such as conservation, classification, and visual perspectivism (see Sinclair, 1969; 1970; 1971). Although information obtained through such a broadened assessment approach may not reveal what specific aspects require intervention, it may provide insights concerning the child's readiness for structured intervention and appropriate strategies for either intervention or compensation.

To summarize the characteristics of our language assessment model, the following factors must be taken into account:

1. Language as a rule-governed symbol system,
2. Language as a generative phenomenon,
3. Language as a social, conventional code,
4. The function(s) of language,
5. The effects of various social contexts, and
6. The developmental nature (content and process) of language.

The employment of this assessment model, or its translation into strategies for obtaining linguistic information, places many demands on the evaluator. First, the evaluator must have an adequate understanding of what rules (both syntactic and semantic) comprise a particular language system. Second, the evaluator must not only understand how sociocultural factors influence language, but, if working with culturally divergent students, must also have a working knowledge of their linguistic system. This is a knowledge of similarities and differences between standard English and the child's language or dialect and of how the child's primary language or dialect interferes with the learning of standard English. Third, the evaluator must understand the nature and various functions of communication, including how these functions place differential cognitive and linguistic demands on the child both as a listener and a speaker. Similarly, the evaluator must be able to analyze a particular social context to determine the degree of familiarity, formality, and abstractness affecting the listener-speaker roles. Fourth, the evaluator must have a strong foundation of knowledge pertaining to both the content and processes of language development. With this foundation, the evaluator can use assessment information to make sensible decisions concerning the what, how, and why of intervention. Finally, in a real sense the evaluator must be an engineer; translating the body of information gained into specific assessment techniques is a rather difficult task. It requires a sound knowledge-base, creative interactional techniques, and a firm understanding of how specific testing paradigms affect the type of language used. Thus, the assessment of language must rest upon a solid base of theory and research. "The most useful and dependable language assessment device is an informed clinician (or educator) who feels compelled to keep up with developments in psycholinguistics, speech pathology, and related fields . . ." (Siegel & Broen, 1976, p. 76, parentheses added).

The remainder of this chapter, while assuming a certain degree of background knowledge as specified by the first four factors above, focuses specifically on the last factor, that is, translating the body of linguistic, psycholinguistic, and sociolinguistic knowledge into sound assessment strategies. Each of the strategies presented throughout this chapter clearly does not embody all of the aforementioned requirements of a model of language assessment. Instead, as Dale (1976) recommends, each of the strategies has a particular diagnostic purpose (e.g., assessing egocentrism in listening). However, various combinations of these tasks should reflect an adequate model of language functioning.

## ASSESSING THE STRUCTURE AND FUNCTION OF LANGUAGE

Before examining various formal and informal assessment strategies, we must first determine the purposes for which assessment is conducted. Also, each strategy attempts to tap a particular area of language and is based on a particular test paradigm or format (e.g., elicited imitation, picture identification, etc.). Both of these factors affect the type of information obtained and how this information can subsequently be used. Let us first consider the purposes of assessment.

Assessment for screening purposes provides information concerning how a child's performance in a given area of language conforms to the norms of a given age group. This information may be presented in the form of percentiles, language ages, and so on. The items of a screening measure are broad in scope, sampling a large number of language abilities. In addition to determining how closely the child's language functioning conforms to given norms, the individual items that the child has passed or failed can provide the evaluator with information as to which linguistic structures the child has mastered and which linguistic structures require further analysis and possible intervention. This evaluative process is facilitated when items in a test are developmentally sequenced. If the test is not set up in a developmentally-based order, the evaluator must rely on personal knowledge of the developmental sequence of language. In essence, assessment for screening purposes answers the following question: Does the child require further assessment and, if so, in what areas of language?

The information derived from screening tests is not, however, sufficient for actually planning an approach to intervention. Several additional questions must first be considered, such as (1) What specifically is the nature of the language problem? (2) What strategies does the child use in processing and producing language? (3) How does the child use linguistic knowledge for the purposes of communication? and (4) What social or cognitive factors contribute to the child's difficulties in the use of language? These questions require in-depth analysis, usually beyond the scope of formal standardized measures.

Just as the purpose of the test influences the type of information it provides, so does the test paradigm, or format. Ideally, the test paradigm should be related as closely as possible to the natural use of language while yielding valuable information. This means that a distinction must be made between assessment techniques that are structured and frequently artificial in nature and those based on the analysis of the natural use of language. In the former situation, we sacrifice information about how a child uses language in the natural process of communication in favor of investigating more closely the structural aspects of language and the possible strategies employed in processing and using language. Assessment based on the use of structured tasks can be designed so that the linguistic features of concern are built into it. For example, if we are interested in exploring the child's understanding of complex sentences representing various logical operations, we can devise structured tasks employing object manipulation or picture identification. In such a case, we could not rely on a spontaneous sample of language, because the linguistic structures of concern may not occur even if several language episodes are recorded and evaluated. Another limitation of a spontaneous language sample paradigm arises out of the kinds of information we are interested in obtaining. Not only are we interested in seeking answers (via a spontaneous sample of language) to questions concerning how the child uses language, but we are also interested in determining what the child knows about language. The latter is best determined through the use of structured assessment tasks, whereby the evaluator can identify and study specific linguistic features and can probe into the bases for the child's responses.

## STANDARDIZED TESTS OF LANGUAGE

Recent literature reflects an apparent trend away from heavy or exclusive reliance on formal, standardized testing toward a strong advocacy for descriptive, informal assessment. Muma (1973; 1978) and Leonard et al. (1978) are prominent among the writers who build a strong case against excessive use of formal tests and for the practice of nonstandardized descriptive assessment. Muma (1973) finds developmental scales and other normative measures of language acquisition to be of questionable value. He maintains that quantified, normative information provides data, but not evidence about the nature of problems in language knowledge and usage. The highly specific, structured tasks characteristic of standardized testing are only remotely related to spontaneous behavior, which varies from context to context and from function to function. Muma (1978, p. 265) urges that, if standardized tests must be administered in order to determine deviance, information beyond the numerical score be gleaned from the formal observation, because "it is more important to learn *how* an individual functions in obtaining a score than *what* the score is."

Teachers, however, should be aware of the most commonly used standardized tests of language because they are of widespread use in language evaluations. Therefore, Table 9.1 presents a number of these tests. The list of tests presented in Table 9.1 is by no means a complete one, and the reader is referred to additional sources (e.g., Bryen & Gallagher, 1982; Wiig & Semel, 1976; 1980; Minifie & Lloyd, 1978; Lloyd, 1976; Muma, 1978; Bloom & Lahey, 1978) where standardized tests of language are catalogued, described, or critiqued.

## SPONTANEOUS LANGUAGE SAMPLES

Obtaining and transcribing a spontaneous sample of language provide us with a tool for analyzing in depth the child's use of language. This analysis can focus on any one of several aspects of language, ranging from syntax to semantics to actual discourse. In addition to supplying a rich corpus with the potential to undergo several forms of linguistic analysis, spontaneous language samples obtained in varying contexts reveal how children use their language for different purposes (e.g., informal interpersonal interaction, giving information).

Stimulating the production of a spontaneous sample of language can be at first a difficult task. The following are some tips to facilitate this effort.

### Tips for Young Children

1. Bring in an unfamiliar toy that requires creative manipulation (e.g., Fisher Price farm or airport). Have another child join the child who is being assessed and simply let the children play together with the toy. If you are interested in how the child uses language when communicating with an adult, have a familiar adult (parent or teacher) interact with the child using the toy. (It is interesting to note that obtaining a sample of a parent/child or teacher/child interaction can provide the evaluator with valuable information concerning not only the child's use of language but also the adult's use of linguistic and discourse strategies. We will develop this point further later in this chapter.)
2. Making and/or using Play-Doh is an excellent stimulus context for promoting children's communication.
3. An animal such as a rabbit, guinea pig, or gerbil is another good stimulus for conversation among children or between an adult and child.

### Tips for Older Children

1. A board game the rules of which children must agree on is a good stimulus for communication. If your interest is assessing how the child uses language for the purpose of giving information, you might utilize a game for which the child already knows the rules and have him teach it to his partner (adult or child).

TABLE 9.1 Commercially Prepared Tests of Language

| Name (Author of Test) | Aspect of Language Measured | Target Population | Purported Purpose | Comments |
|---|---|---|---|---|
| Assessment of Children's Language Comprehension (Foster, Giddan, & Stark, 1973) | Ability of children to identify pictures containing 1, 2, 3, or 4 verbal elements | Preschool through elementary | "To define receptive language difficulty in children and to indicate guidelines for correction" | Available in group or individual form. No expressive ability in children required. Reliability and validity not reported. Not a complete test of language comprehension, as title states (no testing of syntactic comprehension), but useful for measuring number of verbal information bits child can integrate concurrently. |
| Boehm Test of Basic Concepts (Boehm, 1971) | Comprehension of basic vocabulary | Kindergarten through second grade | Comprehension of basic vocabulary used in kindergarten and first grade | Fifty items arranged in increasing difficulty to measure the basic vocabulary of quantity, space, and time. Two alternative forms available. Test can be easily administered individually or in a group. The testing context is similar to that in which the child will generally encounter the word. Standardization sample (K–grade 2) is large and representative geographically, tapping a wide socioeconomic status. In addition to normative data available, de- |

254

| Instrument | Description | Purpose | Age range | Comments |
|---|---|---|---|---|
| Carrow Elicited Language Inventory (Carrow-Woolfolk, 1974) | Expressive language in elicited situation (emphasis on syntax) | To assess a child's productive control of grammar | Ages 3 to 8 | 52 stimulus sentences and phrases are used to elicit responses. Child's responses are taped, require phonemic transcription. Analysis system covers 12 grammatical categories and 5 error types. Provides for in-depth analysis of child's errors on verbs. scriptive error pattern analysis can be done. Validity and test-retest reliability information is provided. |
| Clinical Evaluation of Language Functions (Semel & Wiig, 1980) | A series of subtests measuring a variety of language functions, including both the production and processing of language | To access a variety of language functions, including forming sentences, understanding words and word relationships, memory of spoken discourse, and word retrieval and fluency. | Kindergarten through 10 years | More than 10 subtests measuring many aspects of language that present problems for learning disabled children. Adequate test-retest reliability is reported for subtests, as well as moderate concurrent validity. Response paradigms are varied—including picture identification, imitation, sentence formulation, answering questions, and timed associations. |

TABLE 9.1 (Continued)

| Name (Author of Test) | Aspect of Language Measured | Target Population | Purported Purpose | Comments |
|---|---|---|---|---|
| Detroit Test of Learning Aptitudes (Baker & Leland, 1959) | Reasoning and comprehension, verbal and auditory attentive abilities | Preschool through high school | To identify strengths and weaknesses in faculties directly or indirectly related to language and considered relevant to performance of academic tasks | Nineteen subtests include verbal absurdities, verbal opposites, oral commission, auditory attention span for related syllables, likeness, and differences. Overall reliability is adequate, although there are certain limitations in standardization (e.g., norms are dated, standardization population is restricted). |
| Developmental Sentence Analysis (Lee, 1974) | Expressive syntax in spontaneous speech | Ages 2 to 7 | To evaluate the grammatical structure of child's spontaneous speech | 100 different intelligible spontaneous utterances are taped and analyzed according to length and type. Basic assumption: increasing length a measure of increasing grammatical complexity. Score is weighted for presence of indefinite pronoun or noun modifiers, personal pronouns, main verbs, secondary verbs, negatives, conjunctions, interrogative reversals, and *wh-* questions. Elements |

| Test | Area Measured | Age | Purpose | Comments |
|---|---|---|---|---|
| | | | | that normally occur later are given greater weight. Interjudge reliability = .94; split-half reliability = .73. Validity data supportive. |
| Goldman–Fristoe Test of Articulation (Goldman & Fristoe, 1969) | Articulation | Above age 2 | To assess child's ability to produce speech sounds | Attractively illustrated. Well standardized. Takes about 30 minutes to administer. Measures speech sound production in initial, medial, and final positions in words and sentences. |
| Houston Test of Language Development (Crabtree, 1963) | A variety of expressive and receptive language and language-related tasks | 6 months to 6 years | To assess child's developmental language | Standardization is incomplete. Test has two parts—Part I is a checklist for parent or teacher to check items at the age they were first observed in the child. Part II measures syntactical complexity, intonation, vocabulary, comprehension, and self-identity. |
| Illinois Test of Psycholinguistic Abilities (Kirk, McCarthy, & Kirk, 1968) | Correlates of language such as duplicating a sequence of geometric designs; also vocabulary and expression | Ages 2 to 7 | To identify the psycholinguistic abilities and disabilities of children | Based on a model that separates various skills into expressive, receptive, and organizing aspects, and into representational and automatic levels. Relationship of various subtests to language itself not well established. Overall reliability satisfactory; some subtest reliabilities too low for diagnosis of individuals. Validity unresolved. |

TABLE 9.1 (Continued)

| Name (Author of Test) | Aspect of Language Measured | Target Population | Purported Purpose | Comments |
|---|---|---|---|---|
| Language Comprehension Tests (Bellugi-Klima, 1973) | Selected aspects of language comprehension | Preschool | To test comprehension of linguistic constructions | Child is asked to manipulate real objects in response to examiner's instructions at three levels: (1) active sentences, singular/plural nouns, possessives; (2) negative/affirmative, singular/plural verbs, inflections, adjectival modifications; (3) negative affixes, reflexivization, comparatives, passives, embedded sentences. Items are exemplary rather than comprehensive. Test lends itself well to diagnostic teaching. |
| McCarthy Scales of Children's Abilities (McCarthy, 1970) | Word knowledge, verbal memory, verbal fluency, and analogies | Ages 2.6 to 8.6 years | To assess a variety of faculties related to intellectual functioning | Six scales include verbal, perceptual-performance, quantitative, general cognitive, memory, and motor. Normative data is available for each scale. Test-retest reliability is not presented for each of the 18 subtests that comprise the 6 scales. Standardization, while restricted in age range, is recent and representative. Adequate reliability is reported for the verbal scale. |

| | | | | |
|---|---|---|---|---|
| cal Comprehension, Experimental Edition (Miller & Yoder, 1972) | Syntactic comprehension | Ages 3 to 6 | To assess a child's grammatical comprehension | 42 stimulus sentence pairs spoken by examiner; child points to appropriate picture on plate. Untimed. Not standardized. Internal reliability = .93. Lexical items representative of 5-year-olds. Measures active/passive, prepositions, possessives, negative affixes, pronouns, singular/plural nouns and verbs, verbal inflections, adjectival modifications, reflexivizations. |
| Northwestern Syntax Screening Test (Lee, 1971) | Syntactic expression and comprehension | Ages 4 to 8; standard English speakers | To screen children on the basis of receptive and expressive syntactic usage | 20 receptive items are measured by child indicating which of four pictures is appropriate for sentence. 20 expressive items are similar, except child repeats stimulus sentences as he points. Age norms are presented for small standardization sample. No reliability or validity data reported. |
| Ordinal Scales of Psychological Development (Uzgiris & Hunt, 1975) | Cognitive correlates of language and communication | 2 weeks to 2 years | Six aspects of sensorimotor intelligence—object permanence, imitation, means for achieving de- | Six ordinal scales based on Piaget's theory of sensorimotor development during infancy. Within each scale the eliciting situations are arranged in hierarchical order—simplest to complex. Data yields, for each scale, the stages of cognitive functioning, the child has |

TABLE 9.1 (Continued)

| Name (Author of Test) | Aspect of Language Measured | Target Population | Purported Purpose | Comments |
|---|---|---|---|---|
| | | | sired ends, causality, object relations in space, schemata for relating to objects. | reached. Used widely with normal and handicapped infants, children and severely retarded adolescents and adults. |
| Parsons Language Sample (Spraldin, 1963) | Expressive aspects of language, vocal and nonvocal; comprehension | Children with severe mental handicaps | To sample language behavior according to Skinnerian outline | Considerable use with very low-functioning children. Seven subtests, including vocal and nonvocal. Standardized on mentally retarded children. Overall reliability is satisfactory; subtests too highly correlated to be used diagnostically. Does not measure syntax. |
| Peabody Picture Vocabulary Test (Dunn, 1959) | Receptive vocabulary of standard English | Mental ages 2 to adult | To derive an IQ score | Test is untimed and well standardized. Child points to appropriate picture on plate in response to stimulus word spoken by examiner. May be given by teacher; takes 10–20 minutes. |
| Porch Index of Communicative Ability in Children (Porch, 1974) | Verbal and nonverbal communication | Preschool through 12 years | Assess general communication ability | Two batteries—Basic (15 subtests) and Advanced (20 subtests)—include a variety of verbal, gestural, |

| | | | | |
|---|---|---|---|---|
| | involving verbal, gestural, and graphic skills | | | and graphic communicative tasks related to 10 common objects, which act as stimuli. Extensive study and supervised practice in administration are required. Percentile scores are available for each subtest and modality, as well as for the entire test. Reliability, standardization, and validity data are not reported. |
| Slingerland Screening Tests for Identifying Children with Specific Language Disability (Slingerland, 1970) | Correlates of language such as memory of geometric forms | Children in the early grades | To detect deficits in one or more areas on which receptive and expressive written language is based | Consists of three sets of tests, each with nine subtests—eight for group administration, one for individual. Wall charts, test booklets, and cards are the stimulus materials. Tasks include copying from a model (both written and oral), matching, kinesthetic—motor acts, sound discrimination, sentence completion, among others. No reliability or validity data are presented. |
| Templin–Darley Test of Articulation (Templin & Darley, 1960) | Articulation | Ages 3 to 8 | Screening or diagnosis of articulation | Sound elements tested include 25 consonant blends, 12 vowels, and 6 dipthongs. Child utters sounds in isolation, in words, and in a sentence. Short form (50 items) may be used for screening; all 176 items for diagnosis. |

TABLE 9.1 (Continued)

| Name (Author of Test) | Aspect of Language Measured | Target Population | Purported Purpose | Comments |
|---|---|---|---|---|
| Test for Auditory Comprehension of Language (Carrow-Woolfolk, 1973) | Auditory comprehension of vocabulary, morphology, syntax | Ages 3 to 6 | To measure receptive language in English or Spanish | Test consists of 101 pictorial stimuli plates of three drawings each. One of the drawings is the correct representation, one is the reverse of the stimulus sentence, and the other serves as a distractor. Test is individually administered, with child pointing to appropriate drawing. Provides indication of child's proficiency in vocabulary, morphology, syntax. English and Spanish versions field-tested on native speakers. |
| Test of Language Development (TOLD) (Newcomer & Hammill, 1977) | Receptive and expressive aspects of vocabulary, syntax, and phonology | Ages 4 to 9 | To give indication of child's overall strengths and weaknesses in each are tapped | Test is short and easy to administer. Five principal subtests measure receptive and expressive aspects of vocabulary and grammar. Two supplemental subtests measure articulation and speech sound discrimination. Test subtests correlate with criterion tests, with $r$'s mostly in .70's. Subtests generally internally consistent and stable. |
| Token Test (DeRenzi & Vig- | Verbal directions | Adults with | To assess the | Five parts increase the demands to |

| | | | | |
|---|---|---|---|---|
| dren by Noll, 1970) | of increasing length and complexity | acquired aphasia; revised for children from 3.0 to 12.5 years of age | ability to process and recall verbal directions of increasing length and difficulty | process conjunctions, coordination of clauses, and compound and complex sentences. Response format is the manipulation of a variety of tokens. Highlights comprehension of critical linguistic concepts and relationships and yields analyses of error patterns. Limited standardization information; no reliability reported. |
| Utah Test of Language Development (UTLD) (Mecham, Jex, & Jones, 1967) | Expressive and receptive language, aspects of conceptual development | Ages 1.6 to 14.5 | To derive an overall picture of a child's language development as compared with his peers | Test consists of two sections—one an informant-interview section based on the Vineland Social Maturity Scale, the other a direct test requiring the child to perform such things as repeat digits, recite a story, reproduce geometric forms. Yields score in form of language age. Internal reliabilities high. |
| Vocabulary Comprehension Scale (Bangs, 1975) | Assesses child's ability to follow instructions involving use of various lexical and function words | Ages 2 to 6 language disabled | To provide information on comprehension of pronouns, words of position, quality, size, and quantity | Attractive kit in shape of house. Has manipulative items such as cars, balls. Instructions to child in form of games—Garage, Tea Party, Buttons, miscellaneous. Standardized on culturally diverse middle-income population in Texas. |

Based in part on Bartel, N.R., and Bryen, D.N. Problems in language development. In D.D. Hammill and N.R. Bartel, *Teaching children with learning and behavior problems*. Boston: Allyn and Bacon, 1978, pp. 299-303. Used with permission of the publisher.

2. Trading cards (football, baseball, etc.) are good stimuli for discussion among two children.
3. A recipe for cooking something simple is also a good stimulus for communication.

In addition to creating a suitable context for the interaction, you must be careful of certain other points. Unless you specifically want to determine how the child interacts with you, you should avoid participating in the interaction. The reason for this is twofold. First, your participation may limit the spontaneity of the interaction. Second, if you participate, you will find it difficult to observe, to note visual, contextual details that cannot be picked up on the tape recorder but are an important aspect of the communicative episode. Also, you should minimize the obviousness of your presence as an observer, for this may also affect the spontaneity of the interaction. Finally, unless the children are used to being tape-recorded, you should minimize the machine's visibility as much as possible. Children who are not accustomed to being tape-recorded typically switch to a linguistic code that is formal, stifled, and unnatural when they become aware that they are being tape-recorded.

After you have obtained a sample of language, your next task is to transcribe it. Transcribing a language sample can be a very time-consuming endeavor. The transcript must be a complete and accurate account of the language episode, including both the language recorded on tape and any visual, contextual material related to the interaction. The transcript of the interaction, in contrast to the actual interaction, becomes a permanent representation of the language episode and permits analysis and reanalysis. A well-transcribed sample is valuable not only for identifying the nature and extent of a language problem, but also for determining where to start intervention and for evaluating intervention effects. Some conventions for transcribing samples of language are illustrated by the following samples.

### Sample I: Focusing on Language Problems

1. T:   "What's happening, Peter?"
2. P (points to picture): "It going back. Around . . . . . around . . . . . . . . . again."
3. "That man . . . think . . . . that man knocked out . . . . . (man is lying on the ground). The horse . . ."
4. "On the man and on a rock."
5. "That man and the horse . . . um . . ."
6. "Ho, got on a rock."
7. "In . . (distracted by the tape recorder). I(s) that a mike?"

Several conventions for transcribing a language sample are as follows:

1. Use letters to indicate who is speaking. For example, in the above, the letter *T* is used to represent the teacher and the letter *P* the child (Peter).
2. Use dots to indicate the length of pauses (one dot for approximately each second of pause).

3. Use parentheses to present necessary explanations or context clues, which are part of the communicative episode.
4. Number the lines in the transcript for purposes of later discussion.

### Sample II: Focusing on Articulation Problems

1. T (showing a picture of a boy and a girl washing a dog): "What are they doing?"
2. C: "Dey wash gog." (dog)
3. T: "Why are they washing the dog?"
4. C: "Taw, taw he tiry." (Cause, dirty)

Some helpful conventions here are as follows:

1. Use our regular alphabet (as opposed to the International Phonetic Alphabet, or IPA) to represent as exactly as possible all deviations in articulation (see lines 2 and 4 above).
2. Use parentheses to present necessary explanations of misarticulated words not obvious from the context of the utterance (see lines 2 and 4).

When an accurate transcript has been completed, analysis of the language sample may begin. Several methods for evaluating samples of language exist. For example, Lee (1966) and Lee and Canter (1971) provide a quantitative basis of analysis. Their procedure yields a score that is weighted for sentence length and type and for the presence of eight grammatical features varying in degree of complexity.

Analysis of the transcribed language sample can also show what linguistic rules the youngster does and does not use. In other words, a grammar of the child's language can be written and compared to the grammar of a competent adult language user. Creaghead (1979, p. 118) provides the following language sample from a learning disabled youngster, as well as its linguistic analysis.

### Sample 1

*The elephant ride a bike.*
*The mother fix the supper.*
*The pig cut the meat up.*
*The pig sneak around the meat.*
*Him washing the face.*

### Grammatical Analysis

Phrase structure rules: $S \longrightarrow NP + VP$

$$NP \longrightarrow \left\{ \begin{array}{l} \text{Determiner} + N \\ \text{Pronoun} \end{array} \right\}$$

$$VP \longrightarrow \left\{ \begin{array}{l} V + NP \\ V + PP \end{array} \right\}$$

Morphological rules:  Pronoun $\longrightarrow$ [+ objective]
Progressive $\longrightarrow$ [-*ing*]

If this sample and its analysis were to be compared with a correct version of these same sentences, certain patterns would emerge. To illustrate, let us examine these same sentences in their correct form (Creaghead, 1979, p. 119). Places where the child deviated from the correct sentences are indicated by a circle.

*The elephant (is) rid(ing) a bike.*

*The mother (is) fix(ing) the supper.*

*The pig (is) cutt(ing) the meat up.*

*The pig (is) sneak(ing) around the meat.*

*(He)(is) washing (his) face.*

### Grammatical Analysis

Phrase structure rules:   S $\longrightarrow$ NP + VP

NP $\longrightarrow$ $\left\{\begin{array}{l}\text{Det + N}\\ \text{Pronoun}\end{array}\right\}$

VP $\longrightarrow$ $\left\{\begin{array}{l}\text{Auxiliary + V + NP}\\ \text{Auxiliary + V + PP}\end{array}\right\}$

Morphological rules:   Pronoun $\longrightarrow$ $\left\{\begin{array}{l}\text{[+ subjective]}\\ \text{[+ possesive]}\end{array}\right\}$

Progressive $\longrightarrow$ [*be* + *-ing*]

While there are similarities between the two versions of this language sample (e.g., S $\longrightarrow$ NP + VP), certain systematic differences are apparent. The most noteworthy of these are the absence of the auxiliary in the expanded verb phrases and the almost consistent absence of the progressive verb ending *-ing*. In addition, the youngster reuses the objective form of a pronoun (*him*) in a syntactic position requiring the subjective form (*he*). Finally, the possessive pronoun (*his*) is absent.

If the same patterns are present throughout a large sample of language, the information they contain will be valuable in planning intervention. By comparing the child's grammar to that expected from normal developmental data, one can determine which linguistic features should appear earlier in the child's development and, therefore, should receive initial focus. For the last sample and grammatical analysis, if we compare them to Brown's (1973*a*) data on the acquisition of fourteen morphemes, the focus of intervention should be prioritized as follows:

1. Progressive morpheme *-ing*
2. Auxiliary verb *to be*

Grammatical analysis of a spontaneous sample of language can also be used to study the transformational rules used by a child when producing negative or interrogative sentences. The following sample and grammatical analysis illustrate this.

**Sample 2**

*What that?* (referring to the recorder)
*No! No help.*
*No big book.*
*Where, what, where the police car?*
*What they call those things?*
*What that guy?*

**Grammatical Analysis**

Negation $\longrightarrow No + \left\{ \begin{array}{l} \text{Verb} \\ \text{NP} \end{array} \right\}$

*Wh-* question $\longrightarrow \; Wh + \left\{ \begin{array}{l} \text{NP} \\ \text{NP + V + NP} \end{array} \right\}$

Let us now consider the same sentences in their correct form. Again, the forms that are absent from the child's sentences are indicated by a circle.

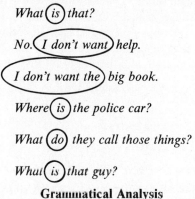

*What* (*is*) *that?*

*No.* (*I don't want*) *help.*

(*I don't want the*) *big book.*

*Where* (*is*) *the police car?*

*What* (*do*) *they call those things?*

*What* (*is*) *that guy?*

**Grammatical Analysis**

Transformations: T neg$\longrightarrow$NP + Aux + Neg + V + NP
wh- $\longrightarrow$ *what* and *where*
T *wh-* question $\longrightarrow \left\{ \begin{array}{l} \textit{wh-} + \text{Aux} + \text{NP ?} \\ \textit{wh-} + \text{Aux} + \text{NP} + \text{V} + \text{NP ?} \end{array} \right\}$

By comparing the two versions of this sample and the grammatical analyses, we can determine that this youngster has not developed the transformational rules for generating either a negative or interrogative type of sentence. To express negation, this youngster simply attaches the negative morpheme *no* to either the verb or noun phrase, rather than embedding it within a sentence or attaching it to the appropriate auxiliary verb. In fact, in both the negative and interrogative sentences, auxiliaries are totally absent. For the interrogative sentences, two general observations can be made. First, *wh-* words are limited to *what* and *where,* and their use is uncertain. This youngster had difficulty determining which *wh-* word was appropriate for asking about location. He switched from *where* to *what* then back to *where* before continuing with his question. Second, obligatory transformational

rules are not present. The youngster used the very parsimonious strategy of pre-
fixing the *wh-* word to the sentence and using the intonational contour of a question form. Auxiliary verbs were not present to be inverted. The information
derived from this analysis in conjunction with available normal developmental
data (e.g., Brown, 1968; 1973*a;* Ervin-Tripp, 1970) is invaluable in identifying
both the linguistic content of intervention as well as the sequencing of intervention targets.

The potential value of spontaneous language samples for analysis is tremendous, and thus a complete description of possible uses is beyond the scope of this
chapter. However, two additional uses suffice to indicate the scope of this value.
The first use is for analyzing syntactic options available to the child, and the second relates to analyzing semantic content.

One characteristic of many youngsters who have language problems is their
limited use of embedded and coordinated sentences. The process of embedding
one proposition within another or coordinating two propositions represents not
only a linguistic achievement but a cognitive one as well. This linguistic versatility
enables the child (or, perhaps, reflects the child's ability) to communicate causal
relationships, part-whole relationships, and so on. The following language sample
illustrates how propositional relationships can either be coordinated within one
sentence or remain relationally and structurally limited.

### Sample 3

| | |
|---|---|
| **(1a)** | *I like candy.* |
| **(1b)** | *It tastes good.* |
| **(2a)** | *John went to the store.* |
| **(2b)** | *He bought some milk.* |

In this sample, each of the four sentences reflects one proposition. The relationship between the first and second sentences of each pair of sentences is neither explicit nor denoted. In contrast to the above, consider the following sentences:

| | |
|---|---|
| **(3)** | *I like candy because it tastes good.* |
| **(4)** | *When John went to the store, he bought some milk.* |

For sentences **(3)** and **(4)**, two facts can be noted. First, within each sentence are
two propositions. Second, and of greater significance, is the fact that the two propositions are related to each other, causally in sentence **(3)** and temporally in sentence **(4)**. These two syntactically complex sentences are more precise in communicating intended meaning and reflect more sophisticated logical abilities than do
the four separate sentences they are derived from. Therefore, samples of language
can be used to note indications of the child's linguistic capabilities and also as
clues to developing cognitive abilities.

In contrast to using a sample of language for the purposes of analyzing syntax,
specific procedures for analyzing semantic relationships do not exist. However, in
some cases Brown's (1973*a*) semantic categories can be helpful for identifying the

range of semantic categories and relationships produced by the child and for determining whether the child embeds one semantic category within another. The following sample provides a basis for semantic analysis.

### Sample 4

*He tried to blow it down.* (agent + action + object + location)

*Blow the house down.* (action + object + location)

*It was strong.* (entity + attribute)

*We fell into the fire house.* (agent + action + location)

*Ate 'im all up.* (action + object + attribute)

In this sample, the child uses semantic relations of up to four terms, including agent, action, object, location, entity, and attribution. However, certain other semantic categories are not evident. These include dative, experiencer, state, possessive, negation, and beneficiary. Also, the child has not demonstrated the ability to embed one semantic relationship within another. If this sample were more extensive, it would be possible to use it to determine whether, in fact, the semantic relationships expressed by the youngster are varied or limited in scope or complexity.

In addition to the procedures described above, several others have been used for analyzing spontaneous samples of language. *The Linguistic Analysis of Speech Samples* (Engler, Hannah, & Longhurst, 1973) outlines a procedure for analyzing patterns of language used by the child for linguistic constructions that are deviant and/or conspicuously absent. Results of this analysis can be used to generate specific intervention strategies for the correction of deviant constructions or the expansion of absent constructions. Similarly, Tyack and Gottsleben (1974) described another method in their *Language Analysis System* whereby the child's utterance is syntactically analyzed, taking into account the communicative intent of the utterance. The utterance is then compared to a complete adult form. Then, expected forms and syntactic constructions that have not been mastered are used as the basis for developing intervention goals. Another analysis procedure is described by Bloom and Lahey (1978). As opposed to the two procedures just mentioned, this one is a semantically-based categorical system for analyzing utterances. Utterances (from single words to complex sentences) are analyzed to secure information about the child's use of various semantic categories, of grammatical morphemes, and of complex forms of connective and relative clauses. This information is then the basis for establishing language goals.

All of the procedures just described are valuable means for obtaining information from which language goals can be established. However, all of these procedures neglect to focus on the broader phenomenon of communication, which includes conversational turn-taking, the use of nonverbal communicative signals, and various communicative functions. In addition, all of these procedures focus exclusively on the child, without taking adequate notice of the child's conversational partner. Since communication involves at least two persons, the interaction between sender and receiver, as well as the physical context, should be analyzed.

This is especially crucial when assessing the communicative interaction of severely language-handicapped persons.

The following paradigm is illustrative of how several features of the communication process can be assessed. In addition to the actual message (i.e., the intended semantic content) and the linguistic construction of the message (i.e., the syntax), other analyzable aspects include the following:

- Conversational turn-taking
- Initiation of conversational topics
- Communicative signals
- Communicative or pragmatic functions

**Conversational turn-taking** is a critical aspect of communication that is generally not assessed. If the child targeted for assessment is not given the opportunity to be both sender and receiver, an incomplete picture of her ability to engage in the cooperative process of communication will result. Therefore, one focus of assessing communication should be an analysis of the time the child (and her conversational partner) spends as both sender and receiver. This can be done by transcribing the interaction of the conversational partners and then calculating the percentage of utterances the child produces in contrast to the percentage directed to the child. The following interaction is an example. A mother (designated as M) and her forty-two-month-old son (designated as C) are playing with a Fisher Price airport toy in a playroom where the mother works.

* 1. C: "Mommy, can I go get people?" (meaning parts of Fisher Price Airport).
  2. M: "I don't know where the people are.
  3. Why don't you draw some?
  4. You could make them into dolls."
* 5. C: "Can I play with that little car?" (indicating toy vehicle on shelf).
  6. M: "That car?" (points to vehicle on shelf and then at C).
* 7. (C smiles affirmatively.)
  8. M: "Well, I guess we could borrow it for a few minutes." (goes to shelf and gets vehicle).
  9. "Oh, that's a big one.
 10. I wouldn't call that a little one.
 11. You could probably sit on that one."
*12. C (sits on car and pushes himself around the round): "Eeee." (sound as if to imitate the sound of wheels turning).
*13. "Mommy." (looks at mother and points to car he's sitting on).
 14. M: "Yes.
 15. I thought you could sit on it.
 16. Your cape's going to get caught." (Mother rolls up cape child is wearing.)

*17. C: "Now I can take the school bus . . . to go to school."
 18. M: "Oh, that's going to be your school bus?"
*19. C: "Uh-huh."
 20. M: "Well, what else do you need to go to school?"
*21. C: "Nothin else."

In this episode there are twenty-one complete utterances (as numbered on the left). Eight of these utterances are from the child (those numbers with asterisks). Therefore, the child spent approximately 38% of the time as the sender. In contrast, the mother spent 62% of the conversational time as the sender. While conversational turn-taking did occur in this episode, the child spent less time as sender than as receiver. It should be noted, however, that the child seemed more interested in playing with the toys than in conversing with his mother, which is not uncommon for a child of his age. It should also be noted that the mother followed the topical interest of her son (i.e., the toys the child was interested in and on which he acted).

**Initiation of conversational topics** is another aspect of communication that is rarely assessed. Its importance stems from an underlying social motivation for communication, that of being affected by one's social environment as well as affecting it. When analyzing a spontaneous sample of language, we can assess to what extent the child is "permitted" to determine the topic or content of the conversation and how well the child performs when the conversational topic is directed by others. Here again, we are viewing communication as a cooperative process with the roles of initiator and responder shifting frequently.

Again using the transcript of the interaction between the mother and her forty-two-month-old son, we can analyze the frequency with which each partner initiates the conversational topic. For this purpose, a conversational topic is defined as any person, event, object, or relationship about which one or both persons communicate. The initiation of the topic can be signaled in many ways (e.g., linguistic reference, actions, gestures, or eye contact). Similarly, the receiver of the message can respond in one of a number of ways—choosing to participate around the initiated topic, to ignore the topical initiation, or to attempt to change the topic by initiating a different one.

In line 1, the child initiates the topic of toy people using language as the communicative signal. In line 2, the mother responds to the child's topical initiation by confirming her son's message and indicating that the location of the toy people is unknown to her. The mother's utterances in lines 3 and 4 initiate a different but related topic (*Why don't you draw some? You could make them into dolls*). However, the child does not acknowledge the mother's topical switch, but rather initiates another topic in line 5 (*Can I play with that little car?*). The mother responds to her son's topical switch in line 6, and the conversation remains on the topic of the child and the car through line 15. The child initiated a new topic three times; all of these were followed by the mother responding to the child's initiation. The mother also initiated new topics on three occasions; however, only once did the child follow the mother's topical direction. On the other two occasions (lines 4 and 5 and lines 16 and 17), the child initiated a new topic.

If we assess the child's ability to affect his social environment by being permitted, and even encouraged, to direct much of the content of the conversation, we have found here a mother who is indirectly teaching her child a very important early message—that language is a powerful communicative tool. From an assessment point of view, this is an important piece of information. The degree of its importance can be seen by contrasting the following interaction with the preceding one.

K is a thirty-three-year-old, severely mentally retarded woman, residing in a residential facility for the mentally retarded. An interaction takes place in K's bedroom at the end of the day after she returns from her educational program. Her conversational partner is K's client care worker (designated as CW).

1. CW (holds cookie in front of K):   "Cookie please!"
2. K:   "Cookie pee, cookie pee." (looks at the cookie while shaking her left hand near her own face).
3. (CW gives K the cookie.)
4. K (eats the cookie and smells her hand):   "Mmm."
5. CW:   "What do you want K?"
6. K (looks at CW):   "Copee, copee."
7. CW:   "Coffee? No."
8. "What about a cookie?"
9. K:   "Cookie, cookie."
10. CW:   "Cookie please."
11. K:   "Cookie pee. Cookie pee."
12. CW:   "Cookie please."
13. (K looks around, appears distracted.)

This interaction, which is an excerpt from a larger yet similar episode, displays a very different pattern as to who is the primary initiator of conversational topics. On three different occasions (lines 1, 5, and 8), the care worker initiates a topic to which K consistently responds (lines 2, 6, and 9). In contrast, K does not initiate at all. Much of the conversation consists of K responding to the care worker's attempts to have K say *Cookie, please*. One interpretation of this interaction is that K has not learned that her communicative signals (linguistic, vocal, or gestural) can actively affect her environment. Instead, she reacts to other's communicative demands.

The implications of this "simulated" assessment for establishing intervention goals should be apparent. First, if we accept that communication is a social process involving at least two persons and that language is a vehicle for communication, then intervention must not focus solely on the language-handicapped person.

Second, if language is to emerge and develop for communicative purposes, the language-handicapped person must understand that all communicative signals can affect the social and physical environment.

The **communicative signals** that serve to convey a message between sender and receiver should also receive assessment. However, the assessment of communication has generally been restricted to the assessment of language. The competent communicator, however, relies on more than language for sending and receiving intended messages. (This is not the case with written forms of communication.) Eye contact, actions, facial expressions, gestures, and vocal intonations serve either to supplement or to take the place of spoken language. The assessment of a child's ability to accurately comprehend and produce a variety of communicative signals is even more important when that child has limited language abilities. Similarly, the competent conversational partner (parent, teacher, or care worker) must be able to interpret the intended meaning of the communicative signals sent by the language-handicapped individual. Finally, since the language-handicapped person may not have adequate access to the complexities of linguistic symbols, such an individual must use other communicative signals to supplement language to make its message understood.

The following interaction between a worker (designated as W) and a brain-damaged, three-year-old child (designated as C) illustrates how we assess a variety of signals used for communication.

> The interaction takes place at a day care center for handicapped children. W and C are at the rear of the room where there is a large therapy ball, some toys, and an exercise mat.
>
> 1. C (in a soft voice with rising and falling intonations):  "Ah-ah-ah-ah." (looks at a musical bell held by W).
> 2. W:  "Yeah, listen to that." (continues to shake the musical bell and smiles at C).
> 3. "Come on. Come on." (melodic intonation and smiles at C).
> 4. (C picks up head and looks at the bells.)
> 5. W:  "Oh my goodness, you're taking everything in."
> 6. "Listen to the bells. See the bells?" (points to the bells, looks at C, and then looks at the bells).
> 7. C:  "Ah-ah-ah-ah." (much breathiness and looks at W).
> 8. W:  "Oh, that's hard work."
> 9. "That's hard work. You're tired." (constantly looking at C).

Here, a variety of communicative signals are used by both the adult worker and the child. For example, the child uses vocalizations (lines 1 and 7) and actions (line 4). All of these signals appear to have communicative value, even if it is not always intentional. The adult's communicative signals include actions (line 2), smiles (lines 2 and 3), vocal intonation (line 3), pointing (line 6), and eye contact (lines 6 and 9). The adult's use of these signals seemed to have several functions—determining whether or not it was time for a topical switch, encouraging further interaction, and referencing targeted objects. Not only did the adult use a variety of signals to encourage further communication, but she was also able to interpret communicative attempts initiated by the child (e.g., looking at bell signaled the child's interest in the bell). Without the use of communicative signals, it is unlikely that the child would have been able to understand or be understood, and communication between the two might have ceased.

Here again, this kind of assessment may lead to the establishment of valuable communicative goals, not only goals for the child (e.g., increase the use of pointing to index the desired object) but for the teacher or parent as well (e.g., interpretation of vocalization or eye contact as potentially meaningful).

**Communicative or pragmatic functions** constitute another variable that can be assessed to provide valuable information for planning strategies for intervention. Communicative functions (as described in Chapters 4 and 6) make up the underlying intent or purpose of the interaction. These functions may be even more fundamental than the actual content of the message itself since they establish the sociopsychological context between conversational partners. Communication is characterized by a degree of reciprocity that makes it imperative that both communicators be assessed to establish the sociopsychological intent of their interactions. Bloom and Lahey (1978, p. 211) summarize the phenomenon of communicative functions, to which they refer as speech acts, as follows:

> Speakers of a language do things with words—they accomplish certain acts with their messages apart from representing the information that is the content of their messages. . . . Acts of requesting, for example, have the same function but can vary in the form of the request.

Several researchers have assessed the communicative functions used by children (e.g., Halliday, 1975; Dore, 1975; Garvey, 1975). Others (e.g., Mazur, Holzman, & Ferrier, 1976; Morgenstern, 1975; Bryen, 1980) have similarly assessed parents and other adult caretakers. These studies have yielded valuable information concerning developmental changes in the acquisition of pragmatics and have provided useful insights into the role that caretakers play in promoting the acquisition of language. Using the communicative functions outlined in Table 9.2, let us analyze the following interactions. The first interaction takes place between a mother (designated as M) and her three-year-old language-delayed youngster (designated as D).

1. D: "Esh." (rising intonation while looking at a picture on a music box). (Q)
2. M: "Yes, see the box?" (I)
3. "Let's hear the music." (MD)
4. D: "Ah . . . ah . . . duh." (stands the box up, then lays it down). (S)
5. M: "That's a long song, isn't it?" (starts singing and then stops). (I)
6. (D bounces on his knees.) (D)

TABLE 9.2   Communicative Functions

| Function | Examples |
|---|---|
| *Nondemanding* | |
| Those messages in which the intent of the sender is not to elicit/demand a response from the receiver. | |
| *Social interpersonal* (S): Messages in which the primary intent is to initiate or maintain a pleasant, positive, warm interaction. Focus is on the interaction rather than on the content of the message. Included are messages to comfort the receiver, responses to receiver's vocalizations, compliance to requests, and messages to keep the conversation going. Also includes those messages whose primary intent is to express the sender's sincere feeling, attitude, or evaluation about a person, situation, activity, or object. | *What a nice boy.* *It's funny.* *Ah, ah, ah.* |
| *Indirect teaching* (I): Messages in which the intent is to comment/report/describe ongoing environmental events. These may include actions performed by receiver or sender, states of being, objects and their attributes, or relational aspects. Emphasis is on indirectly teaching about organization of the environment and how such information might be communicated. Intent is *not* to elicit receiver responses, but simply to provide information. | *That's a big car.* *That's a long song, isn't it?* |
| *Seeking Information* | |
| *Querying* (Q): Messages that are sincere attempts to gain information. | *Want more music?* *Eh?* (pointing to a picture and then looking at adult) |

TABLE 9.2 *(Continued)*

| Function | Examples |
| --- | --- |
| *Demanding* | |
| Those messages in which the intent of the sender is to influence or direct the receiver's behavior. Includes expectation/demand by sender for a response or compliance on the part of the receiver. | |
| *Directive* (D): Includes commands. Also includes attempts to gain receiver's attention. | *Throw the ball.* |
| *Modified directive* (MD): Messages whose intent is to influence or direct receiver's behavior, but softened by using phrases such as *let's* or *it's time to*. Also includes question forms when their underlying intent is to elicit an action, not information. | *Where's the ball?* *Want to throw the ball to mommy?* *Let's wash our hands.* |
| *Tutorial* (T): Messages whose intent is to teach the receiver. Requires a model or initial input of information, followed by a specific intent to elicit that information from the receiver. | *Say coffee please.* |

From Bryen, D.N. *Project: Communication,* 1980. (Based on Mazur et al., 1976). Used with permission of the author.

7. (M resumes singing.) (S)
8. D: "Ah ... da." (smiles at mother). (S)
9. (M continues singing until music stops.) (S)
10. (D bounces.) (D)
11. M: "Oh, music stopped." (I)
12. "Want some more?" (Q)
13. D (points to picture on the music box of a dog): "Eh?" (Q)
14. M: "Dog" (I)
15. D (while waving arms): "Eh." (D)
16. M: "Want some music?" (Q)

Both mother and child use a variety of communicative functions in this interaction. Several of these have the same apparent intent. For example, out of a total of sixteen messages, four are social-interpersonal (two by D in lines 4 and 8 and two by M in lines 7 and 9). Similarly, mother and child both use the information-seeking function twice (D in lines 1 and 3 and M in lines 12 and 16). It is interesting that the child uses three times as many directives (lines 6, 10, and 15) as the mother does (line 3). Even when the mother intends to influence the child's behavior, the directive is softened by using the cooperative form *Let's*. The mother uses the pragmatic function of indirect teacher several times (lines 2, 5, 11, and 14), whereas this function is totally absent from the child's communicative attempts. Also, the total absence of the tutorial function from the mother's language indicates that perhaps the informal give and take of this interaction is more important than the actual direct teaching of language.

Let us contrast the preceding interaction with one between a teacher (designated as T) and her twelve-year-old, profoundly retarded student Marcy (designated as M).

1. T: "Marcy look." (D)
2. "We're going to look at what we wear." (MD)
3. "You try it . . . Look at your hands." (T)
4. (M looks at her hands and cooperates as teacher prompts the sign for "wear.") (S)
5. T: "Wear." (while prompting M's hands). (T)
6. (M cooperates as teacher again prompts.) (S)
7. T (smiling at M): "Very good." (S)
8. (holds up hat) "What is this Marcy?" (Q)
9. (M touches her head.) (S)
10. T: "Good." (S)
11. "It's a hat." (I)
12. "Very good." (S)
13. "We wear a hat on our head." (I)
14. "You say it." (T)
15. "Wear a hat on our head." (while prompting the signs "hat," "wear," and "head.") (T)
16. (M cooperates as teacher prompts.) (S)
17. T: "Very good, Marcy." (S)

The communicative functions used by Marcy and her teacher reflect a very different interactional intent than that in the preceding interaction. The functions used by the teacher with the greatest frequency are the tutorial (lines 3, 5, 14, and 15) and the social-interpersonal (lines 7, 10, 12, and 17). In fact, almost two-thirds of this interaction consists of the teacher directly teaching Marcy and giving social praises for Marcy's cooperative attempts. Other functions are infrequently used by the teacher (directive in line 1, modified directive in line 2, seeking information in line 8, and indirect teaching in lines 11 and 13). Marcy does not appear to be a true conversational partner. In fact, she makes only four communicative attempts and those quite passively. All four can best be described as social-interpersonal; she either actively (line 9) or passively (lines 4, 6, and 16) complies with the communicative demands made of her.

In summary, in contrast to the informal turn-taking in the preceding interaction, the apparent primary intent of this one was to teach the child directly to sign three words. Using this information and other assessment findings, we can develop communicative goals for both adult and child. Of course, our establishing of goals and intervention methodologies is also greatly influenced by our view of how language and communication are learned. This issue was already discussed in Chapter 6 and will be further explored in Chapter 10.

Using spontaneous samples of language has become an important procedure for assessing the structure and function of language. The heavy emphasis of this procedure may be due to its two primary advantages over more formal evaluative strategies. Kretschmer and Kretschmer (1978, p. 172) summarize these advantages as follows:

> ... research on normal language development has focused primarily on spontaneous speech production, resulting in a sizable body of normative data. Second, formal testing situations are generally artificial estimates of performance whereas a conversational format should yield more natural behavior from the child.

However, as a result of the technical and practical problems (e.g., size of sample needed and method of obtaining the sample, need for audio or video equipment, time) involved in obtaining, transcribing, and analyzing conversations, it is often acceptable to use the structured nonstandardized approaches to assessment described in the following section.

## NONSTANDARDIZED APPROACHES TO ASSESSMENT

Leonard et al. (1978) present a strong case (one that teachers and clinicians have consistently articulated) for the use of nonstandardized clinician- or teacher-constructed tasks to assess both the structure and function of language. Their case is supported by three major points. First, clinician-constructed tasks have the potential to allow for study in greater detail of features that seem suspect during formal, standardized testing. Second, through the use of informal testing one is able to assess a "feature that is not assessed at all in a standardized test" (Leonard et al., 1978, p. 374). Third, follow-up testing through informal tasks may help to determine the "cause of a child's difficulty with a particular feature of language" (Leonard et al., 1978, p. 374). In addition to these reasons for using clinician-constructed tasks, another advantage is that one is able to probe further to determine the strategies a child may be using in arriving at a particular linguistic feature.

Strategies for constructing informal language tasks are not presented here, for they have been adequately treated by Leonard et al. (1978). Instead, a series of structured nonstandardized tasks that have been found to be helpful in adding to the information obtainable from standardized tests is given. This section is divided into the following seven assessment areas:

1. Prelinguistic abilities
2. Early language development
3. Language during the preschool years
4. Communication
5. Summary of research-based methodologies
6. Diagnostic teaching
7. Metalinguistics

The evaluative strategies in each area are meant to be suggestive rather than exhaustive. Where feasible, in addition to describing the assessment strategies, their objectives, and procedures, the types of information that can be secured by their use is illustrated via brief case studies. Furthermore, it should be noted that many of the procedures used in the inquiries in Chapters 2 through 5 can be adapted for assessment purposes.

**PRELINGUISTIC ABILITIES**   Many developmentally young children, while having no language, are in the process of acquiring the sociocognitive requisites upon which language and communication are based. Therefore, developing intervention goals for these youngsters demands careful attention. The following nonstandardized tasks are suggestive of the types of strategies that can be used.

ASSESSMENT STRATEGY 1: OBJECT USE OR PLAY. As is described in Chapter 4, one of the cognitive skills that underpins language is the symbolic function. This function can be assessed through the child's use of or play with objects.
   *Objective:* To assess the child's readiness for the symbol system of language.
   *Materials:* Familiar objects, such as a doll, ball, spoon, plastic phone, wash cloth, small mirror, and cup of water.
   *Procedures:* Same as for Inquiry 4.1 (see p. 118).
   *Results:* Identify the stage of object use at which the child is primarily functioning in order to determine readiness for language. Also, determine whether or not the child shows evidence of the following:

1. Sees objects as separate from self.
2. Acts on objects differently depending on their perceptual attributes.
3. Acts on objects differently depending on their social functions.
4. Uses play application (i.e., representational/symbolic play).

   *Example:* The assessment of Scott, a five-year-old, Down's Syndrome child, serves as an illustration.

| Object | Observations | Level |
|---|---|---|
| 1. Doll | Mouths doll, vocalizes *ah-ba-ba,* then bangs other objects with doll, throws doll down. When given the verbal directive, Scott did nothing. | Sensorimotor |
| 2. Ball | Chooses ball as first item. Picks it up, mouths it, throws it, retrieves it, throws it again (not at anyone). It rolls away and his eyes follow it. He retrieves it and throws it again, laughing. | Sensorimotor and self-utilization |
| 3. Spoon | Mouths spoon, bangs it on his foot, puts it in his mouth (as if eating), and says *ga.* | Sensorimotor and self-utilization |
| 4. Plastic phone | Shakes phone, says *ha* into it. Dials, phone rings, and he puts phone to his ear, saying *ba-bah.* | Sensorimotor and self-utilization |
| 5. Wash cloth | Shakes cloth. Taps it against his mouth, waving it. After verbal directive, he picks doll up and throws it down on the floor. | Sensorimotor |
| 6. Small mirror | Mouths it, looks into it while saying *da-da-ah,* then brings mirror to mouth and mouths it. Bangs it. After verbal directive, he bangs the doll and mirror together. Later, he picks up the mirror and makes faces into it. | Sensorimotor and self-utilization |
| 7. Cup of water | Picks up cup and drinks all of the water. When asked if he wants | Self-utilization |

| Object | Observations | Level |
|--------|-------------|-------|
| | some more he says *ga* and makes the sign for more in imitation of the teacher. Given cup with some more water in it, he drinks it. After the verbal directive, he throws the cup on the floor. | |

Scott uses a combination of sensorimotor and functional self-utilization levels of behaviors when interacting with objects. With the doll and the wash cloth, his behavior is exclusively exploratory. However, even at the exploratory level, his schemes are varied, including banging, hitting, mouthing, shaking, and waving. With the ball, the spoon, the phone, the mirror, and the cup of water Scott started out at an exploratory level (e.g., mouthing, banging, and shaking) and progressed to a higher level of object use. He demonstrated self-utilization or functional use of these objects in that his actions on them reflected differentiated and socially determined understanding. Generally, Scott is functioning primarily at the self-utilization level with a continuation of exploratory behaviors. Using this information, we can begin to establish goals for Scott. While Scott does not demonstrate the symbolic function, his readiness for language is emerging. He needs many opportunities to interact with a variety of objects both at the exploratory-sensorimotor and the self-utilization levels.

ASSESSMENT STRATEGY 2: MEANS-END RELATIONSHIPS. An apparent precondition for the emergence of intentional communication and its subsequent symbolic form is the development of means-ends relationships. This sociocognitive structure appears when the child begins to see that both objects and people can be means or instruments for obtaining other objects. This relationship is fully evidenced in both the physical and social sense when the following two conditions exist:

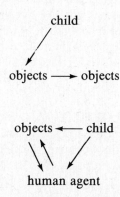

*Objective:* To determine whether or not the child can use objects and human agents to obtain desired objects or actions.

*Materials:* Wind-up toys (e.g., carousel or music box), ball, ruler or stick, cloth, and plastic bowl of cookies.

*Procedures:* To assess the child's instrumental use of objects, the following procedures can be used:

1. Play ball with the child for a short time. Then roll the ball out of the child's physical reach (e.g., under a bed). Place a ruler near the child and observe and note what strategies the child uses to retrieve the ball. For example, does she lose interest in the ball, cry, use her arms to attempt to retrieve it, or spontaneously use the ruler as a tool for retrieval? Hand the ruler to the child and observe.

2. Place a plastic bowl containing two small cookies within easy reach of the child. Say to the child: "Here's some cookies for you. Want the cookies? Here." After the child has eaten the cookies, put more cookies in the bowl and place the bowl out of the child's reach on a movable cloth. Say to the child: "Here's more cookies. Want the cookies? Here." Observe and note what the child does. Does she cry, give up, flail with her arms, attempt to use you as an agent for obtaining the cookies, or pull the cloth to move the bowl within reach? If the child fails to instrumentally use the cloth, demonstrate its use. Then return the bowl to its original position and observe again.

3. Show one of the wind-up toys to the child. Demonstrate how it is wound up and then let the child play with it. After the toy has wound down, observe and note what the child does. Does she try to reactivate the toy? If she fails, does she hand it to you as if to say "More. You do it." Repeat this with another wind-up toy.

*Results:* From your notes determine whether the child (1) uses objects as the means to obtain desired ends (another object) and (2) uses people as agents or means to obtain desired ends (objects or actions). If the child fails to do the first task, the goal would be to encourage continued use of objects exploratorily, functionally, and instrumentally. If the child does not utilize people as agents, this goal can be attained by using gamelike routines where the teacher is both agent and recipient of objects and actions. If, however, the child successfully accomplishes the tasks, then the goal might be to expand the child's repertoire of instrumental use of objects as well as the variety of her intentional communicative signals.

**EARLY LANGUAGE DEVELOPMENT**   Between the ages of nine and eighteen months, the normal child begins to experiment actively with language. However, during this early stage of development, the child's utterances are tied closely to specific situational contexts for the production of meaningful language.

## ASSESSMENT STRATEGY 3: EARLY LANGUAGE COMPREHENSION.

*Objective:* To assess the child's early language comprehension.

*Materials:* None, other than contexts and materials with which the child frequently engages.

*Procedures:* List the contexts of selected commonly occurring activities. Present simple words and phrases related and not related to the contexts. For example, at the table where the child usually eats, say "Want to eat?" or "bye-bye?" At a different part of the room, say "Want to eat?" Observe and note the child's responses.

*Results:* In analyzing the child's responses, note whether or not the child gives either behavioral or verbal indicators that he has understood the meaning of your utterance. Does the child do so only in a well-established situational context (e.g., "bye-bye" only at the door)? Or has the child's early language comprehension become free from specific contexts (e.g., "bye-bye" at the table or sandbox)?

## ASSESSMENT STRATEGY 4: ONE- OR TWO-WORD UTTERANCES.

*Objective:* To assess the child's early meaningful use of one- or two-word utterances.

*Materials:* Toys or objects that the child frequently uses.

*Procedures:* Place the familiar toys or objects in front of the child, one at a time. Engage the child in play with them. Observe the child as he manipulates the objects or engages in activity. Record any utterances and the context in which they occur. If no spontaneous utterances occur, try eliciting utterances by asking "What's this?" or "What's the ball doing?" Note all responses.

*Results:* In analyzing the child's responses, note not only the specific words used but also their apparent semantic intent. This can only be assessed in relation to the particular context in which each utterance is made. For example, is the word *cookie* used to indicate the existence of a cookie, to indicate the recurrence of a cookie, or to indicate the object of an action? This assessment procedure should provide information not only about the words the child produces but also about the semantic function of these words.

**LANGUAGE DURING THE PRESCHOOL YEARS**   As children expand the linguistic capabilities beyond the basic semantic relations period and enter preschool, the following language assessments can be used.

## ASSESSMENT STRATEGY 5: SEMANTIC FEATURES ASSIGNED TO SPECIFIC AND NONSPECIFIC REFERENTS. Dale (1976) suggests that the semantic system of a language is the knowledge that a speaker must have to understand sentences and to relate them to his knowledge of the world. One aspect of the semantic system is what Katz and Fodor (1963) regard as semantic features, each one of which expresses a part of the meaning of a word. For example, *animal*

has, among others, the semantic features [+ animate, − human]. A particular semantic feature may appear in more than one dictionary entry, as in the case of the feature [+ living], which occurs in the dictionary entries of *dog, rose, man, plant,* and so on (Dale, 1976).

Clark (1973) extends the semantic feature approach by asserting that children acquire the meanings of words by sequentially adding specific semantic features. In Clark's semantic features theory, it is argued that the first semantic features acquired are static perceptual features, such as size, shape, color, rather than functional ones (see Nelson, 1974, for a further discussion of the perceptual versus functional features hierarchy). Later, however, features that are more abstract are added. The semantic features theory has been criticized for not taking into account words having no specific referent and figurative aspects of language. However, its approach is useful for understanding the possible reasons why some youngsters have problems with the relative unavailability of certain known words.

*Objective:* To analyze the various semantic features expressed by the child when shown an object as referent and when a word is given without a referent.

*Materials:* Several familiar objects, such as nail, ball, scissors, pencil, and so on, and a list of words without specific referents, such as *animal, toy, hungry,* and *arithmetic.*

*Procedures:* Ask the child to tell you all about each object presented. Probe for a variety of responses by saying "Tell me more." Let the child play with and manipulate the objects. After six referent words, ask the child to tell you about words without particular referents, such as *animal* or *toy* or *hungry.* Record all responses. Probe as much as possible.

*Results:* Analyze how the child's responses varied. What semantic features were imposed on each word? Did the child's responses include (1) label or name of the object, (2) color, (3) shape, (4) major parts, (5) composition, and static perceptual features, such as (6) numerality, (7) class, and (8) example? Or were the child's responses restricted to one feature, such as function? What difficulties, if any, were encountered with the nonreferent words? Did the child rely on specific instances of the word? For example, the child gives *ball, bat, bike,* and *truck* in response to the word *toy* instead of a classificatory description, such as *things you can play with.*

*Example:* The following are the responses that a nine-year-old, learning-disabled youngster gave when asked to tell about the referents and the words without specific referents.

| Referent or Word | Response |
|---|---|
| nail | *Hammer on it. Hammer in walls. Hang up tool. My dad has a tool. I hang up with a nail. My dad has a whole bunch of nails.* |

| **Referent or Word** | **Response** |
|---|---|
| lime-green tennis ball | *Play with a baseball. You throw with bat an' ya bounce it. You roll it, and you throw it up. That's all you do.* |
| animal | *There's a giraffe an' an elephant-giraffe an' an elephant and tigers an um, a, um ostrich, an some bees are animals, and zebras and um seals and dolphins, an sharks.* |
| toy | *It's a thing what you play with . . . You want some toys in ya . . . um in ya . . . your toy chest. That's all 'bout toys.* |

Note that this child uses a restricted set of functional semantic features when describing the two objects. Perceptual features, classification information, and so on are completely absent from his descriptions. In fact, it appears that the meanings of these two objects are defined by two essential features—what actions can be imposed on the object and how the object fits into his particular world. Similarly, when telling about the two words with no specific referents, this child's responses are equally restricted to function (e.g., *you play*) and examples (e.g., *giraffe, elephant,* etc.).

ASSESSMENT STRATEGY 6: SENTENCES AND WORD MEANINGS. The meaning of a word is influenced not only by its semantic features but also by its linguistic context. There are semantic restrictions on the possible combinations that words can take in a sentence in order for that sentence to be meaningful. For example, the sentence *She is my father* violates our notions of truth, because it violates semantic restrictions. That is, the semantic features of *she* [+ human, − female] do not include the semantic features of *father*. Therefore, a full assessment of semantics must cover the child's understanding of isolated words and also of how they are used in meaningful sentences.

*Objective:* To assess the child's semantic knowledge in particular linguistic contexts.

*Materials:* A list of sentences, some of which violate selection restrictions and some of which are semantically correct, should be used as probes. The following sentences are examples of sentences that might be used:

| (1) | *She is my father.* |
| (2) | *My mother has no children.* |
| (3) | *The pony rides the girl.* |
| (4) | *His sister has no brother.* |
| (5) | *The candy eats Carol.* |
| (6) | *My father is a bachelor.* |
| (7) | *My dog writes nice stories.* |
| (8) | *The academic liquid became an odorless audience.* |
| (9) | *The sun danced lightly through the clouds.* |

*Procedures:* After you read each sentence, ask the child to determine if the sentence makes sense (i.e., is a "good sentence") or not (i.e., is a "bad sentence"). After the child has made a judgment about each sentence, ask "Why is it a good (or bad) sentence?" For those sentences the child has judged to be bad, ask the child to "correct it" or "make it better." Record all responses.

*Results:* In analyzing the child's responses, attempt to determine how the child decided which sentences were good or bad. Did he use only the semantic features of isolated words in making judgments? Did he use both semantic features and linguistic context (i.e., selection restrictions) in making judgments? Was the child able to correct semantically anomalous sentences? If not, how many problems did the lack of understanding of the meaning of particular words cause?

*Example:* The following are examples from two children who participated in this assessment task. The first child is an eight-year-old normal child.

Sentence **(1)** *She is my father.*
Judgment: *Bad sentence*
Justification: *Because a girl can't be a father.*
Correction: *Instead of she put he. He is my father.*

Sentence **(3)** *The pony rides the girl.*
Judgment: *Bad sentence*
Justification: *Because a pony can't ride a girl.*
Correction: *The girl is riding the pony.*

Sentence **(4)** *His sister has no brother.*
Judgment: *Bad sentence*
Justification: *If his sister doesn't have no brothers, then how come they said a boy then?*
Correction: *His, his sister has one brother.*

Sentence **(8)** *The academic liquid became an odorless audience.*
Judgment: *Bad sentence*
Justification: *'Cause liquid can't turn into people.*
Correction: *The audience watched him use the um formula.*

The second child is a language-delayed, eight-year-old. The following are her responses to the same questions.

Sentence **(1)** *She is my father*
Judgment: *Good sentence*
Justification: *'Cause you should have a father.*

Sentence **(3)** *The pony rides the girl.*
Judgment: *Good sentence*
Justification: *Because the girl can't ride the pony . . . it's too heavy* (giggles).

Sentence **(4)** *His sister has no brother.*
Judgment: *Good sentence*
Justification: *You don't have to fight.*

Sentence **(8)** *The academic liquid became an odorless audience.*
Judgment: *Bad sentence*
Justification: *Liquids don't become an audience cause that's a liquid not people.*
Correction: *The person became an audience.*

Although both youngsters appear to use several similar strategies (e.g., word order, knowledge of vocabulary, basic semantic features), there are several processing strategies that appear to affect their judgments. For example, in sentences **(1)** and **(4)**, the first child is analytic in processing the sentence, recognizing that pronouns (*she,his*) influence the meaning of the sentence. In contrast, the second child seems to ignore the informational value of these pronouns and opts for a more egocentric strategy of interpretation (i.e., *you should have a father*).

Analyzing children's judgments, justifications, and corrections of anomalous sentences allows us to obtain more information concerning what linguistic strategies youngsters use in processing sentences. Information such as whether the youngster uses word order alone or uses basic semantic relations while ignoring the semantic value of the grammatical morphemes facilitates the planning of a language intervention program.

ASSESSMENT STRATEGY 7: GRAMMATICAL MORPHEMES. Standard English relies heavily on rules that determine the use of particular grammatical morphemes, such as *-ed* markers for the past tense, the *-s* marker for plurality, the *-ing* progressive marker, and the *-er* marker for the agentive role. However, it should be noted that in certain variant dialects of English, these morphological markers may be deleted. In many cases, they are optional rather than obligatory as in standard English.

*Objective:* To analyze the child's production of frequently used standard English morphological markers with familiar and unlearned words.

*Materials:* Use a series of pictures and accompanying stories that act to stimulate the child's production. For each familiar word and accompanying stimulus story, there should be a comparable nonsense story that taps the same morphological marker. For example, the picture stories in Figure 9.1 can be used to tap the *-s* plural marker.

Picture stories can be developed for the *-ed, -s, -ing,* and *-er* markers.[1] In order to assess the use of the past tense *-ed* and plural and possessive *-s* markers in greater depth, the examiner should devise several items that tap the effects of the preceding phonemes on the phonetic realization of the grammatical morpheme (e.g., *church* ⟶ *churchiz, ham* ⟶ *hamz, hat* ⟶ *hats*).

*Procedures:* Present the familiar picture story first, followed by the unfamiliar, nonsense picture story. Say to the child: "I'm going to tell you a story about some pictures. I'm going to leave out a word, so listen carefully. Your job is to fill in the missing word." Read each story and record precisely the child's responses.

*Results:* Analyze the child's responses to determine if she could generate the appropriate grammatical morpheme. Determine if she could do this with unlearned,

FIGURE 9.1   Picture Stories to Tap the Plural Marker

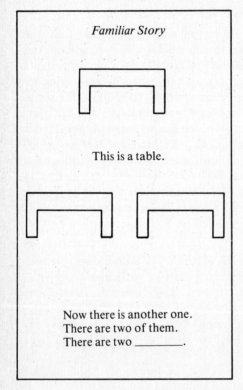

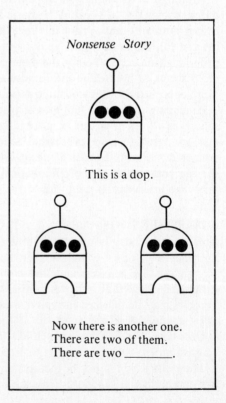

nonsense words as well as with familiar words. If errors did occur, were they isolated to particular markers (e.g., the *-er* marker) or to certain phonological contexts? Develop additional picture stories to probe further these troublesome markers. In addition, pay close attention to determine if the child performs similarly in spontaneous language production. Again, it is vital to remember that certain English dialects may not require the obligatory *-ed, -s,* and *'s* markers. Therefore, the absence of these markers does not necessarily imply a language problem.

*Example:* J.J. is a third-grade student of normal intelligence. He appears to have some language difficulties and is reading and writing at a primer level. The following are his responses to this task. (Items with an asterisk required several probes.)

| Stimulus | Response | Correct morpheme | Appropriate phonetic realization |
|---|---|---|---|
| *Plural* | | | |
| *nad + (z)\** | *ned* | none | none |
| *hotch (+ iz)\** | *hotchiz* | yes | yes |
| *table (+ z)* | *tabelz* | yes | yes |
| *Past tense marker -ed* | | | |
| *lop (+ t)\** | *lopt* | yes | yes |
| *trom + (d)\** | *tromd* | yes | yes |
| *walk (+ t)* | *walkt* | yes | yes |
| *Present progressive* | | | |
| *bine (+ ing)\** | *binding* | yes | yes |
| *swim (+ ing)* | *swimming* | yes | yes |
| *Possessive marker* | | | |
| *nad (+ z)* | *ned* | none | none |
| *girl (+ z)* | *girl* | none | none |
| *Agentive* | | | |
| *bine (+ er)\** | *bine* | none | none |
| *swim (+ er)* | *swimmer* | yes | yes |

In most cases, J.J. was able to generate the grammatical morpheme and its appropriate phonetic realization for both nonsense and familiar words. The main problem occurred with the possessive marker, for which he failed to generate the appropriate morphemic/phonetic marker in both the nonsense and familiar words.

ASSESSMENT STRATEGY 8: GRAMMATICAL MORPHEMES INDICATING RELATIONSHIPS AMONG WORDS. The meaning of sentences is dependent on several linguistic structures—phrase structure rules, transformational rules, and grammatical morphemes. One linguistic function of grammatical morphemes is that of providing important information indicating the logical or temporal relationship between words (*He runs and plays*) and phrases (*He ran fast then fell down*).

*Objective:* To analyze the child's comprehension of grammatical morphemes indicating certain logical (coordination, disjunction) and temporal relationships.

*Materials:* Use familiar objects that children can easily manipulate. Stimulus sentences should also be developed to tap relational morphemes (e.g., *and, or, then, but, not*) linking various sentential elements (e.g., nouns in the NP). The following are examples of sentences that can be used:

**(1)**  *Give me the pencil and the book.* (coordination of two nouns in the VP)

**(2)**  *The book but not the pencil are on the table.* (disjunction in NP)

**(3)**  *Put the book under the table, then hand me the pencil.* (temporal relationship between two propositions)

*Procedures:* Hand the child a book and a pencil (you may use any two familiar objects) and say: "Here is a pencil and a book. I'm going to tell you to do something with them. So listen carefully. You do exactly what I say." Present each stimulus sentence to the child and record what he does with the two objects. After each sentence, return both objects to the table in front of the child before proceeding to the next sentence.

*Results:* In analyzing the child's correct and incorrect responses, note what linquistic features affected the child's performance (e.g., sentence length, type of relational morpheme, what elements of the sentence the morpheme related to). Also, try to determine whether or not the child actually understands the logical relationship represented by each of these morphemes.


**ASSESSMENT STRATEGY 9: SENTENCE IMITATION.** Menyuk (1964) and Miller and Isard (1963) are among the researchers who have studied the value of using the sentence repetition paradigm to assess a child's linguistic capacity. Sentences of various lengths and syntactic complexity are presented to the child to imitate. Findings, especially those of McNeill (1970) and Miller and Chomsky (1963), support the idea that a child will not imitate a particular linguistic feature within a sentence unless that feature is already part of the child's linguistic competence. Therefore, the use of a sentence imitation paradigm is applicable for diagnosing the acquisition of various grammatical rules.

*Objectives:* To determine the child's acquisition of particular grammatical rules.

*Materials:* The only materials necessary for this task are a series of sentences that tap various grammatical structures. These sentences can be developed by referring to any source providing a thorough analysis of syntactic structures and stages in language acquisition. For example, sentences reflecting subordinate clauses of a temporal nature are as follows:

**(1)**        *After he went to the store, he came home to take a nap.*

**(2)**        *He went to the store, and then he came home to take a nap.*

**(3)**        *Before he came home to take a nap, he went to the store.*

*Procedures:* From a series of sentences either tapping a wide range of grammatical features or focusing on a particular set of features, present each sentence to the child and ask the child to imitate it. You may want to follow Menyuk's (1964) procedures, saying:

> "We are going to play the game Follow the Leader. I'm going to say some sentences for you. I want you to say just what I say. If I say 'The boy runs,' I want you to say 'The boy runs'."

Tape-record both your reading of the sentences and the child's responses.

*Results:* Transcribe the child's imitations of the stimulus sentences. Several levels of analysis can be undertaken. First, there is the determination of whether the child provided an exact repetition of the stimulus sentence. If this did occur, it is evidence for the child's competence regarding this particular structure. For example, if the child accurately imitates the following sentences, we could at least tenatively conclude that the associated structures are within the child's linguistic capacity.

$$S \longrightarrow NP + VP$$

$$NP \longrightarrow \left\{ \begin{array}{l} \text{Pronoun} \\ \text{Det} + \text{N} \\ \text{N} \end{array} \right\}$$

$$VP \longrightarrow be + V + \text{-}ing + PP$$

$$PP \longrightarrow \left\{ \begin{array}{l} \text{Prep} + \text{Det} + \text{N} \\ \text{Prep} + \text{N} \end{array} \right\}$$

**(1)**        *He is going to the store.*

**(2)**        *The men are walking down the street.*

**(3)**        *Sally is running to school.*

**(4)**        *I am sitting on the chair.*

If however, deviations occurred in the child's attempts to imitate the stimulus sentences, further analysis should be made. The following deviations from the sentences provide some examples of error analysis.

**(1a)**        *He going to the store.*

**(2a)**        *They are walking down the street.*

**(3a)**        *Sally running school.*

**(4a)**        *Me sitting.*

In sentence **(1a)**, the child, while maintaining the basic semantic relation of agent, action, and location, is not incorporating the auxiliary verb *be* in the present progressive verb phrase. Therefore, the child's knowledge of the syntactic rule

$$VP \longrightarrow be + V + \text{-}ing$$

may be inadequate. This verb phrase structure could then be analyzed in other sentences in various forms, such as follows:

$$VP \longrightarrow \begin{Bmatrix} be + V + \text{-}ing \\ be + V + \text{-}ing + \text{adverb} \\ be + V + \text{-}ing + and + V + \text{-}ing \end{Bmatrix}$$

In contrast, sentence (2a) maintains both the semantic and syntactic structures of the stimulus sentence (2). Even the lexical substitution of *They* for *The men* represents an accurate knowledge of pronouns. Sentence (3a), while maintaining the basic semantic content of the stimulus sentence (3), reflects the following rather unelaborated set of syntactic rules:

$$VP \longrightarrow V + \text{-}ing + PP$$
$$PP \longrightarrow N$$

Finally, in sentence (4a), both semantic and syntactic aspects are limited.

A last note about the use of the sentence imitation paradigm as a diagnostic tool is called for. Sentence imitation provides the examiner with information concerning the child's knowledge of linguistic rules. It does *not* assess the use of this linguistic knowledge in the child's spontaneous use of language. Therefore, it is strongly suggested that assessment be conducted at both levels, that is, spontaneous use of language and sentence repetition. Berry-Luterman and Bar (1968, p. 31) provide a helpful strategy whereby the child's performance can be assessed under the following conditions: "(1) The repetition of grammatically incorrect sentences taken from the child's own spontaneous productions; (2) the repetition of grammatically correct versions of these sentences; and (3) the repetition of the reversed word order of these grammatically correct versions."

The results obtained using the sentence imitation paradigm in conjunction with a spontaneous sample of language are helpful in answering the following questions:

1. What is the difference, if any, between what the child knows about language and how he uses this linguistic knowledge?
2. What is the child's competence to deal with syntactic/semantic structures, such as interrogation, possession, infinitival complement, and so on?
3. At the morphological level, what is the child's competence with verb forms, pluralization, pronoun substitution, and so on?

All this information can be used to determine the need for, starting point of, and progressive steps in language intervention.

**COMMUNICATION**   The ultimate criterion establishing one's competence as a speaker/listener of a particular language is one's ability to utilize accurate and precise expanded language in discourse. For the listener, this means comprehending and retaining the precise meaning of the intended linguistic message as it occurs on an ongoing basis. This is especially important in the school situation, as the child spends a great proportion of the instructional day in the role of listener. For the speaker, communicative competence includes the abilities to (1) determine relevant information to be linguistically coded, (2) code that information from the perspective of the listener, and (3) seek feedback from the listener concerning the accuracy of the message. The following assessment tasks tap various aspects of the speaker/listener role.

ASSESSMENT STRATEGY 10: MAKING COMMUNICATIVE DECISIONS. Every object can be referred to by many words, and many words can represent several different objects. A theory or an assessment of reference must specify how and why this is the case. Presumably, something mediates between the word and the object. This mediational component is meaning, and meaning consists of the experiences of perceiving objects and events in a context. Olson (1970, p. 264) argues that in the word-referent relationship "words designate, signal, or specify an *intended referent relative to the set of alternatives from which it must be differentiated.*" If this is the case, then communicative decisions must be based not only on the knowledge of the intended referent and how it may be referenced, but also on knowledge of the alternatives from which it must be differentiated.

*Objective:* To assess how a child uses (1) knowledge of the referent, (2) knowledge of the various words to symbolize the referent, and (3) knowledge of the alternative referents to communicate effectively.

*Materials:* Although many different objects can be used, the following materials are provided as examples:

1 gold star
1 small, round, white wooden block
1 small, round, black wooden block
1 small, square, black wooden block
1 small, square, white wooden block

*Procedures:* Same as for Inquiry 2.5 (p. 47).

*Results:* After transcribing the directions given by the child, analyze whether or not the child was able to use the alternative context to arrive at an unambiguous message for specifying or signaling the intended referent. Or, was the child somewhat rigid in choosing words to signal the intended referent (e.g., *It's under the round block* regardless of whether the alternatives were round or square)? Information derived from this task should yield relevant hypotheses concerning whether or not the youngster can effectively utilize existing contextual information in the process of communicating.

ASSESSMENT STRATEGY 11: EGOCENTRIC LISTENING. The concept of egocentric thinking and its effects on the ability to communicate have received close attention. However, most of the available research centers on this phenomenon as it relates to the role of the speaker (e.g., Glucksberg & Krauss, 1967; Meissner, 1975; Bearison & Levey, 1977). Egocentric communication may not affect only the speaker's capabilities; it clearly may also affect the listener's ability to process ongoing discourse. Youngsters may confirm messages that are either ambiguous or lack critical information. They may not ask those questions of the speaker that might aid the speaker in recoding the message so that it provides more accurate and adequate information. They may give no feedback at all. In fact, Karabenick and Miller (1977) report, that while improving with age, listeners at the age of seven still have not completely developed the ability to accurately offer or utilize listener feedback. Since youngsters with language delays have a disproportionately higher incidence of linguistic processing problems and much time in school is spent listening, the effects of egocentric listening are critical.

*Objectives:* To assess the child's ability to function as a listener in a communicative task.

*Materials:* Provide a duplicate set of between six and ten blocks that vary in shape, size, color, and configuration (optional). Also needed are a child-size table and two chairs that face each other. Finally, place a visual barrier so that the two children engaging in the block-building task cannnot see one another's blocks.

*Procedures:* Build a configuration with one child's blocks in two stages, that is, first arrange three or four blocks and then add three or four blocks after the speaker has given the first set of directions. Have the child whose blocks are being used for the examiner's construction give directions to the other child (the listener being evaluated); the objective is that the listener be able to construct an identical configuration without seeing the original. Tape-record both the speaker's directions and the listener's verbal feedback. Also, observe and note all listener feedback.

*Results:* From your observations and tape-recording, analyze the nature of the feedback from the listener. Did the listener confirm the adequacy of the message? If so, how? When the speaker's message was either inadequate or inaccurate, what did the listener do? Did the listener simply proceed with the task, apparently thinking (albeit egocentrically) that the information was sufficient for task completion? Or, did the listener provide feedback to the speaker concerning the inadequacy of the message?

The results of this task and similar ones can yield valuable information as to how the child may function as a listener at home or in school. This information can then be used to suggest compensatory classroom strategies (see Chapter 10) as well as therapeutic developmental listening strategies.

ASSESSMENT STRATEGY 12: COMPREHENDING ONGOING DISCOURSE. In addition to providing feedback to the speaker, the listener must be able to process accurately the expanded and frequently abstract language of discourse. In other words, it is not sufficient to determine whether or not the child can comprehend isolated sentences of varying levels of syntactic and semantic complexity. The listener must be able to comprehend the meaning of elaborated language as it occurs (1) where discourse topics may be abruptly shifted, (2) where there is a series of two or more consecutive commands, declaratives, or questions without an intervening interval of silence, or (3) where there is an increased amount of syntactic and semantic variation from sentence to sentence rather than a maintenance of key lexical items or syntactic structures.

*Objective:* To assess the child's comprehension of ongoing language without the aid of extralinguistic cues, such as gestures, contextual clues, and so on.

*Materials:* Provide crayons and drawing paper or construction paper cut-outs of different sizes, colors, and shapes. Devise a script of a fantasy story, which the child will draw following your dictation, or directions, which the child will follow using the cut-out shapes, to construct a design, mask, or scene.

*Procedures:* Say to the child: "I'm going to tell a story and you have to make your picture just like the story I tell." Administer the directions or made-up script to the child two or three sentences at a time. Encourage the child to make the picture or design exactly like the story you tell. Read the entire script and repeat if requested. The following are examples of mini-scripts that might be used.

### Mini-script I

"Hi, I'm Mary Martian from Mars. As you know, I'm a little purple Martian with red, round eyes; a square head, and green, pointed ears. My two little pigtails point up."

### Mini-script II

"Hi, I'm Mary Martian again. Through the window of my spaceship I can see your planet earth. It has a big, round, yellow, smiling sun and blue clouds. It has green trees, flowers, and red birds flying all around."

*Results:* In analyzing the child's picture or design, determine if the child was able to process accurately expanded language. If errors in comprehension did occur, were they errors related to size, shape, color, or position? This error analysis should provide some insight into how the child listens to and comprehends expanded language.

ASSESSMENT STRATEGY 13: REFERENTIAL COMMUNICATION. In order to be an effective communicator, not only must one have competency with various linguistic structures and an adequate vocabulary and related concepts, but one must also be able to take into account what the listener knows and listener feedback. Communicative decisions, such as how precise the linguistic message must be, what constitutes shared speaker-listener knowledge, and so on, must constantly be made. This extralinguistic knowledge, although necessary at all times, becomes even more so when factors such as gestures or contextual cues are absent. The precision, elaborateness, and comprehensiveness of the linguistic information given by the speaker are then critical.

*Objective:* To assess the child's ability to engage in referential communication.

*Materials and Procedures:* Same as those used in assessing egocentric listening (p. 294).

*Results:* From observations and tape-recording, analyze the accuracy, precision, and specificity of the language used by the speaker to give the necessary information. Did the speaker allow for the listener's needs and perspective? For example, did the speaker give directions slowly enough so that the listener had sufficient time to complete each direction? Did the speaker use pronouns, such as *it* or *that one,* for which the listener had a specific referent or did the speaker assume that the listener knew what *it* or *that one* referred to? Was spatial information, such as distance or left-right positioning, given by the speaker? Did the speaker solicit and utilize listener feedback? If so, how?

In summary, recent linguistic and psycholinguistic research certainly provides the educator with a conceptual basis from which to study normal, delayed, and deviant language. Less obvious is the fact that this research offers a wide range of informal assessment strategies and tasks that can add to and enhance the information available through the use of standardized tests. The strategies in the preceding sections have grown out of this research. The following section provides the reader with additional sources and suggestions for transforming current research methodologies into useful assessment strategies.

**SUMMARY OF RESEARCH-BASED METHODOLOGIES**   In this section, descriptions are provided of a few of the psycholinguistic research methods cited by Leonard et al. (1978), plus a few additions from other sources. Selection of research targets for inclusion in this section answers the relative absence of these linguistic forms or functions from most of the widely used standardized tests and reflects the likelihood of the involvement of these forms or functions in the more advanced stages of linguistic competence required by the language of instruction.

In some cases, the material is appropriate for assessment of the young school-aged child. In other cases, the material may be appropriate in its present state for use with older elementary school children or is adaptable through changes in content. Summaries of the selected models are intended to spur further efforts by teachers to study linguistic factors that are possibly related to difficulties in the processing of information in language-dependent academic tasks. Because it is beyond the scope of this chapter to describe each of these strategies, Table 9.3 is meant to provide samples for teacher-initiated application in the form of a few summarized illustrations of how research can be adapted for assessment purposes. Presented in Table 9.3 are the targeted form for assessing, the materials needed, the procedures used, and how these procedures can be adapted for school-related assessment. A detailed listing of various research studies to aid in the development of assessment strategies can be found in Leonard et al. (1978).

Once information is obtained from the nonstandardized assessment procedures described in earlier sections and once goals have been tentatively established and intervention has begun, diagnostic information is continuously available during

TABLE 9.3  From Research to Assessment

| Targeted Form for Assessment | Materials | Procedures | School-related Assessment Tasks | |
|---|---|---|---|---|
| | | | Materials | Procedures |
| Comprehension of Anaphoric Pronoun "it" (Chipman & deDardel, 1974) | Flattened cake of clay, one box containing five marbles, one with twenty marbles, one clear plastic box (empty), and one tray on which is displayed one bar of plasticine chocolate divided into demarcated squares | Present appropriate materials, saying: 1. *There is the clay. Give it to me.* 2. *There is a box with five marbles. Give it to me.* 3. *The chocolate is there. Give it to me.* | A. Any kindergarten or first-grade arithmetic book, pencil or crayon | Say to child, using appropriate materials: 1. *Find the line that has five cats. Point to it.* 2. *Find the picture with more ducks. Put a line under it.* |
| | | | B. Prose passage that is related to subject matter, such as: "Choked with vegetation and ridden with insects, snakes, and disease, the rain forest on the east side of the Andes barred Inca expansion." | After the child reads the passage, say: 1. *Find what barred the Incas from expanding and underline it.* 2. *Find one of the dangers of the rain forest and underline it.* Similar procedures can be used for anaphoric pronouns *them, those, that,* and *the ones.* |

TABLE 9.3 (Continued)

| Targeted Form for Assessment | Materials | Procedures | School-related Assessment Tasks Materials | Procedures |
|---|---|---|---|---|
| Comprehension of Temporal Connectives *before, after,* and *until* (Barrie-Blackley, 1973) | Toy dolls and doll-house | Sentences containing various subordinate clauses beginning with *before, after,* or *until* are said to the child. Children act out the sentences using the toys. 1. *Daddy lies down after he comes in.* 2. *Mommy sits down before Daddy comes in.* 3. *Daddy stands up until Mommy sits down.* | Worksheets appropriate to child's skill levels | Present child with worksheets and give the following directions: 1. *Before you write the number of balloons in the box, put an X on each balloon.* 2. *Do not write the number of balloons in the box until you have put an X on each balloon.* |
| Comprehension of Connectives and Propositional Logical Relations (Paris, 1973) | Paired pictures (e.g., DLM Sequential Picture Cards) related to accompanying sentences in four different truth forms: true-true, true-false, false-true, and false-false. Compound sentences containing the following con- | Picture pairs are displayed and the descriptive sentence is read. Child must decide if the description is true or false. | List of words that the child can read, list of compound sentences containing the connectives. | The child is given the following directions: 1. *Find a word that has a "t" at the beginning and an "a" at the end.* 2. *Draw a line under "jump" but not under "ing."* 3. *Find a word that has either "er" or "est" at the end.* |

| Skill / Objective | Materials | Procedure |
|---|---|---|
| (continued) | nectives: *and* conjunction, *but* conjunction, *both-and* conjunction, *neither-or* disconjunction, *if-then* conditionality, and *if-and only if then* biconditionality.<br><br>4. *If a word has a vowel digraph, then put a circle around it.* | |
| (continued) | Tape-recorded segments of familiar stories (e.g., The Three Little Pigs) or of factual accounts of subjects studied in class (e.g., How Birds Care For Their Young). *Wh*-questions of different types for each segment. | Play each segment. At the conclusion, ask the child the different types of *wh*-questions. In case of failure to respond correctly, replay the segment once to eliminate such possible error-causing factors as inattention or forgetting. Repeat procedure for each segment to secure a number of responses for each type of question. |
| Comprehension of *wh*-Questions *who*, *why*, *when*, and *how* (Cairns & Hsu, 1978) | Brief videotapes of family life, including father, mother, teenage sister, six-year-old brother, and dog. Questions of six types:<br><br>*who* as subject, as in *Who told the boy?*<br>*who* as object using progressive aspect, as in *Who was the Daddy feeding?*<br>*who* as object using *do* support, as in *Who did the boy feed?*<br>*why*, as in *Why did the dog eat it?*<br>*when*, as in *When did the girl feed the dog?*<br>*how*, as in *How did she?* | After being introduced to each character by a photograph, which remains on display, each child watches a taped segment and is then asked the six types of questions. |

Based mainly on material contributed by A. Gerber.

the interaction between teacher and child. Diagnostic teaching can add another valuable dimension to the assessment of language.

**DIAGNOSTIC TEACHING**[2]    During the actual intervention or teaching strategies, the instructional interaction between teacher and child provides another means for confirming, disconfirming, modifying, or generating information about how the child uses language for discourse purposes. The act of teaching can provide information regarding optimal conditions for processing oral or written language, the best way to control the amount of linguistic input to the child, and the child's preference for the oral or written modality. Examples of the kinds of diagnostic tasks embedded in instruction are presented in this section. Once again, these tasks are intended to be suggestive rather than exhaustive.

CONDITIONS FOR PROCESSING ORAL DISCOURSE. In a study by O'Day (1977), a teacher observed a child's overt manifestations of comprehension or lack of comprehension under the following discourse conditions:

1. Isolated questions or statements,
2. Consecutive units of varied and controlled length of sequence with no intervening silence,
3. Consecutive units of varied and controlled length of sequence with pauses to permit time for response to each unit,
4. Repetition of a prior statement or question to which a correct or appropriate response had not been made,
5. Paraphrase of a prior statement or question to which a correct or appropriate response had not been made,
6. Increased or decreased syntactic complexity,
7. Varied or constant key lexical items (nouns and verbs) in a series of sentences involved in a description, and
8. Abrupt shifts of the topic of conversation.

The teacher was able to report that the child responded with a blank or bewildered look, said "huh?," or gave either no response or an inappropriate one under the second, fifth, and eighth conditions. Thus, the child appeared to demonstrate a deficit in the processing of uninterrupted oral language input, seemed not to benefit from a restatement of content in a different linguistic form, and evidenced some momentary inability to respond to sudden topical shifts. In contrast, oral comprehension was facilitated when the teacher allowed additional response time between phrases or sentences, repeated rather than paraphrased declarative sentences, repeatedly used the same key nouns and verbs on picture descriptions, and broke compound commands, declaratives, and questions into a series of short, simple sentences with silence intervals of three to eight seconds between them.

CONDITIONS FOR PROCESSING WRITTEN LANGUAGE. Although the field of reading has existed historically as a separate discipline from that of language, the act of reading is increasingly acknowledged to be the processing of language in the written as opposed to the oral modality (see Chapter 8). Many of the tasks children are required to perform when reading textual material in subject content areas are concerned with their comprehension of the material and their ability to demonstrate that comprehension through some kind of output, either vocal or motor. When a child is not successful at an assigned reading task, it is important to determine whether (1) he could not comprehend the language, (2) he does comprehend the language when he hears it spoken, but has difficulty decoding the visual representation, or (3) he does comprehend the language and content in the visual modality, but was unable to perform the assigned task to demonstrate such comprehension. If the latter, questions must be asked about the conditions imposed by such tasks and how they may be manipulated to determine the nature of the child's difficulty and the variables related to possible success.

The following procedures are suggested when attempting to refine the analysis of the child's difficulties and to compare functioning in written and oral language modalities. The variables controlled are the amount of material to be processed prior to tests of comprehension, the type of questions asked to determine comprehension, retention, and recall, the comparison of visual and oral language processing by the child, and the child's processing of oral reading by the examiner. Illustrations of these procedures are presented in conjunction with results and interpretations of actual evaluations, where such material is available.

COMPREHENSION OF WRITTEN TEXTS. During reading activities, various probing strategies and modifications can aid in identifying possible causes of comprehension problems. These include the following: (1) modifying the type of questions asked of the reader, (2) controlling the amount of reading material presented, and (3) comparing performance on oral and written presentations.

The type of questions asked as comprehension checks may affect the child's performance. Broad questions require more general or inferred responses, which demonstrate comprehension of the total content and, possibly, the ability to abstract an underlying theme (Pollak & Gruenwald, 1978).

Pollak and Gruenwald (1978) report about a child who tended to remain silent when asked to "tell what the story was about." It became the teacher's responsibility to determine whether he had not comprehended what he had just read, had comprehended but not retained the content, or had both comprehended and retained the material but was unable to organize the totality of the information either cognitively or linguistically (i.e., was not able to formulate the response to the broad question). In this type of situation, narrow questioning is helpful. Narrow questions are more specifically factual and tend to facilitate recall.

The same child who did not respond to the broad question readily answered twelve narrower questions about the same story about lost children, indicating accurate recall of factual information and abstraction of underlying meaning. Narrow questions take a number of forms and serve the following functions:

1. *Wh-* questions tap recall, placing demands on the child for retrieval of information (e.g., *When did the children realize they were lost?*).

2. *Yes/no* questions provide information, facilitate recall through inclusion of such cues as key words and phrases (e.g., *Did they realize they were lost when they lost sight of the stream?*).
3. An alternate version of *yes/no* questioning to tap comprehension and recall includes dissonant information that appears to alert the child to the critical element (e.g., *Is the tundra a place with lots of trees?*).
4. Multiple choice questions tap comprehension and retention at the level of recognition in cases where the child is unable to recall the information.

Thus, the kinds of questions to which a child does and does not respond correctly are at least partial guides toward analysis of the nature of the child's problem.

In some cases, errors in processing the questions may be the cause of the difficulty. Some older children with language problems, as well as younger normal children, do not process the *wh-* word but tend to respond instead to implications of the verb phrase.

**Q:**                                   *When are you going on vacation?*

**A:**                                   *To my grandmom's.*

This kind of response calls for further testing of *wh-* words in such simple questions as *When do you go to sleep?, Where do you sleep?, When do you eat dinner?, Where do you eat?,* and so on.

In other cases, a pattern may be suggestive of failure to process *all* critical elements in a question.

**Q:**                                   *What makes our bodies grow?*

**A:**                                   *Trees.*

In this instance the child has evidently focused on the *wh-* word and part of the verb phrase but has failed to process *makes our bodies.* Following-up with a restatement of the question with either intonational highlighting of overlooked elements or rephrasing is necessary in order to decide whether it was failure to comprehend the passage or failure to comprehend the question that caused the error.

In addition to varying the type of questions asked, varying the amount of input may be necessary. If a child demonstrates difficulty in responding to informational questions after the entire paragraph or story has been read, the examiner may mask all but a small portion of the text at a time and question the child only on that information contained in the small segment. Using selected segments from the Paragraph Meaning subtest of the American School Achievement Test, this technique was used with a child. The report (Gerber & Goll, 1978, p. 2) of this evaluation included the following statement:

As the paragraph increased in complexity and number of units, S. was unable to read the total passage and abstract out the embedded units. One of the techniques reported as facilitative to correct responses was "breaking the paragraph into individual components by masking irrelevant information."

Such a performance can be interpreted as either a retention deficit (i.e., a limited capacity as to the amount of information that can be retained) or, possibly, a deficient ability to integrate individual units of information into a higher level of organization that facilitates meaningfulness and, therefore, retention of the individual parts.

Finally comparing the child's performance on oral and written modalities can be helpful. Having a child read aloud is one of the most obvious means of checking on ability to decode the written text. What is frequently noted during oral reading, in addition to difficulty in sounding out the individual words, is a failure to utilize those aspects of linguistic knowledge the child tacitly possesses. For example, "it was noted, also, during oral reading that S. does not seem to respond to sentence boundaries" (Gerber & Goll, 1978, p. 2). This kind of performance pattern by a child who has complete control of the sentences of oral language may be interpreted as evidence that primary linguistic competence is not being invoked in processing language in the written modality. It may be said that failure to process written language through the same system governing the use of oral language is one of the most crucial factors interfering with reading comprehension.

Reading a passage aloud to the child prior to the child's reading and the testing of comprehension and retention has two advantages. If the child responds more successfully to questions about content that has been presented orally, this is evidence that language and the concepts encoded in language are comprehended and adequately processed for related output tasks. In this case, the decoding of written texts may be an area of deficit, or it may be that such supralinguistic variables as stress, intonation, and juncture, although employed by the child in oral language, are not being invoked to enhance meaningfulness during the act of reading written language.

Conversely, some children perform tasks testing comprehension and recall more successfully in the written modality than auditorily. It is possible that such children benefit from the static nature of written language, which is accessible to reinspection for material not apprehended on the initial scan. Transitory auditory information, under ordinary processing conditions, is not as available for reinspection when material has been missed in the ongoing stream of speech.

Even as diagnostic teaching continues and more information is obtained about a child's tacit knowledge of and use of language and language-related processes, one's understanding of the child's abilities and task demands may remain incomplete. The situation is uncomfortable for both teacher and child when gaps in performance are encountered and not fully understood, as when all assessment efforts fail to reveal a language problem and yet the language-related tasks of spelling and writing are continuously troublesome for the child. The following section offers some avenues to explore when such a situation does exist.

**METALINGUISTICS**  One has a tacit knowledge of the rules governing language from the preschool years onward. However, this tacit or unconscious knowledge restricts the linguistic abilities in that language becomes an extension of thinking rather than the object of one's thought. As a child develops both linguistically and cognitively, recursiveness in language furthers the ability to approach language in a highly analytic fashion. Between the ages of eight and twelve, the metalinguistic aspect of recursive thinking is evidenced in children's advancements in the ability to communicate. Youngsters are able to think about their perspective, whether visual or informational, to think about the other person's perspective, and to coordinate the two when coding a linguistic message. When judging the grammaticalness of a sentence, the child can go beyond the semantics and can analytically reflect on both the sense and grammatical knowledge of language in an explicit fashion.

Metalinguistic knowledge, although relatively unresearched, appears to be closely related to the skills of spelling and writing. For example, the task of spelling requires one to explicitly and analytically coordinate what one knows about the grapheme and phoneme relationship. Whereas one's tacit knowledge of linguistic rules may be quite functional in informal daily conversations, it may be insufficient for engaging in a spelling task in which language is both the action and object of one's thinking. Producing written language may also require more than the use of tacit linguistic knowledge. In most situations in which spoken language is used, several factors act to minimize one's need to engage in recursive thinking. First, spoken language is more informal, and one characteristic of this informality is a high degree of familiarity between listener and speaker. This familiarity generally reflects a concomitant degree of shared knowledge between listener and speaker, resulting in less need for recursiveness in thinking, that is, thinking about what one's partner does or does not know. Second, the very nature of informal spoken communication assumes the availability of immediate and ongoing feedback. Therefore, messages that are ambiguous or imprecise have the potential for immediate clarification, depending on the verbal or nonverbal feedback from the listener. As a result, the speaker need not be overly concerned about the exactness of perspective coordination. Finally, in most informal conversations, the existence of a physical and social context supports and frequently disambiguates communicative messages, once again minimizing the need to analytically and consciously organize the content and structure of the message. Greater attention can be paid to the substance or meaning of the message, perhaps while sacrificing structure and precision. In contrast, written communication is generally more formal, cannot rely on immediate feedback, does not presuppose a high degree of shared knowledge, and is not supported by a rich physical and social context. It follows, then, that written language cannot be presuppositional in nature, making many assumptions about shared knowledge. The writer must constantly engage in recursive thinking, deciding not just *what* to write, but precisely *how* to write the message so that it is comprehensive and unambiguous before it is sent. Therefore, written communication requires one to use both linguistic and metalinguistic knowledge.

This point, while having general significance for all school-aged youngsters, may have special significance for language-handicapped youngsters who have a high incidence of both spoken and written language problems. Diagnosed or undiagnosed oral language problems occurring at an early age may be so subtle as not to cause interference with spoken, less formal language. However, these same problems may manifest themselves in written communication, for which both linguistic and metalinguistic demands are greatly increased. Therefore, the assessment of metalinguistic abilities is of considerable importance, even in light of a nonempirically yet logically established relationship between metalinguistics and writing. The following represents one strategy that can be used either orally or in written form to assess a child's ability to incorporate recursiveness as a critical strategy in communicating.[3]

*Objective:* To assess the child's ability to think recursively so that communicative messages (oral or written) produced are reflective of the perspective of the listener.

*Materials:* Tape recorder, if task is to be done orally.

*Procedures:* Give the following directions to the youngster:

"The purpose of this game is to make a series of shopping lists—one for yourself, one for a member of your family, like your mother or brother, and one for a person who does *not* know you but has agreed to do your shopping. You should do (write) your list so that you will get *exactly* what you want from the store."

Have the youngster produce the shopping list for herself first. Then, have her produce the family-oriented shopping list, which should contain the same items as the first one. Finally, have the child do the list, again of the same items, from which the unknown person will do the shopping.

*Results:* Analyze the three shopping lists to determine if the child was able to adapt her thinking and, therefore, her message to the perspective of each recipient. The shopping list developed for self-use is expected to be imprecise and cryptic (e.g., soda, cookies, gum, and fruit), because there is maximal shared knowledge. That is, the child *knows* what kind, the amount, and the brand of the items she desires, and, therefore, only a very cryptic message is needed. In contrast, the shopping list for the *unknown* person cannot be based on the presupposition that "what I know, must also be known by the other." The child must think about what the person needs to know so that the communication will result in obtaining the desired items. This message cannot be imprecise and cryptic, because shared knowledge is minimal. A list of this kind might be as follows:

- one 16-ounce can of Frank's orange soda
- one large package of Oreo cookies
- two pieces of Bazooka bubble gum
- one banana and one Red Delicious apple

## CONCLUDING REMARKS

The position of this chapter is to recommend going beyond the sole use of standardized tests of language and including linguistic and extralinguistic areas in assessment that (1) are not dealt with comprehensively, (2) are not dealt with at all, or (3) do not explore underlying rules or strategies that may account for the child's linguistic performance. Knowledge and use of informal tasks based on linguistic and psycholinguistic research, a sound background in the area of normal language acquisition, and a sensitive and analytic style of interaction are the examiner's most important resources. Application of these resources should provide the foundation for determining the need for and nature of a language intervention program. The following inquiries allow one to put into practice many of the ideas developed in this chapter.

_____                    **INQUIRY 9.1**                    _____

The assessment of language should reflect the effects of social context. Two contextual influences are the perceived formality of the situation and the familiarity of the listener-speaker relationship.

**OBJECTIVES**   The objectives of this inquiry are to:

1. Analyze the effects of social context on the assessment of language.
2. More specifically, analyze the effects of perceived formality of the setting and the familiarity of the listener-speaker relationship on the syntactic construction and the semantic content used by the speaker.

**PROCEDURES**   A child's language is assessed in the following three different social contexts:

1. Child making Play-Doh with familiar peer (familiar and informal context).
2. Child making Play-Doh with examiner (somewhat less familiar and informal context).
3. Child interviewed by the examiner with the tape recorder visible (less familiar and more formal context).

Tape-record approximately ten minutes of interaction in each of the three contexts. Transcribe the three interactions and analyze the transcripts according to the strategies presented on pages 264–269.

**REPORT**   Include the following in your report:

1. Brief descriptions of the child and the three social contexts.
2. Transcripts of the interactions and analyses of the three social contexts.

In addition, address yourself to each of the following questions:

1. What were the effects of the formality and familiarity of the social context on the child's use of syntactic constructions?
2. What were the effects of the formality and familiarity of the social context on the child's use of semantic content?
3. What are the implications of the social-contextual influences for the assessment of children's language?

**EVALUATION**  Did this inquiry develop the specified objectives? If so, how? If not, why? How could the effectiveness of this inquiry be increased?

---

## INQUIRY 9.2

The social context influences the child's use of language and, consequently, the assessment of such language, and so does the testing paradigm. For example, in a structured testing situation, while we may be able to zero in on a particular linguistic feature, we may simultaneously sacrifice important information concerning how the child uses language in a more natural communicative context. On the other hand, if we choose to rely on a spontaneous sample of language as the testing paradigm, it is likely that particular linguistic features of interest may not be produced.

**OBJECTIVES**  The objectives of this inquiry are to:

1. Analyze a structured assessment task (elicited imitation) and a spontaneous language sample as two testing paradigms for yielding information about particular linguistic features used by the child.
2. Evaluate the relative usefulness of each paradigm for the assessment of child language.

**PROCEDURES**  Identify the linguistic features (negative transformations, two-clause constructions containing *before* and *after,* or constructions containing *and/or* or *but not*) to be assessed. Develop a series of stimulus sentences containing the identified constructions for use in the elicited imitation task. Present the stimulus sentences to the child using Menyuk's (1964) procedures (p. 291). Tape-record both the stimulus sentences and the child's repetitions of them. At another time, obtain a spontaneous sample of the child's language. Transcribe and analyze both the child's repetitions and the spontaneous language sample.

**REPORT**  Include the following in your report:

1. Linguistic constructions chosen for assessment and the stimulus sentences used for the elicited imitation task.

2. Transcripts and analyses of the spontaneous sample of language and the elicited imitation task.

In addition, address yourself to the following questions:

1. Did the spontaneous sample of language include the particular linguistic construction of interest? If not, how could the context of the sampling be modified to increase the likelihood of occurrence of these features? If so, what information about these constructions was obtained, and how does this information relate to the findings from the imitation task?
2. What information was obtained from the imitation task concerning the child's knowledge of the particular linguistic constructions assessed? For example, if errors occurred, was semantic content maintained? If there were lexical substitutions, did these substitutions demonstrate semantic and syntactic knowledge?
3. What is the relative usefulness of the two testing paradigms?

**EVALUATION**   Did this inquiry develop the specified objectives? If so, how? If not, why? How could the effectiveness of this inquiry be increased?

## INQUIRY 9.3

Children's performances during language assessment depend not only on their linguistic capabilities but also on the demands of the assessment task. Receptive language testing paradigms, such as picture identification, acting out of commands, or judgment tasks, can yield different results simply because the testing paradigms are different. Similarly, different expressive language tasks, such as elicited imitation, cloze procedures, paraphrasing, and spontaneous usage, can also yield different results as a consequence of the differential linguistic and extralinguistic demands embedded in each task. Therefore, consideration must be given to selecting or developing the content and the format of the language task.

**OBJECTIVES**   The objectives of this inquiry are to:

1. Utilize different testing paradigms for the assessment of particular linguistic constructions.
2. Analyze the various linguistic and extralinguistic demands of each task and how these demands affect the child's language performance.

**PROCEDURES**   Identify a set of linguistic constructions, such as grammatical morphemes *-ed* and plural and possessive *s*, constructions containing *and/or* and *but not,* relative questions, or passive constructions. Determine whether you will be assessing comprehension or expression. Then select at least two testing paradigms to assess the chosen constructions. For example, if the particular feature to be assessed is comprehension of the possessive *'s,* the following test paradigms could be used.

1. *Picture identification:* "Show me the boy's coat" (using various pictorial stimuli).
2. *Acting out:* "Show me Johnny's coat" (using actual children and objects in the classroom.
3. *Judgment:* "Which sentence sounds correct or is a good sentence?"
   a. *The boy coat is on the floor.*
   b. *The boy's coat is on the floor.*
   c. *The coat's boys is on the floor.*

If expressive use of the possessive *'s* is to be assessed, the following test paradigms could be employed:

1. *Elicited imitation:* "Repeat the following sentences."
   a. *The boy's coat is on the floor.*
   b. *He ran down the street after the man's hat.*
2. *Cloze procedure:* "This is a ball. It belongs to the boy. Whose ball is it? The ball is the _____ ."
3. *Paraphrasing:* Tell the child a brief story containing a large number of utterances with the possessive *'s* morpheme. After completing the story, have the child retell it.
4. *Spontaneous usage:* Establish a context where three youngsters can interact with some toys from home. Tape-record their interaction.

Assess the chosen child on the constructions selected. Where appropriate, tape-record the interactions. Finally, analyze the child's performance on each of the tasks.

**REPORT**  Include the following in your report:

1. The particular constructions assessed and whether the focus is comprehension or expression.
2. The task paradigms used to assess the constructions.
3. Analysis of the child's performance on each of the tasks.

In addition, address yourself to each of the following questions:

1. What linguistic and extralinguistic (e.g., memory, perspective-taking) demands are embedded in each of the assessment tasks?
2. What differences in performance, if any, depended on the nature of the testing paradigm? How can performance differences be accounted for, given the varying task demands?

**EVALUATION**  Did this inquiry develop the specified objectives? If so, how? If not, why? How could the effectiveness of this inquiry be increased?

## INQUIRY 9.4

As described in Chapter 7, sociocultural factors such as region, socioeconomic status, and ethnicity influence the structure and use of language. In the assessment of language, sociocultural dialect differences must be taken into account so that language differences are not erroneously diagnosed and treated as language deficiencies. Sensitivity to dialect and language variation is especially important when utilizing formal, standardized tests of language; most of these tests are based on standard English, and any deviation from a standard response is considered to be an error.

**OBJECTIVES**   The objectives of this inquiry are to:

1. Analyze two standardized tests of language to determine the extent to which these tests are biased against a speaker of variant English.
2. Develop alternative testing or scoring procedures to minimize test bias.

**PROCEDURES**   Select and obtain any two standardized tests of language. Utilize the information provided in Chapter 7 or in sources such as Bryen, Hartman, and Tait (1978) and Wolfram and Fasold (1974) to analyze what items of each test, if any, are biased against a speaker of variant English.

**REPORT**   Include the following in your report:

1. The two standardized tests of language used for analysis.
2. An item-by-item analysis of their bias against speakers of variant English.

In addition, address yourself to the following questions:

1. In what ways, if any, are the tests biased against speakers of variant English? Is the bias restricted to one aspect of language, such as phonology, or does it extend to other aspects of language, such as lexicon and syntactic and morphological constructions?
2. How might alternative testing or scoring procedures minimize the impact of dialect differences? Explain.
3. What are the implications of dialect variation for developing and using informal, structured, or spontaneous tasks for the assessment of language?

**EVALUATION**   Did this inquiry develop the specified objectives? If so, how? If not, why? How could the effectiveness of this inquiry be increased?

## INQUIRY 9.5

Criticisms of the usefulness of standardized tests of language were discussed earlier in this chapter. However, despite these criticisms, there continues to be an almost unanimous tendency to rely heavily on these tests. Perhaps this is due to a somewhat superstitious belief in the all-importance of objective, quantifiable data or to a corollary mistrust of subjective judgment. It may also grow out of more practical concerns, such as the expediency with which standardized tests can be utilized. There is, however, little doubt that an examiner's strong foundation in the areas of language and language development are the most powerful diagnostic tools.

**OBJECTIVES**   The objectives of this inquiry are to:

1. Utilize a formal standardized test and an informal, examiner-constructed assessment strategy to assess a particular aspect of language.
2. Analyze the specific value (e.g., screening, in-depth diagnosis) of the standardized and examiner-constructed tests for making decisions as to the need for and the nature of language intervention.

**PROCEDURES**   Select a child who appears to have an undiagnosed language problem. This selection can be accomplished through referrals from teachers or parents. Select a standardized test of language and administer it to the child. In addition, select or develop a series of informal assessment tasks and administer them to the child. The informal tasks can be adapted from any of the inquiries or assessment tasks presented in this book, or they can be constructed on the basis of developmental data and research (see Leonard et al., 1978). After administering the two sets of tasks, analyze the results, focusing on the possible need for and the nature of language intervention.

**REPORT**   Include the following in your report:

1. A brief description of the child and the reason for referral.
2. Standardized test selected and the informal assessment strategies identified or developed.
3. Results of the two sets of testing procedures.

In addition, address yourself to the following questions:

1. What was the nature of the data obtained from the standardized test (e.g., a language age, percentile, subtest standard score)? What information did this data yield that could support tentative decisions about the need for and the nature of language intervention?
2. What was the nature of the data obtained from the informal assessment tasks (e.g., quantitative scores, descriptions of linguistic features utilized by the child)? What information did this data yield that could support

tentative decisions about the need for and the nature of language intervention?

3. Evaluate the relative usefulness of each approach to language assessment.

**EVALUATION**   Did this inquiry develop the specified objectives? If so, how? If not, why? How could the effectiveness of this inquiry be increased?

_____                          **INQUIRY 9.6**                          _____

Leonard et al. (1978, p. 374) provide a strong case for supplementing formal tests with "experimental tasks, guided observations, and protocols" based on current research on normal and disordered language development. Information gathered from tasks derived through this approach not only supplements data from standardized tests, but can also provide a mechanism for studying a particular linguistic feature in greater depth.

**OBJECTIVE**   The objective of this inquiry is to utilize current research on normal and disordered language development as the basis for developing experimental, informal assessment strategies.

**PROCEDURES**   Select a child who appears to have a language problem that has not been diagnosed. As an optional first step, you can administer a standardized language test to obtain a general idea of the presence and/or nature of a language disorder. To supplement this or study a particular aspect in greater depth, develop and utilize an experimental assessment strategy based on current research on normal and disordered language development. Literature citations in Leonard et al. (1978) identify some research from which the experimental tasks can be developed. When the assessment task has been identified, modified, or developed, administer it to the child and analyze the results.

**REPORT**   Include the following in your report:

1. A brief description of the child.
2. Standardized test, if used, and the results obtained from the testing.
3. Aspect of the child's language that was studied in greater depth and the experimental strategy developed from current research. Cite the research from which the assessment task is derived.
4. Results of the experimental assessment task.

In addition, address yourself to the following questions:

1. What additional diagnostic information was obtained from the use of an experimentally-derived assessment task? How did this information sup-

plement or expand the diagnostic information already available about the child's linguistic functioning?

2. How might the experimental assessment task be modified to yield more information of diagnostic value?

**EVALUATION**   Did this inquiry develop the specified objective? If so, how? If not, why? How could the effectiveness of this inquiry be increased?

## INQUIRY 9.7

Dale (1976) correctly concludes that no single assessment task is sufficient to provide a comprehensive evaluation of an individual's language capabilities. The complexity of language dictates an assessment approach whereby several exploratory tasks or observations are called for to arrive at an adequate "hypothesis" concerning the child's linguistic functioning. In Chapters 2 through 5, inquiries were presented exploring various aspects of language. Those inquiries can also be used to assess a child's language development. After several have been judiciously combined into an assessment battery and preliminary results have been obtained, the examiner will possess a relatively comprehensive body of information concerning the linguistic abilities of a child.

**OBJECTIVES**   The objectives of this inquiry are to:

1. Select and administer a battery of assessment tasks to accomplish a relatively comprehensive evaluation of a child's linguistic abilities.
2. Analyze the results of the assessment, specifically focusing on what linguistic and communicative abilities the child has acquired and what ones require further development and possible intervention.
3. Critique the assessment procedures selected with respect to the considerations discussed throughout this chapter.

**PROCEDURES**   Select a child who may have a language problem. From Chapters 2 through 5 choose a battery of language tasks to provide as comprehensive an assessment as possible of the child's language functioning. If appropriate, you may also use standardized tests or experimental tasks based on current research (see Table 9.3 and Inquiry 9.6). Administer the assessment tasks to the child and analyze the results. In analyzing the results, profile both the child's strengths and weaknesses. Finally, specify those areas of linguistic functioning for which further development and, possibly, intervention are indicated.

**REPORT**   Include the following in your report:

1. A brief description of the child.
2. The tasks that you selected to use for the assessment of language.
3. The results of the language assessment.

In addition, address yourself to the following questions:

1. What was the rationale used for selecting each of the assessment tasks?
2. What are the present linguistic strengths and weaknesses of the child as measured by the chosen language tasks?
3. What areas of the child's language need further development? In other words, what specific areas would you include in a language intervention program for this child?
4. How do each of the assessment tasks answer the various considerations discussed in the beginning of this chapter (i.e., influences of testing paradigm, dialect variation, purpose of the testing, and effects of social context)?
5. What additional information, if any, is required to provide a comprehensive assessment of this child's language abilities?

**EVALUATION**   Did this inquiry develop the specified objectives? If so, how? If not, why? How could the effectiveness of this inquiry be increased?

### NOTES

1. The procedures in the following are adapted from Berry and Talbott (1966).
2. Much of the material for this section has been contributed by A. Gerber.
3. The procedures are based on Elasser and John-Steiner (1977).

# 10

# Language Problems and Classroom Approaches

Language plays a critical role in most aspects of our daily lives. When we are very young children, language serves a socialization function, transmitting and coding many culturally based features of both the physical and the social environment. It is through language as a cultural institution that very young children form attachments not only to their immediate families but also to the larger cultural group. Until children are approximately school-aged, language serves primarily a social function; its social function remains important throughout life. This does not mean that early language serves no other function. Studies of mother-child interactions have yielded evidence that maternal linguistic input also has tutorial and regulatory functions. However, when children enter school, language takes on additional importance since it is the primary medium for instruction. Concepts are taught via this conventional symbol system. Facts and information are shared between teacher and pupil and among pupils using language as the primary medium. Students are requested to tell, to ask, to talk about and so on. Students' readiness for certain academic tasks, their achievement, and their aptitude are usually assessed through the use of language-mediated tests. There is little doubt that language is one of the most critical factors influencing children's access to both the social and the pedagogical worlds. Therefore, it is surprising that the role of language in the classroom has, until recently, received rather limited attention.

Assuming that teachers do not verbalize solely for the sake of making noise, it follows that the structure and function of their linguistic input to their students should be analyzed to determine how they affect pupil access to information and instructional encounters within the classroom. Such analysis is obviously necessary in light of the fact that students are bombarded with a tremendous quantity of language during an average school day. To underscore this point, Conn and Richardson (1976, p. 130) calculated the quantity of language used by teachers of mentally retarded youngsters in England. One teacher, they reported, produced

315

4870 linguistic syllables in just over one hour. Concerning this large quantity of linguistic input, the following questions arise:

1. Do teachers take into account the various linguistic capabilities of their pupils?
2. Do students process and understand the linguistic input?
3. How are students encouraged to use their linguistic capabilities in the classroom?
4. In what way is the language of instruction different from the language of everyday social intercourse?
5. What are the effects of language problems given the instructional demands of schooling?
6. How can teachers compensate for the language problems of their youngsters while simultaneously encouraging the further growth of linguistic abilities?

The purpose of this chapter is to address each of these questions in order to provide some insight into the role of language in the classroom.

## THE LANGUAGE OF INSTRUCTION AS A SPECIFIC LINGUISTIC CODE

In Chapter 6, the structure and function of the linguistic input of a parent to a language-learning child—a speech register termed motherese or baby talk—was characterized as a simplified linguistic code more or less tuned into the cognitive and linguistic abilities of the child. It is a tryadic system, including the parent, the child, and the objects and events shared by the two. Its function is primarily social in nature, apparently with some tutorial and regulatory functions that are subordinated in importance. Communication is usually concrete, making effective use of context and gestures as supportive aids, and is usually child-centered and -oriented.

In contrast, the language of instruction, the **teacher register,** has quite different purposes and features. First, and perhaps foremost, the teacher register clearly has a different purpose. Whereas the purpose of baby talk is understanding and being understood by the child (i.e., maintaining the interaction between parent and child), the function of the teacher register is primarily tutorial and regulatory. The teacher's job has traditionally been defined as one of instructing and maintaining behavioral and social order (regulatory function) in the classroom. Therefore, when children enter school, they are likely to encounter language being used for different purposes.

Second, parent-child interactions are essentially dyadic or tryadic in nature; however, in school the communicative context is one of teacher and group. This change in context results in several critical modifications for the child. First, the child spends a greater amount of time as a listener, in dramatic contrast to the almost one-to-one ratio of listener and speaker roles in the parent-child interaction. Second, topics of "conversation" are usually adult-oriented and -initiated, which is also in contrast to the dominant child-orientation of parent-child interactions. Third, because language is directed to a group, rather than to the individual, there may be reduced attention to feedback regarding the students' comprehension of the message. Again, this is in contrast to parent-child interactions in which the parent appears to be particularly attuned to the child's linguistic and nonlinguistic feedback regarding comprehension. As a result of the group context and its reduced capabilities for individual feedback, teachers are not as likely to adjust their linguistic input to the capabilities of individual children. Linguistic modifications by teachers with regard to vocabulary, syntactic construction, the need for repetition and expansion, and effective use of context are likely to be less prevalent than those of parents (Ray, 1980).

Finally, the language of instruction is generally more abstract than that used in familiar social discourse. In all likelihood, there is less shared knowledge (i.e., familiarity) between teacher and pupils. Therefore, pupils must accommodate their linguistic messages accordingly. Gestures may not be used as frequently as supplements to language. The use of context by the teacher to clarify what is being said may also occur less frequently. As a result, students are faced with increased linguistic and cognitive demands in encountering the communicative style of the classroom. For most youngsters entering school, the transition from the parental linguistic code to the language of instruction appears to present few major problems. However, children who are delayed or deficient in the acquisition of language may experience quite serious problems.

**THE INSTRUCTIONAL CODE AND THE LINGUISTICALLY UNREADY CHILD** Teachers of the lower grades may be faced with children who are unready for the linguistic code found in the typical classroom. Who are these children, and what are their problems? Linguistically unready children may be preschool or elementary-school children who are quite normal, but who are somewhat slower in their acquisition of language. They may be youngsters who suffer from mild to moderate hearing losses not previously detected. They may be youngsters who are mildly mentally retarded or learning-disabled. They may be youngsters who, due to emotional problems, are preoccupied with fantasies and subsequently have problems maintaining their attention to the ongoing flow of speech. They may be children who are not motivated to use their linguistic knowledge for the purposes of communication. Because the growth of language is influenced by many environmental, cognitive, and social factors, the linguistically unready child may be the product of any of these factors.

Linguistic problems are as diverse as the causes for linguistic unreadiness. The linguistically unready child may not be motivated to actively engage in the cooperative process of communication. Having not adequately received the message that communicative attempts can powerfully affect the social and physical environment, this child may not initiate communication. Consequently, such a child may not say to the teacher *I don't understand this,* thus actively soliciting the other's help. Instead, the child may struggle in an attempt to independently resolve the lack of understanding. In doing so, frustration and potential failure may result, which once more underscore the child's conviction of powerlessness.

The linguistically unready child may also be delayed in the acquisition of the structures and content of language. As a result, the child may have available only limited semantic units and syntactic constructions. Communicative attempts may often be cryptic, with several semantic constituents deleted. Comprehension of language may also be affected, such that complex sentences may not be adequately processed.

Youngsters who are mentally retarded are most likely to be delayed in the acquisition of the basic semantic categories and syntactic constructions. As the severity of the retardation increases, so does the degree to which language is delayed. For example, in a study of severe and profoundly retarded individuals conducted by Featherman (1974), the following delays in language were noted. Only 17.1% of these mentally retarded persons used one-word, utterances to express such semantic relations as agent, action, object, location, or possession. When the demands for expressive language were increased to include two-word utterances that serve basic semantic functions, such as location (e.g., *there book*) or negation (e.g., *no hungry*), the percentage of individuals using these language structures dropped to 12.9%. Further analysis revealed that these individuals were also deficient in internal phrase development. For example, only 8.6% of the population used expanded noun phrases as independent units for modification. Articles, demonstrative and possessive pronouns, and descriptive and quantitative adjectives were used minimally when attached to nouns. In addition, only 8.6% of these subjects used nouns differentially, and pronouns were infrequently substituted for noun phrases (e.g., *hit it* for *hit the ball*). When their language was analyzed to investigate the inclusion of noun phrases as subjects of longer units of language (e.g., *The old man is there.*), the percentage of individuals passing the criterion behavior was only 5.7%.

A similar pattern existed for the development of the verb phrase. Only 10.0% of these individuals used expanded verb phrases of three and four words, and when verb tense was required even without appropriate inflection (e.g., *I no fall down*), the percentage was further depressed to 7.1%. Inflectional markers added to verbs to denote noun-verb agreement, past tense, and so on occur later in the normal development of the verb phrase. The fact that among this population there was a further decrease in this criterion attainment to only 4.3% provides further evidence for the concept of language invariance even among a population as severely retarded as the one studied. There was also a relatively infrequent use (4.3%) of verb phrases attached to the subject of a sentence.

Such youngsters as these are the most linguistically unready for the typical classroom instructional code. In some cases, not only are they unready for the language used in the classroom, but they may be unready for language in general. These severely delayed youngsters, while having rudimentary forms of communication, may not have developed the necessary cognitive requisites for dealing with any symbol system, let alone a conventional symbol system such as language. As a result of their greatly reduced linguistic abilities, these youngsters may be denied access to communicative encounters unless the teacher accommodates to their level.

Learning disabled youngsters may also be delayed, although not as severely, in the acquisition of language. This delay may include (1) difficulties in producing and comprehending reversible grammatical constructions, such as active and passive voice, (2) omissions of grammatical morphemes, such as prepositions, conjunctions, auxiliary verbs, and articles, and (3) errors in word order. Some of the most common structural problems are presented in Tables 10.1 and 10.2.

As a result of these structural problems, the learning-disabled youngster may be unready for the complex commands and ongoing discourse requiring the processing of numerous propositions that are so typical of the instructional linguistic code. It is not surprising that learning-disabled youngsters have been characterized as being unattentive, restless, and distractible, for it is likely that they cannot process many of the linguistic interchanges occurring in the classroom.

LIMITED VOCABULARY. Limited vocabulary can also affect the child's access to the instructional linguistic code. This is true for verbal exchanges within the classroom and for beginning reading instruction. All children acquiring language are constrained by their limits in vocabulary, but the parental register appears to be particularly attuned to this fact. Parents engage in several discourse strategies to aid their children in the comprehension and development of apparently unfamiliar words. For example, parental self-repetition that emphasizes particular words may make these unfamiliar words more perceptually salient to the child. This repetition, in conjunction with the utilization of the physical context as a

TABLE 10.1 Structural Problems Found in Learning-disabled Youngsters: Noun Phrase

| Structure | Example |
|---|---|
| Omission of noun phrase | *Ran down the street.* |
| Use of personal pronouns | *I seen Bobby Clarke and it had no teeth.* |
| Absence of possessive inflection | *It is Mary dress.* |
| Absence of plural marker | *He has fifty cent.* |
| Use of grammatical morphemes: | |
|   1. Articles | *I want a apple.* |
| | *I want apple.* |
|   2. Prepositions | *I wanna go this game.* |
| | *Next year we might go Florida.* |
|   3. Conjunctions | *I climb in almost got hurt.* |

TABLE 10.2    Structural Problems Found in Learning-disabled Youngsters:
Verb Phrase

| Structure | Example |
| --- | --- |
| Absence of present progressive auxiliary | *He going.* |
| Subject/verb agreement for third person singular omitted | *He run.* |
| Regularization of irregular past tense verbs | *He runned.* |
| Absence of regular past tense marker | *Yesterday, he walk.* |
| Absence or irregular past tense marker | *Yesterday, he run.* |
| Absence or substitution of auxiliary verbs | *He been here.* |
| | *He have been here.* |
| Interrogation: Problems inverting the auxiliary verb (*be, have, do, can*) and the subject | *Where he did go?* |
| | *I can have cookies?* |
| Negation: Problems attaching the negative morpheme to auxiliary verb | *I no want cookie.* |
| | *I not have money.* |
| Appropriate use of transitive and intransitive verbs | *He fell a striped cat.* |
| | *He ran a bucket of water.* |

communicative supplement, may in fact help the child learn new words. However, in a classroom situation where the teacher is interacting with the group rather than the individual child, repetition and context clues may not be employed. Consequently, some children may not comprehend the unfamiliar vocabulary that is embedded in the mass of verbalization heard in the classroom context.

CONTEXT- AND ACTION-BASED LANGUAGE. As stated earlier, the instructional linguistic code is generally more abstract than the parental register and perhaps more abstract than language that serves a social, interpersonal function. Language used in the classroom is frequently displaced from the here and now and from the child's ongoing actions, and therefore it cannot be supplemented by gestures and contextual clues. Most children entering the elementary grades no longer require language that is context- and action-based. However, some children, especially preschool or mentally retarded or learning-disabled youngsters, continue to require the aid of physical context or their own actions in the comprehension and production of language. This is a psychological factor that has been recognized as important in the learning of basic arithmetic concepts and has been incorporated in the teaching of arithmetic. However, it has not been expanded to cover other aspects of the teaching-learning process in which language plays a key role. Children who are unready to deal with language that is completely abstracted from a physical context are likely to miss much of the information communicated in the classroom.

PROBLEMS COORDINATING MORE THAN ONE DIMENSION. Any child who spends time in a classroom typically must process complex language coordinating more than one proposition or dimension. The preschool child continually hears requests, such as *Get your coat and form a line at the door.* The school-aged child is requested to *Take out your pencil, turn to page forty-two of your arithmetic book, and complete all of the addition problems there.* In order to follow these directions, a child must be able to comprehend all dimensions of these complex linguistic messages. For some children who are cognitively or linguistically immature, following directions such as these is problematic. In some cases, a child processes only the first dimension of the message (e.g., gets his coat but does not join the other children in forming a line at the door). In other cases, the child processes only part of the message and waits for a nonlinguistic cue from other children (e.g., children walking to the door) to compensate for the unprocessed linguistic message. In still other cases, the child randomly processes one dimension of the sentence ignoring others (e.g., begins arithmetic work having not processed the page number of the assigned task). Children who have these difficulties not only find classroom interactions and assignments confusing and frustrating but also create frustrations for their teachers who do not understand the nature of the problem.

PROBLEMS WITH LANGUAGE IN USE. For the majority of children in regular classes, language problems evidenced may be quite subtle and not based on specific linguistic structural delays such as those described earlier. If assessed on their ability to produce and comprehend single sentences measuring different syntactic and semantic structures, these youngsters do fine. However, these same youngsters may not adequately comprehend connected speech as it occurs in the classroom. For some youngsters, an increase in background noise interferes with their ability to accurately process ongoing language. For others, the natural rate of speech is frustratingly fast. Other youngsters may require pauses between complex sentences to allow them adequate processing time. These youngsters may also need the presence of exaggerated stress and the heightening of pitch for critical information in ongoing speech to make such information more perceptually salient.

Some youngsters have difficulty comprehending ongoing language because of rapid changes in the listener and speaker roles. In a typical dyadic context, the child is either the speaker or the person spoken to. Therefore, dyadic-based pronouns such as *you, me,* and *I* are somewhat more stable. However, as the size of a group increases beyond two, the listener and speaker roles increasingly vary. To illustrate, using the personal pronouns *I, you, me, we, us, he, she, they,* and *them,* in a dyadic interaction, the child is referred to only as *you* [+singular, +listener], *we* [+plural, +speaker, +subjective case], *I* [+singular, +speaker, +subjective case], or *me* [+singular, +speaker, +objective case]. In contrast, in a tryadic or larger interactional context, the child may be additionally referred to as *he* or *she* [−listener, −speaker, +singular, +objective case], or *they* [−listener, −speaker, +plural, +objective case]. To further complicate the situation, other children in the group may also be referred to as *you, I, they, we,* or *me* depending on the shifts in the listener and speaker roles.

Pronouns other than those relating to the speaker-listener relationship may cause problems in comprehending ongoing language. Pronouns that refer to previously specified entities either within the sentence or between sentences may not be accurately coordinated with those entities. For example, in the sentence *The boy had a car and he gave it to me,* a child may not recognize that the pronoun *he* refers back to the noun phrase *the boy* and the pronoun *it* refers to the noun *car* in the verb phrase. Pronouns can also refer to information specified in a previous sentence, such as in the following: *Your arithmetic work begins on page 14. When you finish it, you may have free time.* Some youngsters may not understand that the pronoun *it* in the second sentence refers to the phrase *your arithmetic work* in the first sentence.

To complete this section on the instructional code and the linguistically unready child, brief mention must be made of those youngsters who, while apparently having adequate language abilities, may not be ready for language-related processes such as reading and writing. In Chapter 9, arguments were presented for assessing metalinguistic abilities extending beyond the tacit knowledge of language. The rationale for this position is that instruction in reading, spelling, and writing requires more than the use of language. Given the manner in which reading, spelling, and writing are traditionally taught, children must think about speech and language in addition to thinking about their use. For example, when the phonics approach to reading is employed or when spelling is taught, children must be quite analytic about their speech. They must think about how words are segmented into phonemes and how these segmented phonemes are more or less represented by graphic symbols. Similarly, when writing, children must analytically segment the natural flow of language so that each word can be accurately and precisely represented graphically.

For many youngsters, the transition from naturally occurring, ongoing, verbal language to the more formal, consciously arrived at, written form is not an easy one. For some youngsters, this transition is extraordinarily difficult. The reasons for this difficulty are not that clear at present. Some (e.g., Goodman & Goodman, 1977; Smith, 1971) suggest that the difficulty is based more on differences in how oral and written language are taught than on differences in how they are learned. Others (e.g., Vellutino, 1977) use direct and indirect evidence to demonstrate the relationship between literacy problems and dysfunction in the semantic, syntactic, or phonological aspects of language. Still others (e.g., Elasser & John-Steiner, 1977) maintain that "poor writing" is connected to certain inherent cognitive and social demands of the writing process itself and to the cognitive and social readiness of the writer. Regardless of the position one takes, there is clear evidence that learning a spoken language has met with considerably greater success than have attempts at teaching written language.

Linguistic problems such as those just discussed are only representative of the variety of language problems likely to be encountered in the classroom. Unfortunately, it is beyond the scope of this chapter to adequately address the growing body of literature describing the nature and severity of language problems found in preschool and school-aged youngsters. Interested readers are encouraged to pursue this topic in greater depth in sources such as Berry, 1968; 1976; Bloom and Lahey, 1978; Gerber and Bryen, 1981; Leonard, 1979; Morehead and Morehead, 1976; Muma, 1978; and Schiefelbusch and Lloyd, 1974. In any case, because so much of what occurs in the classroom is language-based, there is a need for heightened sensitivity to the linguistic needs of various youngsters in relation to the linguistic demands of the classroom. Where mismatches between the two do occur, children may not only be denied adequate access to the ongoing informational exchanges but they may also defensively "turn off" to language-based activities in general.

## APPROACHES TO LANGUAGE
## INTERVENTION IN THE CLASSROOM

In this section, the discussion concerns approaches to language intervention in the classroom, including (1) issues and considerations in developing strategies for intervention, (2) formal language programs, (3) informal approaches to language intervention, and (4) adapting classroom interactions to facilitate communication.

The assumption underlying most intervention approaches is that language, its structure, and its functions can be formally isolated from ongoing interactions and taught. However superficially appealing it may be, this assumption calls for some analysis. The following section attempts to explicate this issue, in addition to addressing other considerations regarding language intervention.

**ISSUES AND CONSIDERATIONS IN DEVELOPING STRATEGIES FOR INTERVENTION** The basis of all formal language intervention programs (see Table 10.3), as well as of many informal approaches, is that the structure and function of speech and language can be isolated during "language time" and formally taught. Therefore, children who demonstrate delays in language acquisition or deficits in particular aspects of speech and language are frequently referred to speech and language specialists for specified time periods to receive language therapy or training. This common practice has recently been challenged on several points (see Michaelis, 1978); however, the fundamental question underlying such challenges is whether language can be taught. The most radical challenge comes from the nativistic position (see Chapter 6), which argues that language is neither taught nor learned, but is instead acquired by the child. While one can argue that the differences among these terms are more superficial than real, the implications from the three perspectives for the development of language and the treatment of language-handicapped youngsters are substantially different. If one assumes that language is acquired by children, then the role of the environment is rather a benign one both for the child who is acquiring language normally and for the child who is evidencing language delays. Unless one can modify the biological or neurological make-up of the language-impaired child, the most that the environment can do is to compensate for existing language problems.

In contrast, the perspective that language is learned suggests an active learner as well as an active mediator for learning. Children bring to the language-learning situation certain biological, neurological, and psychological conditions that greatly influence what and how they learn. The environment, however, variously interacting with the learner, can clearly either facilitate or create barriers to the learning process. Given this interactional influence both the learners and their environment are continuously active, each affecting the other. Research concerning parent-child interactions most clearly supports this position (see Chapter 6). If one accepts the psychological validity of this position, then one's approaches to language problems will be neither wholly pessimistic (according to the nativistic view) nor wholly deterministic (according to the behavioral view). Rather, one will believe that while the environment plays an important role in enabling the child to discover or construct basic linguistic structures and communication strategies, it is clearly the child who must do the learning.

The view that language is taught assumes that the child is basically a passive recipient of the linguistic information that is systematically and lawfully transmitted by the environment. This is the deterministic position already presented in Chapter 6, and it requires little reconsideration here. What does require consideration is the issue of teaching language to language-impaired youngsters. It is frequently argued that the position that language is learned obviously accounts for the child who has adequately developed language. But what about the child who, given optimal learning conditions, has not adequately learned language? Doesn't such a child demonstrate the need to be taught language more formally? On the surface, this logic may seem quite flawless. However, if this position is examined more critically, the conclusion is not quite so clear. The problem involves what is being taught. Clearly, one's goal in language intervention is not the teaching of particular sentences. If that were the case, one would need to teach language continuously for many, many years. Instead, the goal of any language program must be the learning of underlying linguistic principles or rules that generate sentences and of underlying strategies for how language is effectively put to use. Otherwise, the child will need to be taught a new sentence for every new heard or expressed linguistic proposition. The very nature of language is that it is generative, that is, from a finite set of underlying rules, the language user is capable of understanding and generating a potentially infinite number of well-formed sentences.

The question as to why these underlying rules cannot be directly taught may arise. The answer to this question derives from the nature of the data that can be transmitted to the child. All that we can expose the child to is a corpus of particular sentences such as the following:

> *The boy is running.*
> *The child is crying.*
> *The man is fighting.*

> *The lady is singing.*
>
> *The dog is barking.*
>
> *The girl is playing.*

It is up to the child to learn that their underlying linguistic principle is as follows:

NP [+agent, +singular] + *is* + V (progressive action) + *-ing*

Without applying this underlying principle, the child might utter the following sentences:

> *The broom is sweeping.*
>
> *The chairs is running.*

   In conclusion, it is plausible to teach isolated sentences, in the same way that isolated vocabulary is taught. However, it is most unlikely that language as a generative symbol system can be formally taught. It is the child, whether handicapped or not, who must learn the linguistic principles underlying the corpus of the language.

STRUCTURE VERSUS FUNCTION. Another issue that must be examined when approaching language intervention is that of structure versus function. It should become clear that this issue to a large extent reflects the more basic question of whether language can be formally taught. Children who are identified as having language problems are typically so recognized on the basis of delayed or deviant structural aspects of speech or language. They may have only minimally acquired the basic semantic relations, may be delayed in developing syntactic constructions and grammatical morphemes, or may commit errors in word order. As a result, language approaches are generally designed to focus on developing or correcting these structural problems. The problem is that, in order to formally intervene, one needs to isolate each structure in need of development or correction, which generally means separating the structure of language from its function of communication. For example, a child of seven has not acquired the auxiliary verb *be,* which is necessary for the production of certain negative and interrogative transformational sentences. Negative sentences requiring the embedding and verb marking of *be* are produced by the child as follows:

> *He not running.*
>
> *I not go out.*
>
> *That boy not sharing with me.*

If one of the goals of language intervention is to directly teach the child to embed the auxiliary *be* between the noun phrase and the negative morpheme *not,* while also teaching that the auxiliary marks tense and agreement, then the intervention needs to specifically focus on this structure. Teaching strategies such as imitation of sentences representing this structure, or having the child respond to *Tell me about this picture,* are designed to focus on this particular negative transformation. Similarly, when directly correcting this child's spontaneous utterances, one should focus on the particular structure, as can be seen from the following interaction:

> Child (pointing outside): "Look, look! It not raining anymore."
> Teacher: "It's not raining anymore. Say *it is not raining anymore.*"
> Child: "It is not raining anymore." (Walks away from the teacher.)

However, in teaching or correcting any particular linguistic feature, the structure of language is separated from its communicative function. The function of language is not that of "labeling or matching pictures to words, or repeating what someone else says" (Holland, 1975, p. 518). The structure of language has no raison d'être other than to be used for the purpose of communication, and communication is an active, interpersonal interchange.

Polanyi (1964) suggests that speech and language are subsidiaries to the focal functions of communication (e.g., persuading, giving directions, or arguing). When we shift attention to the speech and language particulars of which we were previously aware only in their subsidiary role, we run the risk of interfering with the focal function of communication. Polanyi's point is illustrated in the preceding interaction between teacher and child. The child initially employs the focal function of communication by calling the teacher's attention to a change outdoors (*It not raining anymore*). In attempting to formally correct the linguistic structure, the teacher focuses on the subsidiary aspect of the correct use of *is not.* In doing so, the teacher shifts her attention from the focal role of communication to the subsidiary aspect of language. As a result, the child also shifts attention, and communication is terminated.

The alternative to teaching linguistic particulars directly is to focus on the various functions of language through which the particulars of speech and language derive their meaning. In so doing, we can focus only indirectly on structure, by employing discourse strategies such as repetition, expansion, and stress, as illustrated in the following:

> Child (pointing outside): "Look, look! It not raining anymore."
> Teacher: "*It's* not raining anymore?" (stress and intonation are heightened on *it's*). "Do you think we can have recess now?"
> Child: "I get my coat and tell the other children." (Runs to inform the other children).

Clearly, in this interaction the teacher focuses on the child's communication, the focal function of language. As a result, communication continues. The teacher has not separated the structure of the language particular to be taught from its function. The teacher has indirectly stressed the targeted language structure by repeating the child's utterance, expanding it to include the particular feature of concern, and making it perceptually salient by adding stress and heightening pitch. Note that the teacher is not directly teaching language, but rather is providing an interactional context through which the child's learning of language is facilitated.

The controversy over structure versus function is far from resolved in curricular approaches to language. For example, the structural approach to teaching language continues to be advocated by many (see Mellon, 1969). Relatively few professionals have favored the development of general language arts curricula based on the function of language rather than its structure (see Cazden, 1972; Smilansky, 1968; Shaftel & Shaftel, 1967; and Moffett, 1968*a*; 1968*b*). The concept of the focal function of communication is even less prevalent in approaches to language intervention (see Holland, 1975; Michaelis, 1978; Rees, 1973; and Bryen, 1980). Notwithstanding the current approaches to language curricula, the issue of structure versus function remains central to language intervention.

THE CONTEXT OF LANGUAGE INTERVENTION. Young, normal children begin to use their emerging communication and language skills as extensions of their actions and as a means for representing the concrete, the here and now. This contextual orientation continues through the preschool years and into elementary school. Youngsters talk about objects and events that are perceptually present long before they use the same semantic structures to describe, recall, or anticipate objects and events that are distanced in time and space. Paramount consideration should be given to this phenomenon when planning and implementing intervention approaches for language-delayed youngsters. Attention must be paid not only to the linguistic aspects in need of development, but also to the child's cognitive readiness for using language that is temporally and spatially abstracted from the immediate context. For many children with language problems, the focus of the language context should be on doing and talking about what is being done (e.g., *What's Carol doing?* or *How can we make the building taller?*) before focus is placed on events distanced in time and space (e.g., *What happened to Carol?* or *What will happen if the building is too tall?*). The context is as important as the process of intervention.

SCOPE AND SEQUENCE OF LANGUAGE INTERVENTION. Children's language is characterized by a continuous growth in structure and function until it approaches that of the mature adults in the speech community. During this growth, both structure and function may differ qualitatively from that of adult language. The learning of language is not simply an additive process whereby new structures are linearly added to old ones. For example, the child does not learn the adult form *There is a ball* in the additive manner shown:

Time I:     *ball*

Time II:    *a ball*

Time III:   *is a ball*

Time IV:    *There is a ball.*

Instead, children learn language by abstracting from the adult corpus semantic and syntactic rules that most parsimoniously represent meaning and that may differ both quantitatively and qualitatively from adult linguistic forms. Therefore, in learning the adult form *There is a ball,* the following stages or sequence emerge:

> Time I:  *ball*
>
> Time II:  *There ball*
>
> Time III:  *There a ball*
>
> Time IV:  *There is a ball.*

Similarly, the functions of children's language may vary qualitatively from those of adult language. Young children use language to inform and demand, whereas adults may also use it to teach, persuade, and hypothesize.

The differences between a developmental and an additive approach are reflected in the scope and sequence of various language intervention programs. Some programs, such as the Monterey Language Program (Gray & Ryan, 1972), reflect an additive model in scope, sequence, and instructional methodology. Others, such as *Emerging Language* (Hatten, Goman, & Lent, 1973), are based on a developmental model.

Clearly, decisions concerning the choice of an intervention program or the development of intervention strategies should consider the assumptions underlying the scope and sequence of the approach. This consideration, as well as (1) whether language is seen to be learned, taught, or acquired, (2) a focus on the issue of structure versus function, and (3) the context of language intervention, form the basis for this decision making. In the remaining sections of this chapter, descriptions of various formal and informal approaches to language intervention are presented.

**FORMAL LANGUAGE PROGRAMS**  As language and language problems began to receive serious attention in the late 1960s and early 1970s, many language kits and programs were developed and published for use with language-handicapped children. A summary of some of the most widely used language programs appears in Table 10.3. By examining Table 10.3, it should become apparent that many of these programs assume that language can be taught through carefully sequenced activities and the use of behavioral techniques such as imitation, differential reinforcement, and shaping (e.g., Peterson, Brener, & Williams, 1974; Engelmann & Osborn, 1970; Gray & Ryan, 1972; Kent, 1972; McDonald & Blott, 1974). In contrast, only a few of the listed programs view language intervention from the perspective of the interaction between an active learner with an equally active environment (e.g., Miller & Yoder, 1974; Bricker, Dennison, & Bricker, 1975; Moffett, 1968a).

Similarly, most of the programs summarized in Table 10.3 focus either primarily or exclusively on the structure of language, relegating the function of language to a separate and secondary role (e.g., Engelmann & Osborn, 1970; Gray &

TABLE 10.3 Summary of the Most Widely Used Language Development Kits and Programs

| Name (Author of Kit) | Target Population | Type of Approach | Comments |
|---|---|---|---|
| Constructive-Interactive Adaptation Approach to Language Learning (Bricker, Denison, & Bricker, 1978) | Moderately to severely handicapped | Developmental; psycho-linguistic | Purpose is to facilitate the learning of a generative language system, not simply isolated phrases. Based on the view that the child learns language through interaction with the environment. Includes cognitive prerequisite, early receptive, and expressive basic semantic relations. |
| DISTAR I, II, III (Engelmann & Osborn, 1970) | Preschool and older | Drill and repetition; task analytic; imitation and reinforcement | Highly structured and organized. Emphasis on expressive aspect of language. Moves from the familiar and simple to the more complex. Instructional groups based on performance levels. Heavy use of question-answer form of instruction (Teacher: *What's this?* Pupils, together: *That's a pencil!*). Appears successful in teaching specific responses to specific stimuli; less adequate in generalizing to other situations. |
| Emerging Language (Hatten, Goman, & Lent, 1973) | All children with language problems | Developmental; Chomskyian | Consists of carefully sequenced expressive language objectives and activities ranging from one-word utterances to basic transformations. Primarily focuses on the syntactic structures of language. |

329

TABLE 10.3 (Continued)

| Name (Author of Kit) | Target Population | Type of Approach | Comments |
|---|---|---|---|
| Environmental Language Intervention (McDonald & Blott, 1974) | Moderate to severe language delays | Semantically based scope and sequence; use of imitation | Attempts to train rules governing the semantic functions of early two-word utterances. Use of both linguistic and nonlinguistic (environmental context) cues. Stress on imitation, conversation, and play. |
| Fokes Sentence Builder Kit (Fokes, 1975) | Learning-disabled, deaf, hard of hearing, borderline to mild mentally retarded | Cognitive-psycholinguistic; stimulative | Highly structured. Unique design for teaching syntactic rules and structures, not as rote responses. |
| GOAL: Language Development-Games Oriented Activities for Learning (Karnes, 1976a) | Normal to moderately handicapped | Developmental; stimulative | Highly structured. Based on *Illinois Test of Psycholinguistic Abilities* model. Lessons in game format. Criteria for mastery of each lesson not predetermined. |
| An Integrated Curriculum in Language Arts (Moffett, 1968a) | K–grade 12, all children | Communication-based | Curriculum sequence based on increasing distance between listener and speaker and distancing one's self in time and space. |
| Karnes Early Language Activities (Karnes, 1976b) | All mentally handicapped | Developmental; stimulative | Downward extension of GOAL with 200 model lessons. Provides instructional ideas only; actual items must be supplied by user. |
| Language Acquisition Program (Kent, 1972) | Moderately to severely handicapped | Early receptive and expressive language; behavioral | Emphasis on preverbal skills, such as attending and imitation, and early receptive and expressive language. |

| Program | Population | Approach | Description |
|---|---|---|---|
| | | | Includes modifications for use with sign language. Tries to integrate structure/function structured in play. |
| Minnesota Early Language Development Sequence (Clark, Moores, & Woodcock, 1975) | Hearing- and language-impaired youngsters | Developmental, visual approach (rebuses) | Use of rebuses (pictographs) designed to facilitate language for children who have difficulty with spoken languages. Individual rebuses and rebuses combined into phrases and sentences. |
| Monterey Language Program (Programmed Conditioning for Language) (Gray & Ryan, 1972) | All children needing help in language | Behavioral; operant | Highly structured. User must be trained and certified by distributor. Includes pretests and posttests, placement tests, branching provisions, specific criteria. Good data showing effectiveness, including transference. |
| MWM Program for Developing Language Abilities (Minskoff, Wiseman, & Minskoff, 1972) | Ages 3 to 11 with evidence of language deficits | Developmental; stimulative | Rationale is based on the model of the *Illinois Test of Psycholinguistic Abilities*. Comprised of a teacher's guide, inventory, manual, and materials. Provisions for diagnostic screening; remediation of weak areas according to model. Activities sequenced by difficulty level. |
| An Ontogenetic Language Teaching Strategy for the Retarded (Miller & Yoder, 1974) | Moderately to severely handicapped | Developmental; semantically based | A series of strategies designed to facilitate the learning of basic semantic relations. Focuses primarily on communicative interaction. |
| Peabody Language Development Kits | All children | General developmental; stimulative | Purpose is to stimulate oral language, heighten verbal intelligence, and |

## TABLE 10.3 (Continued)

| Name (Author of Kit) | Target Population | Type of Approach | Comments |
|---|---|---|---|
| (Dunn & Smith, 1966) | | | enhance school progress. Overall language stressed. Attractive and motivating. Kits contain manual, lessons, manipulative materials, reinforcement chips, and picture cards. Group instruction format. Research showing effectiveness is inconclusive. |
| Project MEMPHIS (Quick, Little, & Campbell, 1973) | Mild to severely handicapped | Developmental | Emphasis on language for verbal and nonverbal communication. Has 260 lesson plans based on three steps: plan, implement, evaluate. |
| SYNPRO (Syntax Programmer) (Peterson, Brener, & Williams, 1974) | All ages with mild problems | Operant; drill | Can be used by professionals or aides. Provides a highly structured way of programming syntactic strings. |
| Transformational Sentence-Combining (Mellon, 1969) | Junior and senior high school students | Syntax; Chomskyian; written language | Attempts to teach students to combine syntactically simple sentences into complex ones. Encourages syntactic variety in written language. |
| Visually Cued Language Cards (Foster, Giddan, & Stark, 1975) | Normal to profoundly retarded | Stimulation of functional language | Consists of 5 series of picture cards. Related to Assessment of Children's Language Comprehension Test. May be used at home or school. |
| Wilson Initial Syntax Program (Wilson, 1973) | Those with syntax problems, especially TMR | Stimulation; Chomskyian | Emphasis on improving receptive syntactic skills. Can be used by aides. |

Based partly on Bartel, N.R., and Bryen, D.B. In Hammill, D.D., and Bartel, N.R., *Teaching children with learning and behavior problems*, 2nd ed. Boston: Allyn & Bacon, 1978, pp. 316–17. Used with permission of the publisher.

Ryan, 1972; Peterson, Brener, & Williams, 1974; Kent, 1972; Clark, Moores, & Woodcock, 1975; Mellon, 1969). Only the programs of Miller and Yoder (1974), Moffett (1968a), and Bricker, Dennison, and Bricker (1975), explicitly focus on communication, recognizing that the particulars of language have no meaning outside the context of a communicative, interactive context. The primacy of communication is reflected in these programs through the use of environmental contexts that capitalize on children's ongoing actions and interactions with the physical and social world. In contrast, those programs focusing primarily on the structure of language utilize a context that is somewhat artificial and is certainly not child-oriented or -initiated. Instead, they place heavy reliance on the use of line drawings, picture cards, and adult-selected objects as language stimuli.

The influence of developmental language research regarding the sequence and stages of normal language growth is reflected in most of the intervention programs summarized in Table 10.3. The only exceptions are the programs developed by Gray and Ryan (1972), Engelmann and Osborn (1970), and Peterson, Brener, and Williams (1974). However, some of the developmentally based programs were explicitly influenced by Chomsky's theories. Therefore, the focus of these programs is on syntactic development (e.g., Foster, Giddan, & Stark, 1975; Hatten, Goman, & Lent, 1973; Mellon, 1969). In contrast, the programs developed by Bricker, Dennison, and Bricker (1975), McDonald and Blott (1974), and Miller and Yoder (1974) embody the view that semantics is the basis of language. The focus of these latter programs is that of developing basic semantic relations, such as agent+action+object, recurrence, possession, and location, rather than noun phrases, verbs, and so on.

Although many of these language programs were developed for use with mildly and moderately handicapped children, a substantial number include those youngsters who are severely handicapped and may be completely nonverbal. Yet very few of these programs explicitly take into account the cognitive prerequisites to language development. The exceptions are the programs of Kent (1972) and Bricker, Dennison, and Bricker (1975). Even these two programs show a considerable discrepancy in specifying just what constitutes prerequisite skills and abilities. For example, Kent (1972) having a somewhat strong behavioral orientation, focuses exclusively on developing attention and motor and vocal imitation. The underlying assumption is that a child who cannot attend, sit still, and imitate is not ready for the development of language. Bricker, Dennison, and Bricker (1975) also focus on the development of imitation and attention, but they additionally recognize the importance of certain cognitive attainments, such as object permanence and symbolic play.

It is interesting to note that so many of these language programs rely so heavily on imitation, either as a prerequisite skill to learning language or as a method for teaching language. However, the importance of imitation and its role in learning language has not been clarified. Ramer (1976) suggests that imitation is one mechanism for learning or practice that assists in general development. However, she goes on to argue that imitation cannot be considered a specific requisite for language acquisition due to the wide range of variability in its use by young children. Prutting and Connolly (1976) and Dale (1976) concur with Ramer's position that imitation is not the primary determinant of language acquisition. In support of this position, Leonard and Kaplan (1976, p. 454) provide evidence against the interpretation that "imitation functions solely as a process for lexical acquisition." On the other hand, there is equally compelling evidence for viewing imitation as an important precursor to language. For example, Bates et al. (1977) found that imitation was one of the important predictors of both gestural communication and verbal language. In studying the language and communication of severely and profoundly mentally retarded persons, Kahn (1975) and Capuzzi (1978) found that those retarded persons who utilized verbal or nonverbal communication systems had all developed imitation, as defined by Piaget (1952; 1962). In contrast, those who had not adequately developed imitation, did not demonstrate the use of expressive language. Both researchers concur that imitation is a necessary but not sufficient condition for language production. Further support for the importance of imitation as a process in language acquisition is provided by Bloom, Hood, and Lightbrown (1974). From research on children learning new words, they conclude that imitation *may* serve to introduce new words into the child's growing vocabulary.

While the role of imitation continues to be studied in normal and handicapped populations, heavy reliance on its use as an intervention strategy may be premature. Such a strong imitative focus may be erroneous, not solely because of the equivocal evidence regarding its importance in language acquisition. Children who are continually exposed to imitation as a language strategy may begin to view their utterances as functionless. They may not learn the critical "lesson" that language only derives its meaning through its use as a communicative vehicle. It may be due to the heavy reliance on imitation that there continues to be such widespread concern over the generalization of learned structures outside the training session (see Michaelis, 1978; Baer & Guess, 1973).

Most language intervention programs outlined in Table 10.3 are restricted to oral language (exceptions are those of Clark, Moores, & Woodcock, 1975 and Kent, 1972). However, there is growing evidence to support the position that nonverbal language intervention systems are beneficial not only to deaf youngsters, but also to hearing-autistic and severely mentally retarded children. This is reflected in the widespread use of language programs based on manual signs with severely retarded, moderately retarded, cerebral-palsied, and autistic populations (Goodman, Wilson, & Bornstein, 1978). Extrapolating from a nationwide survey, Goodman, Wilson, and Bornstein (1978) speculated that manual sign programs were being used with well over 10,000 handicapped individuals. Recognition of the applicability of gestural and manual language systems with severely handicapped populations is also acknowledged by increased coverage in professional journals (e.g., Brady & Smouse, 1978; Bonvillian & Nelson, 1976; Carr et al., 1978; Casey, 1978; Elder & Bergman, 1978, Fristoe & Lloyd, 1977; 1978; Harris,

1978; Reich, 1978; Salisbury, Wambold, & Walter, 1978; Stremel-Campbell, Cantrell, & Halle, 1978; Topper, 1975).

One final note about this section on formal approaches to language intervention. The assumption underlying most of the programs summarized in Table 10.3 (and to a large extent underlying several of the informal approaches described in the following pages) is that language is learned during specific language periods and is then generalized to a more natural situation outside the training context. This assumption clearly contradicts how children normally acquire language. They are not exposed to language learning only during specific language periods. Language learning occurs throughout the day as part of the normal routine of feeding, dressing, play, and social interaction.

In summary, during the 1970s there was a dramatic growth in the availability of language intervention programs. Several concerns exist in regard to the assumptions underlying their use. One of the most vital criteria to be used in selecting or developing an intervention program has been articulated by Holland (1975, p. 519). Language intervention must be viewed as a "communication microcosm" that "should provide a model of the language world to the child and should present him or her with opportunities to participate fully in using that model."

**INFORMAL APPROACHES TO LANGUAGE INTERVENTION** The scope of this chapter makes it unfeasible to describe all of the multiplicity of informal options available to the teacher to facilitate language development or remediate a language problem. With this in mind, the following are representative of the strategies that can be integrated into the classroom curriculum. Each activity is geared to a particular aspect of language and can be utilized with the entire class, in small groups, or in a one-to-one format. Before describing these activities, it should be noted that, since assessment and instruction are essentially two sides of the same coin, the informal assessment techniques presented in Chapter 9 can easily be adapted to instructional activities. Also, since language is an interpersonal phenomenon, and communication is its main function, all activities must stress these aspects. This means that imitation should be kept to a minimum and that the language activities should reflect the child's ongoing activities rather than more passive activities, such as labeling pictures.

FACILITATING THE DEVELOPMENT OF COGNITIVE CORRELATES OF LANGUAGE. Because so little attention has been traditionally paid to the importance of facilitating the development of early cognitive correlates of language in severely handicapped youngsters, this section gives extensive coverage to this area (see also Morehead & Morehead, 1974; Bricker, Dennison, & Bricker, 1975; and the *Guide to Early Developmental Training*, 1977, pp. 230–319). Following is a sequentially ordered series of activities to facilitate the development of object permanence, object use, and imitation. These strategies can be used after assessment determines that the prelinguistic child has not attained the necessary conditions for the symbolic function of language. Some of the instructional strategies can also be used to facilitate the development of intentional, nonverbal communication. Because the stages are sequentially based within each area (object permanence, imitation, and object use), when the child has successfully attained a stage, the teacher can begin to expand simultaneously the child's repertoire horizontally and vertically. To expand it horizontally, the teacher can add new objects so that the newly acquired schemas can be generalized. By introducing the child to the next developmental level, the teacher can expand the child's repertoire vertically.

It should also be noted that, while exposing the child to the various activities, the teacher should use a variety of communicative signals and functions to code the ongoing actions. This is important for several reasons. First, ongoing communication enhances the social-interpersonal nature of the interaction. Second, one of the early and important features of communication, turn-taking, can be built into the teaching-learning context. Third, by using the child's communicative signals, whether intentional or not, as cues for topical continuation or switching, the teacher can help the child have the opportunity to learn the critical lesson that communicative attempts can affect the environment. Finally, the child may incidentally learn various verbal or nonverbal ways to code actions, objects, relations, and so on. (These activities can be coordinated with the assessment strategies described in Chapter 9.)

INTERVENTION STRATEGY 1: VISUAL PURSUIT AND PERMANENCE OF OBJECTS. One of the cognitive precursors to language is the concept of object permanence. This means that objects are viewed as permanent, regardless of the context in which they occur and any actions taken upon them.

*Objective:* To facilitate the development of object permanence.

*Procedures:* The development of object permanence begins with visual pursuit of slowly moving objects and culminates with the retrieval of an object that is invisibly displaced under several screens. At Stage 1, the child is encouraged to visually pursue a slowly moving object. To begin, simply have the child visually fixate on objects of interest. This can be encouraged by presenting the child with an object that makes a sound or by letting the child hold an object. As soon as the child looks at an object, expand the types of objects presented to the child. Some objects can be musical, some movable, and so on. At all times encourage the child to look at the object, and talk to the child using selected discourse strategies described in Chapter 6 (e.g., self-repetition, heightened pitch, stress, and intonation).

When the child can successfully fixate on a variety of objects, encourage the child to visually follow individual objects as you slowly move them horizontally. To encourage this, use objects with sounds, or let the child hold the object, or help her to turn her head toward the slowly moving object. Utilize different objects of interest, and eventually omit the sound and the physical prompting. Repeat this procedure with objects that are moved vertically. Remember, during all activities, to interact with the child using discourse strategies, such as the following:

> While moving the object say "See the ball? Where's the ball?" (pointing at the ball) "Here's the ball."

In Stage 2, the child is encouraged to notice the disappearance of slowly moving objects. To accomplish this, show the child an object that is familiar and interesting. Once the child fixates on the object, move it past her shoulder and then behind her head. Encourage the child to watch the object. If she loses interest in the object when it moves out of her visual field, use a musical object, move it slowly to where it would disappear, then hold it there briefly and gradually leave less of the object in the child's view. Use a variety of objects, some that produce sound and others that do not. When the child's eyes linger on the spot where the object was last seen, it is evidence for the beginning of object permanence.

Finding objects that are partially hidden is characteristic of Stage 3. Skills prerequisite to this stage include the ability to visually fixate on stationary and slowing moving objects and the ability to grasp objects. Strategies to encourage this involve using objects with sound or objects the child can hold, slowly moving the object under a pillow, cup, or other screen; and leaving the object partially visible. Use other objects, and hide more and more of each object. Remove the presence of sound as a perceptual clue and also discontinue the child's action of holding. Use a gamelike interactive approach as in the following:

> While slowly hiding an activated music box under a pillow say "Where's the music box? Where is it? Where did the music box go? Go get the music box? Go get it." (Lift the pillow off the music box.) "Here it is. Here's the music box."

When the child can retrieve objects that are partially hidden, continue to Stage 4, in which the child finds completely hidden objects after observing their visual displacement. Let the child watch you while you place an object under a screen. At first the screen should be thin and flexible (e.g., a cloth), so that the presence of the object is noticeable by the bulging of the screen. Also, musical objects should be used initially, so that there are auditory cues to their presence. When the child begins to find the hidden objects, use screens that are thicker and objects that do not produce sound. At this point, you have created the context for hide-and-seek games, which promote object permanence.

Activities for achieving Stage 5 are essentially the same as those for Stage 4. However, the new objective is for the child to find objects totally hidden in one of two places. Increasing the possible displacement to more than one location is intended to demonstrate to the child that the existence or permanence of an object is not dependent on its physical context.

In Stage 6, the child is encouraged to find objects that are hidden or displaced in three places alternately. Activities to foster this ability are quite similar to those described for Stage 4.

For Stage 7, the activities are changed slightly. While the child is watching, first place an object into a container and then hide the container behind or under a screen. The child must retrieve the container and then find the hidden object within it. In so doing, the child must be able to retain a mental image of the object since she never sees the actual object being hidden behind the screen (i.e., an invisible displacement). Use strategies similar to those already described, as well as discourse strategies to promote atte ition and interaction. The final stage, Stage 8, is characterized by the child's successful retrieval of objects that have been invisibly displaced under one of several screens. Activities to achieve this can be much like those previously described. They should culminate in the child's recognition that objects exist more or less permanently regardless of actions taken upon them and regardless of their locations.

INTERVENTION STRATEGY 2: DEVELOPMENT OF OBJECT USE OR PLAY. Children need to develop an interest in and an understanding of objects for the following reasons: (1) to achieve a precursor to the later semantic relations of agent + object, action + object, and object + attribute, (2) to learn about the functions and attributes of objects, and (3) to understand that things can represent other things (i.e., representation). Children generally learn about objects through their actions upon them.

*Objective:* To learn to interact with objects exploratorily, functionally, and symbolically.

*Procedures:* Like object permanence, the development of object use moves through a number of continuous stages, beginning with visual inspection of objects and culminating with the symbolic use of objects. Activities are briefly presented here for each of the seven stages. It must be reiterated that all activities should be gamelike in nature and accompanied by selective discourse strategies as described in Chapter 6. The use of accompanying discourse strategies is designed to maintain a warm and positive interaction, to encourage the child's maintenance of attention, and to indirectly teach the child how objects, actions, and attributes are encoded linguistically.

During Stage 1, the child should be encouraged to visually inspect objects. This can be accomplished by simply providing the child with interesting objects to watch. Objects that change position, emit sounds, or have bright colors should be used because they are likely to interest the child and hold her attention. During Stage 2, the child should also be encouraged to hold objects. Place objects in front of the child that are interesting and easily grasped. Observe whether or not the child grasps the object (i.e., coordinates looking and grasping). If the child does not grasp the object, place it in her hand. Help the child grasp it, if necessary, but do not force the child's grasping action. Vary the objects presented to the child with respect to texture, weight, shape, color, and so on.

During Stage 3, the child is encouraged to mouth safe objects. Mouthing is an important early schema for learning about the attributes of objects (e.g., taste, hardness, temperature). Place an object in the child's hand, and observe whether or not she brings it to her mouth. If she does, vary the objects presented to her.

Observe whether she mouths all objects or only certain objects. Selective mouthing demonstrates that the child has begun to discriminate among the properties of objects. If the child does not mouth objects, hold a safe object near her mouth and encourage mouthing. If the child still does not mouth, put syrup or another sweet-tasting substance on the object and encourage oral exploration.

The use of simple undifferentiated motor schemas to explore objects is characteristic of Stage 4. Present various objects one at a time. Observe what the child does with each one (e.g., rubs, shakes, waves, bangs). If the child does nothing, model, in a gamelike fashion, different actions on the objects. Repeat with a variety of objects and actions (e.g., pound the table with a spoon).

Stage 5 is characterized by the use of differentiated motor schemas. During this stage, the child should be encouraged to adjust her motor schemas to the physical properties of objects. For example, the child:

1. Slides certain objects on a flat surface.
2. Bangs metallic objects because of an interesting resultant sound.
3. Tears or crumbles soft or papery objects.

If the child does not spontaneously explore objects using different motor schemas, encourage her to do so by modeling in gamelike activities. Vary the type of object used.

In contrast to the exploratory object play of Stages 1 through 5, in Stage 6 the child should be encouraged to use objects in a socially-determined and functional manner. If the child does not spontaneously use objects functionally, the following procedures can be used. Select objects familiar to the child, and determine what responses are considered functional for each object (e.g., given a cup she drinks from it or fills it with sand and then spills it out). Have one set of objects for the child and a duplicate set for yourself. In a gamelike atmosphere, demonstrate one function of an object and ask the child to do what you do. Communicate about the object and your actions upon it. Repeat the activity with other objects.

Stage 7, which is symbolic use of objects, is the culminating stage and is a major precursor to language. Successful attainment of this stage demonstrates the child's emerging representational abilities as evidenced by the child's representing one object (e.g., a truck) by another (e.g., a block). Encourage the child to use familiar objects, such as blocks, a box, or a pot to represent other objects, such as cars, a house, and a bathtub. To do so, have one set of objects for the child and a duplicate set for yourself. Demonstrate, and encourage the child to pretend with you. Describe what you are doing, using a variety of discourse strategies. Repeat the activity with other objects.

INTERVENTION STRATEGY 3: DEVELOPMENT OF VOCAL IMITATION. Along with object use and object permanence, vocal imitation is a precursor to the emergence of language. To achieve vocal imitation, the ability to coordinate the vocal and hearing schemas and the ability to accommodate to novel utterances are necessary.

*Objective:* To facilitate the development of vocal imitation.

*Procedures:* Reflexive crying is the earliest vocalization, and, in Stage 1, it should receive adult attention. Respond to the child's crying as though the cry was intentional (see Chapter 6 for interactional strategies).

When the child begins to produce vocalizations other than crying, respond to these in order to increase their frequency and variety. Strategies for increasing vocalizations in Stage 2 include imitating the child's vocalizations and attributing meaning to them. In addition, increase the child's opportunities to vocalize by utilizing activities that encourage frequent vocalization (e.g., rough-housing, tickling). Imitate all of the child's spontaneous vocalizations.

Stage 3 focuses on encouraging the child to repeat familiar and self-initiated vocalizations. Young children begin to imitate the sounds people make only when those sounds are similar to ones they can already produce. Also, in the early stages of vocal imitation, children imitate only if they initiate the vocal interaction. Repeat all child-initiated sounds (e.g., gurgles, coos) throughout the day. Use games (e.g., peek-a-boo) to stimulate imitations.

In contrast to those for Stage 3, activities for Stage 4 are designed to encourage the child's imitation of familiar but other-initiated sounds. At first, note which sounds the child makes most frequently, including both segmental and suprasegmental features of intonation, stress, and pitch. In addition, note the contexts in which these sounds most frequently occur. In the same contexts, listen for the child's vocalizations, wait a few seconds, and then imitate them. Encourage the child to imitate. Increase the lapsed time between the child's vocalization and your imitation. In a gamelike atmosphere, use containers and paper towel tubes to make sounds into. Encourage the child to do the same.

Imitating new sounds is the focus of Stage 5. Activities to encourage this include the following procedures. First, select unfamiliar sounds from those that are easiest for the child to produce, such as vowels, labial consonants (e.g., /ba/, /ma/, /pa/), and back consonants (e.g., /ka/, and /ga/). Initially, produce sounds the child already spontaneously makes and then gradually introduce new sounds during daily routines. Encourage the child to imitate. Relate these new, other-initiated sounds to meaningful activities as illustrated by the following:

> Eating⟶ *mm*
> Banging a spoon ⟶ *ba ba ba*
> Pushing a truck ⟶ *rm, rm, rm*
> Dog barking ⟶ *ruh, ruh, ruh*

Also use games with associated sounds, such as peek-a-boo (*boo*), swinging the child (*whee*), and who's in the mirror (*hi*). Encourage the child's imitation of these sounds as part of the game's routine.

In Stage 6, encouraging the child to imitate new words is the focus. Words selected for imitation should reflect the child's understanding of objects, events, and interests and should be easy for her to articulate. Engage in high-interest activities or games, meanwhile addressing short phrases to the child with the targeted word repeated several times as follows:

To the child holding a spoon say: "See the spoon?" "Where's the spoon?" "Here's the spoon." (stress on the word *spoon*).

Encourage the child to imitate your words.

INTERVENTION STRATEGY 4: DEVELOPMENT OF MOTOR IMITATION. Facilitating the development of motor imitation has several purposes, including the following: (1) it may aid in the development of vocal imitations; (2) it fosters the coordination of the visual and motor schemas; and (3) it aids in learning the socially determined use of objects. The development of gestural imitation begins at Stage 1 with an increase in motor schemas and culminates at Stage 6 with deferred imitation.

*Objective:* To facilitate the development of gestural imitation.

*Procedures:* In order to increase motor schemas at Stage 1, identify motor activities involving objects that the child finds enjoyable. Using gamelike routines, provide many opportunities for interaction with those objects. While you and the child are interacting with the objects, employ appropriate discourse strategies to create a warm, interpersonal atmosphere, to facilitate the child's maintenance of attention, and to describe ongoing action.

Stage 2 focuses on the imitation of motor schemas that are familiar and child-initiated. As they do in vocal imitation, children first begin to imitate the motor schemas others produce only when those schemas are familiar and child-initiated. Watch the child, and note which motor schemas she spontaneously produces. When she ceases an action, imitate it, then pause, and encourage the child's imitation. Again, be sure to accompany the activity with selected discourse strategies.

In contrast to those in Stage 2, activities in Stage 3 are designed to encourage imitation of familiar but other-initiated actions. First, note which motor schemas the child spontaneously produces. Initiate those schemas, and encourage the child to imitate them. For example, bang a spoon on the table while saying, "bang, bang, bang." Hand the spoon to the child and encourage her imitation of the banging action. Also, you can use a duplicate set of objects to encourage imitation.

During Stage 4, the child is encouraged to imitate familiar actions that are visible. The factor of visibility is important here, for the child must be able to see not only your production of the action, but her own as well. By so doing, she may be better able to accommodate her production of the action to the one produced by you. When selecting actions to be modeled, you should consider whether or not they are familiar and have pleasurable effects. Examples of such activities are clapping games, such as "patty-cake," and numerous action songs, such as "Incy-bincy Spider." Act out these games, and encourage the child to imitate some of the actions. If she does not spontaneously imitate, gently prompt the targeted action.

Imitating unfamiliar and nonvisible motor schemas is the focus of Stage 5. Since its nonvisibility requires the child to perform the action without actually seeing her own production of it, she must have attained a certain degree of mental imagery. Obtain the child's attention while performing an action that the child cannot see herself do (e.g., wrinkle your nose, blink your eyes). Observe the child's reaction. If the child imitates, repeat the process with other actions. However, if the child does not spontaneously imitate, provide further encouragement and clues, for example, by adding sound to the action (e.g., smacking your lips).

Deferred imitation, or imitation without the model present, is the culminating stage. Since the child must perform an action at a later time, she must remember (i.e., have a mental image of) the action. Perform an action that is unfamiliar to the child. Observe the child at a later time to determine if she reconstructs the action without a model present. Also, ask the parent or other caretaker to note occurrences of the action in other contexts. If deferred imitation is evidenced, repeat the steps with other, more complex, actions. If deferred imitation is not noted, perform an unfamiliar action that utilizes an object or objects (e.g., tapping a drum with drumsticks). At a later time, hand the child the object(s), and note whether or not deferred imitation occurs. The object(s) used should act as a context clue to the initial action.

INTERVENTION STRATEGY 5: ACHIEVING DESIRED ENDS. An important area of cognitive development focuses on children's learning that they, agents using objects as instruments, can achieve their ends. This is an important factor in the development of intentional communication. The development begins with simple hand-watching and culminates when the child can obtain a desired object using an unrelated object as an instrument.

*Objective:* To facilitate the development of means-ends relationships.

*Procedures:* In Stage 1, the child is encouraged to watch his hands (an object to the child). This is done by gently moving his hands into his visual field and adding interesting actions, such as tickling or gently moving his fingers. At this early stage, the intent is to begin the coordination of vision and prehension. Here, and throughout the following suggested activities, accompany your actions with selected discourse strategies as already described.

Reaching and grasping for objects is characteristic of Stage 2. This requires the rudimentary coordination of visual and motor schemas, which is an ability that is necessary for motor imitation and functional object use. Hold a familiar and attractive object in front of the child. Observe his reaction. If the child grasps the object, repeat with other objects in a gamelike manner. Also, allow the child to have an opportunity to explore the whole object. If the child does not grasp but merely reaches for the object, help him to grasp it. Be certain, however, that the child is visually focusing on it. If the child neither reaches for nor grasps the toy, move it closer to him and help him grasp it.

When the child can successfully reach for and grasp a variety of objects, he is ready for Stage 3, which involves letting go of one object in order to reach for another. Here, as in the previous stage, the child is learning that his hands can be very effective instruments for obtaining desired objects. Hand the child two familiar and attractive objects, placing one in each of his hands. Offer the child a third, favorite object, by holding it in front of him within reach. Observe if and how the child obtains the third object. Does he try to obtain it while still holding the other objects? Does he let go of one of the two objects before reaching for the third one? If the child exhibits anticipatory letting-go, repeat with other objects in a game-like, turn-taking atmosphere. Repeat this routine frequently throughout the day. If the child does not let go of the held objects, encourage this behavior by asking for one of them and offering the third object in return.

The child must learn that, in addition to his hands, other objects can be instrumental in obtaining desired objects. This usage is first witnessed in Stage 4, which involves obtaining a desired object by using a support. After interesting the child in an object, place it out of reach on a support (e.g., a cloth or tray) that is within reach of the child. Observe the child's reaction. If he does not attempt to obtain the object by pulling at the support, encourage the child by saying "Where's the object? Go get the object." If the child still does not use the support, model its use. Repeat the activity at different times with different objects in a gamelike atmosphere.

Obtaining a desired object by using another unrelated object as an instrument is the culminating stage. After interesting the child in an object, tie a string around the object while the child is looking. Then place the object out of the child's reach, but keep the string within reach. Follow the same procedures described for Stage 4. Repeat this activity, using a twelve-inch ruler as the instrumental object. Repeat at different times during the day with different objects.

INTERVENTION STRATEGY 6: ENCOURAGING NONVERBAL COMMUNICATION. In addition to working with the cognitive correlates of language, the teacher can also focus on enabling the child to use nonverbal communicative signals. This can be done during daily routines, such as dressing, eating, or playing.

*Materials:* No materials other than those generally used in daily routines are needed.

*Procedures:* During daily routines, consciously begin to use gestures in addition to spoken language when communicating with the child. For example, while talking, pointing can be used to index the following:

|  **people**  |  **objects**  |
|---|---|
| *you, me* | *ball, car* |
| *he, she* | *spoon, food* |
| *him, her* | *dog, shoe* |
| *we, us, they* | |

|  **location**  |  **possession**  |
|---|---|
| *there, here* | *mine* |
| *hall, bathroom, classroom* | *yours* |
| *outside* | *her, his* |
| *in, on, under* | |

After several days of using gestures as an additional communicative signal, encourage the child to do so also. This can be done by modifying the daily routine so that an unexpected state or event occurs. For example, during feeding do not place any food in the child's bowl. Wait for some type of child-initiated communicative attempt (e.g., confused facial expression, vocalization, point to the empty plate) signaling that an unexpected event has occurred. If the child does in some way signal, interpret the signal by saying (and gesturing) *There's no food,* thereby confirming the child's communicative attempt. Then place the food in the child's bowl and say (with accompanying gestures) *Here's your food.* Continue the normal eating routine. If the child does not initiate any communicative attempt, with exaggerated intonational and gestural stress, say *Where's your food? There's no food here!* Wait for any responses from the child (e.g., gazing at empty bowl, pointing). Present the food after confirming the child's signal and continue with the daily routine.

Continue to use gestures and other nonverbal signals as supplements to spoken language and encourage the child to use a variety of nonverbal communicative signals. Other strategies, both verbal and nonverbal, can be found in Hart and Rogers-Warren (1978).

**ADAPTING CLASSROOM ACTIVITIES TO FACILITATE COMMUNICATION**   When developing intervention strategies to increase and expand communication, the teacher must again take into account several cognitive and linguistic factors. The teacher must consider the child's communicative development, in addition to development in the semantic/syntactic aspects of language. For example, is the child still primarily egocentric in the use of language, or is language socialized? When facilitating the child's communicative development, the teacher must start with the here and now and only very gradually introduce talking about past events or speculating about what will happen in the future. Finally, the context of the intervention strategies should be as much as possible a microcosm of the real world. Language should be used to send or receive information, ask and answer questions, and describe activities and states. The following informal strategies are a small sample of the kinds of activities that can be developed and expanded for incorporation in the classroom program.

INTERVENTION STRATEGY 7: TALKING ABOUT ONGOING ACTIONS. Both teachers and therapists can develop stimulating activities to encourage children to talk about events, to share their feelings and perspectives about their experiences, to recall and describe the sequences of events, and to share information. Trips to the zoo, the police station, the firehouse, and so on can be followed by teacher-directed questions such as *What happened?, Where did you go?, What did you see?,* and *When did you see the giraffe?* If they answer at all, children with language and/or cognitive problems respond with minimal verbal information. For developmentally young children, the task of describing what occurred in the past, whether remote or recent, may require linguistic and cognitive abilities that are not yet present within their psychological schemas. It is, therefore, important to begin a language intervention strategy by encouraging the child to describe ongoing actions. Activities such as cooking, playing with clay, doing carpentry, and painting can generate related questions by the teacher. The perceptual attributes of the objects and their relationships aid the child in describing ongoing actions. The teacher's questions should focus the child's attention on particular aspects of the immediate events, while also providing the structure for appropriate responses. Only after the child develops the facility to describe ongoing actions should the focus shift to describing actions and events that occurred in the past.

*Objective:* To strengthen the child's ability to describe ongoing actions.

*Procedures:* It is important to first select several activities that include observable, discriminative events naturally occurring in a classroom. Such activities include painting, playing with clay, building with blocks, making cookies, and eating lunch. It is also important that the children find the activity to be stimulating and enjoyable. Opportunity should be given for the children to spend as much time as they need engaging in the activities before descriptions of their actions are requested. The following is one possible sequence of the various stages that could be built into the strategy:

| Stage | Teacher input | Child output |
|---|---|---|
| 1. Gaining familiarity with the activity | None | Ongoing actions with the objects |
| 2. Following instructions | *Squeeze clay.* | Appropriate motor response |
| 3. Reporting simple ongoing actions of the child | *What are you doing?* *Where is the clay?* | *Squeeze* or *Squeezing clay* or *I'm squeezing the clay.* |
| 4. Reporting simple ongoing actions of others | *What am I doing?* *What is Wayne doing?* *Where is Carmen's clay?* | *Squeeze* or *Squeezing clay* or *You're squeezing the clay.* |
| 5. Following instructions involving two-component actions | *Squeeze the clay and roll the clay.* | Appropriate motor response |
| 6. Reporting two-component ongoing actions of the child | *What are you doing?* *What's happening?* | *Squeeze clay; roll clay* or *Squeezing and rolling clay* or *I'm squeezing and rolling the clay.* |
| 7. Reporting two-component ongoing actions of others | *What am I doing?* *What is Jack doing?* | *Squeeze clay; roll clay* or *Squeezing and rolling clay* or *You're squeezing and rolling the clay.* |
| 8. Reporting simple actions of the child that occurred in the recent past | *What were you doing?* *Where was the clay?* | *Squeeze clay* or *Squeezed clay* or *I squeezed the clay* or *I was squeezing clay.* |

| Stage | Teacher input | Child output |
|---|---|---|
| 9. Reporting simple actions of others that occurred in the recent past | *What was I doing?* *What was Jack doing?* *What happened?* | *Squeeze clay* or *Squeezed clay* or *Jack was squeezing clay.* |
| 10. Reporting two-component actions of the child that occurred in the recent past | *What were you doing?* *What was happening?* *What happened?* | *Squeeze and roll clay* or *Squeezed and rolled clay* or *I squeezed and rolled the clay.* |
| 11. Reporting two-component actions of others that occurred in the recent past | *What was I doing?* *What was Carol doing?* *What happened?* | *Squeeze and roll clay* or *Squeezed and rolled clay* or *Carol was squeezing and rolling the clay.* |

Increase the time that elapses between the activity and the verbal description.

Several considerations must be mentioned at this point. The complexity of the language response should be consonant with the child's structural development. For example, a child functioning at a two-word utterance level should not be required to respond with a complete sentence. You should be more concerned with the appropriateness of the content of the response rather than its structure. Also, for linguistically delayed youngsters, the temporary use of a modeled response may be necessary. However, modeling by the teacher as a prompt should be discontinued as soon as possible. Finally, a gamelike atmosphere should be used for motivation. For example, one child might leave the room, and if she can then identify the action as described by another child, it would be the latter's turn to be "it."

INTERVENTION STRATEGY 8: ASKING QUESTIONS. At a very young age, children begin to ask questions. This questioning increases the child's curiosity about the world and also provides a forum for receiving factual information about the world. Parents of normally developing children often complain that at about two years of age their children persistently ask *Why this?* and *Why that?* While at times it might be annoying, this questioning is motivated by the child's desire to receive factual information about place, name, time, and so on and causal explanations. Children's *why* questions can be described in three basic categories (Piaget, 1955):

| Category | Example |
|---|---|
| 1. Causal explanations about physical objects | *Why is it so heavy?* |
| 2. Motivation: Purpose or motive for a human activity or state | *Why are we going?* *Why don't you know?* |
| 3. Justification for a rule or social convention | *Why do we have to salute the flag?* |

Each of these questions reflects a very real social and cognitive need in the child. While the structure of children's questions may vary, their intent, that is, to obtain information remains relatively stable. This can be seen in the following examples:

| Content | Example |
|---|---|
| 1. Questions relating to facts, location, events, and time | *Are there also little fishes round the edge?* |
| | *Where is my ball?* |
| 2. Questions about human actions and about rules | *Who do you like best, John or me?* (actions) |
| | *Do grown-ups make mistakes, too?* (actions) |
| | *Who said I have to?* (rules) |
| 3. Questions about classification and calculation | *What does hassle mean?* |
| | *What is a bachelor?* |

Most children spontaneously ask questions and need little, if any, encouragement to do so. However, there are some children who are reluctant to ask questions. Such reluctance handicaps children in that many internal questions, misunderstandings, and confusions stay unresolved. These children must receive special attention from the teacher/clinician to encourage the asking of questions. The rationale for such encouragement is more than merely a cognitive one, for asking and answering questions is a social interaction reflecting the human communicative process.

*Objectives:* To develop strategies to encourage the asking of questions, taking into account the various purposes and content of questions.

*Procedures:* In developing your strategies, you should be especially concerned with the context of the teaching or therapeutic setting. If you provide activities or objects that are completely familiar, the child may feel no need to ask questions. Therefore, the activities, games, or events should be novel enough to motivate the child to ask questions. In addition, the child should be an active participant in the action, so that curiosity is triggered. Besides the context of the session, you should consider other ways to encourage the timid and reluctant child to ask questions. The use of puppets and role playing can be helpful. The following example shows one way that a puppet can facilitate the child's asking of questions.

> Two children and the teacher/clinician are seated on the floor. The teacher is holding a puppet, watching the two children cooperatively working on a new puzzle. The puppet is shy, so he has to ask the children to ask questions for him. He might ask Juan to ask Peter *Why can't I have my turn, now?*

The teacher/clinician's role here is that of observing the children as they are engaged in their activity in order to identify key moments when questions can be asked. Also, the puppet can model specific questions by asking one child to ask various questions of the other child or teacher.

Whether or not puppets or role-playing are used, it is important to consider (1) the context, (2) the purpose of the questions, and (3) the structure of the questions. It is equally important to be aware that if children's questions consistently go unanswered or are ridiculed for being stupid, they may become more reluctant to ask questions. Finally, in developing strategies to encourage the asking of questions, the intent should be of primary concern, instead of its structure. Whether the child says *Like me?* or *Why you not like me?* or *Why don't you like me?* the intent of the question should be stressed. You can repeat and expand the question, saying *Why don't I like you?,* before answering the child. However, this strategy is not the same as directly correcting the structure of the child's question.

INTERVENTION STRATEGY 9: REFERENTIAL COMMUNICATION. "Communication of a specific object, event or relationship to another is the simplest kind of communication. . . ." (Dale, 1972, p. 226). While this may be true, for many children having language problems or who are developmentally young, referential communication poses many problems. One reason for this difficulty is that a particular referent may be referred to by many names. Consider a block that is red in color, triangular in shape, and small in size. It may be appropriately called *a block, a small block, a red block, a triangular block, it,* or *that one.* While each description accurately refers to the particular block, some subset of these descriptions may have to be used by the speaker in a particular context to communicate effectively to the listener which block to select. The speaker must, therefore, consider the set of alternatives from which the listener must select the intended block. While this may seem to be a rather easy task, for most young children and many older ones, this is a difficult linguistic and cognitive task. As already mentioned, much of young children's language is egocentric. Therefore, the speaker may not consider the set of alternatives from which the listener must operate. In neglecting to do so, the speaker may say *Move this one* without considering that the listener does not know to what referent *this one* applies.

In order to encourage children as speakers to be more effective communicators, the teacher must not only help them to expand their use of language but also sensitize the children to the need to consider the listener's perspectives.

*Objective:* To expand the role of the speaker, taking into account the linguistic skills as well as the cognitive demands of the speaker (i.e., consideration of the listener).

*Procedures:* Many activities can be developed that require the speaker to communicate information about specific objects, events, or relationships. The block-building activity described on pages 84–87 is one such activity. Others, such as building with Tinkertoys or erector sets, puzzles, or making masks with various shapes cut out of colored construction paper, can be used. The range of possible activities is endless. In using activities for the context of a language intervention, certain content considerations should be explored. The cognitive demands placed on the speaker should gradually be increased. Therefore, you might want to start with an activity that only minimally requires the speaker to consider the set of alternatives from which the listener must operate. Consider the following situation:

> Two children are seated at a table, separated by an opaque screen. Each child has a toy dog and a toy truck. The speaker's role is to verbally communicate to the listener which toy is to be picked up.

In this situation, the speaker need only consider the most minimal set of alternatives from which the listener must operate—the names of the toys. The teacher and the entire audience (i.e., the rest of the class) can probe both the listener and the speaker to determine whether or not the information given is sufficient.

As the children become more effective communicators, the cognitive and linguistic demands presented by the situation should be increased. The following illustrates a possible setting:

> Two children separated by an opaque screen are seated at a table in front of the class. The listener is blindfolded, thus pretending to be blind. Both children have before them the same collection of six blocks varying in shape, and/or size. The speaker builds a construction using all of the blocks, and the speaker's task is to provide enough information so that the listener can replicate the construction.

This situation is much more cognitively complex than the preceding one. Here, the speaker must be aware of the visual limitations of the listener and of the wide set of alternatives from which the listener must choose. The speaker must talk about shape, size, relationships, positions, and so on. Again, both the teacher and audience should participate by probing to determine if the information given by the speaker was adequate. Encourage the children to shout out such queries as *What do you mean by this one?* in reaction to nonspecific information.

Activities can be designed to gradually increase the cognitive and linguistic demands placed on the speaker. The teacher need only consider the children's readiness for the increase of these demands and the necessity for a variety of activities to maintain motivation.

INTERVENTION STRATEGY 10: COMMUNICATION BASED ON IN-CREASED DISTANCE BETWEEN LISTENER AND SPEAKER. Moffett (1968a) suggests that the development of communicative abilities includes the dimension of increasing the distance between the listener and speaker—the *I-you* dimension. This is not only important in spoken communication, but becomes increasingly important as youngsters learn to communicate via written language. Children must learn that as the spatial or temporal distance between listener and speaker increases, certain discourse strategies (e.g., gestures, use of existing physical context) are no longer effective. As a result, they must linguistically build in the context.

*Objective:* To facilitate communication when the distance between listener and speaker is increased.

*Materials:* All that is needed are a tape recorder and another class of students and their teacher to be partners in this interaction.

*Procedures:* In conjunction with another class, decide on a joint project in which each class will independently participate (e.g., building a model of the neighborhood, growing plants, solving classroom disputes). Each day the children in each class will communicate via taped messages to the other class concerning the progress, events, or mishaps of the project. As part of the activity, both teacher and students can provide feedback to the other class concerning the effectiveness of their communication attempts. Questions asking for clarification of ambiguous or inadequate messages can be sent between classes, as can requests for additional or more explicit information. This process can continue throughout the school year. In addition, a class in another school can join this communicative partnership.

INTERVENTION STRATEGY 11: PERSUASIVE COMMUNICATION. Whereas communicating about a specific object, event, or relationship is the simplest function of language, language may be used for other purposes. One such function is that of persuasion. Language can have the power of influencing another person's point of view or position on a particular topic. As a social tool, this function of language is well worth developing.

*Objective:* To expand the role of the speaker to include the cognitive and linguistic skills of persuasion.

*Procedures:* Although this activity is geared primarily for use with older children, young children can begin to engage in persuasive activities, although their strategies will be less sophisticated. Establish a series of role-playing situations wherein a student must persuade an adult (e.g., teaching aide) or another student to do something that he or she might not normally want to do. For example, the speaker must convince the aide to give a particular child or the entire class additional free time for play. Although one child is the persuader, the audience (i.e., the rest of the class) can help the persuader develop this argument. The teacher should encourage the persuader to go beyond simple pleas and descriptions of why it is important to the child or class (e.g., *We want to play longer*). Instead, the persuader should be encouraged to consider the attitudes or values of the listener in the argument to make it valid from the perspective of the listener (e.g., *If we have additional time for play, we will be more alert for the science lesson*).

**APPROACHES TO SEMANTICS AND SYNTAX**  Whether an intervention approach is designed for an individual with pervasive language problems or for an individual with a few specific problems, several considerations are important. First, it is crucial to determine whether the problem is primarily a syntactic or a semantic problem. For example, a child may have the semantic function of negation without the appropriate syntactical structure to express it (e.g., *I not go home* instead of *I don't go home*). Second, children's language problems can affect either the reception or expression of language. Generally, intervention should begin with reception. Finally, children with language problems should begin with concrete experiences before moving on to more abstract language activities.

Therefore, language activities should begin with the here and how rather than with objects that are absent or events that are distanced in time.

INTERVENTION STRATEGY 12: EXPANDING NOUN PHRASES AND VERB PHRASES. One of the most common difficulties a child may experience is restricted usage of either the verb phrase or noun phrase of a sentence. When either type of phrase is restricted either in expression or reception, much potential information is lost.

*Objective:* To develop and expand the child's capacity to use (receptively and expressively) expanded noun phrases or verb phrases.

*Materials:* Familiar objects around the classroom that require more than a simple name or label to be identified can be used. For example, two desks or balls or books could be used. Children in the class can also be used.

*Procedures:* A Sherlock Holmes gamelike approach can be used, in which one child describes a hidden object or a child without actually naming it. This would constitute the clues. The mystery is solved when the children in the class identify the hidden object or the child on the basis of the clues. In using this strategy, you must first identify which phrase (noun or verb) you wish to develop. Once you have done this, it is then important to determine the sequencing of structures to be developed. The following is a list of objects or children to be identified and the increasingly more difficult expanded noun phrases or verb phrases needed as the clues.

| Objects/People | Expanded Phrase Taught |
|---|---|
| 1. Two flowers (one green and one blue) | Color + Noun (NP) |
| 2. Three books (one large blue book, one small blue book, and one large green book) | Size + Color + Noun (NP) |
| 3. Two girls (one girl with a yellow skirt and one with a brown skirt) | Noun + embedded NP |
| 4. Two balls (one is on the box and one is in the box) | Expands VP to Verb + NP |
| 5. Two children walking (one child walking slowly and one walking fast) | Expands VP to Verb + Adverb |
| 6. Two children pretending (one child wanting to play a piano and one child wanting to ride a horse) | Expands VP to V + Complement |

INTERVENTION STRATEGY 13: DEVELOPING NEGATIVE AND INTERROGATIVE TRANSFORMATIONS. Many children who have developed the semantic bases for negation and interrogation have not yet developed the structural transformations for expressing these sentence types. For example, a child might use the sentence *I no like him* to express a negative proposition or *I go home?* with rise in intonation to express interrogation. In both cases, the child has mastered the content of each sentence type but not its structure.

*Objective:* To develop the appropriate transformational structures for expressing negation and interrogation.

*Materials:* Puppets can be used as simulated speakers and listeners.

*Procedures:* It is first necessary to determine where the child is in developing the appropriate transformations. The transformational operations for negation and *yes/no* questions are as follows:

### Negation

Terminal Structure: NP + Aux + Neg + Verb (+ NP) (*I do not like you*) (*I don't like you*)

Declarative: NP + Verb + NP (*I like you*)

T (neg I): NP + Aux + V + NP (*I do like you*)

T (neg II): NP + Aux + Neg + V + NP (*I do not like you*)

T (neg III): Contraction of Aux + Neg (*I don't like you*)

(See pp. 111 for developmental stages.)

### Interrogation (*Yes/No* Questions)

Terminal Structure: Aux + $NP_1$ + V (+ $NP_2$) (*Do you like me?*)

Declarative: $NP_1$ + Verb + $NP_2$ (*You like me.*)

T (*yes/no* I): $NP_1$ + Aux + Verb + $NP_2$ + ? (*You do like me?*)

T (*yes/no* II): Aux + $NP_1$ + V + $NP_2$ + ? (*Do you like me?*)

(See pp. 109 for developmental stages.)

For example, using the above sequences it can be seen that the child who said *I no like him* has not yet reached the first negative transformation where the obligatory auxiliary verb is included. Instead, this child is simply embedding the negative morpheme *no* between the noun phrase and the verb. Similarly, saying *I go home?* shows that the child has not yet developed the first transformation of interrogation where the auxiliary verb is included. Here the child indicates question content by using the structure of a declarative sentence with the appropriate intonation (i.e., rise in pitch at the end of the sentence). Intervention for this child should start with the inclusion of the appropriate auxiliary verbs. The child and teacher can begin with one puppet each. The teacher tells the child to tell his puppet to say the following sentences:

> *I <u>do</u> like you.*
>
> *I <u>can</u> play ball.*
>
> *You <u>are</u> coming to my party.*

In this way, the teacher acts as the model, and the child produces the particular structure by talking for the puppet. When the child can generate the appropriate auxiliary verb, he is ready for the next stage in both negation and interrogation. Similar puppeting strategies can be used for each successive stage.

INTERVENTION STRATEGY 14: PRONOMINALIZATION. Another linguistic problem of many children is the difficulty in accurately comprehending or producing pronouns. The use of pronouns, both personal and impersonal, requires the ability to classify with respect to animate versus inanimate (i.e., *I, you, she* versus *it*) singular versus plural (*i.e., I* versus *we, he* versus *they*), gender (i.e., *he* versus *she*), and shifts in speaker and listener roles and spatial aspects (i.e., *I* versus *you, this* versus *that*). For example, if a child is standing next to his female teacher and another child comes by and says *She is happy* referring to the teacher, the first child must know that *She* expresses the categories [+animate, +female, +listener]. If the teacher concurs, saying *I am happy*, the child must comprehend that *I* expresses the categories [+animate, +female, +speaker]. Both spoken sentences refer to the same person, but the pronouns used have varied. This can be a very confusing linguistic concept for some children.

*Objective:* To develop the use of personal and impersonal pronouns.

*Materials:* All that is needed are a ball and some pictures of objects to be pinned to the children's clothing.

*Procedures:* Select a particular set of pronouns that conrast with one another with respect to a particular category. For the case of male versus female, have the children sit in a circle, girls alternating with boys. Each child's task is to roll the ball to another child, but before doing so the child must determine if the recipient is a *he* or a *she* and state which.

When the children are successful at this, the additional category of animate versus inanimate can be added. Some children wear pictures of familiar objects, such as car, ball, or house, while the remaining children retain their animate identities. Now before a child rolls the ball he must make two decisions; i.e. animate/inanimate and male/female before committing himself to *he, she, it*. This game-like strategy can be used to develop the static pronominal categories just described as well as the more temporally and spatially changing pronouns such as *I/you, you/me,* or *this/that*.

The preceding informal activities are by no means exhaustive or fully representative of the ways in which language intervention can be integrally incorporated into the classroom curriculum. Additional activities can be found in Muma (1978), Moffett (1968*a;* 1968*b,* Smilansky (1968), and Shaftel and Shaftel (1967). However, it must be reiterated that language intervention should not be limited only to those times designated as "language time." Language strategies should be incorporated into the school environment throughout the child's day. The following section draws attention to the classroom as a continuing communicative context.

## THE CLASSROOM AS A COMMUNICATIVE
## CONTEXT

Awareness of language problems should not be limited to the one period each day set aside for language activities and intervention. This linguistic awareness should be operative throughout the school day, for it is largely through language that children have adequate access to the informational and social exchanges that occur in the classroom. In this section, the view that the classroom should be an ongoing communicative context is discussed from two different but compatible perspectives: (1) the use of compensatory communicative strategies and (2) the facilitation of communication. The set of compensatory strategies concern particular language problems that may interfere with the child's access to linguistically mediated information and present specific modifications teachers can make to minimize these problems. The second series of strategies are designed to encourage communication in the classroom. These strategies have generalized use with normally developing youngsters as well as with those who have language problems.

**COMPENSATORY COMMUNICATIVE STRATEGIES**   Several modifications in the linguistic input by the teacher should facilitate the comprehension, and perhaps even foster the development, of language in children who are experiencing language difficulties. These strategies should be used continuously throughout the school day.

COMPENSATORY STRATEGY 1: MODIFICATION OF GRAMMATICAL CONSTRUCTIONS. For those youngsters who have difficulty processing complex constructions, such as structures with expanded noun phrases or embedded clauses, the teacher can simplify the sentences directed to the children to facilitate comprehension. Sentences such as the following compress quite a bit of information into them, and for some children this information compression may be too much to process.

**(1)**   *Take your coats and books and prepare to form a line at the door to go home.* (compound sentence)

**(2)**   *Find the picture of the boy who is tall, fat, and running.* (expanded noun phrase)

**(3)**   *Here is a picture of some dogs. Find the big dog that is barking in the street.* (embedded clause)

Informal feedback from the children or information derived from structured assessment tasks (see Chapter 9) should help to identify children with this problem. By simplifying sentences, reducing the amount of information contained in each sentence, the teacher should be able to increase comprehension. The following simplifications of sentences **(1)** through **(3)** should serve as examples:

**(4)**   *Gather your coats and books.* (Pause until the children do so.) *It is time to go home. Form a line at the door.*

**(5)**   *Find the picture of the boy. The boy is fat. He is tall. The boy is running.*

**(6)**   *Here is a picture of some dogs. One dog is barking and is in the street.*

Simplification of linguistic input should cover vocabulary as well as grammatical construction.

COMPENSATORY STRATEGY 2: REDUCING THE LINGUISTIC AND COGNITIVE DEMANDS. The abstract instructional code imposes linguistic and cognitive demands, which some children cannot meet and which therefore must be reduced by the teacher. This can be done by using nonverbal and contextual clues whenever possible. For example, if the teacher is conducting a lesson on baking cookies, nonverbal clues could be used to supplement the verbally based directions. First, materials to be used should be visible to all children, so that while saying *Take two and a quarter cups of flour,* the teacher can supplement this message by actually pointing to the cups of flour. In addition, each child could have a pictorially represented set of directions to follow, such as the ones presented in Figure 10-1. These sequentially ordered pictures can help the child follow the flow of the verbal directions.

COMPENSATORY STRATEGY 3: MODIFICATIONS IN THE QUALITY, RATE, AND PROCESSING TIME. For those children who have difficulty processing the frequently quick rate of connected speech, the teacher can employ several changes. Most simply, the rate of speech itself can be decreased. Second, pauses between sentences can be increased and/or lengthened. Both of these modifications result in additional processing time for those children who are in need of it. Third, judicious use of added stress, juncture, and pitch can highlight the key elements of the verbal message. This increases the segmentation of the speech flow, making critical informational units perceptually more salient.

Use of self-repetition also serves to highlight new or important information, again segmenting it from the ongoing flow of speech and allowing additional processing time. This is demonstrated in the following example:

Teacher (pointing to a triangular block): "See the block? See the . . . triangle . . . block? Here's the triangle block. It's a triangle."

In addition to utilizing self-repetition, the teacher can also expand the child's incomplete or incorrect utterances. This process of expansion appears to serve two functions. First, it confirms for the child that her intended message has been received and understood. Second, it provides the child, in an indirect fashion, with the complete or correct linguistic model. Directly correcting the child interrupts and can even interfere with communication. The following is an example of the use of expansion:

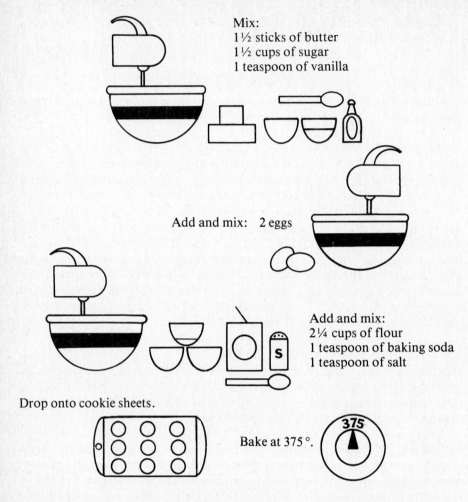

Mix:
1½ sticks of butter
1½ cups of sugar
1 teaspoon of vanilla

Add and mix:   2 eggs

Add and mix:
2¼ cups of flour
1 teaspoon of baking soda
1 teaspoon of salt

Drop onto cookie sheets.

Bake at 375°.

FIGURE 10.1   Pictorially Represented Directions for Making Cookies

Child (showing the teacher a box turtle): "Look what I brang!"
Teacher: "Look what you brought?" (stress on *brought*). "You brought in a turtle!"

The teacher can also enlarge or extend information on the topic proposed by the child, as is seen when the teacher continues the preceding interaction as follows:

Teacher: "The turtle has a hard shell to protect it. All turtles have shells."

Here the teacher does more than confirm the child's message and model the standard linguistic form. The teacher utilizes the child's communication as a basis for supplying information about a topic of apparent interest to the child.

Because the use of anaphoric pronouns causes problems for many youngsters, these pronouns making references to previously specified information should be used cautiously. This caution relates to anaphoric pronouns occurring within a sentence (e.g., *Take the apple and give it to Jon*) and especially to those used across sentence boundaries (e.g., *The spaceship went to the moon. It carried two astronauts and lots of equipment*). With some children, the teacher should completely avoid using anaphoric pronouns. For other children, the use of these pronouns needs to be supplemented with additional information. For example, repetition strategies can be used as in grouped sentences **(7)** and **(8)**.

**(7)**     *Take the apple and give it to Jon.*
         *Give the apple to Jon.*

**(8)**     *The spaceship went to the moon.*
         *It carried two astronauts and lots of equipment.*
         *In the spaceship were two astronauts and much equipment.*

In addition to repetition, references made by pronouns can be supplemented with gestural references to the specified objects. This is illustrated by sentence **(9)**

**(9)**         *Take the apple and give it* (gestures to the apple) *to Jon.*

COMPENSATORY STRATEGY 4: NONVERBAL FEATURES. Important communicative components such as posture, gestures, and facial expressions serve to supplement the linguistic symbols by decreasing ambiguity. They also add to the richness of the communicative episode by creating intimacy between the listener and speaker and by supplying affective nuances. To create a minimally ambiguous and maximally rich communicative context, the teacher should make effective use of this nonverbal dimension in the classroom.

**FACILITATION OF COMMUNICATION**   Rather than focusing on the language problems of children through the exclusive use of intervention and compensatory strategies, the teacher should recognize and encourage the communicative capabilities of youngsters. All children, even the most severely handicapped, have some system for communication, and it should be reinforced. Cazden (1972, p. 243) accurately argues that while "reinforcement seems impotent in affecting the child's learning of grammatical rules," it probably is quite effective in activating the use of these linguistic rules in communication. Therefore, what should be reinforced is not the subsidiary particulars of speech and language, but rather the child's attempts at communication.

Studying language should not be confused with using language for the purposes of informing, persuading, hypothesizing, and so on. However, it is not uncommon to find youngsters engaged in learning what a noun or an adjective is instead of using their tacit knowledge of these lexical categories to create explicit and creative descriptions of their physical, social, psychological, or fantasy worlds. Whereas metalinguistic awareness, that is, a conscious awareness of the particulars of language and speech, may have some value for learning to spell and to communicate through writing, Cazden (1972) stresses that there is no evidence that learning to be aware of one's tacit linguistic knowledge makes any difference in one's spoken language abilities.

The types of questions posed by teachers also affect the quality of communication occurring in the classroom and the types of thought processes underlying the communication. Language by its very nature is a creative process, and the question strategies employed by the teacher should recognize and capitalize on this. Questions such as the following require convergent thinking and typically result in brief, simple answers:

Question: *What do we call this?* (pointing to a rectangular block).
Required answer: *Rectangle.* (a label)

Question: *Where do we go to borrow books?*
Required answer: *To the library.* (locative)

In contrast, questions can be asked (1) that do not require one correct answer, (2) that foster divergent thinking, and (3) that typically call for more linguistically complex answers. Examples of these types of questions are as follows:

Question: *What do you think might happen next?* (showing a picture to the
    class of a child running into a busy street after a rolling ball).
Possible answers: *He'll get hit by a car.*
                  *His mother will punish him.*
                  *He'll get the ball.*

Question: *How can you tell when it's going to rain?*
Possible answers: *It gets cloudy outside.*
                  *The leaves look different.*
                  *My mother calls me to come in from playing.*

Finally, the nature of the activities presented to children also influences the type of language they use. Activities that are static in nature stimulate labeling and describing. In contrast, activities that involve the transformation of substance or any change in attributes can facilitate predicting, hypothesizing, recalling, in addition to labeling and describing current states. In developing activities to foster growth in both thinking and communication, the teacher should keep two dimensions in mind. Moffett (1968a) identified them as the *I-you* dimension and the *I-it* dimension. As children begin to develop communicative competence, the distance between the listener and speaker should be able to be increased. This *I-you* dimension has already been discussed (see p. 349). The distance between the child and the palpable environment (i.e., the *I-it* dimension) should also be able to be increased as the child develops cognitively and linguistically. If it does, the child can begin to progress from talking about the present to talking about the past and hypothesizing about or anticipating the future.

In summary, language is one of the most powerful tools available to humans. Its interpersonal, instructional, and even political capabilities are far-reaching. There is little doubt that the development of language as a communicative vehicle should be one of the principal goals in the education of all youngsters.

## INQUIRY 10.1

Modifications in linguistic input by teachers are frequently needed to compensate for the language problems of handicapped youngsters. These modifications include reducing syntactic and semantic complexity and using discourse features to facilitate language comprehension. While it is well known that parents adapt their language to accommodate to the linguistic abilities of their youngsters, it is less clear that teachers do the same.

**OBJECTIVES**   The objectives of this inquiry are to:

1. Analyze how teachers modify their linguistic input to accommodate to the linguistic abilities of their students.
2. Determine how discourse strategies are used by teachers to facilitate the comprehension of language by their students.

**PROCEDURES**   Select a student who is known to have or is suspected of having a language delay. Have the child's teacher interact with him in a dyadic situation. The context of the interaction should be a quasi–teaching situation in which the teacher is instructing the child to make something (e.g., building with an erector set). Tape-record the interaction. After the teacher-child interaction, have the teacher interact with you (teacher-adult dyad) in describing the child and giving an estimation of how he performed on the task. Tape-record this interaction.

Transcribe both interactions and analyze the two transcripts. Your analysis should include, but not necessarily be limited to, differences in the teacher's input to each of the two dyads in the following areas:

1. Mean length of utterance (syntactic complexity).
2. Type-to-token ratio (the number of *different* words used compared to total number of words used—vocabulary complexity).
3. Use of context clues.
4. Repetitions.
5. Expansions.
6. Use of anaphoric pronouns.
7. Use of questions.

**REPORT**   Include the following in your report:

1. Brief descriptions of the teacher and the child and the context in which the teacher-child interaction took place.
2. Transcripts of the two dyadic interactions.

3. Analysis of the teacher's linguistic input to the child and the adult. The following format can be used:

| Feature | Teacher-Child Frequency | (%) | Teacher-Adult Frequency | (%) |
|---|---|---|---|---|
| 1. MLU | 3.6 | | 5.2 | |
| 2. Tape-to-token ratio | .36 | | .67 | |
| 3. Repetitions | 8 | (12) | 0 | ( 0) |
| 4. Pronouns | 3 | ( 5) | 12 | (18) |

In addition, address yourself to the following questions:

1. In what ways, if any, did the teacher modify the syntactic/semantic complexity of the input to the child?
2. In what ways, if any, did the teacher utilize discourse strategies to aid the child's comprehension of linguistic input? How did this differ from the discourse features used in the teacher-adult dyad?
3. How might the classroom teaching context affect the teacher's ability to make necessary linguistic modifications? How might the teacher overcome any of the obstacles identified?

**EVALUATION**   Did this inquiry develop the specified objectives? If so, how? If not, why? How could the effectiveness of this inquiry be increased?

_____                **INQUIRY 10.2**                _____

The instructional code, that is, the language used in the classroom for instructional purposes, has been described as (1) linguistically complex, (2) group-oriented, (3) reduced in shared knowledge (familiarity), (4) abstracted from the here and now, (5) quick in rate, and (6) less prone to use listener feedback. In light of these features, it is quite possible that linguistically delayed or unready children may experience considerable difficulty in comprehending ongoing communication in the classroom.

**OBJECTIVES**   The objectives of this inquiry are to:

1. Describe the characteristics of the instructional code used in a typical classroom.
2. Analyze the linguistic and cognitive demands embedded in the instructional code.
3. Speculate on how a linguistically delayed child might have difficulty comprehending information delivered via the instructional code.

**PROCEDURES**   Observe and tape-record a lesson being presented by an elementary school teacher in a typical classroom. Transcribe the tape, noting all uses of contextual clues by the teacher. Analyze the teacher's linguistic input, taking into account the descriptive features of the instructional code given above.

**REPORT**   Include the following in your report:

1. Brief descriptions of the classroom and the lesson being presented.
2. A transcript of the lesson presented.
3. Analysis of the teacher's linguistic input, including the following:
   a. Linguistic complexity (e.g., MLU and type-to-token ratio).
   b. Group orientation and use of listener feedback (verbal and nonverbal).
   c. Rate of speech flow.
   d. Degree of use of shared knowledge.
   e. Abstraction from the present, palpable context.

In addition, address yourself to the following questions:

1. What characteristics of the instructional code were observed to be used by the teacher in presenting a lesson to the class?
2. What linguistic and cognitive demands are placed on the child by these characteristics of the teacher's linguistic input to the class?
3. How might a linguistically delayed or unready child have difficulty comprehending the information delivered via the language used by the teacher?

**EVALUATION**   Did this inquiry develop the specified objectives? If so, how? If not, why? How could the effectiveness of this inquiry be increased?

_____                     **INQUIRY 10.3**                     _____

Recent ecological studies of children's behavior have focused on the classroom as an environment that either facilitates the development of certain behaviors and/or interactions or hinders the development of specific abilities. When considering language as a potentially valuable and effective communicative ability, one should be aware of the relationship between the curricular approach to teaching and the fostering of communication. Each curricular approach makes very real assumptions, whether explicit or implicit, about the roles of the listener and speaker. In examining the relationship between curricular approach and communication, one should note the typical interactional patterns between the teacher and the child that are implicit in the various curricular approaches.

Weikart (1972) provides a conceptual model he used in examining various preschool programs for the disadvantaged. Although this model relates specifically to early childhood education programs, it is equally relevant as a framework for examining primary and secondary education programs for normal and mildly or profoundly handicapped youngsters. The following shows how some curricular approaches focus on the interaction between the teacher and the child:

|  | **Teacher initiates** | **Teacher responds** |
|---|---|---|
| **Child initiates** | Open education approach | Child-centered approach |
| **Child responds** | Academic or programmed approach | Custodial approach |

Obviously, each curricular approach implies a pattern of language usage on the part of the teacher and student. Superimposing Weikart's model onto Piaget's notions of language use in children, one could hypothesize about the various types of language whose development would be encouraged in children by these approaches. For example, the custodial approach might facilitate the increased development of egocentric speech, since (1) its classroom environment may be devoid of activities in which children collectively engage, (2) stimulating materials may be absent, or (3) in the extreme case, children may be kept isolated in cubicles. In sharp contrast, the open education approach probably encourages the increased development of both egocentric speech and of socialized speech (i.e., adapted information, criticism, questions, and answers). This can be hypothesized of this approach because both teacher and child initiate interactions, and therefore the child is encouraged to ask questions, share information, provide answers to others' questions, and verbalize judgments about personal actions and the actions of others.

Not only do these curricular approaches make implicit assumptions about the relative importance of various aspects of communication, but they also make implied assumptions about the relative importance of the roles of listener and speaker in the learning process. These implicit assumptions may have considerable effect on the development of language.

**OBJECTIVES**   The objectives of this inquiry are to:

1. Analyze a classroom structure with respect to Weikart's model of curricular approaches and its effect on language usage.
2. Suggest an alternative curricular approach that might facilitate the development of language usage in children.

**PROCEDURES**   Visit a classroom where interaction is occurring between the teacher and the children. This can be during reading, arithmetic, social sciences, or art. First, note the seating arrangement of the teacher and students (e.g., teacher is at the front of the room, and children are seated in rows). After you have observed for a while and have thus become less obtrusive, tape-record about five minutes of class interaction. While you are tape-recording, make notes of any nonverbal types of communication occurring in the classroom (e.g., gesturing among students, body contact, etc.). Transcribe the tape using the following format:

| Utterance | Teacher initiates | Child initiates | Teacher responds | Child responds |
|---|---|---|---|---|
| 1. *What day is it today class?* | Q | | | |
| 2. Entire class: *Thursday.* | | | | A |
| 3. *John, what day is it today?* | Q | | | |
| 4. John: *Thursday.* | | | | A |
| 5. Sally: *How 'bout me, teacher?* | | Q | | |
| 6. *Okay, Sally. Tell us what day it is today.* | | | D | |
| 7. Sally: *It Thursday.* | | | | A |

Code: Q = Questions; A = Answers; C = Criticism; I= Adapted information; D = Demands, commands, orders, threats; M = Motor responses (e.g., writes a word, colors a picture); O = Other responses (e.g., reads a story, spells a word).

Calculate the total number of teacher-initiated, teacher-responded, child-initiated, and child-responded incidents. Also calculate the number of times that various forms of language (i.e., answers, questions, etc.) were used by the children. Finally, roughly calculate the amounts of time children spent as listeners and as speakers.

**REPORT** Include the following in your report:

1. Transcript and analysis according to the format described above.
2. Calculations of:
   a. Types of interactional incidents.
   b. Forms of language use.
   c. Time children spent as listeners and speakers.

In addition, address yourself to the following questions:

1. How would you describe the curricular approach of the classroom you observed? Use Weikart's model in describing the classroom, as well as your own insights.
2. Analyze the language interaction between the teacher and children using the data you obtained. Take special notice of the assumptions implicitly made concerning the relative importance of various forms of language used and of the children's roles as speakers and listeners.
3. Describe an alternative curricular approach that might facilitate the development of language in children. In describing this approach, take into account seating arrangements, learning activities, context, and so on.

**EVALUATION**   Did this inquiry develop the specified objectives? If so, how? If not, why? How could the effectiveness of this inquiry be increased?

_____                **INQUIRY 10.4**                _____

Questioning is used quite frequently as a conversational and information-requesting strategy by teachers and parents. It serves several functions, including (1) providing turn-taking opportunities in conversations, (2) checking comprehension, and (3) requesting youngsters to give factual information or hypothesize about causal relations and motivations. Certain types of questions—those termed "fishing" questions—require that the child give a predetermined correct answer (e.g., *This ball is big. What is this ball?*, while pointing to a small ball). Typically, these questions require that the child observe and report, and the answers are necessarily linguistically simple (e.g., *It's small*). Other question forms require children to go beyond observing and reporting and encourage them to identify relationships, hypothesize about motives and purposes, or justify rules or social conventions.

**OBJECTIVES**   The objectives of this inquiry are to:

1. Analyze the types of questions teachers ask the youngsters in their classes.
2. Determine the quality of thinking and linguistic responses necessary to answer the questions presented.

**PROCEDURES**   Observe and tape-record a lesson being presented by a teacher in a typical classroom. Transcribe the tape, noting the type of questions proposed by the teacher and the answers given by the youngsters. Analyze the questions and responses using the following format:

| Question | *Wh-* form | Purpose of question | Response by child |
|---|---|---|---|
| 1. *Where is the big fat fish?* | *Where* | Observe and report | Child points. |
| 2. *Why is this ball of clay so heavy?* | *Why* | Causal explanation | *There is more clay in it.* |

**REPORT**   Include the following in your report:

1. Brief descriptions of the class and the lesson being presented.
2. Transcript and analysis of the questions proposed by the teacher and responses to them given by the children, using the format presented above.

In addition, address yourself to the following questions:

1. What types of questions were posed by the teacher to the children?
2. What were the purposes of these questions, and what were the responses given by the children?
3. How does the type of questioning affect the quality of thinking and linguistic responses necessary to answer?

**EVALUATION** Did this inquiry develop the specified objectives? If so, how? If not, why? How could the effectiveness of this inquiry be increased?

————————— **INQUIRY 10.5** —————————

In developing language activities or an intervention approach, one must consider the basic assumptions underlying the approach. Some of these considerations are as follows:

1. Is language directly taught, learned, or acquired?
2. Should the focus be on structure or function?
3. What should be the context of the language activities?
4. How does one arrive at the scope and sequence of a language approach?

**OBJECTIVES** The objectives of this inquiry are to:

1. Develop a series of language activities or an intervention approach that can be used to foster the development of a particular aspect of language or communication.
2. Analyze the assumptions (specified above) underlying the developed activities.

**PROCEDURES** Develop a series of language activities to be used with an individual child, a small group of children, or an entire class. In doing so, specify the following:

1. Objectives of the activities.
2. Materials needed.
3. Procedures.

If possible (this is optional), try out the activities you have developed and keep an ongoing log of the results.

**REPORT** Include the following in your report:

1. The language activities developed, including the objectives, materials, and procedures.
2. An ongoing log of your trial use of these activities (optional).

In addition, address yourself to the following questions:

1. What was the rationale used in selecting the objectives, materials, and procedures of the language activities?
2. How do your activities reflect the considerations outlined in the introduction to this inquiry?

**EVALUATION**   Did this inquiry develop the specified objectives? If so, how? If not, why? How could the effectiveness of this inquiry be increased?

# APPENDIX

# Transcripts of Children's Language and Communication

A variety of transcripts of children's language and communication appear in this appendix. These transcripts represent various levels of linguistic development, ranging from the prelinguistic period to complete linguistic competence. A variety of social contexts and communication demands are also represented in these transcripts—from highly interpersonal parent-child interactions to classroom instruction.

These transcripts can be used as data for many of the inquiries in this book; they are referenced to specific inquiries (see below) in order to facilitate such use. It must be noted, however, that no matter how accurate and precise the transcripts of language interactions are, a great deal of valuable information is lost if one does not actually observe the interaction. The conventions used to transcribe these interactions and samples of speech do not follow the International Phonetic Alphabet (IPA). In most cases, standard English orthography is used to represent speech, and intonation, stress, and pitch are not coded.

The following transcripts are included:

*Prelinguistic Communication (Inquiries 1.2, 2.1, 2.2, and 5.1)*

Transcript 1: Laura (7 months)
Transcript 2: Christopher (12 months)
Transcript 3: Anne (5½ months)

*Mother/Child Dyads (Inquiries 2.4, 3.4–3.6, 5.3, and 6.1–6.5)*

Transcript 4: Mother and Twins (Robert and Andrew, 14 months)
Transcript 5: Mother and Rachael (17 months)
Transcript 6: Mother, Father, and Sashie (20 months)
Transcript 7: Mother and Scott (30 months)
Transcript 8: Mother and Son (42 months)

*Father/Child Dyad (Inquiries 2.4, 3.4–3.6, 5.3, and 6.1–6.5)*

Transcript 9: Father and Steven (24 months)

*Object Interactions (Inquiry 3.1)*

Transcript 10: Michael (3 months)
Transcript 11: Eric (18 months)
Transcript 12: Jimmy (17 years, profoundly retarded)

*Child/Child Dyads (Inquiries 2.3 and 4.1)*

Transcript 13: Jon (5:2 years) and Ben (5:6 years)
Transcript 14: Julie (8 years) and Rachel (7 years)

*Adult/Adult Interactions (Inquiries 1.1 and 6.2)*
Transcript 15: Husband and Wife—Sandy (24 years) and Joe (25 years)
Transcript 16: Adult and a Group of Adults

*Language in the Classroom (Inquiries 10.2–10.4)*

Transcript 17: Teacher and Three-year-olds in Nursery Class
Transcript 18: Teacher and an Elementary School Class

*Dialect Variations*

Transcript 19: Regionally Based Dialect Variation (Inquiry 7.1)
Transcript 20: Ethnicity and Dialect Variation (Inquiry 7.2)
Transcript 21: Dialect Variation and Social Context (Inquiry 7.3)
Transcript 22: Dialect Variation and Social Context—Reading, Writing, and Speaking (Inquiry 7.7)

## PRELINGUISTIC COMMUNICATION

### TRANSCRIPT 1: LAURA (7 MONTHS)[1]
Laura is a seven-month-old child. She is the first child born to her parents. The setting for this inquiry is the living room and kitchen in her home. The session was taped as she interacted with her mother, father, and grandmother, but primarily her mother. The mother's reasons for some of her responses are placed in brackets, [ ], following the responses.

#### Kitchen
1. (Laura, held by her mother, gives short cry and a little squirm of her body.)
2. Mother (in soft, high-pitched tone throughout the taping session): "What? You want to get down. You want to get in your walker?" (puts Laura in her walker).
3. L: "Ah."
4. M (to husband outside storm door): "Your daughter's looking for you."

[Ah is her sound for her mother and father, and Laura was looking in the direction of the storm door.]

5. (L, in walker trying to open cabinets and touching things in kitchen that are level to her walker, whimpers.)

6. M: "What do you want? What do you want? You want to get into trouble?" [She attributed meaning to Laura's whimper because the walker is constructed in such a way that it has a little table on the front, and because of this table Laura is not able to open the cabinets even though she has a good grasp on the cabinet handle.]

7. (L touches jacket on chair.)

8. M: "Who's coat is that? Is that ah's coat? Mommy's coat?" [No real intent, just conversing with Laura.]

9. (L, after playing game of peek-a-boo with her mother, laughs.)

10. M: "Again?" [Laura seemed to enjoy the game, so interpreted her laugh as wanting to play some more.]

11. (L looks up toward door.)

12. M: "Oh, you saw Daddy, didn't you?" [Laura saw her father outside the storm door.]

13. (L, walker stuck between chair and doorway, cries and scowls.)

14. M: "Oh, what's the matter? Push, push! Come on! Push, push! That's it! Yeah! Come on! Awh! Tell Mommy. What's the matter?" [Laura cried because her walker was stuck.]

15. (L, while her mother is playing and tickling her with a stuffed monkey on her face, puts her face down on walker table and smiles with a happy look in her eyes.)

16. M: "Does that tickle? Yea! That's your monkey." [Mother took Laura's behavior as one of enjoyment.]

### Living Room

17. (L coughs then cries immediately following.)

18. M: "Awh, come on, come on. I'll get a diaper for you. Hold on, I'll be right back." [Mother's reason was that sometimes when she gets kind of fussy, you can kind of figure that that's what it is.]

19. L: "*u*" (then high pitched sound) "*u*" (laying on back while getting diaper changed and also rubbing her eye with her hand).

20. M: "Ah, someone's getting sleepy." [She usually takes an afternoon nap.] (She sits Laura up after changing her diaper.)

21. (L rubs sides of shoes back and forth several times while sitting up.)

22. M: "You want your shoes off? Let's take them off. Oh, that feels better, doesn't it?" [Mother said sometimes she feels Laura's feet get tired in those baby shoes.]

23. (L crawls near grandmother and tugs on her pant leg and looks toward her.)

24. Grandmother (grabbing Laura's hands): "Come on, stand up, Laura." (Laura grabs grandmother's hands and pulls herself up on her feet.) [She likes attention.] (Grandmother and mother were talking at the time and not attending to Laura.)

## TRANSCRIPT 2: CHRISTOPHER (12 MONTHS)[2]

1. (Christopher carries music box that is playing and walks away from Mother.)
2. Mother (points to the picture on the music box): "Look at the picture."
3. (C looks at the picture.)
4. M: "See? See the little boy."
5. (C looks and points to another part of the picture.)
6. M: "There's a boy with a sailboat."
7. (C looks away and grabs the box.)
8. M (removes C's hand and points): "Look. Look, Christopher." "Duck . . . quack, quack, quack."
9. C: "Ah! Ah!" (grabs the box and walks away).
10. M: "Okay."
11. C: "Ga . . ga."
12. M: "Come here." (shakes rattle).
13. (C turns toward M.)
14. M: "Look, Christopher." (shakes rattle).
15. (C looks at the rattle.)
16. M: "Do you want this?" (holds out the rattle to him).
17. C: "A . . da . . . uh . . . a . . . da." (turns away holding the music box).
18. M: "No? Okay."
19. (C walks away.)
20. M: "Are you going to dance?"
21. C: "Ahda."
22. M: "Ah . . dance?"
23. (C squats and places the box on the floor, then touches the picture on the box.)
24. M: "Oh look. Look at that."
25. C: "Esh."
26. M: "Yes, see the boy?"
27. C: "Ahsha."
28. M: "Yes, see."
29. (C leans his hand on the picture.)
30. M (points to the picture): "See?"
31. C: "A . . . a . . . duh." (stands the box up, then lays it down, looks away and starts to stand up).
32. M: "That's a long song, isn't it?" (begins to sing to the music).
33. (C bounces on his knees.)

34. (M continues to sing and begins to sway to the music.)
35. (C starts waving his arms.)
36. (M sways more obviously, still singing.)
37. C: "Ahda."
38. (M sings and sways, then the music stops.)
39. (C bounces.)
40. M: "Oh, music stopped . . . Want some more?"
41. C (points to the picture): "Eh."
42. M: "Dog."
43. C (waving arms): "Eh."
44. M: "Want some music?"
45. C (bending over the box): "Ah, ah . . . ye, ye."
46. M: "Ha! It stopped."
47. C (pointing to the picture): "Daheda."
48. M: "Yes . . . it stopped."
49. C: "Ashya . . . ya." (stands up). "Ka."
50. M: "Here." (gets the ball).
51. C (squats down and points to the box): "Ahdaya . . . ahyada." (holds knob of the music box).
52. M: "Want more music? Want me to turn it?" (turns on the music).
53. C (mouthing the box, then pointing to the picture): "Ahjah."
54. (M sings to the music.)
55. (C begins bouncing on his knees.)
56. (M continues to sing.)
57. (C pats the box, then stands up.)
58. M (holds out the ball to C): "Here."
59. (C turns toward M and takes the ball, mouths it while starting to walk away.)
60. M: "Want to throw mommy the ball?" (holds out her arms and physically turns C towards her). "Hey!"
61. (C throws the ball to M.)
62. M: "Yey!"
63. (C looks at the ball rolling away.)
64. M (retrieves the ball and hands it out to C): "Here ya go."
65. (C takes the ball.)

## TRANSCRIPT 3: ANNE (5½ MONTHS)[3]

Mother brings in bottle to give to Anne in her lap. Anne wiggles all over her body, and there is intense eye contact between Anne and her mother.

1. Mother: "It's all right, get so excited even when you're eating, you can't stop moving even for one minute."
2. (Anne makes loud sucking noises on the nipple, while keeping steady eye contact with her mother. She is at the same time clutching and un-

clutching her fingers, touching them together, moving her hands and feet. Her mother tries to remove bottle from A's mouth. She succeeds, but A makes a face and tries to hold on to the bottle to show that she doesn't want to give it up.)

3. M: "Okay we'll go right back to it, just sit up one minute and we'll give you a little burp." (Anne screws up face.) "Just a minute."

4. A: "*E, eh, e.*" (She becomes progressively louder and cries making high-pitched sounds. While she does this, she looks at the bottle sitting on the table.)

5. M (gives her a quick burp and gives her back the bottle): "Say, I'm starving."

6. (A sucks vigorously on the bottle with rhythmic sucks. She holds tightly to the bottle and blinks hard several times, while looking at her mother.)

7. M: "Slow down Anne."

8. A (very softly): "*Eee.*" (while continuing to suck on the bottle). (She unclutches her hands, but still touches fingers.) "*Eee.*"
(There is a bang on the next door wall.) "*Eee.*" (A looks in the direction of the noise.)

9. M: "What's that?"

10. (A lightly and briefly touches her mother's breast with her hand, as if to reassure herself that the noise is not a threat because her mother is here. As A touches her mother, M responds.) "What? Yea." (as if to reassure A that there is nothing to be concerned with. M's voice is soft and quiet when she says this.)

11. M: "All right." (takes out bottle). (The *all right* announces what she is about to do. As she takes out the bottle, A reaches towards it. Her mother rescrews the cap, as A slowly sinks down into her mother's lap.)

12. M: "I think this is dripping here." (A begins to suck on the bottle again, but this time focusing on the light on the ceiling. Her mother rubs A's toes and looks at her while she is drinking her bottle.)

13. M: "Where's this all going Anne, huh, where is this all going?"

14. A (looks at her mother): "*E*" (pause) "*E*" (softly spoken as if to answer her mother. Then she begins to wiggle.)

15. M: "Okay, all right, relax, relax." (She takes the bottle out of A's mouth.)

16. M: "Okay Anne, let's have another little burp here. Otherwise we're going to have a little problem."

17. A: "*t t E E*" (A seems to answer her mother.)

18. M: "Sit up, sit up over this way, okay?" (A plays with magazine as her mother burps her.) "Alright, just a minute."

19. A: "*E, E*"

20. M: "Where'd that all go." (A burps and says) "*E E*"

21. M: "What the matter, what's the matter?" (A's mother seems to be re-

sponding to *E* sounds as if A had indicated she was not pleased with something.)

22. A: *"E, E"* (A seems to terminate the conversation by getting in the last word and beginning to play with the magazine pages again.)
23. M: "Okay want more?" (pitch goes up on more). "Hmmm? Here we go, want more?" (She offers A the bottle.)
24. (A closes her mouth and slightly turns her head away from her mother's body.)
25. M (picks up the non-verbal clues) "No? Okay, just a minute. I'll put that there for a minute." (The bottle is put down.)

## MOTHER/CHILD DYADS

### TRANSCRIPT 4: MOTHER AND TWINS
### (ROBERT AND ANDREW, 14 MONTHS)[4]

1. (Mother talking to Robert): "How big are you Robert? How big are you? How big are you babe? Say sooooo big."
2. (Robert and Andrew both respond by lifting their hands into the air.)
3. R: "Sooooooo."
4. M: "Sooo big . . . yeah. And where's the plane, where's the plane?"
5. R (points upward out of kitchen window): "Deeee."
6. M (to observer): "He says *deeee* for D.C. whatever, because Jeffrey always says DC-8, 9, 10." (To R): "Where's the plane, where's the plane?"
7. R: "Deeeeeee."
8. M: "Deeee. Yeah. Good boy; good boy."
9. A: "Naaaa."
10. M (looks over at A and says in same intonation as his remark): "Yeah." (To R: "An where's ma-ma? Ma-má." (more loudly) "Ma-má."
11. (A bangs spoon in his high chair.)
12. M: "Ma-ma, where's ma-ma?"
13. R: "Uhn."
14. M: "And where's da-da? Da-da. Say daddy."
15. (R starts whimpering.)
16. A: "Uhn."
17. M (to R): "Make nice. Come make nice."
18. A: "Niiiiiie."
19. R: "Niiiiie." (Both boys rub their own heads, first A, then R.)
20. "Say nice."
21. R: "Niiiiiie."
22. M: "Nice." (to herself) "What else can we do?" (to R): "You wanna try something new? Oh Cheerios, Cheerios, Cheerios, Cheerios, ch, ch, ch."
23. R: "Cheeeeee."

24. (A bangs spoon.)
25. M (laughingly to A): "You're playing with your cheerios?"
26. M: "Cheerios."
27. R: "Cheeeeee." (Both boys are playing with cheerios.)
28. M: "Good boy. Good little boy."
29. A: "Ummm."
30. M (looks over at Andrew): "Oh, ummmmm. Good food, ummm. Is it ummmm? Is it ummm good?"
31. (R and A both bang spoons on their high chairs.)
32. M (to R): "Oh, you want some juice, you want some juice? Ju, ju, juice. J . . . j . . . juice, some juice, j . . j . ." (to A): "Would you like some juice, Andrew? Juice. Juice."
33. A: "Ummmm."
34. M: "Ummm? Is that um-um good?" (to R): "Say Debbie, where's Debbie? Say Deb-bie, Say Debbie."
35. R: "Mom."
36. M: "Mom? Yeah, here's mom." (points to herself). "Where's Debbie and Jeffrey, Jeffrey, Jeffrey?"
37. R (loudly): "Eh."
38. M: "Jeffrey, where's Jeff?"
39. R (in blowing motion): "Ffffff."
40. M: "Ffffff fffff fffff."
41. R: "Fffffff."
42. M (runs fingers against lips): "Wuh-wuh-wuh-wuh."
43. R (begins hitting his hand against his mouth in Indian sing-song fashion): "Ah-ah-ah-ah."
44. M: "Andrew, you too. Wuh-wuh-wih-wuh."
45. (A does the same as his brother.)
46. (R goes back to blowing *ffffff* sounds.)
47. M: (to R, pointing to utensils): "Fork, fork, plate, plate, plate."
48. (R begins to get interested in the tape recorder; then begins to cry when his mother takes his plate away from him.)
49. M: "I'll give you something else."
50. R: "Nya."
51. M: "Dry?" (picks R up from high chair). "Are you dry or are you wet?" (takes Robert into dining room to be changed). "There we go." (hands him a rattle).
52. (R makes a cooing sound.)
53. M: "Yeah, you like that? You wanna talk to Andrew? Say, Andrew."
54. (R looks at observer.)
55. M: "Is that Carol? Say, Carol."
56. R: "Uh."
57. M: "Yeah." (hands him a shoe to play with while changing his diaper

and he immediately puts it up to his mouth). "Shoe . . . shoe . . Don't eat the shoe."

58. A (from kitchen): "Da da, da ya."
59. M (powders Robert and blows the powder): "Whuuuh."
60. R (imitates M's blowing): "Whuuuuh."
61. A (from kitchen): "Ah, ah."
62. M: "Robert." (whistles). "Robert, Andrew's talking to you Robert." (She kisses R.) "Say ma, ma, ma. Where's mommy? Where's mommy?"
63. R: "Ma, ma, ma."
64. M (smiles): "Where's mommy?" (gives him a big kiss). "Ah!"
65. R (smiles widely): "Yea, yea, yea."
66. M (kisses him again): "Yea, yea, yea."
67. (R looks at observer.)
68. M (points to observer): "Carol. Carol. Say hi."
69. R: "Uh."
70. M: "Yeah. That's Jeffrey and Debbie's favorite lady." (stands R up on changing table). "Now you're dry. Say soooo big. How big are you? So big. Soooo big."
71. R (lifts hands up into the air as M says *soooo big*): "La la . . . . . eah"
72. M: "Eah, yeah. We're going to walk over to the playpen. Come on." (They walk together through the kitchen. Robert stops at the wall oven and turns on the light.)
73. M: "What's that? Light? Light?"
74. R: "Da!"
75. M: "Light. Light." (R continues to play at the oven.)
76. M: "No, come on, no. Come on, come on . . ."
77. (R starts to whimper as his mother pulls him away.)
78. M: "Come on, good boy, good boy. Come on . . . No more, no more." (They continue walking into the family room and M lifts R into the playpen. R immediately begins playing with toys. M shows him other toys and turns on the TV. Sesame Street is on.)
79. (A reaches out his arms as if to indicate that he wants to be picked up as M comes back into the kitchen.)
80. M (kisses him as she picks him up. This makes A very excited and he giggles.): "How big are you kid? How big are you Andrew? Come on, how big?"
81. A: "Aaaaaah."
82. M (smiles): "How big are you? Let me see your finger. Let me see your finger."
83. (A laughs.)
84. M (kisses him): "Nice."
85. A: "Na Na." (rubs top of his head).
86. M: "Nice, Nice, Nice." (words are drawn out and emphasized).

87. A: "Ah, ah, ah . . . . ah, ah, ah."
88. M (hides his eyes with her hands): "Peek-a-boo. Play peek-a-boo?" (in a higher voice) "Peek-a-boo."
89. (R in other room, starts playing peek-a-boo by hiding his eyes.)
90. M (takes A into dining room to be changed; while on the changing table, she says *shoe* in a playful manner, moving the shoe up to A's face as she speaks.): "Shoe, shoe."
91. (A laughs.)
92. M: "Are you wet? Soaked. You are ssssoaked." (playfully). "Soaked, soaked, soaked. Peek-a-boo! Play peek-a-boo?" (whispers quickly) "Peek-a-boo." "How big are you Andrew? How big are you? Say sooo big." (puts on powder and blows as she did with R) "Whuuuuh."
93. (A laughs excitedly at first and then starts crying.)
94. R (babbling in the playpen in response to the TV): "Ah, ah, ah."
95. M (to A): "Where's Jeffrey? . . . . Do you hear Robert? What's he saying? Can you tell me what he's saying? Hey, peek-a-boo."
96. (A laughs excitedly, then touches his socks.)
97. M: "Socks, socks. Can you say socks?" (hugs A while pulling up his overalls). "Uhn, uhn, uhn."
98. A: "Uhn, uhn, uhn . . . . . . . uhn . . . . . . . uhn, uhn."
99. M: "Uhn, uhn, uhn, uhn." (louder and with emphasis) "Uhn."
100. A: "Uhn"
101. M: "Uhn."
102. A: "Uhn." (bites his mother's neck).
103. M: "Uhn, owww, don't bite!"
104. (R shrieks excitedly from the other room.)
105. A: "Eh, eh, eh."
106. M: "Uhn, uhn, uhn . . . . . uhn! Ba, ba, ba"
107. A: "Ba, ba, ba." (bites his mother's neck again).
108. M: "Don't bite, don't bite. There we go. Now you look like a cute mensch." (M lifts his hands while standing him on the changing table, then assists him as he jumps up and down.) "Jumpee, jumpee, jumpee." (intersperses this with kisses). (A laughs excitedly.) "Yeah! Yuh, oop." (She takes him down.) "You wanna take a walk too? Come on. You've got cold hands." (M leads A by the hand as he walks.) "Here we come Robert."
109. (A cries when placed in the playpen.)
110. M (takes A out of the playpen; he then crawls up to the TV and points to the Sesame Street characters. M then takes R out of the playpen too.): "Ernie, Ernie!"
111. A: "Yuh."
112. M: "Yeah."
113. R (crawls over to the fish tank and points to the fish): "Deee." (He then begins fingering the wires.)

114. M: "No, don't touch that."
115. R: "Deeee."
116. M: "Noooo. No . . . look at the fish. Where are the fish?"
117. R: "Wah."
118. M: "Fish? Fish. Fish." (last word said in higher pitch).
119. R: "Deah" (raises pitch on second syllable as if imitating his mother).
120. M: "Fish . . . fish . . . fish."
121. (A begins babbling to the TV.)
122. M: "TV . . . . This is TV . . . TV."
123. (R now walks over to the TV and back to the fishtank.)
124. M: "Where are the fish . . . sh . . . sh . . . sh?"
125. A (to TV): "I de da."
126. M (to A): "Show. Show." (A begins hitting the screen with an open palm.) "Hi, say hi, can you say hi? (in a higher pitched voice) "Hi, hi."
127. (R comes over to the TV and begins hitting the screen like A.)
128. M: "Look, children." (holds onto their hands to stop them from hitting the screen). "Uhn, uhn, uhn, no, no, no, no, no, no."
129. (A continues to bang on the screen despite his mother's protests.)
130. M: "No, no, no, don't hit. No, don't."
131. (R moves away from the TV and starts to walk to the observer.)
132. M (to R): "Go head, go head." (to A) "No, no, no." (this is said in angrier tones).
133. A (whines and continues hitting the screen): "Uhn, uhn, uhn, no, nnno, no, no."
134. R (returns to fishtank): "Teah."
135. A: "Eeah, eeeah, eeeah."
136. M: "Here we go. Yeah."
137. A: "Yeah, yeahahah, go, da." (says this as he crawls over to the laundry basket and begins pulling clothes out).
138. M: "There you go. You're going to take everything with you?"
139. (A shrieks happily.)
140. M: "You're going to take all of Mommy's clothes out of here? I knew it. I know it!" (to observer) "Andrew's favorite thing is to mess up and Robert puts it all back." (She smiles.)
141. M (to R): "Here Robert, you clean up. Yeah, you put it all back. You put it all back for me. You put it back? You put it back for me? In. In." (M shows the boys and all three put the clothes back.)
142. R (crawls back over to the fishtank): "Teee."
143. M: "Fish . . . fish."
144. R (starts fingering wires): "Uhn, uhn, oh, no, no, no."
145. (M takes R away from the tank.)
146. A: "Eeah."
147. M: "Yeah." (Both boys crawl excitedly toward the kitchen as if in a

game. M puts both boys back in the playpen and turns up the volume on Sesame Street.)

148. (Both boys stand facing the TV with arms around each other's shoulders. Left alone in the room with just the TV, they occasionally talk back to the TV with expressions such as *ah, ya, da*. When the TV is turned off, the boys play in the playpen. R sits and looks at a cloth book and babbles to the book. A, standing above him, babbles to R.)
149. (R picks up the toy telephone, and M sees this from the kitchen.)
150. M (from kitchen): "Hi, hi, how are you?"
151. R (into receiver): "Ya, awwie." (While playing, the boys utter sounds as well as squeals. Sometimes they appear to be speaking to each other, but often they are engaged in solitary play. Every once in a while one twin will grab a toy away from his brother; the first twin will start to cry a little. Sometimes they work out their disagreement themselves, and sometimes M intervenes by separating them or by saying *make nice*.)

## TRANSCRIPT 5: MOTHER AND RACHAEL (17 MONTHS)[5]

1. Rachael: "Wa gaat?"
2. Mother: "What? You have new clothes? . . Hm?"
3. R: "Iss sat?"
4. M (softly, almost under her breath): "What's that? Where're your shoes Rachael? Where are your shoes? Wanna get your shoes? Where are your shoes, huh? . . . Are they in the other room? Wanna go look for it? Yeah. Where are your shoes?"
5. R: ". . . Iss a iss."
6. M: "Your shoes, yeah." (M goes to the next room. Next interchange is unintelligible.)
M: "There they are . . Want me to put em on? Come on. Let's put on your shoes."
7. R: "Co?"
8. M: "There."
9. R: "Co."
10. M: "What? Is it cold, hm?"
11. R: "Cos."
12. M: "Cold?"
13. R: "Cos . . . Wis sat?"
14. M: "What's what?"
15. R: "Cos. Co."
16. M: "Cold? Is that what you're saying?"
17. R: "Cos. Cos. *Cod.*"
18. M: "Cold? Is it cold, you have to put on your shoes? Yeah?"
19. R: "Uh oh." (pointing to loose Mickey Mouse decal on sneaker).
20. M: "Oh what? Uh oh . . . Who's that? Where's Mickey Mouse?" (whispering).

21. R: "Mickey."
22. M: "Yeah. Where's Mickey Mouse? There. Bring him back."
23. R: "Uh oh."
24. M: "Uh oh. Mickey Mouse is coming off." (laughs) "Hm?"
25. R: "Uh oh."
26. M: "Uh oh. Mickey Mouse is coming off" (sing-song). "There. . . . Hm?"
27. R: "Mum."
28. M: "Um hm."
29. R: "Go ousi!" (points to door).
30. M: "(Unintelligible) let Floyd out? Should we let Floyd out?" (Unintelligible exchange as door is opened to let cat out).
31. R: "Was sat. Was sat?"
32. M: "What's what? . . . It's raining out there."
33. R: "Uppie." (raises arms to be picked up).
34. M: "What? You wana look at Floyd. Uppie, uppie uppie. Uppie, uppie, uppie, uppie. There. Where's Floyd?. . . . . . . . . . . . . . Where's Floyd? . . . . . . . . . . . ."
35. R: "Was sat?"
36. M: "A picture."
37. R: "Ohh. Ohh wass." (sing-song).
38. M: "Rachael, can you see the picture?"
39. R (bangs on the window for a while): "Was sat?"
40. M: "A nail . . . nail . . ."
41. R: "Iss . . Uppie."
42. M: "Uppie Uppie with me."
43. R (yelling): "Was da."
44. M: "What?"
45. R: "Da."
46. M: "What?"
47. R: "Was dat?"
48. M: "Floyd? Outside? Oh, look how wet it is." (whispering). (M puts R down and tries to interest her in a puzzle or blocks.)
49. R (going over to the door): "Ehh?"
50. M: "No, it's raining outside, Rachael. It's raining outside."
51. R: "Iss Cod."
52. M: "It's cold. That's right. It's cold outside."
53. R: "Co."
54. M: "Cold."
55. R: "Cos."
56. M: "Yes, it's cold outside."
57. R (pointing to sweater, one which she usually wears outside): "Seter."
58. M: "Sweater, I know you have it on, but it's raining. Rachael, it's raining outside. Water. It's raining outside. It's wet. Look." (M opens the

door and they go out for a minute. R gets her hands wet. There are several unintelligible exchanges.) "See? It's raining outside. It's all wet." (M laughs at the wet hands, then closes the door.)

59. (R starts to fuss and cry.)
60. M: "No, we have to stay inside. Uh uh."
61. R: "Ehh! Ehh!"
62. M: "Rachael, it's cold and it's raining outside."
63. R: "Ousi."
64. M: "Yes, that's right. It's wet. Is your hand wet?"
65. R: "Waher."
66. M: "Yes, Water. Wet. It's wet."
67. (R looks at the water on her hands. Then she rubs her hands together.)
68. M: "Rachael, you're cleaning your hands. You're cleaning your hands. Yeah." (laughs).
69. (Rachael again begins playing *was dat?* with M and leads her back to the lock on the door. Then R again says *co* ten times while M tries to distract her by leaving the room, introducing new toys, etc. Finally, M again opens the door and R gets more water on her hands.)
70. M: "Wet. Wet. There. All done. All done. There. Well. No more. No more. Uh uh. No more. That's all. That's all."
71. R: "Was dat?"
72. M: "What's that? That's outside. No more."
73. R: "Uppie?"
74. M: "No. No more."
75. (Now M manages to get R interested in books. They read one with animal noises.)

## TRANSCRIPT 6: MOTHER, FATHER, AND SASHIE (20 MONTHS)[6]

1. Mother: "Sashie."
2. Sashie: "Hm, mm." (looking out window).
3. M: "Do you remember how to play with Shapo?" (picking up toy).
4. S: "Yesth."
5. M: "Which one do you want to put in first?"
6. S (looking towards door): "Da-dy."
7. M: "Is that Daddy coming?"
8. S: "Da-ie." (pauses to look) "Da-ie."
9. M: "Say 'Hi Daddy.' "
10. S: "Aw ite, Da-ie. Hi, Da-ie."
11. M: "Do you want Daddy to come here?"
12. S: "Ear."
13. M: "Can you tell him that?"
14. S: "C'mear."
15. Daddy: "Hi, Sash."

16. M: "Shall we play with this? Show Diane how you play with this?"
17. (S shakes head yes, then begins hitting toy on floor causing part to swing around.)
18. M: "Does that mean yes?"
19. S (continues hitting toy): "Doe wu'."
20. D: "Hey!"
21. S: "Doe-wu' " (spoken slowly). "Dwu" (spoken quickly). (He continues to bang on toy to make part go around.) "M,mm."
22. M: "Sash."
23. S: "Gog! Gog! Ga-yog!" (excitedly hitting window looking at dog outside).
24. M: "Sash."
25. S: "Huh?" (stops tapping).
26. M: "Sash, let's do this." (indicating playing with the toy).
27. S: "No."
28. M: "No?"
29. S: "Yeh."
30. M: "Well, you know what maybe we can do?"
31. S: "Huh?"
32. M: "Maybe we can go into the other room and water the plants." (pause, no response). "Would you like to do that?"
33. S: "Yeh."
34. M: "Can you tell me what you'd like to do?"
35. S: "Hyeh."
36. M: "What shall we do? Shall we get water?"
37. S: "H-yeahs."
38. M: "Can you tell me that? What should we get?" (sound of electric saw coming from outside. S goes to window to look out, begins hitting at the window).
39. M (sawing stops): "Sash" (whispered).
40. S: "Humm."
41. M: "Shall we show Diane how we water the plants?" (S does not respond but begins trying to make paper clip stay on frame of a window pane. He continues attempt for about twenty seconds of clip falling, picking it up, and trying again. Finally, success!)
42. M (clapping): "Yea."
43. D (clapping): "Hooray."
44. M: "Can you say *Hooray?*"
45. S: "Wa izis?"
46. M: "That's a tape recorder." (Sawing noise begins again.)
47. S: "Uh."
48. M: "Up?" (S looks out window.)
49. D: "Sashie."

50. S: "Buk." (putting hand on window).
51. M: "That was a bug."
52. "Did you see a bug? What were you trying to do? What did you do to the bug?"
53. S: "He et."
54. M: "That's right, you hit."
55. D: "Sashie, what can we do in there?" (pointing towards the next room).
56. S: "Huh, mum."
57. D: "Huh?"
58. S: "Mm, water."
59. D: "You want to water?"
60. S: "Yesth."
61. D: "Ok, let's do that." (S and D leave the room, enter hall.)
62. S: "Da-ie" (pointing to mat on the floor).
63. M: "That's Superman."
64. D (in hall): "That's Superman."
65. S: "Huh,h."
66. D: "That's a picture of Superman."
67. S: "Whadat?"
68. D: "That's a big house."
69. S: "Dere?"
70. D: "That's a big stick."
71. S: "Da-ie."
72. D: "Huhmm."
73. S: "Whazis?"
74. D: "That's a big giant, whoa, a, with a big stick."
75. S: "Tick."
76. D: "That's right a big stick." (D and S move to other room to water plants; M also enters same room.)
77. M: "What did you just throw down? What was that?"
78. S: "Ro, ro, rari." (runs after toy racquet just thrown).
79. M: "And what do you do with a racquet?"
80. S: "Um, hiye."
81. M: "When Daddy plays tennis, Sashie, what does he do?"
82. S: "Hi hit."
83. M: "Hit what? Sash, be careful of your fingers. No, no, no. That's not good. What does Daddy do with the racquet?" (removes child's fingers from between door and door frame).
84. S: "No, no."
85. M: "What does Daddy do with the racquet?"
86. S: "Bye." (closes door to the room).
87. M: "Bye, bye."
88. S: "Where dadie?"
89. M: "Daddy's downstairs. Where's Sasha?"

90. (S points to himself and smiles.)
91. (M laughs.)
92. S: "Where book?"
93. M: "The book is on the shelf."
94. S: "Huh?"
95. M: "The book is on the shelf. Who's coming?" (footsteps heard coming upstairs).
96. S: "Da-de. Who izit?"
97. M: "Do you want to fill it up with water?" (giving empty milk jug).
98. S: "Da-ee, da-ee."
99. D: "What?" (S leaves with father to get water from bathroom and returns to room with books.)
100. M: "What is that?"
101. S: "Book."
102. M: "How many books?"
103. S: "Here."
104. M: "How many books is this?"
105. S (leaves room to go with Daddy): "Da-dee."
106. D: "What are you doing?"
107. S: "Da-dee, cey books Momee."
108. D: "How many books did you give her?"
109. S: "Two. Water, here." (returning to room where there are plants to be watered).
110. D: "Where?"
111. S: "In'ere."
112. M: "Should Daddy put it in there?"
113. S: "Yea."
114. D: "Where?"
115. M: "On the plant?"
116. D: "Is this like in your book. There's the little boy who puts water on the plant?"
117. S: "Yea."
118. M: "And he sprinkled the ground with water."
119. D: "We'll give some to the flower." (S walks to plant as it's watered.)
120. S: "Water, mm." (walks to another plant). "Mm. Inere." (excitedly).
121. M: "Good idea, right in there."
122. D: "Where else, Sashie?"
123. S: "Da, inere." (pointing to a plant).
124. D: "Okay."
125. M: "All very good ideas."
126. D: "Where else should Daddy put water?"
127. S: "Inere." (again pointing to a plant).
128. D: "Okay."
129. S: "Here."

130. D: "Where?"
131. S: "Nere."
132. D: "Oh, in there."
133. S: "Yeah."
134. D: "Oh."
135. S: "Nere." (S just looking at a plant near him).
136. D: "Where? Oh, in there."
137. S: "Mmm, hmm."
138. D: "Oh."
139. S: "Nere." (again pointing towards a particular plant).
140. D: "Oh, we already gave that water. It has enough water. Shall we put some here?" (gesturing with his head toward another plant).
141. S: "Yeah, hyeah." (pause, walks to another plant, points). "More water."
142. M: "How about in there, Sash?" (Mother walks toward one plant.)
143. S: "Hm."
144. M: "Did that one get any?"
145. S: "Wer?"
146. M: "Should that one get some?" (pointing to plant on desk).
147. S: "Yeah, in, inere."
148. D: "In there?"
149. S: "Yeah."
150. D: "Okay."
151. S: "Mant more water."
152. D: "We'll have to get more water."
153. S (emphatically): "More water. More water in ere." (pointing to bathroom).
154. D: "Mommy will go get it with you."
155. S (from bathroom): "More water inear."
156. M: "You're right."

## TRANSCRIPT 7: MOTHER AND SCOTT (30 MONTHS)[7]

Ellen and her son Scott are the participants involved in this interaction. Scott is a thirty-month-old child who is functioning age-appropriately. The setting of this interaction is the bedroom of the researcher's home. It should be noted that Ellen, a personal friend of the researcher, appeared agitated by the taping, which resulted in a seemingly unnatural interaction (her speech was very high-pitched and fast-paced through the session).

1. Mother: "Wanna play a game?"
2. Scott: "Yeh. What's this? What's this, ma?" (picks up and looks at a cassette).
3. M: "See the flowers? Where's the flowers?"
4. S: "Here." (holds up the cassette). "This is mud. This is mud."

5. M: "Can you read that?" (refers to the label on the cassette).
6. S: "Yeh. This is mud. It is mud."
7. M: "It is mud? Can you read those letters by any chance? Do you wanna try and read those letters?"
8. S: "No. It's mud."
9. M: "What are you gonna do with the mud?"
10. S: "I . . . I . . . I . . . I . . . I canke this shovel here."
11. M: "You're gonna e . . . a . . . t it?"
12. S: "Yes." (laughs).
13. M: "Oh. I don't think you should eat mud."
14. S: "Why?"
15. M: "I don't think it tastes very good."
16. S: "You can e . . . e . . . e."
17. M: "What?"
18. S: "What's this?" (looks out the window).
19. M: "What's outside? Whose car is that outside?"
20. S: "Come-ba. But I wanna g . . . o."
21. M: "Why do you want to go home?"
22. S: "Cause Daddy's home."
23. M: "Why?"
24. (S walks over to a container of electric curlers and plays with them.)
25. M: "Do you know what those are? What are they? You didn't tell me what those are yet. Okay, bring them over to me and I'll show you what you do with them and you can tell me what they are. Okay?"
26. S (repeatedly carrying armfuls of curlers from the container to the bed): "It's a comb-brush."
27. M: "Yeh. It's like a comb or brush. But, here. Here. Can you bring me one please and I'll show you then." (holds a curler up to her hair and then drops it). "Oops!"
28. S: "You drop them!"
29. M: "They're curlers. Oh, my hair isn't long enough."
30. S: "That one's not big."
31. M: "That one's not big enough?"
32. S: "Ne."
33. M: "Which one's bigger?"
34. S (points from one curler to another—then finally to the larger one): "That one—all the big . . . coilers . . . we . . . will." (trying to replace the curlers in their case on the graduated peglike pieces).
35. M: "Give me that."
36. S: "Yeh."
37. M: "Well, now I'll show you what we do with them. Put a few of them in." (places some in).
38. S: "I can try and do it!"
39. M: "Okay."

40. S: "This one and this one and this big one."
41. M: "Here, let's see. Is it, is it the same size?"
42. S: "Yes it is."
43. M: "Oh, okay. How many do you have here?"
44. S: "T . . two."
45. M: "Two. What are you gonna do with them? Watch out for your feet. Watch."
46. S (tries to put some in and drops some): "You drop them. You drop."
47. M: "You're not supposed to drop them. You can't do it with Mommy's." (holds up curler to her hair).
48. S: "These are for all the people."
49. M: "Who?"
50. S: "Marcy."
51. M: "She does?"
52. S: "Yeh."
53. M: "I don't think Aunt Marcy wears these."
54. S: "Oh."
55. M: "Who uses them?"
56. S: "Uncle Brien."
57. M: "Uncle Brien!"
58. S: "Who uses them?"
59. M: "Well, I'll tell you."
60. S: "Oh."
61. M: "What are these called? Do you know?"
62. S: "Koo-kay . . . kooch . . ay."
63. M: "Curlers."
64. S: "Coilers."
65. M: "Now, who uses curlers?"
66. S: "Jane—Janie!"
67. M: "Jane uses curlers, that's right! Tell Andy who Janie is."
68. S: "O . . h. Happa boray."
69. M: "Janie's the babysitter. Janie's mother's birthday is April 10th. Whose else's birthday is April 10th?"
70. S: "Your borday."
71. M: "When's your birthday?"
72. S: "When *your* borday?"
73. M: "When is it?"
74: S: "When is it?"
75. M: "March 31st."
76. S: "Boom!" (pretends to hit his mother).
77. M: "When is your birthday?"
78. S: "Now . . . now I'm going to put the mud in." (goes looking for the cassette).
79. M: "Okay, but tell me when your birthday is."

80. S: "Where's the mud?"
81. M: "I don't know. What did you do with it?"
82. S: "Mud, where's the mud? That's the mud." (gets the cassette). "That's mud too." (picks up the microphone).
83. M: "I don't know what that is."
84. S: "Mud."
85. M: "I don't think so."
86. S: "Mud."
87. M: "I better check it out."

## TRANSCRIPT 8: MOTHER AND SON (42 MONTHS)[8]

The setting is a playroom in mother's place of employment. Child is playing on the floor with a Fisher-Price airport toy. Mother is sitting at a table with crayons, scissors, and paper. Observer (recorder) is in a corner of the room.

1. Mother: "Boy, that is a giant box of crayons. Wow, there are some of the big fat kind."
2. Child: "Let me see fat one. Let me see."
3. M: "See them." (shows child the box of crayons).
4. C: "Put them down here." (indicates floor beside the table). "Over here."
5. M (places crayons on floor as child has indicated): "Here's some paper. You can draw on this paper."
6. C: "No." (looks around room. Begins to play with Fisher-Price airport again.)
7. M: "What did you find in the airport?"
8. (C gives no response.)
9. M: "Are there any parts in the airport?"
10. (C gives no response.)
11. M: "Or is there nothing in it?"
12. C: "But there nothin' in it."
13. M: "There's nothin in it?"
14. M: "You know, there's scissors here, too, if you want to cut. Do you want to cut?"
15. C: "No."
16. M: "Do you want to make a puzzle?"
17. C: "No."
18. M: "No. You want to play with the airport, huh?"
19. (C gives no response.)
20. C: "Mommy, can I go get people?" (meaning parts for Fisher-Price airport toy).
21. M: "I don't know where the people are. Why don't you draw some. You could make them into dolls."
22. C: "Can I play with that little car?" (indicates toy vehicle on shelf).

23. M: "That car?" (points to vehicle on shelf). "Well, I guess we could borrow it for a few minutes." (goes to shelf and gets vehicle).
24. M: "Oh, that's a big one. I wouldn't call that a little one. You could probably sit on that one."
25. C (sits on car and pushes himself around the room): "Eeeee." (makes sound as if to imitate sound of wheels turning).
26. C: "Mommy." (looks at mother and points to car she's sitting on).
27. M: "Yes. Uh, huh. I thought you could sit on it."
28. M: "Your cape's going to get caught." (Mother rolls up cape child is wearing.)
29. C: "Now I can take the school bus . . . to go to school."
30. M: "Oh. That's going to be your school bus?"
31. C: "Uh-huh."
32. M: "Well, what else do you need to go to school?"
33. C: "Nothin else."
34. M: "Nothing else? You might need a book."
35. C: "No I didn't."
36. M: "You don't need a book for school?"
37. C: "No."
38. M: "How about your lunch?"
39. C: "I got my lunch in . . . the . . . room where you keep my lunch."
40. M: "You're right. Your lunch is in the other room where the refrigerator is."
41. M: "I think I'm going to draw something with these crayons." (picks out several crayons and a piece of paper). "Maybe I'll draw a big gorilla."
42. C: "A giant gorilla. And could you put on this?" (points to vehicle).
43. M: "What?"
44. C: "Could you put on this school bus?"
45. M: "You mean put the school bus in the picture?"
46. C: "Put the school bus."
47. M: "Well, turn it around so I can see it."
48. (C turns vehicle around.)
49. M: "You come over here and tell me if I'm doing this right."
50. C: "Kay. Make his face first."
51. M: "The gorilla?"
52. C: "Yea."
53. M: "Okay. I'll draw his face."
54. C: "Just like King Kong. Just like King Kong."
55. M: "I don't think I know how to make a gorilla." (laughs). "It'll end up looking like a teddy bear."
56. C: "Oh. That's the way should be."
57. M: "Can you make his ears? He needs his ears to hear."
58. C: "You do it."
59. (M continues drawing.)

60. C: "Not like that!"
61. M: "Well show me. How do you make a gorilla?"
62. C: "He doesn't have this." (points to a part of mother's drawing).
63. M: "He doesn't? I thought he had a big one like a teddy bear." (Mother continues drawing.)
64. C: "Ah ... ah ... What you doing? Oh no he doesn't. Like King Kong."
65. M: "What?"
66. C: "Like King Kong."
67. M: "Well that's what I'm trying to make. Does that look like King Kong?"
68. (C gives no response.)
69. M: "Does that look the way King Kong does?"
70. C: "Yea."
71. M: "It does?"
72. C: "Make him giant."
73. M: "Okay, I'll make him giant."
74. C: "Now make him outta dawls."
75. M: "Huh?"
76. C: "Doll, doll."
77. M: "Doll?"
78. C: "Yea. And cut 'em all."
79. M: "Cut him? Why?"
80. C: "So he can be like ... like have children ... make outta children."
81. M: "So he can what?"
82. C: "Made outta children."
83. M: "Are you saying children?"
84. C: "Yea. Children."
85. M: "King Kong will be made out of children?"
86. C: "Yea."
87. (M laughs.)
88. C: "Make 'em like this." (tries to fold paper). "You get one scissors."
89. M: "Oh. You want to make it into a puzzle?"
90. C: "No."
91. M: "Well what do you want to do with the scissors?"
92. C: "Well ... make ... see ... children."
93. M: "Make children with the scissors?"
94. C: "Yea."
95. M: "You mean cut out some little children?"
96. C: "Yea."
97. M: "Oh. Do you want to draw one for me?"
98. C: "Well, you do."
99. M: "Will you cut it out?"
100. C: "You cut it out!"

101. M: "No, you don't want to cut it out?"
102. C: "No."
103. M: "Okay."
104. C: "Like they show on TV."
105. M: "They show you that on TV?"
106. C: "And they go . . . like . . . this." (pulls hands apart). "They pull it."
107. M: "Oh! You mean those paper dolls?
108. C: "Yea."
109. M: "Oh. I know what you mean now. Well, we'll need a strip of paper like this." (cuts paper).
110. M: "Then we have to fold it like this." (shows child how to fold paper).
111. M: "Okay. Now. I don't know what these are going to look like. Are these going to be girls or boys?"
112. C: "Boys."
113. M: "Boys?"
114. (C laughs.)
115. M: (begins to draw paper doll): "Here's his head and arms and feet."
116. C: "And then he . . . he doesn't have eyes."
117. M: "No. We have to draw the eyes on."
118. M: "Now we need to cut him out. Here's a pair of scissors."
119. C: "That's the way should be."
120. M: "Do you want to cut? I'll help you."
121. C: "Kay."
122. M (helps child hold scissors): "We'll start here. Go around his foot."
123. C: "Why do that? You're ripping him!"
124. M: "No. I'm not ripping him."
125. C: "Yea you are. It won't be good."
126. M: "Here we go around his arm. Up around his head now."
127. (C whimpers.)
128. M: "Does this hurt your finger? Is that what's wrong?"
129. C: "No. I'm just worried about . . . you're gonna mess him up."
130. M: "Oh. Well . . . if we mess him up, we can always make more. There's a lot of paper." (continues to help child cut).
131. C: "Paper dolls are not like that."
132. M: "Okay. Do you want to open it up?"
133. C: "Yea." (opens up dolls).
134. M: "See?"
135. (C laughs.)
136. M: "See. Here he is. He's got all his brothers. Okay? There he is. There's the King Kong. Now what?"
137. (C gives no response.)
138. M: "You could draw faces on those kids. Do you want to put on their eyes?"
139. C: "No."

140. M: "They could be going around in a circle too."
141. C: "But . . . but how do you make them go round a circle? They won't go together."
142. M: "Now wait. I'll show you what I'll do." (takes scissors and cuts slits in dolls). "I'll make a slit to hook them." (hooks dolls together to form a circle).
143. C (laughs): "How they dance? They can't dance."
144. M: "Sure they can."
145. C: "Let's see."
146. M: "You know what they look like? They almost look like a little crown."
147. C: "Let me have it." (puts circle of dolls on top of his head and laughs).
148. M: "Now they're dancing on your head. Don't shake your head or they'll fall off."

## FATHER/CHILD DYAD

### TRANSCRIPT 9: FATHER AND STEVEN (24 MONTHS)[9]

The following is a transcript of a language interaction between a father and his two-year-old son in the child's playroom. The child is on his bicycle when the father enters the room.

1. Father: "What are you doing, huh?"
2. Steven: "Ih a ih boke."
3. F: "That's not broke, you have to push hard. Let me see ya go. Push the pedals. First this pedal and then the other one. Go ahead. Push hard!"
4. S: "Ooo go ga." (Steven gets off the bike and gets a ball.)
5. F: "What's that?"
6. S: "Ooo guk, ha ga."
7. F: "Wanna have a catch with this ball?" (He throws the ball to Steven.) "Whoooa!"
8. S: "Um mish."
9. F: "You missed?"
10. S: "Ooo fum . . . bah."
11. F: "Here you try it."
12. S (whines): "Uh."
13. F: "What?"
14. S: "Ooo sum mish."
15. F: "You missed? Go get the ball and we'll try it again. Okay . . . okay. Throw it over here. . . . Come on."
16. S: "Uh gah guck."
17. F: "What happened?"
18. S (trying to get the ball): "Guck."
19. F: "What is it Steven? What is it?"

20. S: "Ih bah."
21. F: "Ooohh. Here, throw it again." (Steven throws the ball.) "Do it again."
22. S: "Okay."
23. F: "Wanna try to catch it? Put your arms out. Okay now, here it comes. Be ready. Here comes the ball. Catch it."
24. S: "Uhh!"
25. F: "Almost. . . . Almost."
26. S: (looking out the window): "Uh main . . . go main? Ga go main? Kay?"
27. F: "It's raining out, that's right. And when it rains out we have to stay in and play inside."
28. S: "Oon gah! Is ih goo gah . . . ou-si?"
29. F: "That's outside."
30. S: "Da-ee?"
31. F: "Yes?"
32. S: "Bok. Bok." (pointing to his blocks).
33. F: "Okay." (dumps out blocks).
34. S: "Boo boks! Ooz a car."
35. F: "A little wooden car! Look at that! Where did this come from? Rrrrrrrrrrrr. Vroom vroom vroom vroom vroom."
36. S: "Um um um."
37. F: "Vroom vroom vroom vroom."
38. S: "Um um." (playing with blocks). "Um gah . . . tem . . . em . . . Da?" (the blocks fall down.)
39. F: "Look. What did you do?"
40. S: "Oo bok. Oo shoe bok."
41. F: "Did you hit your shoe into the block? Is that what you did? Well let's see if we can do that again. Only this time you help me build. Here's a block for you . . . a block for you and a block for Daddy."
42. S: "Ish a oon bok?"
43. F: "You put the block over there, and we'll build it high. Alright now, put this block on top of those. Ooops. Okay?"
44. "Yea."
45. "Yea, that's good. Let's build another one. Alright put another block on there." (Blocks fall.)
46. S: "Ish a oon bok?"
47. F: "What happened to the blocks? What happened?"
48. S: "Oo shoe bok."
49. F: "Hum?"
50. S: "Oo shoe bok."
51. F: "I see. Well let's try it again, Steve."
52. S: "Kay . . . oo shoe. Oo shoe . . . gah. Oo gah. Oo gah."
53. F: "What's this here?"

54. S: "Gah."
55. F: "What is it?"
56. S: "Bok."
57. F: "A block!"
58. S: "Eee"
59. F: "And what's this?"
60. S: "Oo go bok."
61. F: "A bucket? And . . ."
62. S: "Emm . . ."
63. F: "And . . ."
64. S: "Emm . . ."
65. F: "What's this?"
66. S: "A gah."
67. F: "What is it?"
68. S: "A gah."
69. F: "It's a bucket. Lemme hear ya say bucket."
70. S: "Buk-kee."
71. F: "That's right!"

## OBJECT INTERACTIONS

### TRANSCRIPT 10: MICHAEL (3 MONTHS)[10]

Michael is sitting on a lap with objects on the floor within reach.

#### First Set of Objects

*Crocheted doll*—Doll held his attention for one minute. He looked at the doll, smiled (while fixating on the face of the doll). He reached out and touched the doll slightly, appearing to be fingering the texture of the doll.

*Ball*—He just glanced at it while looking around at all of the objects. He did not try to grasp it even when it was held up to him.

*Spoon*—He glanced at the spoon on the floor with the other objects. When I picked up the spoon, he fixated on it for thirty seconds. He then reached out for it and grasped it in his hand. The spoon fell back against the side of his head. He tried to lick it, then managed to put it in his mouth just before he lost his grip, and the spoon fell to the floor.

*Box of Kleenex*—Beyond an initial glance, when the box was later brought to his attention, he fixated on the box for thirty seconds. (The box had a bright pattern on it.) He did not try to touch the box.

#### Second Set of Objects

*Plastic phone*—He just glanced at the phone when initially looking at all of the objects. (At this point, Michael began to cry. I could not quiet him even by trying to play with him with the doll. His mother came in and picked him up. His crying then changed to sounds of *unch, unch*. We then took a short break so Michael could breast-feed his dinner.)

*Doll hat*—He glanced at this when it was on the floor. I held it up, and he grasped it and put it to his mouth. It shortly fell out of his hand.

*Wash cloth*—Once again, he glanced at it. When I held it up to him, he grasped it and fingered it for a moment then put it to his mouth, sucking on it.

*Mirror*—This was the object that held Michael's attention the most and that received the most reactions. He looked down at the mirror and saw his own image and smiled. He saw my image in the mirror when I held it up for him, and he smiled again. He fixated looking in the mirror at himself, while I was still holding it, for a minute and fifteen seconds. He continually smiled, and he also made the sound *cua, cua* after he watched himself dribble. He then grasped the handle and got the mirror to his mouth, whereupon he sucked it before he lost his grip.

### Third Set of Objects

*Toothbrush*—As with the rest of the objects, he glanced at it while it was on the floor. He grasped the toothbrush when I held it up to him, and got it to his mouth where he sucked it. As before with the spoon, doll hat, wash cloth, and mirror, he could not hold onto these objects for very long. After a short time, the toothbrush fell to the floor.

*Hairbrush*—He glanced at the baby brush. When I held it up, he grasped it, and it rubbed against his hand as a result of the way he was holding it. He looked toward the brush momentarily out of the corner of his eye. Then he looked back at the mirror, laying on the floor in front of him, for thirty seconds. He then tried to put the brush in his mouth. He could no longer hold it, however, and it fell to the floor. He then put his hand in his mouth.

*Small pillow*—The pillow had a bright pattern on it and held Michael's attention for thirty seconds. When I picked it up, he opened his mouth and tried sucking on it. (I was holding it about one and a half inches from his face.)

## TRANSCRIPT II: ERIC (18 MONTHS)[11]

### First Set of Objects (ball, spoon, doll, and cup)

Eric said "boom" and threw the ball. Then he pointed to the cat that walked in, and he made lots of conversational noises. He picked up the spoon and hit it against the table and then the lamp. While still holding the spoon, he looked at the cup and asked for juice, "cu, cu." He picked up the cup to drink. While doing so, the doll fell off the table, and he said "boom." He returned his attention to the spoon and made more banging noises with it. When directed to do so, he fed the doll with the spoon and said "mm . . . mm."

### Second Set of Objects (doll, tissue, and wash cloth)

Eric put the tissue to the doll's nose (after pointing out its nose) and then to his own nose. He put the wash cloth over his face and then over the cup. His interest returned to the spoon and cup, which had been set aside. He played with the spoon in the half-emptied cup, and it fell over. He said "boom." He then played in the spilled juice. He handed me the spoon and drank juice from the cup, which had been refilled. Eric would not give any to the doll until his own thirst was satisfied. When given more juice he gave the doll some, saying "mm . . . mm."

### Third Set of Objects (hat, phone, mirror, hairbrush, and doll)

When given the hat and asked to put it on the doll, he said "na" and refused to do so. I handed him the phone, which elicited a big "ohh . . . da . . oh," but he did not play with it. He noticed the spoon off to the side, picked it up, and fed me with it. He fed himself and laughed and said "ga." He took the hairbrush and brushed his hair, saying "aah." He then brushed my hair and said "umm." When verbally directed to do so, Eric also brushed the doll's hair. He did not always use the correct side of the brush, but the function was consistently correct. He returned once more to the spoon and tried to brush his hair with it. I then handed him the mirror. He talked a little, using front consonantal sounds, while holding the mirror but did not seem to be very interested in it.

## TRANSCRIPT 12: JIMMY (17 YEARS, PROFOUNDLY RETARDED)[12]

Focusing on the movement of my hands, Jimmy looked down to the floor. His first action that related to the objects was to pick up the spoon. Out of the first four objects placed in front of him, the spoon was the only object upon which he acted independently. (The examiner did not hand the spoon directly to him.)

### First Set of Objects

*Spoon*—Jimmy put the spoon directly to his mouth. The spoon was grasped by the handle and inserted upside down in his mouth. His mouth remained open with the spoon still in it as he started to make his nasal sound. Jimmy then turned the spoon sideways in his mouth and moved it toward the front of his teeth and gums. He proceeded to bite down on the spoon as it remained in this position. (The examiner removed the spoon from his mouth to attract his attention to the box.)

*Box*—After having been shown the box, Jimmy took the box from the examiner's hands and held it with both of his. Changing the position of the box, he held it with his middle fingers, one on each side of the box's length, and started swinging the box back and forth. This action was stopped momentarily, and then Jimmy put the edge of the box to his mouth and bit the corner.

*Ball*—When Jimmy was handed the ball, he took it in his hands holding it at chest level. He threw the ball toward the teacher by pushing it forcefully away from himself with both hands.

*Doll*—The plastic doll was handed to Jimmy in an upright position with the doll's face in front of Jimmy's. He took hold of the doll by one leg and raised it to his mouth, biting on the foot. Next, he looked at the doll and when doing so became still. By this it is meant that he had no body movements or noises. Jimmy then started pulling on the doll's right leg and also attempted to move it back and forth, but with little success. Again, he put the doll's foot into his mouth and bit down.

### Second Set of Objects

*Mirror*—Although Jimmy held the mirror to his face he did not appear to look into it to see his image. He quickly put the object into his mouth and started to bite down as if teething on it.

*Doll hat*—The hat was held in front of Jimmy's face to draw his attention. He grabbed the hat by the string and swung it back and forth a couple of times. After this, the hat was swung and let go of onto the floor.

*Phone*—Jimmy picked up the phone receiver and managed to hold it by his two middle fingers and thumbs. The twirling motion with the phone receiver began and along with this, he initiated the nasal sounding noise and rocking motion. Next, Jimmy put the dial receiver to his mouth and mouthed on the object, also with his rocking movement.

*Wash cloth*—With his left hand, Jimmy swung the wash cloth back and forth and then threw it sideways to the floor.

### Third Set of Objects

*Pillow*—Jimmy picked the pillow up with both hands and immediately drew it to the right side of his face, leaning his neck to the right to rest on the pillow. His action looked as though he were hugging the pillow in the sleeping position. This lasted for only a few seconds and then he brought the pillow back in front of him. He watched the pillow as he swung it with two hands back and forth directly in front of his body.

*Toothbrush and cup of juice*—Jimmy grasped the handle of the toothbrush with his left hand and put the bristles in his mouth, keeping his mouth open. Seeing the cup, he took the toothbrush out of his mouth with his right hand and picked up the cup with his left hand and drank the juice. Meanwhile, he continued holding the toothbrush in his right hand. When he finished drinking all the juice, he handed the cup to his teacher and looked at his teacher's face. When the teacher put the empty cup on the floor, Jimmy put the toothbrush to his open mouth and began rubbing his gums with the bristles.

*Hair brush*—The examiner hit the hairbrush on the floor to draw attention to it and Jimmy picked it up and twirled it as he did the other objects (with two fingers and thumb). Seeing the cup again, he dropped the brush on the floor and picked up the cup. He looked in the cup and then handed the cup to Nick. Nick put the cup down, and Jimmy picked it up once more, this time failing to look inside but drinking from the empty cup. He then handed the examiner the cup and looked at her.

## CHILD/CHILD DYADS

### TRANSCRIPT 13: JON (5:2 YEARS) AND BEN (5:6 YEARS)[13]

The setting is a small carpeted room with a desk and chair for the recorder. Children manipulated the Fisher-Price village toy placed on the floor.

1. Jon: "Where's the baby?"
2. Ben: "He has the garage up." (cranks lift in garage to elevated position).
3. J: "Look what I'm gonna do to that man." (aiming a rubber band at toy figure of a man).
4. B: "Uh-hmm."
5. J: "Should I do dat to the man?"
6. B: "No, do it to a, do it to the other man."
7. J: "You mean like this?" (aims rubber band at a different toy figure).
8. B: "Yeh."
9. J: "Kay. Watsh. Here I go." (shoots man with rubber band).
10. J: "Where's the garage in here?"
11. B: "That's the fixing shop."
12. J: "Is this a garage? Is it?" (looks at recorder and points to the garage section of the village).
13. B: "Yes."
14. J: "See. Told ya."
15. B: "He's parkin'. He's gettin' fixed." (moves toy car and man).
16. J: "Hey! Look." (uses a high-pitched voice and points to figure of the man as he balances it on the roof).
17. B: "He has it goin', he's goin' on a trip. Kay?" (indicates man figure).
18. J: "Yeh. Sho I got a guy? Yeh. He's goin' somewhere."
19. B: "I got the 'frigerator." (picks up toy refrigerator).
20. J: "He's goin' somewhere."
21. B: "Well, he can. Kay?"
22. B: "We need this." (indicates toy car and trailer). "We need a chair, sink." (puts these toy items on the toy trailer as they are named).

23. J: "Yeh. This might fit in here." (tries to put play suitcase in the toy re-frigerator). "Ya know."
24. B: "We need this." (indicates toy table). "We need a bed too, Jonathan."
25. J: "Yeh, we do."
26. B: "Na, how will this fit in?" (tries to fit bed on the trailer with other items).
27. J: "I don't know. Dontcha know?"
28. B: "Yeh."
29. (J gives unintelligible exclamation.)
30. B: "But . . . no more fits on. Can't bring anthin' else."
31. J: "Not even a little suitcase?"
32. B: "Yeh. We can bring the suitcase."
33. B: "They'll be moving. First bring the 'frigerator. First he's bringin' the 'frigerator."
34. J: "No, still wait. It not fit on." (has difficulty putting suitcase on trailer).
35. J: "First he brings the 'frigerator." (says this quietly to himself as he takes the refrigerator off the trailer).
36. B: "Yeh."
37. J: "Yeh. An it's getting this wet." (indicates suitcase).
38. B: "An . . . and that man's helping. This man."
39. J: "Hey, look!" (high-pitched voice). "He's got a suitcase."
40. B: "But, put, he's driving back. Okay? Now put more in."
41. J: "Then we'll, then I'll put it in. Do we need any . . ."
42. B: "He's gonna drive the car back. Kay? Cause he has to carry the, the. . . . 'frigerator all the way up the steps . . into the house."
43. J: "Yeh, an he's doin' dis stuff." (indicates other toy items).
44. J: "Uhhh, look how he does it."
45. B: "Zooomm." (makes car sound as he moves car around).
46. B: "You next! You could drive and I carry the stuff up. Okay?"
47. J: "Someone need somemore that."
48. J: "Need any more? We . . ."
49. B: "Take the whole thing." (indicates toy car and trailer).
50. B: "He, he crosses the light." (pushes man across bridge). "An he ge, gets the light thing on the top."
51. J: "Here. Here's two more sings (things) and then. . . ."
52. B: "All right! I have some stuff."
53. B: "Where could the sofa go?" (says this softly as if to himself). "There. Right there." (places sofa in a room of the village).
54. J: "Where could that carrin go?" (shows B the toy baby playpen).
55. J: "Up on that roof?"
56. B: "Yeh. the baby sleeps up on the roof." (places playpen on roof).
57. (J and B both laugh.)
58. J: "The baby might fall down."
59. B: "Big deal."

## TRANSCRIPT 14: JULIE (8 YEARS) AND RACHEL (7 YEARS)[14]

The following interaction takes place in the children's second-grade classroom during an indoor recess period. They are working on a social studies project involving construction of buildings for a model community.

1. Rachel: "What are you making?"
2. Julie: "An apartment. That's good." (nodding toward R's project).
3. R: "Thank you. That's good too."
4. J: "Thank you. I didn't finish it yet. I just started."
5. R: "I'm almost finished."
6. J (struggling with her project): "I'm putting too much glue on there."
7. J (pounds paper onto the carton she is using): "There."
8. R: "Everything's sticking."
9. J (in conversational tone): "Aaagh."
10. R: "What?"
11. J: "Those lumps. Look what happened." (showing R).
12. R: "I'll fix it." (reaching over to J's box).
13. J: "That's better" (taking box from R).
14. R: "Can't do it. Yich." (struggling with carton).
15. J: "Did you finish all your *Daily News?*"
16. R: "Yeah, I'm done all my work. This is my center." (pointing to carton).
17. R: "Same with me. This is my center."
18. (Both work quietly for a few moments.)
19. J: "Know what I did to make this the exact size? I put it on; what I thought was too big, I cut it. This is my own scissors."
20. R: "Are you gonna have anything on the back?"
21. J: "What?"
22. R: "The back!"
23. J (pointing to R's project): "You should attach that to this."
24. R: "I am."
25. J: "Oooh that's good. Whataya makin'?"
26. R: "I'm making . . . making a bakery stuck to a hotel."
27. J: "I'm making an apartment. Know what I'm gonna call it?"
28. R: "What?"
29. J: "Kinger's apartment."
30. R: "I'm calling my bakery *Rustic.*"
31. J: "Rustic?"
32. R: "Rustic Bakery and the hotel, the Rustic Hotel." (Pause in conversation). "Rustic—um—Rustic Tavern burnt down, so I decided to make it the Rustic."
33. R: "Stuff—stuck together."
34. J: "It's good. You gonna make anything else after this?"

35. R: "Yeah, makin' three things."
36. J: "God!"
37. R: "Julie you know what I'm making now?"
38. J: "What?"
39. R: "Something out of an egg carton."
40. J: "Whataya makin'?"
41. R: "I dunno."
42. J: "Are you allowed to make somethin' from egg cartons?"
43. R: "Yeah. That's why they're in there. You can make anything you want."
44. J: "Teacher said not to make anymore hotels. Said there's too many hotels."
45. R: "So you're making an apartment."
46. J: "I know. I'm not making a hotel. I'm making an apartment."
47. R: "I made a hotel. I wanted to make a hotel."
48. J: "I might make a garage."
49. R (talking over J): "See what I'm making now."
50. J: "A gas station!"
51. R: "Sort of a funny gas station." (pointing to original project). "There's the door."
52. J: "I like that. . . . I really do. It's cool."
53. (Pause in conversation while R goes to get more materials for her project.)
54. J: "Look at mine now; it's really comin' out good."
55. R: "Aaagh. What's going on? I put the glue right in the middle too."
56. J: "Hurry up. It's gonna come off again."
57. R: "Where's the glue?" (pause in conversation). "I know what I'm making, Julie."
58. J: "What are you making?"
59. R: "It's really funny."
60. J: "Well tell me!"
61. R: "A movie—where you get to see movies—a cinema."
62. J: "Are those the seats?"
63. R: "Yeah. The other side is."
64. J: "I think this is the best center she ever put up."
65. R: "What?"
66. J: "The one we're doing."

## ADULT/ADULT INTERACTIONS

## TRANSCRIPT 15: HUSBAND AND WIFE—SANDY (24 YEARS) AND JOE (25 YEARS)[15]

1. Sandy: "Joe, would you like some carrots flambée?" (holding out dish of carrots).

2. Joe: "No. I don't eat that shit. Sandy, I don't like that. I didn't like it at Janis."

3. S: "You told me you liked it."

4. J: "That was to be polite. I liked the broccoli."

5. S: "Thanks for tellin' me now . . ."

6. J: "You're welcome." (sarcastically).

7. S: ". . . after I made carrots flambée all night. I slaved over it."

8. J: "Ummm. It probably took you all night to peel the carrot. Good practice. Out in El Paso they love carrots flambée."

9. S: "What do you think if I put lettuce, tonight, if I put a bed of lettuce and then put the carrots flambée and the dressing over it, instead of serving it like this?" (pointing to carrot mixture in bowl).

10. J: "Okay. Ah, well, it'll screw up the lettuce. Ha-ha-hah."

11. S: "Why? The carrots taste just like salad dressing."

12. J: "Uhch! Blech! Drek from blech! Ha-ha-hah. Burp."

13. S: "What a pain!"

14. J: "That's why you love me."

15. S: "Doin' that at the dinner table." (shakes her head from side to side).

16. J: "Sandra, I need something to eat, quickly."

17. S: "What?" (preoccupied with the newspaper).

18. J: "I said I need something to eat, quickly. Please. Don't stare at me with your little eyes like that."

19. S: "I offered you carrots flambée."

20. J: "How about some tea, some orange juice. Thank you. This lady walks into the delivery room last night. She had her kid at home. Came in just to have the afterbirth delivered. She didn't want any prenatal care. Uh, it looked like the hippyish types. The husband had a long scraggly beard and long hair, and naturally the kid died. The baby died."

21. S: "Well a lotta kids are born in cabs and born at home and . . ."

22. J: "Yeah, but, uh, most people have prenatal care. Ya know if there's gonna be a problem. This lady she never saw a doctor."

23. S: "Ya want tomato juice?"

24. J: "No."

25. S: "Uh lot of people don't believe in doctors."

26. J: "Neither did this one. She had a dead baby."

27. S: "Did she stay in the hospital after that?"

28. J: "She went right home. Maybe she did stay. I'm not sure."

29. S: "She should have stayed."

30. J: "Oh great. Isn't that criminal negligence! It's stupidity."

31. S: "Did she give any reason?"

32. J: "I guess. An this other lady told us she had a little girl . . . I don't want it! KEEP IT." (J exclaims in a loud voice.)

33. S: "What?"

34. J: "Uh, told us she gave birth to a little girl and then shouted KEEP IT! I want a boy. Work so hard to have a baby an ya don't git wha ya want."

35. S: "Do any of em have it natural?"
36. J: "Not on purpose. Huhn. They come in too late—they get one."
37. S: "It's painful, huhn?"
38. J: "No. Not if they had a lot of kids before."
39. S: "It's not painful?"
40. J: "This morning in the delivery room, the nurse delivered. While I was scrubbin' up, the baby came out."
41. S: "What did the nurse say? Was she surprised?"
42. J: "Yeah."

## TRANSCRIPT 16: ADULT AND A GROUP OF ADULTS[16]

This is a transcript of a recording made in a classroom of fourteen graduate students, all over twenty-one years of age. The main speaker is a professor (P). Students are designated by S. The professor uses the blackboard at the beginning of the tape.

1. P: "That, uh, would indicate that curriculum, from the point of view of the school (pause) must be integrated with (pause) the (pause) person's approach to learning. So you have, you have in the school, something called curriculum (writes on board) and over here you have (pause) a child's experience. (pause) This is rather an adult conclusion about what should be taught. Here, here you have something which is called (pause) real (pause) to a child."
2. P: "What's the first thing that you remember, as you were growing up? That, uh, was a constant, a real thing that happened to you, that you can hold on to and, uh, (pause) use? Could be a word, could be a location. What's the first thing you remember that, that was constant, and still remains now, as true? Something you learned when you were very young and it has not changed? It is still true, it is still real, it still has a relationship to you that is (pause) something you can use (pause) in judgment. Something you can use in comparison, something you can use in, um, um, like a differential way of thinking about people, locations, space, time, um, anything. What's the earliest thing you remember that was real to you?"
3. S: "I guess a child's first experience is its parents and usually that's the most stable and . . ."
4. P: "And that remains constant."
5. S: "Suppose . . ."
6. P: (interrupting) "You have a mother and a father."
7. S: (interrupting): "You can say, well, let's say your feelings for your family, which is something . . ."
8. P: "That's good. Got into the affective thing early, which is, uh, really a good thing. And that is still the same."
9. S: "Well, the same as—you know I'm generalizing."

10. P: "I'm saying, be specific."
11. S: "Well, let's say, uh, hopefully, uh, the emotion for the family, uh, it's different but . . ."
12. P: "So, family. I belong to a family. And I belong in a family and there's hardly any way of excluding me. Anything else that you remember, you know, like, I'd like to go prekindergarten about feelings and relationships. How many of you have older brothers and sisters? Did you ever think you're gonna catch up in age? Did you? The perception of that (pause) is something that you have to deal with. I'll give you a personal example. I thought I would get older than my older brother (pause) at some point. He's two years older and I thought, I'm, I'm gonna catch up. I know he's eight and I'm six, but when I get older than he is, which is, you know, stupid kind of thinking, but I said I'm, when I get older than he is, I'm gonna beat him up cuz he beat me up and I figured I'm gonna get bigger, better, faster, than he is. Uh, anything else from preschool years where you, you learned a concept of, um, who you were, who you . . . what's a cousin? (pause) to a four-year-old? What is a cousin?"
13. S: "A name."
14. P: "Yeh, Margie is my cousin. What is cousin? Margie. You can't really separate those two. Margie is my cousin and that's my cousin. Who is she? My cousin. What does cousin mean? Margie. You know. You really can't separate them. (pause) Going to school. What were your ideas about who you were and (pause) to whom you were related? Or your ideas about things?"

## LANGUAGE IN THE CLASSROOM

### TRANSCRIPT 17: TEACHER AND THREE-YEAR-OLDS IN NURSERY CLASS[17]

1. T: "Okay, are we ready?"
2. T: "Do you know what we are going to make over here? Hmmm. What are we going to make?"
3. L: "Playdough."
4. T: "We're going to make playdough." (Voice slowly enunciates words as if repeating and expanding what Larry has just said.)
5. T: "Anyone know what this is?" (holds up flour and puts some in a glass measuring cup).
6. A: "Yea."
7. J: "Yea."
8. T: "What is it?"
9. A: "Playdough."
10. T: "No." (still holding flour in cup). "Anybody know what this is?" (voice lilts upwardly).

11. T: "It's white, wanna smell it? What's it smell like?" (moves it around the children so that they can smell it).
12. J: "Nothing."
13. T: "Smell like anything to you?" (L shakes head no.)
14. T: "No?" (responding to L. shaking his head).
15. L: "I wanna sit over here." (As he says this, he gets up from his chair and moves to another empty chair.)
16. T: "You wanna sit there? Okay."
17. T: "Here, I'm gonna give half of this to Jon." (She measures flour from large measuring cup into a metal cup for Jon.)
18. T: "See how it makes a dusty powder." (As she pours, the dust from the flour rises.)
19. (J reaches for the glass measuring cup.)
20. T: "Not this cup. I'm gonna give it to you in a metal cup."
21. J: "Let me do it."
22. T: "Hmmm." (ignores J's demand and pours flour into metal cup for children and puts one in front of J).
23. A: "Oh, what is it?" (refers to what they are making, not to just the flour).
24. T: "Hmm?"
25. A: "What is it?"
26. T: "I'm gonna let you do it, alright?"
27. A: "Your gonna let me do it?"
28. T: "I'm gonna let *you* do it."
29. T: "I'm gonna put some in this cup for you." (puts flour in cup and hands it to A).
30. T: "Now this is called flour."
31. A: "Flour."
32. T: "Would you like some flour? Alica has flour. Did you want some flour too, Gwan?"
33. (G shakes head yes. Teacher gives some to Gwan.)
34. T: "Pour it in." (refers to pouring flour into individual mixing bowls).
35. A: "Flour and?" (Children pour flour into their mixing bowls.)
36. T: "Alright now we're going to give everybody some of this."
37. T: "Do you know what this is?"
38. T: "What is it?"
39. J: "Flour."
40. T: "No, do you know what this is? Your mommy uses it at home. Salt."
41. J: "Salt."
42. A: "Salt."
43. T: "This one's for Alica, some salt. Here's your salt."
44. T: "What are you doing Jennifer?" (J doesn't answer.) "What do you have in your hand?"
45. T: "Mix it together, Alica. With your hands." (A bit hesitant).

46. G: "Where's my salt?" (his voice rises with a touch of indignation).
47. T: "Here's your salt. We're gonna pour it right in here." (pours salt in Gwan's bowl).
48. T: "And give you some salt." (said to Jennifer).
49. J: "I want a little bit."
50. T: "You want a little bit, okay?"
51. T: "*Now* you know what we're going to put in there? We're going to shake the color."
52. T: "Would you like green or blue?"
53. T: "I want blue."
54. T: "You want blue?" (shakes it in bowl).
55. T: "You want some green, Alica?"
56. A: "Yea."
57. T: "Stand up Alica, you're so short, stand up." (said softly and kindly).
58. T: "Gwan, here's some green for you." (G. begins to mix it up as does A.)
59. T: "Good, now mix it up."
60. T: "You're gonna need some more green, Alica."
61. J: "I want more."
62. T: "Look at that. How does it feel? How does it feel?"
63. G: "I'm making a ball."
64. T: "Gwan's making a ball."
65. A: "I'm making a ball. See the ball?"
66. T: "Look how she is making a big fat ball."

## TRANSCRIPT 18: TEACHER AND AN ELEMENTARY SCHOOL CLASS[18]

1. Teacher: "I'm going on a hike."
2. Eric: "Oh, no." (a groaning interruption).
3. T: "And I'm going to climb up this big something hill."
4. Hal: "Uhh." (raising hand, straining to get teacher's attention).
5. T (points to words *craggy* and *quaggy* on the board): "This or this?"
6. (Janet and Richard raise hands. Some mumbling among students.)
7. T: "Leslie."
8. Leslie: "I—I can't pronounce the word."
9. H: "Oh, come on."
10. (Amy, Janet, and some of the boys laugh at Leslie's remarks.)
11. Richard (gives clues to Leslie): "Cr, cr . . . . ."
12. Amy (moves over next to Leslie and whispers): "Craggy."
13. L: "Craggy, craggy."
14. T: "Okay. What kind of hill is a craggy hill?"
15. (Amy whispers to Leslie.)
16. L: "Huh?" (to teacher). "Will you shut up, Amy!" (turns toward Amy).
17. T: "Well, it's bumpy. What makes it bumpy?"

18. R: "Usually, it's rrrocky."
19. T: "What is it, Richard?"
20. R: "It's rocky."
21. (Hal, in back, reads a book on the table.)
22. L (looks and points at Hal in tell-tale voice): "He's reading. Oh . . . ." (turns to talk to Amy).
23. T: "Yes, usually if it's craggy, it's usually rocky. Okay. Why didn't you say quaggy?"
24. Carl: "Uh." (groaning and turning toward Richard). "I hate that word."
25. T: "Janet."
26. R (directed toward Carl): ". . . . and then they . . . ."
27. T: "What was quaggy? Do you remember? I'll show you the picture." (shows pictures in book). "Here's a craggy hill."
28. (Amy and Leslie sitting with arms on Amy's desk whispering together.)
29. T: "What was the quaggy? What is it?"
30. E: "Not very hilly."
31. T: "Amy." (touching Amy on head)
32. A: "Rough?"
33. T: "Quaggy is rough?"
34. (Several children talking at once, Amy and Leslie still talking together. Eric, Carl, and Richard talking. Tape unclear.)
35. (Kathy apparently answers, but can't hear on tape.)
36. Janet (turning to Amy, in an annoyed voice): "Take a hike Amy!"
37. E: "Flooded."
38. T: "Good for you, Kathy. What was it?"
39. K: "Flooded."
40. J: "Flooded."          (All said more or less simultaneously.)
41. E: "Flooded."
42. T: "Remember, I talked about a quagmire. You get stuck in the quagmire. It's all oozy, thick mud. It's quaggy."
43. H (interrupting at teacher's pause in conversation): "What's oozy?"
44. T: "We don't use that word very much, but you do hear the word quagmire."
45. L (calling out, interrupting): "Mrs. Valla."
46. T: "Animals were stuck, prehistoric animals got stuck in quagmire in the tarpits, and, uh, were buried there. And that's where we find the bones."
47. L: "Mrs. Valla." (louder this time).
48. T: "Yea?"
49. L: "Do you have any kids?"
50. T: "Yea. I have four. Why?"
51. L: "Huh, I was just thinking."
52. T: "I have two boys and two girls, so I'm not prejudiced."
53. (Janet, Carl, Richard, and Eric laugh.)

54. A (to teacher): "You're lucky."
55. (Eric, Richard, and Carl laugh.)
56. L: "You should have four girls." (said simultaneously with Janet).
57. J: ". . . three sisters." (hard to hear, laughter and Leslie talking).
58. T (to Janet): "Huh? You have three sisters?"
59. (Many people talking now, tape not clear. Teacher now talking to Janet.)
60. T: "That's nice."
61. L (directed to teacher): "I have one brother, two brothers and one little sister." (Richard is also talking to Amy and Leslie at this point.)
62. J: "Oh, you have two and two in your family, too."
63. R: "I got two boys and two girls."
64. J: "I get stuck with the cat." (hard to hear, everyone is now talking).
65. T: "You get stuck with the cat?"
66. (Everyone talking now. Amy and Richard standing, talking near Richard's desk.)
67. T: "Shhh!"
68. T (pauses) "Shhh!" (some less noise).
69. T: "Are you the youngest in the family?"
70. J: "Oldest."
71. T: "How come you get stuck with the cats?"
72. (Can't hear answer. Richard talking again to Carl and others also talk.)
73. L (pointing at Amy): "She gets stuck with the dog."
74. T: "Well, families, we have animals and we have lots of people. We have to get along with them all, don't we? (To Janet) Do you like your three sisters? Do you get along with them?"
75. J: "No."
76. A (pointing at Hal): "Look what Hal's doing." (Hal's playing with books. Richard and Carl turn and talk to one another, but stop to pay attention to what Amy says.)
77. T: "Sure, everyone has problems."
78. C (annoyed tone): "Hal!"
79. R: "Hal—quit it, Hal!"
80. C (critically): "Hey, Hal."
81. (Teacher continues talking to others, can't make out words on tape.)
82. T: "Okay. Let's see about these two . . . . ." (words mumbled, points to next two words and pictures on board).
83. L (at the same time): "Hey, Hal, all you do is your classwork!"
84. T: "Sh!" (loudly, directed to Leslie and class in general). "Let's see about these two words. Then I'm going to go on and read to you about Egypt."
85. E (groans): "Uuh!"
86. T: "This is *dismal* and what's this?" (pointing to word *picturesque* on board).

87. L: "Picturesque." (Also, several children raise hands, others shout out *picturesque.* One shouts out *dismal.*)
88. T: "Good, picturesque. I stood on the hill and I looked down at the" (pauses).
89. (Almost all children raise hands, several ooh's.)
90. T: "Little picturesque village?" (teacher finishes sentence). "Everyone knows it. What is it?"
91. (Several answer at once, Kathy, Richard, Eric, and Amy.): "Picturesque."
92. T: "What kind of day would you say today is?"
93. R: "A dismal . . ."
94. E: "Dismal." (Others answer, too.)
95. T: "A dismal. I looked out on a picturesque village, but today is what?"
96. (Several children say *dismal.*)
97. T: "Because it's gray and cloudy."
98. R: "Rainy."

## DIALECT VARIATIONS

### TRANSCRIPT 19: REGIONALLY BASED DIALECT VARIATION[19]

Speaker 1 (northerner): "Jus' put it in neuhe. Theuhe isn' any couhnuhs in nis who(l)e bow'. Yea—but if you—. Well, I'm not gonna do i(t). You' goin be sorry. Are you bad? Down here i' says green giant. She brang me here first. Mines is blue. Theuhe isn't no white in this."

Speaker 2 (southerner): "Look at tha' wha' I kill' (pause)—a turkey, righ' in the hea'. The train it crash'. She um—mauhied de man. Um—she was still stauh o' de rif'e. I' was a apple on top o' this—um—doll's—poodle's hea(d). She was layin in be' an' she die(d). Da' why dey call 'er . . . . Like scauhy movie', like Dracula. Da's goo' one. Um—he le' us stay up, whi'e he go 'o be'. So they wuhe wonduhin who was doin it—dey . . . A(ll) dey could do was jus' le' 'im—le' im ge' 'um. An' you lock youuh door. They 'cor'in me?"

### TRANSCRIPT 20: ETHNICITY AND DIALECT VARIATION[20]

Speaker 1 (black): "We' gonna make some gook. 'Cause de fa(t) beas' scauhes you, right? Whi'e I' been jus' gookin' aroun', just tink o' how I' make a postuh—. . . slap dis all ovuh his face. 'Somebo'y rub' dis on 'im fuh vaseline intinsive care lotion, den he'll really have intinsive cauhe. Don't dis look like—? Dis feel like I'm smashin' up . . . . Dis like Jill' butt openin . . . Den he take' a doo doo."

Speaker 2 (white): "I know—ge's youuh hands all dirty an' . . . Why ' you sayin I'm a goof ba(ll)? My fav'ri(t)e color's blue. Green's one o' my fav'ri(t)e colors. She' gonna heauh dat on ne tape recorder. Man, nis is a big room. God—yours is red. Gi'e me a li'le piece more an' I'll give you—... If you'll gi'e me a piece, I'll give you a piece."

## TRANSCRIPT 21: DIALECT VARIATION AND SOCIAL CONTEXT[21]

Situation I (peer interaction): "Why should you be fightin fuh dem when dey' sittin back heuhe loungin? Like de—de people da(t) give you ouhduhs, dey' still sittin behind de' des'es whi'e you ' ou(t) fightin, killin people. You ha(d)—i(t) seem' like people da(t) get high, dey' ha(d) 'lot o' fun."

Situation 2 (interview): "My brothuh an' I live wi' my grandmothuh and dey live wi' my mothuh . . . . The exuhcise (is, i's) good. It doesn' seem long, you know, once you firs' get to i(t). Really, it only takes twenty minutes to get deuhe. All o' 'um auhe good—most of 'um."

## TRANSCRIPT 22: DIALECT VARIATION AND SOCIAL CONTEXT—READING, WRITING, AND SPEAKING[22]

Situation 1 (interview): "I' all depinds on how things is runnin. Nouh-feastuhn University in Boston, Massachusetts. How long ago? Hm-m. I's been so long, I' done fuhgot. I's a' righ(t). I's not too much violence ouh loud, you know. My fa(th,v)uh, he didn't go to college eithuh. Anything tha's—hol's youuh interes'."

Situation 2 (reading): "A long flowin beauhd clings to his chin, giving those who observe him a pronounce' feeling of the utmos' respec'. Fouh example, i' is exceedingly hot in Deaf Valley in southern Calfouhnia an' at the same time, the neighboring mountains have been covuhed with ice. If theuhe is little aiuh, the plane' (is, i's) col' fuh the same reason."

Situation 3 (writing): "The problems facing me after I graduate is first finding a summer job. I might have to deal with prejudice feelings. There is a lot of racial tention going around. A person can put theirselves into this same state of mind. This word has been handed down through the ages."

## NOTES

1. McCadden, M. Inquiry 2.2. Unpublished paper, Temple University, 1978. Used with the permission of the author.
2. Coren, A. S. Analysis of videotaped mother-child interaction. Unpublished paper, Temple University, 1979. Used with the permission of the author.
3. Lombardi, J. A. Mother-child interaction. Unpublished paper, Temple University, 1978. Used with the permission of the author.
4. Hirschfeld, C. Mother-twin interaction. Unpublished paper. Temple University, 1978. Used with the permission of the author.
5. Stevens, S. Mother-child interaction. Unpublished paper, Temple University, 1979. Used with the permission of the author.
6. Gallagher, D. Inquiries into child language: Inquiry 1. Unpublished paper, Temple University, 1978. Used with the permission of the author.

7. Coren, A. Analysis of videotaped mother-child interaction. Unpublished paper, Temple University, 1979. Used with the permission of the author.
8. Roberts, P. Parent-child interaction. Unpublished paper, Temple University, 1979. Used with the permission of the author.
9. Mihalisin, R. Y. Analysis of father's speech to his two-year old son. Unpublished paper, Temple University, 1978. Used with the permission of the author.
10. Zidow, S. Inquiry 3.1. Unpublished paper, Temple University, 1978.
11. Patterson, C. Inquiry 3.1. Unpublished paper, Temple University, 1979. Used with the permission of the author.
12. Chicorelli, L. Child-object interaction. Unpublished paper, Temple University, 1978. Used with the permission of the author.
13. Roberts, P. Child-child interaction. Unpublished paper, Temple University, 1979. Used with the permission of the author.
14. Patrich, L. Child-child interaction. Unpublished paper, Temple University, 1979.
15. Eisenstein, P. The adult language model. Unpublished paper, Temple University, 1976. Used with the permission of the author.
16. Fernbach, L. The adult language model. Unpublished paper, Temple University, 1976. Used with the permission of the author.
17. Lombardi, J. A. Classroom interaction. Unpublished paper, Temple University, 1978. Used with the permission of the author.
18. Wolf, B. Classroom interaction. Unpublished paper, Temple University, 1978.
19. Bryen, D. N., Hartman, C., and Tait, P.E. *Variant English: An introduction to language variation.* Columbus, Ohio: Charles E. Merrill, 1978, p. 170. Used with the permission of the publisher.
20. Ibid., p. 176. Used with the permission of the publisher.
21. Ibid., p. 188. Used with the permission of the publisher.
22. Ibid., pp. 189–90. Used with the permission of the publisher.

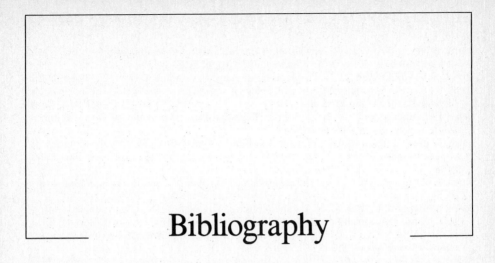

# Bibliography

Alvy, K. The development of listener adapted communications in grade-school children from different social class backgrounds. *Genetic Psychological Monographs,* 1973, *87,* 33–104.

Ames, W. S., Rosen, C. L., and Olson, A. V. The effects of non-standard dialect on the oral reading behavior of fourth grade black children. In C. Braun (ed.), *Language, reading, and the communication process.* Newark, Del.: International Reading Association, 1971.

Anderson, R. C., Reynolds, R. E., Schaller, D. L., and Goetz, E. T. Frameworks for comprehending discourse. *American Educational Research Journal,* 1977, *14,* 367–82.

Atkinson-King, K. Children's acquisition of phonological stress contrasts. Working Papers in Phonetics, No. 25. Los Angeles: UCLA, 1973.

Austin, J. *How to do things with words.* New York: Oxford University Press, 1962.

Baer, D. M., and Guess, D. Teaching productive noun phrases to severely retarded children. *American Journal of Mental Deficiency,* 1973, *77,* 498–505.

Baker, H. J., and Leland, B. *Detroit test of learning aptitudes.* Indianapolis, Ind.: Test Division of Bobbs-Merrill, 1959.

Baldie, B. J. The acquisition of the passive voice. *Journal of Child Language,* 1976, *3,* 331–48.

Baldwin, A. L., and Baldwin, C. P. The study of mother-child interaction. *American Scientist,* 1973, *182,* 714–21.

Bangs, T. *Vocabulary comprehension scale.* Austin, Tex.: Learning Concepts, 1975.

Baratz, J. C. Teaching reading in an urban Negro school system. In J. C. Baratz and R. W. Shuy (eds.), *Teaching black children to read.* Washington, D.C.: Center for Applied Linguistics, 1969*a*.

Baratz, J. C. Linguistic and cultural factors in teaching reading to ghetto children. *Elementary English,* 1969*b*, *46,* 199–203.

Baratz, J. C. Should black children learn white dialect? *American Speech and Hearing Association,* 1970, *12,* 415–17.

Barrie-Blackley, S. Six-year-old children's understanding of sentences adjoined with time adverbs. *Journal of Psycholinguistic Research,* 1973, *2,* 153–65.

Bartel, N. R. A review of the *Illinois Test of Psycholinguistic Abilities* and the *Parsons Language Sample.* Unpublished paper, Indiana University, 1967.

Bartel, N. R. Problems in language development. In D. D. Hammill and N. R. Bartel, *Children with learning and behavior problems.* Boston: Allyn & Bacon, 1975.

411

Bartel, N. R., and Axelrod, J. Nonstandard English usage and reading ability in black junior high students. *Exceptional Children,* 1973, *39,* 653–55.

Bartel, N. R., and Bryen, D. N. Problems in language development. In D. D. Hammill and N. R. Bartel, *Teaching children with learning and behavior problems,* 2nd ed. Boston: Allyn & Bacon, 1978, 262–340.

Bates, E. Language and context: Studies in the acquisition of pragmatics. Doctoral dissertation, University of Chicago, 1974.

Bates, E. Pragmatics and sociolinguistics in child language. In D. M. Morehead and A. E. Morehead (eds.), *Normal and deficient child language.* Baltimore: University Park Press, 1976a.

Bates, E. *Language and context: the acquisition of pragmatics.* New York: Academic Press, 1976b.

Bates, E., Benigni, L., Camaioni, L., and Volterra, V. Cognition and communication from 9–18 months. A correlation study. Unpublished paper, University of Colorado, 1977.

Bates, E., Camaioni, L., and Volterra, V. The acquisition of performatives prior to speech. *Merrill-Palmer Quarterly,* 1975, *21,* 205–26.

Beard, R. M. *An outline of Piaget's developmental psychology for students and teachers.* New York: Basic Books, 1969.

Bearison, D. J., and Levey, L. M. Children's comprehension of referential communication: Decoding ambiguous messages. *Child Development,* 1977, *48,* 716–20.

Bellugi-Klima, U. Language comprehension tests. In C. Lavatelli (ed.), *Language training in early childhood education.* Champaign, Ill.: University of Illinois Press, 1973.

Bereiter, C., and Engelmann, S. *Teaching disadvantaged children in preschool.* Englewood Cliffs, N.J.: Prentice-Hall, 1966.

Berko, J. The child's learning of English morphology. *Word,* 1958, *14,* 150–77.

Berry, M. F. *Language disorders of children.* Englewood Cliffs, N.J.: Prentice-Hall, 1968.

Berry, M. F., and Eisenson, J. *Speech disorders.* New York: Appleton-Century-Crofts, 1956.

Berry, M. F., and Talbott, R. *Exploratory test of grammar.* Rockford, Ill.: Author, 1966.

Berry, P., ed. *Language and communication in the mentally handicapped.* Baltimore: University Park Press, 1976.

Berry-Luterman, L., and Bar, A. The diagnostic significance of sentence repetition for language impaired children. *Journal of Speech and Hearing Disorders,* 1968, *36,* 29–39.

Bever, T. G. The cognitive basis for linguistic structures. In J. R. Hayes (ed.), *Cognition and the development of language.* New York: John Wiley & Sons, 1970, 276–352.

Birdwhistell, R. L. *Kinesics and context.* Philadelphia: University of Pennsylvania Press, 1970.

Blachowicz, C. L. Z. Semantic constructivity in children's comprehension. *Reading Research Quarterly,* 1977–1978, *13,* 188–99.

Blachowicz, C. L. Z. Factors affecting semantic constructivity in children's comprehension. *Reading Research Quarterly,* 1978–1979, *14,* 165–81.

Blank, M., Rose, S. A., and Berlin, L. J. *Preschool language assessment instrument: The language of learning in practice.* New York: Grune & Stratton, 1978.

Bloom, L. *Language development: Form and function in emerging grammars.* Cambridge, Mass.: MIT Press, 1970.

Bloom, L., *One word at a time.* The Hague: Mouton, 1973.

Bloom, L., Hood, L., and Lightbrown, P. Imitation in language development: If, when, and why. *Cognitive Psychology,* 1974, *6,* 380–420.

Bloom, L., and Lahey, M. *Language development and language disorders.* New York: John Wiley & Sons, 1978.

Bloom, L., Rocissano, L., and Hood, L. Adult-child discourse: Developmental interaction between information processing and linguistic knowledge. *Cognitive Psychology,* 1976, *8,* 521–52.

Bloomfield, L. Linguistics and reading. *Elementary English,* 1942, *19,* 125–30, 183–86.

Bloomfield, L., and Barnhart, C. L. *Let's read: A linguistic approach.* Detroit: Wayne State University Press, 1961.

Blount, B. G. Ethnography and caretaker-child interaction. In C. E. Snow and C. A. Ferguson (eds.), *Talking to Children.* London: Cambridge University Press, 1977, 297–308.

Boehm, A. E. *Boehm test of basic concepts.* New York: Psychological Corporation, 1971.

Bonvillian, J. D., and Nelson, K. E. Sign language acquisition in a mute autistic boy. *Journal of Speech and Hearing Disorders,* 1976, *41,* 339–47.

Bowerman, M. *Early syntactic development.* London: Cambridge University Press, 1973.

Brady, D. O., and Smouse, A. D. A simultaneous comparison of three methods for language training with an autistic child: An experimental single case analysis. *Journal of Austism and Childhood Schizophrenia,* 1978, *8,* 271–79.

Bransford, J. D., Barclay, J. R., and Franks, J. J. Sentence memory: A constructive versus interpretive approach. *Cognitive Psychology,* 1972, *3,* 193–209.

Bransford, J. D., and Johnson, M. K. Contextual prerequisites for understanding: Some investigations of comprehension and recall. *Journal of Verbal Learning and Verbal Behavior,* 1972, *11,* 717–27.

Bransford, J. D., and McCarrell, N. S. A sketch of a cognitive approach to comprehension: Some thoughts about understanding what it means to comprehend. In W. B. Weimer and D. S. Palermo (eds.), *Cognition and the symbolic processes.* New York: John Wiley & Sons, 1974, 189–230.

Bricker, D., Dennison, L., and Bricker, W. *Constructive-interactive adaptation approach to language.* Monograph Series, No. 1. Miami, Fla.: Mailman Center for Child Development, University of Miami, 1975.

Broen, P. A. The verbal environment of the language-learning child. Monograph No. 17. American Speech and Hearing Association, 1972.

Brown, C. *Manchild in the promised land.* New York: Macmillan, 1965.

Brown, C. The language of soul. In T. Kochman (ed.), *Rappin' and stylin' out.* Urbana, Ill.: University of Illinois Press, 1972.

Brown, R. How shall a thing be called? *Psychological Review,* 1958, *65,* 14–21.

Brown, R. The development of questions in child speech. *Journal of Verbal Learning and Verbal Behavior,* 1968, *7,* 279–90.

Brown, R. The first sentences of child and chimpanzee. In R. Brown (ed.), *Psycholinguistics.* New York: The Free Press, 1970.

Brown, R. *A first language: The early stages.* Cambridge, Mass.: Harvard University Press, 1973*a.*

Brown, R. Development of first language in the human species. *American Psychologist,* 1973*b, 28,* 97–107.

Brown, R. Introduction: The place of baby talk in the world of language. In C. Snow and C. Ferguson (eds.), *Talking to children.* London: Cambridge University Press, 1977, 1–27.

Brown, R., and Bellugi, U. Three processes in the acquisition of syntax. *Harvard Educational Review,* 1964, *34,* 133–51.

Brown, R., Cazden, C., and Bellugi-Klima, U. The child's grammar from I to III. In A. Bar-Adon and W. S. Leopold (eds.), *Child language readings.* Englewood Cliffs, N.J.: Prentice-Hall, 1971.

Bruner, J. S. The ontogenesis of speech acts. *Journal of Child Language,* 1975, *2,* 1–21.

Bryen, D. N. Speech-sound discrimination on linguistically unbiased tests. *Exceptional Children,* 1976, *42,* 195–201.

Bryen, D. N. *Project: Communication—staff training curriculum for nonvocal severely/profoundly impaired individuals.* Unpublished manuscript, Temple University, 1980.

Bryen, D. N., and Gallagher, D. The assessment of language and communication. In B.

Bracken and K. Paget (eds.), *Psychoeducational assessment of preschool and primary age children.* New York: Grune & Stratton, 1982.

Bryen, D. N., Hartman, C., and Tait, P. E. *Variant English: An introduction to language variation.* Columbus, Ohio: Charles E. Merrill, 1978.

Buchanan, C. D. A programmed introduction to linquistics. Lexington, Mass.: D. C. Heath, 1963.

Buckhalt, J. A., Rutherford, R. G., and Goldberg, K. E. Verbal and nonverbal interactions of mothers with their Down's syndrome and nonretarded infants. *American Journal of Mental Deficiency,* 1978, *82,* 337–43.

Cairns, H. S., and Hsu, J. R. Who, why, when and how: A developmental study. *Journal of Child Language,* 1978, *5,* 477–88.

Capuzzi, L. Cognition and communication in the severe and profoundly impaired. Unpublished doctoral dissertation, Temple University, 1978.

Carr, E. G., Binkoff, J. A., Kologinsky, E., and Eddy, M. Acquisition of sign language by autistic children. *Journal of Applied Behavior Analysis,* 1978, *11,* 489–501.

Carrow, E. *Test for auditory comprehension of language.* Austin, Tex.: Learning Concepts, 1973.

Carrow-Woolfolk, E. *Carrow elicited language inventory.* Austin, Tex.: Learning Concepts, 1974.

Caselli, R. Keys to standard English. *The Elementary School Journal,* 1970, *71,* 86–89.

Casey, L. D. Development of communicative behavior in autistic children: A parent program using manual signs. *Journal of Autism and Childhood Schizophrenia,* 1978, *8,* 45–59.

Cazden, C. B. *Child language and education.* New York: Holt, Rinehart & Winston, 1972.

Cazden, C., John, V., and Hymes, D., eds. *Functions of language in the classroom.* New York: Teachers College Press, 1972.

Chafe, W. L. *Meaning and the structure of language.* Chicago: University of Chicago Press, 1970.

Chappell, G. E., and Johnson, G. A. Evaluation of cognitive behavior in the young nonverbal child. *Language, Speech and Hearing Services in Schools,* 1976, *1,* 17–24.

Chipman, H., and deDardel, C. Developmental study of the comprehension and production of the pronoun "it." *Journal of Psycholinguistic Research,* 1974, *3,* 91–100.

Chomsky, C. S. *The acquisition of syntax in children from 5 to 10.* Cambridge, Mass.: MIT Press, 1969.

Chomsky, C. S. Reading, writing and phonology. *Harvard Educational Review,* 1970, *40,* 287–309.

Chomsky, N. *Syntactic structures.* The Hague: Mouton, 1957.

Chomsky, N. A review of Skinner's *Verbal Behavior. Language,* 1959, *35,* 26–58.

Chomsky, N. *Aspects of the theory of syntax.* Cambridge, Mass.: MIT Press, 1965.

Chomsky, N. *Language and mind,* enlarged ed. New York: Harcourt Brace Jovanovich, 1972.

Chomsky, N., and Halle, M. *The sound pattern of English.* New York: Harper & Row, 1968.

Chubrich, R. E. Comments on "Analysis of a father's speech to his language learning child." *Journal of Speech and Hearing Disorders,* 1975, *40,* 545–46.

Clark, C. R., Moores, D. F., and Woodcock, R. W. *Minnesota early language development sequence.* Minneapolis, Minn.: University of Minnesota Research, Development and Demonstration Center in Education of Handicapped Children, 1975.

Clark, E. V. On the acquisition of the meaning of "before" and "after." *Journal of Verbal Learning and Verbal Behavior,* 1971, *10,* 266–75.

Clark, E. V. What's in a word? In T. E. Moore (ed.), *Cognitive development and the acquisition of language.* New York: Academic Press, 1973.

Clark, H. H., and Clark, E. V. *Psychology and language: An introduction to psycholinguistics.* New York: Harcourt Brace Jovanovich, 1977.

Condon, W. S., and Sander, L. W. Neonate movement is synchronized with adult speech: Interactional participation and language acquisition. *Science,* 1974, *183,* 99–101.

Conn, P., and Richardson, M. Approaches to the analysis of teacher language in the ESN (S) classroom. In P. Berry (ed.), *Language and communication in the mentally handicapped.* Baltimore: University Park Press, 1976, 129–41.

Cook, M. Gaze and mutual gaze in social encounters. *American Scientist,* 1977, *65,* 328–33.

Corrigan, R. Language development as related to stage 6 object permanence development. *Journal of Child Language,* 1978, *5,* 173–89.

Crabtree, M. *Houston test of language development.* Houston, Tex.: Houston Press, 1963.

Creaghead, N. A. Speech and language performance. Unpublished paper, 1979.

Cross, T. Mother's speech adjustments: The contributions of selected variables. In C. Snow and C. Ferguson (eds.), *Talking to children.* London: Cambridge University Press, 1977, 151–87.

Dale, P. S. *Language development: Structure and function.* Hinsdale, Ill.: Dryden Press, 1972.

Dale, P. S. *Language development: Structure and function.* New York: Holt, Rinehart & Winston, 1976.

Davitz, J. R. *The language of emotion.* New York: Academic Press, 1969.

Deese, J. *Psycholinguistics.* Boston: Allyn & Bacon, 1970.

DeRenzi, E., and Vignolo, L. A. The token test: A sensitive test to detect receptive disturbances in aphasia. *Brain,* 1962, *85,* 665–78.

Dillard, J. L. *Black English: Its history and usage in the United States.* New York: Random House, 1972.

Dittman, A. T. Developmental factors in conversational behavior. *Journal of Communications,* 1972, *22,* 404–23.

Dore, J. Holophrases, speech acts, and language universals. *Journal of Child Language,* 1975, *2,* 21–40.

Downing, J. *Comparative reading.* New York: Macmillan, 1973.

Dunn, L. M. *Peabody picture vocabulary test.* Minneapolis: American Guidance Services, 1959.

Dunn, L., and Smith, J. O. *Peabody language development kits.* Circle Pines, Minn.: American Guidance Services, 1966.

Durkin, D. *Phonics, linguistics and reading.* New York: Teachers College Press, 1972.

Edgerton, W. F. Ideograms in English writing. *Language,* 1941, *17,* 149.

Edmonds, M. H. New directions in theories of language acquisition. *Harvard Educational Review,* 1976, *46,* 175–98.

Edwards, M. L. Perception and production in child phonology: The testing of four hypotheses. *Journal of Child Language,* 1974, *1,* 205–19.

Eibl-Eibesfeldt, I. Similarities and differences between cultures in expressive movements. In R. A. Hinde (ed.), *Nonverbal communication.* London: Cambridge University Press, 1972.

Eimas, P. D., Sigueland, E. R., Jusczyk, P., and Vigorito, J. Speech perception in infants. *Science,* 1971, *171,* 303–306.

Eisenberg, R. B. Auditory behavior in the human neonate: Functional properties of sound and their ontogenetic implications. *International Audiology,* 1969, *8,* 34–45.

Elasser, N., and John-Steiner, V. P. An interactionist approach to advancing literacy. *Harvard Educational Review,* 1977, *47,* 355–69.

Elder, P. S., and Bergman, J. S. Visual symbol communication instruction with nonverbal, multiply handicapped individuals. *Mental Retardation,* 1978, *16,* 107–12.

Elkonin, D. B. U.S.S.R. In J. Downing (ed.), *Comparative reading.* New York: Macmillan, 1973.

Engelmann, S., and Osborn, J. *Distar language.* Chicago: Science Research Associates, 1970.

Engler, L., Hannah, E., and Longhurst, T. Linguistic analysis of speech samples: A practical guide for clinicians. *Journal of Speech and Hearing Disorders,* 1973, *38,* 192–204.

Ervin-Tripp, S. Discourse agreement: How children answer questions. In Hayes (ed.), *Cognition and the development of language.* New York: John Wiley & Sons, 1970.

Falk, J. S. *Linguistics and language.* Lexington, Mass.: Xerox College Publishing, 1973.

Fasold, R. W. *Tense marking in black English: A linguistic and social analysis.* Washington, D.C.: Center for Applied Linguistics, 1972.

Fasold, R. W., and Shuy, R. W., eds. *Teaching standard English in the inner city.* Washington, D.C.: Center for Applied Linguistics, 1970.

Fasold, R. W. and Wolfram, W. Some linguistic features of Negro dialect. In R. W. Fasold and R. W. Shuy (eds.), *Teaching standard English in the inner city.* Washington, D.C.: Center for Applied Linguistics, 1970, 41–86.

Featherman, J. Assessment of educational characteristics of severely and profoundly impaired school-age children. Unpublished doctoral dissertation, Temple University, 1974.

Ferguson, C. A. Baby talk as a simplified register. In C. Snow and C. A. Ferguson (eds.), *Talking to children.* London: Cambridge University Press, 1977, 209–35.

Fillmore, C. The case for case. In E. Bach and R. Harms (eds.), *Universals in linguistic theory.* New York: Holt, Rinehart & Winston, 1968.

Fokes, J. *Fokes sentence builder kit.* Boston: Teaching Resources, 1975.

Ford, J., Lewis, S., Hicks, S., Williams, D., Hoover, M. R., and Politzer, R. Report on the working conference on the SCRDT black English tests for teachers. Occasional Paper No. 15. Stanford University Center for Research and Development in Teaching, 1976.

Ford, W., and Olson, D. The elaboration of the noun phrase in children's description of objects. *Journal of Experimental Child Psychology,* 1975, *19,* 371–82.

Foster, H. L. *Ribbin' jivin' and playin' the dozens.* Cambridge, Mass.: Ballinger, 1974.

Foster, R., Giddan, J. J., and Stark, J. *Assessment of children's language comprehension test.* Palo Alto, Calif.: Consulting Psychologists Press, 1973.

Foster, R., Giddan, J. J., and Stark, J. *Visually cued language cards.* Palo Alto, Calif.: Consulting Psychologists Press, 1975.

Fouts, R. Acquisition and testing of gestural signs in four young chimpanzees. *Science,* 1973, *182,* 978–80.

Fouts, R. Transfer of signed responses in American Sign Language from English vocal stimuli to physical object stimuli by a chimpanzee. *Learning and Motivation,* 1976, *1,* 458–75.

Francis, W. N. *The structure of American English.* New York: The Ronald Press, 1958.

Fraser, C., Bellugi, U., and Brown, R. Control of grammar in imitation, comprehension and production. *Journal of Verbal Learning and Verbal Behavior,* 1963, *2,* 121–35.

Fristoe, M., and Lloyd, L. L. Manual communication for the retarded and others with severe communication impairment: A resource list. *Mental Retardation,* 1977, *15,* 18–21.

Fristoe, M., and Lloyd, L. L. A survey of the use of non-speech systems with the severely communication impaired. *Mental Retardation,* 1978, *16,* 99–103.

Gardner, B. T., and Gardner, L. A. Teaching signs to a chimpanzee. *Science,* 1969, *165,* 664–72.

Gardner, B. T., and Gardner, L. A. Two way communication with a chimpanzee. In A. Schrier and F. Stollnitz (eds.), *Behavior of nonhuman primates,* vol. 4. New York: Academic Press, 1971.

Gardner, B. T., and Gardner, L. A. Early signs of language in child and chimpanzee. *Science,* 1975, *187,* 752–54.

Garnica, O. K. Some prosodic and paralinguistic features of speech to young children. In C. Snow and C. Ferguson (eds.), *Talking to children.* London: Cambridge University Press, 1977, 63–88.

Garvey, C. Requests and responses in children's speech. *Journal of Child Language,* 1975, *2,* 41–63.

Gerber, A., and Bryen, D. N. *Language and learning disabilities.* Baltimore: University Park Press, 1981.

Gerber, A., and Goll, P. Clinical diagnostic report. Unpublished paper, Temple University Speech and Hearing Center, 1978.

Giattino, J., and Hogan, J. G. Analysis of father's speech to his language-learning child. *Journal of Speech and Hearing Disorders,* 1975, *40,* 524–37.

Gibson, E. J., and Levin, H. *The psychology of reading.* Cambridge, Mass.: MIT Press, 1975.

Ginsburg, H., and Opper, S. *Piaget's theory of intellectual development.* Englewood Cliffs, N.J.: Prentice-Hall, 1969.

Gladney, M. R. A model for teaching standard English to nonstandard English speakers. *Elementary English,* 1968, *45,* 758–62.

Gleason, J. B. Fathers and other strangers: Men's speech to young children. Georgetown University 26th Round Table on Languages and Linguistics. Washington, D.C.: Georgetown University, 1975, 289–97.

Gleason, J. B. Some notes on feedback. In C. Snow and C. Ferguson (eds.), *Talking to children.* London: Cambridge University Press, 1977, 199–205.

Glucksberg, S., and Krauss, R. M. What do people say after they have learned how to talk? Studies of the development of referential communication. *Merrill-Palmer Quarterly,* 1967, *13,* 309–16.

Goldman, R., and Fristoe, M. *Goldman-Fristoe tests of articulation.* Circle Pines, Minn.: American Guidance Services, 1969.

Gonzales, A. *The blackborder: Gullah' stories of the Carolina coast.* South Carolina: The State Company, 1922. Cited by S. S. Baratz and J. C. Baratz in Early childhood intervention: The social science base of racism, *Harvard Educational Review,* 1970, *40,* 29–50.

Goodman, K. S. *Study of children's behavior while reading orally.* Final report, Project No. S425, Contract #OE-6-10-136. Washington, D.C.: U.S. Office of Education, 1968.

Goodman, K. S. Analysis of oral reading miscues: Applied psycholinguistics. *Reading Research Quarterly,* 1969, *5,* 9–30.

Goodman, K. S., and Goodman, Y. M. Learning about psycholinguistic processes by analyzing oral reading. *Harvard Educational Review,* 1977, *47,* 317–33.

Goodman, L., Wilson, P. S., and Bornstein, H. Results of a national survey of sign language programs in special education. *Mental Retardation,* 1978, *16,* 104–106.

Gordon, D., and Lakoff, G. Conversational postulates. In *Papers from the Seventh Regional Meeting of the Chicago Linguistic Society.* Chicago: University of Chicago, 1971.

Gray, B. B., and Ryan, B. P. *Monterey language program (programmed conditioning for language).* Palo Alto, Calif.: Monterey Learning Systems, 1972.

Greenfield, P., Smith, J., and Laufer, B. Communication and the beginnings of language. Unpublished paper, Harvard University, 1972.

Grice, H. P. The logic of conversation. Unpublished paper, University of California at Berkeley, 1968.

Grimes, J. *The thread of discourse.* The Hague: Mouton, 1975.

Gruber, J. S. Topicalization in child language. *Foundations of Language,* 1967, *3,* 37–65.

Hall, E. T. Provemico. *Current Anthropology,* 1968, *9,* 83–95, 106–108.

Hall, R. W. A muddle of models: The radicalization of American English. *English Journal,* 1972, *61,* 705–10.

Halliday, M. A. K. *Learning how to mean—Explorations in the development of language.* London: Edward Arnold, 1975.

Halliday, M. A. K. *Explorations in the functions of language.* New York: Elsevier, 1977.

Halliday, M. A. K., and Hasan, R. *Cohesion in English.* London: Longmans, 1976.

Harris, R. Children's comprehension of complex sentences. *Journal of Experimental Child Psychology,* 1975, *19,* 420–33.

Harris, T. L. The language spectrum: Using total communication with the severely handicapped. *Education and Training of the Mentally Retarded,* 1978, *16,* 85–89.

Hart, B., and Rogers-Warren, A. A milieu approach to teaching language. In R. Schiefelbusch (ed.), *Language intervention strategies.* Baltimore: University Park Press, 1978, 194–235.

Hatten, J., Goman, T., and Lent, C. *Emerging language.* Westlake Village, Calif.: The Learning Business, 1973.

Hayhurst, H. Some errors of young children in producing passive sentences. *Journal of Verbal Learning and Verbal Behavior,* 1967, *6,* 634–39.

Hilgard, E. R., and Bower, G. H. *Theories of learning.* Englewood Cliffs, N.J.: Prentice-Hall, 1975.

Hockett, C. F. *A course in modern linguistics.* New York: Macmillan, 1958.

Holland, A. L. Language therapy for children: Some thoughts on context and content. *Journal of Speech and Hearing Disorders,* 1975, *40,* 514–23.

Hooper, P. P., and Powell, E. R. Note on oral comprehension in standard and nonstandard English. *Perceptual and Motor Skills,* 1971, *33,* 34.

Hoover, M. E. R. *Appropriate use of black English by black children as rated by parents* (Technical Report No. 46). Stanford, Calif.: Stanford Center for Research and Development in Teaching, 1975.

Hopmann, M. R., and Maratsos, M. R. A developmental study of factivity and negation in complex syntax. *Journal of Child Language,* 1978, *5,* 295–309.

Horner, V. M., and Gussow, J. D. John and Mary: A pilot study in linguistic ecology. In C. B. Cazden, V. P. John, and D. H. Hymes (eds.), *Functions of language in the classroom.* New York: Teachers College Press, 1972, 155–94.

Huey, E. B. *The psychology and pedagogy of reading.* Cambridge, Mass.: MIT Press, 1968.

Hume, A. *Of the orthographie and congruitie of the Britain tongue.* Edited with an introduction by H. B. Wheatley. London: EETS publication No. 5, 1865.

Huttenlocher, J. The origins of language comprehension. In R. L. Solso (ed.), *Theories in cognitive psychology.* New York: John Wiley & Sons, 1974.

Hymes, D. Competence and performance in linguistic theory. In R. Huxley and E. Ingram (eds.), *Language acquisition: Models and methods.* New York: Academic Press, 1971.

Hymes, D. Ways of speaking. In R. Bauman and J. Sherzer (eds.) *Explorations in the ethnography of speaking.* London: Cambridge University Press, 1974.

Ingram, D. Phonological rules in young children. *Journal of Child Language,* 1974, *1,* 49–64.

Ingram, D. Sensorimotor intelligence and language development. In A. Lock (ed.), *Action, gesture and symbol: The emergence of language.* New York: Academic Press, 1976*a.*

Ingram, D. Current issues in child phonology. In D. M. Morehead and A. E. Morehead (eds.), *Normal and deficient child language.* Baltimore: University Park Press, 1976*b.*

*An introduction to manual English.* Vancouver, Wash.: Washington State School for the Deaf, 1972.

Irwin, O. C. Infant speech: Equations for consonant-vowel ratios. *Journal of Speech and Hearing Disorders,* 1946, *11,* 177–80.

Irwin, O. C. Infant speech: Consonant sounds according to place of articulation. *Journal of Speech and Hearing Disorders,* 1947, *12,* 397–401.

Irwin, O. C. Infant speech: Development of vowel sounds. *Journal of Speech and Hearing Disorders,* 1948, *13,* 31–34.

Jakobson, R. *Kindersprache, aphasie, und allgemeine lautgesetze.* Uppsala: Almquist & Wiksell, 1941.

Johnson, H. The meaning of "before" and "after" for preschool children. *Journal of Experimental Child Psychology,* 1975, *19,* 88–99.

Johnson, K. R. Teacher's attitude toward nonstandard Negro dialect: Let's change it. *Elementary English*, 1971, *48*, 176–84.

Jones, B. J. A study of oral language comprehension of black and white, middle and lower class, pre-school children using standard English and black dialect in Houston, Texas, 1972. Doctoral dissertation, University of Houston, 1972. *Dissertation Abstracts International*, 1973, *33*, 3957A-3958A. University Microfilms No. 73-4318.

Kagan J., and Lewis, M. Studies in attention in the human infant. *Merrill-Palmer Quarterly*, 1965, *11*, 95–127.

Kahn, J. V. Relationship of Piaget's sensorimotor period to language acquisition of profoundly retarded children. *American Journal of Mental Deficiency*, 1975, *79*, 640–43.

Karabenick, J. D., and Miller, S. A. The effects of age, sex, and listener feedback on grade school children's referential communication. *Child Development*, 1977, *48*, 678–83.

Karnes, M. B. *GOAL: Language development—Game oriented activities for learning*. Springfield, Mass.: Milton Bradley, 1976*a*.

Karnes, M. B. *Karnes early language activities*. Champaign, Ill.: GEM, P.O. Box 2339, Station A, 1976*b*.

Katz, J. J., and Fodor, J. A. The structure of a semantic theory. *Language*, 1963, *39*, 170–210.

Keenan, E. Conversational competence in children. *Journal of Child Language*, 1974, *1*, 163–83.

Kendon, A. Movement coordination in social interaction. *Acta Psychologica*, 1970, *32*, 100–125.

Kent, L. A language acquisition program for the retarded. In J. E. McLean, D. E. Yoder, and R. L. Schiefelbusch (eds.), *Language intervention with the retarded*. Baltimore: University Park Press, 1972.

Kievman, E. L. A pilot study designed to expand the linguistic versatility of socially disadvantaged kindergarten Negro children. Doctoral dissertation, University of California, 1969. University Microfilms No. 69-1113.

Kimball, J. P. Seven principles of surface structure parsing in natural language. *Cognition*, 1973, *2*, 15–47.

Kintsch, W. *The representation of meaning in memory*. Hillsdale, N.J.: Lawrence Erlbaum Associates, 1974.

Kirk, S. A., McCarthy, J. J., and Kirk, W. D. *Illinois test of psycholinguistic abilities*. Urbana, Ill.: University of Illinois Press, 1968.

Klima, E. S., and Bellugi-Klima, U. Syntactic regularities in the speech of children. In D. Reibel and S. Schane (eds.), *Modern studies in English*. Englewood Cliffs, N.J.: Prentice-Hall, 1969.

Knapp, M. L. *Nonverbal communication in human interaction*. New York: Holt, Rinehart & Winston, 1978.

Kochman, T. *Rappin' and stylin' out*. Urbana, Ill.: University of Illinois Press, 1972.

Kretschmer, R. R., and Kretschmer, L. W. *Language development and intervention with the hearing impaired*. Baltimore: University Park Press, 1978.

Labov, W. *The social stratification of English in New York City*. Washington, D.C.: Center for Applied Linguistics, 1966.

Labov, W. Some sources of reading problems for Negro speakers of nonstandard English. In A. Frazier (ed.), *New directions for elementary English*. Champaign, Ill.: National Council of Teachers of English, 1967, 140–67.

Labov, W. Variation in language. In C. E. Reed (ed.), *The learning of language*. New York: Appleton-Century-Crofts, 1971.

Labov, W. The logic of nonstandard English. In J. S. DeStefano (ed.), *Language, society and education: A profile of black English*. Worthington, Ohio: Charles A. Jones, 1973, 10–44.

Labov, W. Speech presented at Conference on Language in the Classroom: The Positive

Implications of Cultural and Linguistic Diversity, at University of Pennsylvania Graduate School of Education, Philadelphia, 1975.

Lakoff, G. Language in context. *Language,* 1972, *48,* 907–27.

Lakoff, R. Ifs, ands and buts about conjunction. In C. Fillmore and T. Langendoen (eds.), *Linguistic universals.* New York: Holt, Rinehart & Winston, 1971.

Lakoff, R. The logic of politeness: Or minding your P's and Q's. In *Papers from the Ninth Regional Meeting of the Chicago Linguistic Society.* Chicago: University of Chicago, 1973.

Lee, L. Developmental sentence types: A method for comparing normal and deviant syntactic development. *Journal of Speech and Hearing Disorders,* 1966, *31,* 311–30.

Lee, L. *Northwestern syntax screening test.* Evanston, Ill.: Northwestern University Press, 1971.

Lee, L. *Developmental sentence analysis.* Evanston, Ill.: Northwestern University Press, 1974.

Lee, L., and Canter, S. Developmental sentence scoring: A clinical procedure for estimating syntactic development in children's spontaneous speech. *Journal of Speech and Hearing Disorders,* 1971, *36,* 315–40.

Lefevre, C. *Linguistics and the teaching of reading.* New York: McGraw-Hill, 1964.

Lenneberg, E. Language disorders in childhood. *Harvard Educational Review,* 1964, *34,* 152–77.

Lenneberg, E. *Biological foundations of language.* New York: John Wiley & Sons, 1967.

Lenneberg, E., Rebelsky, F., and Nichols, I. The vocalizations of infants born to deaf and hearing parents. *Human Development,* 1965, *8,* 23–37.

Leonard, L. B. Language impairment in children. *Merrill-Palmer Quarterly,* 1979, *25,* 205–32.

Leonard, L. B., and Kaplan, L. A note on imitation and lexical acquisition. *Journal of Child Language,* 1976, *3,* 449–55.

Leonard, L. B., Perozzi, J. A., Prutting, C. A., and Berkley, R. K. Nonstandardized approaches to the assessment of language behaviors. *American Speech and Hearing Association,* 1978, *20,* 371–79.

Levin, H, and Watson, J. The learning of variable grapheme-to-phoneme correspondences. In *A basic research program on reading,* Final report, Project No. 639. Washington, D.C.: Cornell University and U.S. Office of Education, 1963.

Lewis, M. M. *Language, thought and personality in infancy and childhood.* Toronto: Hanrap & Co., 1963.

Lieberman, P. *Intonation, perception, and language.* Cambridge, Mass.: MIT Press, 1967.

Lin, S. C. *Pattern in the teaching of standard English to students with a nonstandard dialect.* New York: Columbia University Press, 1965.

Lindfors, J. *Children's language and learning.* Englewood Cliffs, N.J.: Prentice-Hall, 1980.

Lloyd, L. L., ed. *Communication assessment and intervention strategies.* Baltimore: University Park Press, 1976.

Lopez, N. *Making a movie.* Unpublished paper, Temple University, 1975.

Macnamara, J. Cognitive basis of language learning in infants. *Psychological Review,* 1972, *79,* 1–13.

Maratsos, M. Preschool children's use of definite and indefinite articles. *Child Development,* 1974, *45,* 446–55.

Mattingly, I. G. Reading, the linguistic process, and linguistic awareness. In J. F. Kavanagh and I. G. Mattingly (eds.), *Language by ear and by eye: The relationships between speech and reading.* Cambridge, Mass.: MIT Press, 1972.

Mazur, E. F., Holzman, M., and Ferrier, L. A pragmatic analysis of mothers' speech to prelinguistic infants. Paper presented at First Annual Boston University Conference on Language Development, Boston, October, 1976.

McCarthy, D. *McCarthy scales of children's abilities.* New York: Psychological Corporation, 1970.

McDavid, R. I. Go slow in ethnic attributions: Geographic mobility and dialect prejudices. In R. W. Bailey and S. L. Robinson, *Varieties of present-day English.* New York: Macmillan, 1973.

McDonald, J. D., and Blott, J. P. Environmental language intervention: The rationale for a diagnostic and training strategy through rules, context, and generalization. *Journal of Speech and Hearing Disorders,* 1974, *39,* 244–56.

McNeill, D. Developmental psycholinguistics. In F. Smith and G. A. Miller (eds.), *The genesis of language.* Cambridge, Mass.: MIT Press, 1966.

McNeill, D. *Acquisition of language.* New York: Harper and Row, 1970.

Mecham, M. J., Jex, J. L., and Jones, J. D. *Utah test of language development.* Salt Lake City: Communication Research Associates, 1967.

Meissner, J. A. Use of relational concepts by inner-city children. *Journal of Educational Psychology,* 1975, *67,* 22–29.

Mellon, J. C. *Transformational sentence-combining: A method for enhancing the development of syntactic fluency in English composition.* Champaign, Ill.: National Council of Teachers of English, 1969.

Menyuk, P. A comparison of grammar of children with functionally deviant and normal speech. *Journal of Speech and Hearing Research,* 1964, *7,* 109–22.

Menyuk, P. *The acquisition and development of language.* Englewood Cliffs, N.J.: Prentice-Hall, 1971.

Mercer, J. R. I.Q.: The lethal label. *Psychology Today,* 1972, *6,* 95–97.

Michaelis, C. T. Communication with the severely and profoundly handicapped: A psycholinguistic approach. *Mental Retardation,* 1978, *16,* 346–49.

Miller, G. A., and Chomsky, N. Binary models of language users. In D. Luce, R. Bush, and G. Gallanter (eds.), *Handbook of mathematical psychology,* vol. 2. New York: John Wiley & Sons, 1963, 419–92.

Miller, G. A., and Isard, S. Some perceptual consequences of linguistic rules. *Journal of Verbal Learning and Verbal Behavior,* 1963, *2,* 217–28.

Miller, J., and Yoder, D. *Miller-Yoder test of grammatical competence,* experimental ed. Madison, Wis.: University of Wisconsin Bookstore, 1972.

Miller, J., and Yoder, D. An ontogenetic language teaching strategy for retarded children. In R. L. Schiefelbusch and L. L. Lloyd (eds.), *Language perspectives: Acquisition, retardation and intervention.* Baltimore: University Park Press, 1974.

Minife, F. D., and Lloyd, L. L. (eds.), *Communicative and cognitive abilities—early behavioral assessment.* Baltimore: University Park Press, 1978.

Minskoff, E., Wiseman, D. E., and Minskoff, G. *The MWM program for developing language abilities.* Ridgefield, N.J.: Educational Performance Associates, 1972.

Moerk, M. L. Process of language teaching and training in the interaction of mother-child dyads. *Child Development,* 1976, *47,* 1064–78.

Moffett, J. *An integrated curriculum in the language arts, K–12.* Boston: Houghton Mifflin, 1968*a.*

Moffett, J. *Teaching the universe of discourse.* Boston: Houghton Mifflin, 1968*b.*

Montagu, A. The skin, touch and human development. *Somatics,* 1977, *1,* 3–8.

Moore, D. Competence and performance factors in the development of copulative sentences in children of different social classes. Unpublished paper, University of Illinois, 1968.

Moore, T., ed. *Cognitive development and the acquisition of language.* New York: Academic Press, 1973.

Morehead, D. M., and Ingram, D. The development of base syntax in normal and linguistically deviant children. *Journal of Speech and Hearing Research,* 1973, *16,* 330–52.

Morehead, D. M., and Morehead, A. E. From signal to sign: A Piagetian view of thought and language during the first two years. In R. L. Schiefelbusch and L. L. Lloyd (eds.), *Language perspectives: Acquisition, retardation, and intervention.* Baltimore: University Park Press, 1974.

Morehead, D. M., and Morehead, A. E. *Normal and deficient child language.* Baltimore: University Park Press, 1976.

Morgenstern, G. R. An attendant training program for increasing verbal responding in institutionalized severely retarded adolescents. Paper presented at the Convention of the American Speech and Hearing Association, Washington, D.C., 1975.

Moskowitz, A. The two-year-old stage in the acquisition of English phonology. *Language,* 1970, *46,* 426–41.

Muma, J. R. Language assessment: Some underlying assumptions. *American Speech and Hearing Association,* 1973, *15,* 331–38.

Muma, J. R. *Language handbook: Concepts, assessment, intervention.* Englewood Cliffs, N.J.: Prentice-Hall, 1978.

Nelson, K. Structure and strategy in learning to talk. *Monographs of the Society for Research in Child Development,* 1973, *38* (Serial No. 149), 1–2.

Nelson, K. Concept, word, and sentence: Interrelations in acquisition and development. *Psychological Review,* 1974, *81,* 267–85.

Nelson, K., and Benedict, H. The comprehension of relative, absolute and contrastive adjectives in young children. *Journal of Psycholinguistic Research,* 1974, *3,* 333–42.

Nelson, K., Garskaddon, C., and Bonvillian, J. D. Syntax acquisition: Impact of experimental variation in adult verbal interaction with the child. *Child Development,* 1973, *44,* 497–504.

Newcomer, P., and Hammill, D. D. *Test of language development (TOLD).* Austin, Tex.: Empiric Press, 1977.

Newport, E. L., Gleitman, H., and Gleitman, L. R. Mother I'd rather do it myself: Some effects and noneffects of maternal speech style. In C. Snow and C. Ferguson (eds.), *Talking to children.* London: Cambridge University Press, 1977, 109–49.

Noll, J. D. The use of the token test with children. Paper presented at the 46th Annual American Speech and Hearing Association Convention, New York, 1970.

O'Day, P. Clinical diagnostic report. Unpublished paper, Temple University Speech and Hearing Center, 1977.

Olson, D. Language and thought: Aspects of a cognitive theory of semantics. *Psychological Review,* 1970, *77,* 257–73.

Orton, S. "Word-blindness" in school children. *Archives of Neurology and Psychiatry,* 1925, *14,* 581–615.

Orton, S. *Reading, writing, and speech problems in children.* London: Chapman & Hall, 1937.

Osgood, C. E. On understanding and creating sentences. *American Psychologist,* 1963, *18,* 735–51.

Osser, H., Wang, M., and Zaid, F. The young child's ability to imitate and comprehend speech: A comparison of two subcultural groups. *Child Development,* 1969, *40,* 1063–76.

Ostwald, P. F. *The semiotics of human sound.* The Hague: Mouton, 1973.

Paris, S. Comprehension of language connectives and propositional logical relationships. *Journal of Experimental Child Psychology,* 1973, *16,* 278–91.

Peterson, H. A., Brener, R., and Williams, L. L. *SYNPRO* (Syntax Programmer). St. Louis, Mo.: Mercury Company/Division of EMT Labs, 1974.

Pfuderer, C. Some suggestions for a syntactic characterization of baby-talk style. Working Paper 14. Berkeley, Calif.: Language Behavior Research Laboratory, University of California, 1969.

Phillips, J. Syntax and vocabulary of mothers' speech to young children: Age and sex comparisons. *Child Development,* 1973, *44,* 182–85.

Piaget, J. *The origins of intelligence in children.* New York: International Universities Press, 1952.

Piaget, J. *The language and thought of the child.* New York: Meridian, 1955.

Piaget, J. *Play, dreams and imitation.* New York: Norton, 1962.

Piaget, J. *Psychology and intelligence.* Paterson, N.J.: Littlefield, 1963.

Piaget, J. *Six psychological studies.* New York: Random House, 1967.

Piaget, J., and Inhelder, B. *The psychology of the child.* New York: Basic Books, 1969.

Pierce, J. A study of 750 Portland, Oregon children during the first year. *Papers and Reports in Child Language Development,* 1974, *9,* 19–25.

Polanyi, H. *Personal knowledge: Towards a postcritical philosophy.* New York: Harper & Row, 1964.

Politzer, R. L. Auditory discrimination and the "disadvantaged": Deficit or difference. *The English Record,* 1971, *21,* 174–79.

Politzer, R. L. Problems in applying foreign language teaching methods to the teaching of standard English as a second dialect. In J. DeSefano (ed.), *Language, society, and education: A profile of black English.* Worthington, Ill.: Charles A. Jones, 1973, 238–50.

Pollak, S. A., and Gruenwald, L. J. *A manual for assessing language interaction in academic tasks.* Madison, Wis.: Midwest IGE Services, 1978.

Porch, B. E. *Porch index of communicative ability in children.* Palo Alto, Calif.: Consulting Psychologists Press, 1974.

Premack, D. The education of Sarah. *Psychology Today,* 1970, *4,* 54–59.

Premack, D. Language in chimpanzee? *Science,* 1971, *172,* 808–22.

Premack, D. Teaching language to an ape. *Scientific American,* 1972, *227,* 92–97.

Prutting, C. A., and Connolly, J. E. Imitation: A closer look. *Journal of Speech and Hearing Disorders,* 1976, *41,* 412–22.

Quick, A. D., Little, T., and Campbell, A. *Project MEMPHIS.* Belmont, Calif.: Fearon, 1973.

Ramer, A. The function of imitation in child language. *Journal of Speech and Hearing Research,* 1976, *19,* 700–717.

Ray, V. Modifications of language input by preschool teachers as a function of young children's language competencies. Unpublished dissertation, Temple University, 1980.

Rebelsky, F., and Hanks, C. Fathers' verbal interaction with infants in the first three months of life. *Child Development,* 1971, *42,* 63–69.

Rees, N. Basis of decision in language training. *Journal of Speech and Hearing Disorders,* 1973, *37,* 283–304.

Reich, R. Gestural facilitation of expressive language in moderately/severely retarded preschoolers. *Mental Retardation,* 1978, *16,* 113–17.

Rommetveit, R. *On message structure.* New York: John Wiley & Sons, 1974.

Rosen, C. L., and Ames, W. S. Influence of nonstandard dialect on the oral reading behavior of fourth grade black children under two stimuli conditions. In J. A. Figurel (ed.), *Better reading in urban schools.* Newark, Del.: International Reading Association, 1972.

Ross, S. B. On syntax of written black English. *TESOL Quarterly,* 1976, *10,* 115–22.

Rystrom, R. C. The effects of standard dialect training on Negro first graders learning to read. Unpublished doctoral dissertation, University of California at Berkeley, 1969.

Rystrom, R. C. Dialect training and reading: A further look. *Reading Research Quarterly,* 1970, *40,* 581–99.

Sachs, J. The adaptive significance of linguistic input to prelinguistic infants. In C. Snow and C. Ferguson (eds.), *Talking to children.* London: Cambridge University Press, 1977.

Salisbury, C., Wambold, C., and Walter, G. Manual communication for the severely handicapped: An assessment and instructional strategy. *Education and Training of the Mentally Retarded,* 1978, *13,* 393–97.

Sapir, E. Language. In D. G. Mandelbaum (ed.), *Edward Sapier: Culture, language and personality.* Berkeley, Calif.: University of California Press, 1970.

Savin, A. B. What the child knows about speech when he starts to learn to read. In J. F. Kavanagh and I. G. Mattingly (eds.), *Language by ear and eye: The relationship between speech and reading.* Cambridge, Mass.: MIT Press, 1972.

Schane, S. A. *Generative phonology.* Englewood Cliffs, N.J.: Prentice-Hall, 1973.

Schiefelbusch, R. L., and Lloyd, L. L., eds. *Language perspectives: Acquisition, retardation and intervention.* Baltimore: University Park Press, 1974.

Schlesinger, I. M. Relational concepts underlying language. In R. L. Schiefelbusch and L. L. Lloyd (eds.), *Language perspectives: Acquisition, retardation, and intervention.* Baltimore: University Park Press, 1974.

Schlesinger, I. M. The role of cognitive development and linguistic input in language acquisition. *Journal of Child Language,* 1977, *4,* 153–69.

Schlesinger, I. M., and Namir, L., eds. *Sign language of the deaf.* New York: Academic Press, 1978.

Schwartz, R. G., Leonard, L. B., Wilcox, M. J., and Folger, M. K. Again and again: Reduplication in child phonology. *Journal of Child Language,* 1980, *7,* 75–87.

Semel, E. M., and Wiig, E. H. *Clinical evaluation of language functions.* Columbus, Ohio: Charles E. Merrill, 1980.

Shaftel, F., and Shaftel, G. *Words and action.* New York: Holt, Rinehart & Winston, 1967.

Shuy, R. W. Teacher training and urban language problems. In R. W. Fasold and R. W. Shuy (eds.), *Teaching standard English in the inner city.* Washington, D.C.: Center for Applied Linguistics, 1970, 120–41.

Shuy, R. W. Language problems of disadvantaged children. In J. V. Irwin and M. Marge (eds.), *Principles of childhood language disabilities.* New York: Appleton-Century-Crofts, 1972, 185–208.

Shuy, R. W. Speech presented at Conference on Language in the classroom: The Positive Implications of Cultural and Linguistic Diversity, at the University of Pennsylvania Graduate School of Education, Philadelphia, 1975.

Shuy, R. W., Baratz, J. C., and Wolfram, W. *Sociolinguistic factors in speech identification.* Final Report, NIMH Grant #15048. Washington, D.C.: National Institute of Mental Health, 1969.

Shuy, R. W., Wolfram, W. A., and Riley, W. K. *Field techniques in an urban language study.* Washington, D.C.: Center for Applied Linguistics, 1968.

Siegel, G. M., and Broen, P. A. Language assessment. In L. L. Lloyd (ed.), *Communication assessment and intervention strategies.* Baltimore: University Park Press, 1976, 73–122.

Sinclair, H. Developmental psycholinguistics. In D. Elkind and J. Flavell (eds.), *Studies in cognitive development.* New York: Oxford University Press, 1969.

Sinclair, H. The transition from sensorimotor behavior to symbolic activity. *Interchange,* 1970, *1,* 119–26.

Sinclair, H. Sensorimotor action patterns as a condition for the acquisition of syntax. In R. Huxley and E. Ingram (eds.), *Language acquisition: Models and methods.* New York: Academic Press, 1971.

Skelly, M. *Amer-Ind gestural code based on Universal American Indian hand talk.* New York: Elsevier, 1979.

Skinner, B. F. *Verbal behavior.* New York: Appleton-Century-Crofts, 1957.

Slingerland, B. H. *Slingerland screening tests for identifying children with specific language disability,* 2nd ed. Cambridge, Mass.: Educators Publishing Service, 1970.

Slobin, D. I. Cognitive prerequisites for the development of grammar. In C. A. Ferguson and D. I. Slobin (eds.), *Studies of child language development.* New York: Holt, Rinehart & Winston, 1973.

Smilansky, S. *Effects of sociodramatic play on disadvantaged preschool children.* New York: John Wiley & Sons, 1968.

Smith, A. L. *Language, communciation in black America.* New York: Harper & Row, 1972.

Smith, F. *Understanding reading: A psycholinguistic analysis of reading and learning to read.* New York: Holt, Rinehart & Winston, 1971.

Smith, F. The uses of language. *Language Arts,* 1977, *54,* 638–44.

Smith, N. *The acquisition of phonology: A case study.* London: Cambridge University Press, 1973.

Snow, C. Mothers' speech to children learning language. *Child Development,* 1972, *43,* 549–65.

Snow, C. The development of conversation between mothers and babies. *Journal of Child Language,* 1977*a, 4,* 1–22.

Snow, C. Mothers' speech research: From input to interaction. In C. Snow and C. Ferguson (eds.), *Talking to children.* London: Cambridge University Press, 1977*b,* 31–49.

Somerville, M. A. Dialect and reading: A review of alternative solutions. *Review of Educational Research,* 1975, *45,* 247–62.

Spraldin, J. E. Assessment of speech and language of retarded children: The Parsons language scales. *Journal of Speech and Hearing Disorders,* Monograph Supplement 10, 1963, 8–31.

Stark, R. E. Features of infant sounds: The emergence of cooing. *Journal of Child Language,* 1978, *5,* 379–90.

Stauffer, R. G. *Directing reading maturity as a cognitive process.* New York: Harper & Row, 1969.

Stelle, T. W. *Language: An introduction for parents of deaf children.* Washington, D.C.: Gallaudet College Press, 1978.

Stern, D. *The first relationship: Infant and mother.* Cambridge, Mass.: Harvard University Press, 1977.

Stewart, W. A. On the use of Negro dialect in the teaching of reading. In J. C. Baratz and R. W. Shuy (eds.), *Teaching black children to read.* Washington, D.C.: Center for Applied Linguistics, 1969.

Stone, N. W., and Chesney, B. H. Attachment behaviors in handicapped infants. *Mental Retardation,* 1978, *16,* 8–12.

Stremel-Campbell, K., Cantrell, D., and Halle, J. Manual signing as a language system and as a speech initiator for the non-verbal severely handicapped student. In E. Sontag (ed.), *Educational programming for the severely/profoundly handicapped.* Reston, Va.: Council for Exceptional Children, 1977, 335–47.

Sylvester-Bradley, B., and Trevarthen, C. Baby talk as an adaptation to the infant's communication. In N. Waterson and C. Snow (eds.), *The development of communication.* New York: John Wiley & Sons, 1978, 75–91.

Templin, M. C. *Certain language skills in children: Their development and interrelationships.* Institute of Child Welfare Monograph No. 26. Minneapolis, Minn.: University of Minnesota Press, 1957.

Templin, M. C., and Darley, F. L. *The Templin-Darley tests of articulation.* Iowa City, Iowa: Bureau of Educational Research and Service, State University of Iowa, 1960.

Thomas, P. *Down these mean streets.* New York: Knopf, 1967.

Tonkova-Yampol'Skaya, R. V. Development of speech intonations in infants during the first two years of life. In C. A. Ferguson and D. I. Slobin (eds.), *Studies of Child Language Development.* New York: Holt, Rinehart & Winston, 1973, 128–38.

Topper, S. T. Gesture language for a non-verbal severely retarded male. *Mental Retardation,* 1975, *13,* 30–31.

Trudgill, P. Sex, convert prestige and linguistic change in the urban British English of Norwich. *Language in Society,* 1972, *1,* 179–95.

Tulkin, S. R. Social class differences in infants' reactions to mother's and stranger's voices. *Developmental Psychology,* 1973, *8,* 137.

Turner, G. H. Oral reading errors of fifth grade students. Unpublished doctoral dissertation, Temple University, 1979.

Tyack, D., and Gottsleben, R. *Language sampling, analysis, and training: A handbook for teachers and clinicians.* Palo Alto, Calif.: Consulting Psychologists Press, 1974.

Uzgiris, I. C., and Hunt, J. McV. *Assessment in infancy: Scales of psychological development.* Chicago: University of Illinois Press, 1975.

Velletutti, P. Language of the mildly retarded: Cognitive deficit or cultural differences? *Exceptional Children,* 1971, *37,* 455–59.

Vellutino, F. R. Alternative conceptualizations of dyslexia: Evidence in support of a verbal deficit hypothesis. *Harvard Educational Review,* 1977, *47,* 334–54.

Venezky, R. L. *The structure of English orthography.* The Hague: Mouton, 1970.

Venezky, R. L. *Theoretical and experimental base for teaching reading.* The Hague: Mouton, 1976.

Venezky, R. L., and Chapman, R. S. Is learning to read dialect bound? In S. L. Laffey and R. Shuy (eds.), *Language differences: Do they interfere?* Newark, Del.: International Reading Associates, 1973.

Wabash Center for the Mentally Retarded, Inc. *Guide to early developmental training.* Boston: Allyn & Bacon, 1977.

Waddell, K., and Cahoon, D. Comments on the use of the *Illinois Test of Psycholinguistic Abilities* with culturally deprived children in the rural South. *Perceptual and Motor Skills,* 1970, *31,* 56–58.

Wadsworth, B. *Piaget's theory of cognitive development.* New York: David McKay, 1969.

Webb, P. A., and Abrahamson, A. A. Stages of egocentrism in the use of "this" and "that": A different point of view. *Journal of Child Language,* 1976, *3,* 349–68.

Weikart, D. P. Curricular approaches in early childhood. In J. Stanley (ed.), *Preschool programs for the disadvantaged.* Baltimore: John Hopkins University Press, 1972.

Weintraub, F. J. Recent influences of law on the identity and placement of children in programs for the mentally retarded. In *A very special child.* Washington, D.C.: President's Committee on Mental Retardation, 1971, 12–13.

Whorf, B. L. *Language, thought, and reality.* Cambridge, Mass.: MIT Press, 1956.

Wier, R. Some questions on the child's learning of phonology. In F. Smith and G. A. Miller (eds.), *The genesis of language.* Cambridge, Mass.: MIT Press, 1966, 153–68.

Wiig, E. H., and Semel, E. M. Development of comprehension of logico-grammatical sentences by grade school children. *Perceptual and Motor Skills,* 1974, *38,* 171–76.

Wiig, E. H., and Semel, E. M. *Language disabilities in children and adolescents.* Columbus, Ohio: Charles E. Merrill, 1976.

Wiig, E. H. and Semel, E. M. *Language assessment and intervention for the learning disabled.* Columbus, Ohio: Charles E. Merrill, 1980.

Wilbur, R. B. The linguistics of manual language and manual systems. In L. L. Lloyd (ed.), *Communication assessment and intervention strategies.* Baltimore: University Park Press, 1976, 423–500.

Williams, F., and Whitehead, J. L. Language in the classroom: Studies of the Pygmalion effect. *The English Record,* 1971, *21,* 108–13.

Wilson, M. S. *Wilson initial syntax program.* Cambridge, Mass.: Educators Publishing Service, 1973.

Wolfram, W. A. Nature of nonstandard dialect divergence. *Elementary English,* 1970, *47,* 739–48.

Wolfram, W., and Fasold, R. W. *The study of social dialects in American English.* Englewood Cliffs, N.J.: Prentice-Hall, 1974.

Wood, B. S. *Children and communication: Verbal and nonverbal language development.* Englewood Cliffs, N.J.: Prentice-Hall, 1976.

# Author Index

427

# Subject Index

## ABOUT THE AUTHOR

Diane N. Bryen, Ph.D., has been a faculty member in the Department of Special Education at Temple University since 1973. Her primary involvement has been in teaching graduate-level courses in child language and language disorders, for which she was a recipient of the Christian Lindbach Award for Distinguished Teaching. She has also consulted and written extensively on topics related to language development and disorders. Dr. Bryen has authored and coauthored various articles and chapters of books on child language, as well as two books. Her involvement in cross-cultural teaching and research has included work with students from Puerto Rico and continued professional/student exchange programs with Israel.